# Australia's Military History

FOR

DUMMIES®

by David Horner

WILEY

Wiley Publishing Australia Pty Ltd

**Australia's Military History For Dummies®**

Australian Edition published by
**Wiley Publishing Australia Pty Ltd**
42 McDougall Street
Milton, Qld 4064
www.dummies.com

Copyright © 2010 Wiley Publishing Australia Pty Ltd

The moral rights of the author have been asserted.

National Library of Australia
Cataloguing-in-Publication data:

| | |
|---|---|
| Author: | Horner, D. M. (David Murray), 1948–. |
| Title: | Australia's Military History For Dummies/ David Horner. |
| ISBN: | 978 1 74216 983 5 (pbk.) |
| Notes: | Includes index. |
| Subjects: | Military history. |
| | Australia — Armed Forces — History. |
| | Australia — Military policy — History. |
| | Australia — History, Military. |
| Dewey Number: | 355.00994 |

All rights reserved. No part of this book, including interior design, cover design and icons, may be reproduced or transmitted in any form, by any means (electronic, photocopying, recording or otherwise) without the prior written permission of the Publisher. Requests to the Publisher for permission should be addressed to the Contracts & Licensing section of John Wiley & Sons Australia, Ltd, 42 McDougall Street, Milton, Qld 4064, or email auspermissions@wiley.com.

Cover image: © Sally-Anne Kerr/iStock

Typeset by diacriTech, Chennai, India

10 9 8 7 6 5 4 3 2 1

Limit of Liability/Disclaimer of Warranty: THE PUBLISHER AND THE AUTHOR MAKE NO REPRESENTATIONS OR WARRANTIES WITH RESPECT TO THE ACCURACY OR COMPLETENESS OF THE CONTENTS OF THIS WORK AND SPECIFICALLY DISCLAIM ALL WARRANTIES, INCLUDING WITHOUT LIMITATION, WARRANTIES OF FITNESS FOR A PARTICULAR PURPOSE. NO WARRANTY MAY BE CREATED OR EXTENDED BY SALES OR PROMOTIONAL MATERIALS. THE ADVICE AND STRATEGIES CONTAINED HEREIN MAY NOT BE SUITABLE FOR EVERY SITUATION. THIS WORK IS SOLD WITH THE UNDERSTANDING THAT THE PUBLISHER IS NOT ENGAGED IN RENDERING LEGAL, ACCOUNTING, OR OTHER PROFESSIONAL SERVICES. IF PROFESSIONAL ASSISTANCE IS REQUIRED, THE SERVICES OF A COMPETENT PROFESSIONAL PERSON SHOULD BE SOUGHT. NEITHER THE PUBLISHER NOR THE AUTHOR SHALL BE LIABLE FOR DAMAGES ARISING HEREFROM. THE FACT THAT AN ORGANISATION OR WEB SITE IS REFERRED TO IN THIS WORK AS A CITATION AND/OR A POTENTIAL SOURCE OF FURTHER INFORMATION DOES NOT MEAN THAT THE AUTHOR OR THE PUBLISHER ENDORSES THE INFORMATION THE ORGANISATION OR WEB SITE MAY PROVIDE OR RECOMMENDATIONS IT MAY MAKE. FURTHER, READERS SHOULD BE AWARE THAT INTERNET WEB SITES LISTED IN THIS WORK MAY HAVE CHANGED OR DISAPPEARED BETWEEN WHEN THIS WORK WAS WRITTEN AND WHEN IT IS READ.

**Trademarks:** Wiley, the Wiley logo, For Dummies, the Dummies Man logo, A Reference for the Rest of Us!, The Dummies Way, Making Everything Easier, dummies.com and related trade dress are trademarks or registered trademarks of John Wiley & Sons, Inc. and/or its affiliates in the United States and other countries, and may not be used without written permission. All other trademarks are the property of their respective owners. Wiley Publishing Australia Pty Ltd is not associated with any product or vendor mentioned in this book.

# About the Author

**David Horner** is Professor of Australian Defence History in the Strategic and Defence Studies Centre at the Australian National University. A graduate of the Royal Military College, Duntroon, the Australian Army's Command and Staff College, the University of New South Wales and the Australian National University, he served as an infantry platoon commander in Vietnam in 1971 and had various regimental and staff appointments until he retired from the Army as a lieutenant colonel in 1990.

He is the author or editor of 28 books on Australian military history, strategy and defence, including *Crisis of Command* (1978), *High Command* (1982), *SAS: Phantoms of the Jungle* (1989), *Inside the War Cabinet* (1996), *Blamey: The Commander-in-Chief* (1998), *Defence Supremo* (2000), *Making the Australian Defence Force* (2001) and *Strategic Command, General Sir John Wilton and Australia's Asian Wars* (2005). He is the editor of the Australian Army's military history series and has been the historical consultant for various television programs. As an Army Reserve colonel, from 1998 to 2002 he was the first Head of the Australian Army's Land Warfare Studies Centre.

In 2004 Professor Horner was appointed the Official Historian of Australian Peacekeeping, Humanitarian and Post-Cold War Operations, and in 2009 was made Member of the Order of Australia for service to military history.

He lives in Canberra, with his wife, Sigrid.

# Dedication

To the men and women of the Australian Defence Force, who serve the nation at home and overseas with professionalism, dedication and sacrifice.

## Publisher's Acknowledgements

We're proud of this book; please send us your comments through our online registration form located at http://dummies.custhelp.com.

Some of the people who helped bring this book to market include the following:

*Acquisitions, Editorial and Media Development*

**Project Editor:** Catherine Spedding

**Acquisitions Editor:** Bronwyn Duhigg

**Editorial Manager:** Hannah Bennett

*Production*

**Graphics:** Wiley Art Studio

**Cartoons:** Glenn Lumsden

**Proofreader:** Charlotte Duff

**Indexer:** Karen Gillen

The authors and publisher would like to thank the following copyright holders, organisations and individuals for their permission to reproduce copyright material in this book.

Cartographer: GIS Services, College of Asia and the Pacific, The Australian National University

Every effort has been made to trace the ownership of copyright material. Information that will enable the publisher to rectify any error or omission in subsequent editions will be welcome. In such cases, please contact the Permissions Section of John Wiley & Sons Australia, Ltd.

# Contents at a Glance

Introduction .................................................................................. 1

## Part I: The Essentials of Australian Military History ....... 9
Chapter 1: Exploring Why Australia Goes to War ................................................ 11
Chapter 2: Coming to Grips with the Military ..................................................... 21

## Part II: The Wars of Colonial Australia ........................ 37
Chapter 3: Colonial Conflicts ............................................................................... 39
Chapter 4: Battling the Boers, 1899–1902 .......................................................... 55

## Part III: The First World War: Australia's Greatest Tragedy ........................................................ 71
Chapter 5: Australia Goes to War, 1914 .............................................................. 73
Chapter 6: Creating the Anzac Legend at Gallipoli, 1915 ................................... 89
Chapter 7: Enduring the Horrors of the Western Front, 1916–17 ..................... 105
Chapter 8: Riding to Victory in Palestine, 1916–18 ............................................ 121
Chapter 9: Hammering the Huns, 1918 ............................................................... 137

## Part IV: The Second World War: The Empire Beckons .. 155
Chapter 10: Winning the First Battles, 1940–41 .................................................. 157
Chapter 11: New Theatres, New Allies and New Enemies, 1941 ........................ 173
Chapter 12: Defeating the Afrika Korps, 1941–42 ............................................... 189
Chapter 13: Our Airmen in Europe, 1939–45 ....................................................... 203

## Part V: Our War in the Pacific ..................................... 219
Chapter 14: The Japanese are Coming! 1941–42 ................................................ 221
Chapter 15: New Guinea Battles — A Jungle Hell, 1942–44 ............................... 245
Chapter 16: Fighting to the Finish, 1944–45 ....................................................... 269
Chapter 17: The Civilian Side of the War ............................................................ 285

## Part VI: The Aussies Do Their Bit in the Cold War ....... 301
Chapter 18: Taking up Arms for the United Nations in Korea, 1950–53 ............ 303
Chapter 19: Backing the Brits in Malaya and Borneo, 1950–66 ......................... 321
Chapter 20: Fighting Alongside the Yanks in Vietnam, 1962–72 ........................ 335

## Part VII: On Overseas Service .................................................. 359
Chapter 21: Peacekeeping Near and Far, 1947–2010 ........................................... 361
Chapter 22: Flying the Flag in Iraq and Afghanistan, 1990–2010 ............................ 377

## Part VIII: The Part of Tens .................................................. 393
Chapter 23: Ten Top Australian Military Leaders ............................................ 395
Chapter 24: Ten Famous Australian Battles ................................................. 405
Chapter 25: Ten Myths of Australian Military History ...................................... 413

## Index .................................................................. 421

# Table of Contents

## Introduction ........................................................................... 1
About This Book ................................................................. 1
Conventions Used in This Book ........................................ 2
What You're Not to Read .................................................. 3
Foolish Assumptions ......................................................... 3
How This Book Is Organised ............................................ 4
    Part I: The Essentials of Australian Military History ....... 4
    Part II: The Wars of Colonial Australia ........................ 4
    Part III: The First World War: Australia's Greatest Tragedy ....... 4
    Part IV: The Second World War: The Empire Beckons ....... 5
    Part V: Our War in the Pacific ....................................... 5
    Part VI: The Aussies Do Their Bit in the Cold War ....... 5
    Part VII: On Overseas Service ...................................... 6
    Part VIII: The Part of Tens ........................................... 6
Icons Used in This Book ................................................... 6
Where To Go from Here .................................................... 7

## Part I: The Essentials of Australian Military History ....... 9

### Chapter 1: Exploring Why Australia Goes to War ................. 11
Where Australians Have Fought ..................................... 12
Why Australians Have Fought ........................................ 13
    Australianists and Imperialists ................................... 14
    Global conflicts that shaped the nation ..................... 15
    Supporting our friends ............................................... 16
    Doing good in the world ............................................. 16
Remembering Our Military History ............................... 17
    Revisiting the stories of Australia at war .................. 17
    Honouring the Anzac legend ...................................... 18

### Chapter 2: Coming to Grips with the Military ..................... 21
How Do We Fight? ............................................................ 22
    Fighting alongside allies ............................................. 22
    The pollies are in charge ............................................ 23
Her Majesty's Forces Down Under ................................ 24
    Royal Australian Navy ................................................ 24
    Australian Army .......................................................... 25

Royal Australian Air Force ................................................................. 27
Forming the Australian Defence Force ............................................... 28
The Diggers ................................................................................................... 30
Amateurs, Regulars and Nashos ......................................................... 30
On the front-line: Those doing the fighting ..................................... 31
Knowing when to salute ....................................................................... 33
Honouring the brave ............................................................................ 34

## Part II: The Wars of Colonial Australia ....................... 37

### Chapter 3: Colonial Conflicts . . . . . . . . . . . . . . . . . . . . . . . . . . . . . . . . . . . . .39

Garrisoning the Colonial Outpost .............................................................. 40
The Battle of Vinegar Hill .................................................................... 40
The Rum Rebellion ............................................................................... 41
Defending Sydney ................................................................................. 41
Securing the vast continent ................................................................. 42
Soldiers versus miners — the Eureka Stockade .............................. 42
Raising volunteers ................................................................................ 43
Building forts ......................................................................................... 44
Skirmishes and Massacres — the Frontier Wars ..................................... 44
Aboriginal warfare ................................................................................ 45
Settler, military and police methods .................................................. 46
Pacifying the frontier — 130 years of warfare .................................. 47
The massacre at Myall Creek ............................................................... 48
The great Australian silence ................................................................ 49
Responding to the Call of Empire ............................................................... 49
To New Zealand, for Empire and a farm ............................................ 50
Soldiering in Sudan ............................................................................... 51
Getting ready for Federation ............................................................... 52
Beating the Boxers at Beijing .............................................................. 52

### Chapter 4: Battling the Boers, 1899–1902 . . . . . . . . . . . . . . . . . . . . . . . . .55

Sending Colonial Volunteers ....................................................................... 56
The Black Week of the British Empire ............................................... 56
Asking and offering: The colonies come to the party ..................... 58
Questioning our involvement .............................................................. 59
Arriving in South Africa ....................................................................... 60
Skirmishing at Sunnyside .................................................................... 60
Advancing to Pretoria ................................................................................... 61
Winning respect at Colesberg ............................................................. 62
Marching hard to Bloemfontein .......................................................... 63
Riding with Hutton's mounted brigade ............................................. 63

Countering the Boer Raids ..................................................................... 65
    Enter the Bushmen ........................................................................ 65
    Learning a lesson at Koster River ................................................. 65
    Defending Eland's River ............................................................... 66
Patrolling the Veldt............................................................................... 67
    Continuing the commitment........................................................ 68
    Pursuing General de Wet............................................................. 68
    Humiliation at Wilmansrust......................................................... 68
    Breaker Morant breaks the law ................................................... 69
    Australian Commonwealth Horse ............................................... 70
Counting the Cost................................................................................. 70

## Part III: The First World War: Australia's Greatest Tragedy .................................................. 71

### Chapter 5: Australia Goes to War, 1914 ........................... 73
Defending the Commonwealth............................................................ 74
    An Army for a nation .................................................................... 74
    Compulsory service for boy soldiers........................................... 76
    A Navy of our own ........................................................................ 77
Joining the Empire's War — To the Last Shilling ............................... 79
Looking After our Backyard ................................................................. 80
    Mounting the first expedition...................................................... 80
    Seizing German New Guinea — No more 'Um Kaiser.
        God save 'Um King .................................................................. 82
Falling In with Britain ........................................................................... 83
    Raising the Australian Imperial Force ........................................ 83
    *Sydney* versus *Emden* — 'Beached and done for' ..................... 85
    Anzacs in Egypt — desert marches and pyramids..................... 87

### Chapter 6: Creating the Anzac Legend at Gallipoli, 1915 ........... 89
Landing at Anzac Cove......................................................................... 90
    Clambering ashore under fire — the stuff of legend ................. 91
    Thrusting inland: The confusing first day ................................. 92
    Digging in for life .......................................................................... 92
    Our daring submariners — entering the Sea of Marmara ......... 93
Holding On............................................................................................. 94
    Charging the Turkish line at Helles............................................. 95
    Repelling the Turkish attack at Anzac........................................ 95
    Surviving the worst conditions.................................................... 96

False Hope in the August Offensives ..................................................97
    Seizing Lone Pine for no advantage ..........................................98
    Dying at the Nek for no purpose ................................................99
    Climbing Chunuk Bair for no gain ............................................100
Sneaking Away ......................................................................................101
    Reporting unpalatable truths to London ................................101
    Deciding to depart ...................................................................102
    Tricking the Turks ....................................................................102
Reassessing and Remembering ........................................................103

## Chapter 7: Enduring the Horrors of the Western Front, 1916–17 ....105

Adapting to a New Theatre ................................................................106
    Enlarging the AIF .....................................................................106
    Deploying to France .................................................................108
Attacking Under Fire ..........................................................................109
    Australia's worst day: Tragedy at Fromelles ..........................110
    Attempting the impossible on the Somme ............................111
    A nation divided: Voting for or against conscription ...........112
The Coldest Winter .............................................................................113
    Advancing to the Hindenburg Line .........................................113
    Bungling and bravery in the Bullecourt battles ....................114
Success Ends in Failure in Flanders .................................................114
    Making their mark: The 3rd Division at Messines ................115
    Side by side on the Menin Road ..............................................115
    Struggling through the mud to Passchendaele .....................116
Modern Industrial Warfare .................................................................117
    Living in the trenches ..............................................................118
    Dominating the battlefield: The big guns ..............................118
    Gas, gas, gas! .............................................................................119
    Above the maelstrom: The air war ..........................................120

## Chapter 8: Riding to Victory in Palestine, 1916–18 ................121

Our Light Horse Tradition ..................................................................122
    Setting up the Light Horse ......................................................123
    No place for horses at Gallipoli ...............................................123
Clearing the Turks from Sinai ............................................................124
    Reforming the mounted troops ...............................................124
    A decisive victory at Romani ...................................................125
    Marching across the desert to Magdhaba ..............................126
Third Time Lucky at Gaza ...................................................................127
    Disappointment at the first battle of Gaza ............................128
    The second battle of Gaza and the Desert Mounted Corps .........128
    Charging the enemy lines at Beersheba .................................129

Pausing for Breath in Palestine.................................................................130
    Christmas in Jerusalem.................................................................130
    The Australian Flying Corps over the desert ...............................131
    Raiding beyond the Jordan River.................................................132
  A Perfect Victory .............................................................................133
    Deceiving the Turks: Planning the breakthrough ........................133
    The greatest cavalry feat in history ............................................134
    Entering Damascus in triumph.....................................................135

### Chapter 9: Hammering the Huns, 1918 ........................137
  Crushing the German Offensive.....................................................138
    Determination at Dernancourt......................................................139
    Saving Hazebrouck .......................................................................140
    Valour at Villers-Bretonneux.........................................................140
  The Counteroffensive that Won the War ......................................142
    Trying out new methods at Hamel ..............................................144
    Black day for the Germans at Amiens ........................................145
    Storming Mont St Quentin ...........................................................146
    Breaking the Hindenburg Line.....................................................146
  Gallant Airmen: The Australian Flying Corps...............................147
  Sailing the Seas: The Navy's Experience......................................149
  Lest We Forget.................................................................................151
    Counting the casualties................................................................151
    Reaping political benefits ............................................................152
    Commemorating the fallen ..........................................................153

## Part IV: The Second World War: The Empire Beckons.. 155

### Chapter 10: Winning the First Battles, 1940–41...................157
  Australia Neglects Its Security.......................................................158
    The war-weary nation ..................................................................158
    Still tied to Britain..........................................................................159
    Penny-pinching depletes our defences .......................................160
    Belatedly re-arming.......................................................................160
  Not Another War!.............................................................................161
    Gearing up......................................................................................162
    Recruiting a new force..................................................................163
    Training in Palestine .....................................................................164
    Supporting the motherland ..........................................................164
  Gaining Control of the Oceans ......................................................165
    Patrolling the coast at home .......................................................165
    Contesting the Mediterranean ....................................................166
    Sinking Italian ships......................................................................166

Helping out at Berbera ................................................................... 167
Fighting the French at Dakar ........................................................ 167
Backing a coup in New Caledonia ............................................... 167
Upholding the Digger Legend in the Middle East ............................. 168
Baptism of fire at Bardia ............................................................... 169
Capturing the fortress at Tobruk .................................................. 170
Outmanoeuvring the Italians ........................................................ 170
Sideshow at Giarabub .................................................................. 171

## Chapter 11: New Theatres, New Allies and New Enemies, 1941 ...173

Blitzkrieg and Bombing in Greece ....................................................... 173
Reviving the Anzac Corps ............................................................. 174
Meeting the German panzers at Vevi .......................................... 175
Plugging gaps in northern Greece ............................................... 176
On the run ..................................................................................... 177
Last stand at Brallos .................................................................... 177
Evacuation .................................................................................... 178
Desperate Defences in Crete ................................................................ 179
Digging in with the Kiwis again .................................................... 179
Shooting German paratroopers ................................................... 180
Futile defence at Retimo .............................................................. 180
Saved by the navy ........................................................................ 181
Fierce battles at sea ..................................................................... 181
Invading Syria ........................................................................................ 182
Crossing the frontier .................................................................... 183
The French counterattack at Merjayoun .................................... 184
Closing in on Damascus ............................................................... 184
Victory at Damour ........................................................................ 185
Watching over the Persian Gulf ................................................... 185
The Jitters Set in at Home .................................................................... 186
Recognising the Japanese threat ................................................ 186
Reinforcing Malaya ....................................................................... 187
Changing our political leaders .................................................... 187
*Kormoran* sinks *Sydney* ............................................................... 188

## Chapter 12: Defeating the Afrika Korps, 1941–42 ................189

The Benghazi Handicap: Australia's Part in the Retreat ...................... 190
Deploying to the desert ............................................................... 190
Falling back to Tobruk .................................................................. 191
Surviving the Siege of Tobruk .............................................................. 192
Repulsing the Desert Fox's tanks ................................................ 192
Patrolling the perimeter .............................................................. 193
Running the gauntlet — our ships sustain the garrison ............ 194
Demanding relief — Blamey becomes the most hated
    man in the Middle East ........................................................... 195

Scaling Down Australia's Forces in the Middle East ............................. 196
Bitter Battles: Preventing the Germans from Reaching the Nile .......... 196
    Keeping the Germans off-balance at Tel el Eisa ........................... 197
    Losing a battalion at Ruin Ridge ................................................ 198
    Australian airmen patrol in the desert ....................................... 198
Winning at El Alamein ................................................................................ 199
    Plans and preparations ................................................................ 200
    Crossing the start line ................................................................. 201
    Drawing in the German reserves ................................................ 201
    Breaking through the line ........................................................... 202
    Heading home .............................................................................. 202

## Chapter 13: Our Airmen in Europe, 1939–45 .................... 203

An Air Force of Our Own ............................................................................ 204
    Forming the Royal Australian Air Force .................................... 205
    Struggling for survival ................................................................ 205
A Last Call of Empire: The Empire Air Training Scheme ....................... 206
    Losing our identity ...................................................................... 206
    Training and serving around the world ..................................... 208
Fighters and Flying Boats .......................................................................... 211
    A few of the few: Our airmen in the Battle of Britain ................ 211
    Finding tasks for the fighters ..................................................... 211
    Searching the seas: Coastal Command protects the convoys ..... 212
Bombing: The Deadliest of Jobs ................................................................ 213
    Night stalking .............................................................................. 214
    Bomber Command's war ............................................................ 214
    Surviving a sortie over Germany ............................................... 216
    Supporting the Normandy landing ............................................ 216
    Strategic bombing: Necessary evil? ........................................... 217

# Part V: Our War in the Pacific ........................................ 219

## Chapter 14: The Japanese are Coming! 1941–42 ................ 221

Reeling from the Japanese Thrust ............................................................. 222
    Jungle ambushes ......................................................................... 224
    Trapped at Parit Sulong .............................................................. 225
    The worst disaster: The fall of Singapore ................................. 226
Garrisoning the Islands to the North: Hostages to Fortune .................... 228
    The shock at Rabaul ................................................................... 230
    More troops are sacrificed: The loss of Ambon ........................ 231
    Caught unawares in Darwin ....................................................... 232
    Guerrilla war in Timor ................................................................ 233
    Overpowered in the fight for Java .............................................. 234
    Curtin demands that our troops come home ............................ 234

Uncle Sam to the Rescue ........................................................................ 235
    MacArthur takes charge.................................................................. 236
    The Yanks are here!........................................................................ 237
Thwarting Japan's Plans ......................................................................... 239
    Assessing enemy intentions ......................................................... 241
    Saving Port Moresby: The Battle of the Coral Sea ...................... 242
    Threatening our shores: Submarines sneak into
        Sydney Harbour........................................................................ 243
    Breathing more easily: The Battle of Midway tips the balance ... 243

## Chapter 15: New Guinea Battles — A Jungle Hell, 1942–44 ....... 245

Halting Japan's South Pacific Offensive ................................................ 246
    The Japanese landing at Buna...................................................... 248
    Guadalcanal and the sinking of HMAS *Canberra*
        at Savo Island............................................................................ 249
    Breaking the Japanese spell at Milne Bay................................... 249
    Retreating over the Kokoda Trail................................................. 250
MacArthur Orders a Counterattack ....................................................... 252
    Regaining Kokoda ........................................................................... 252
    Trapping the enemy at Oivi–Gorari .............................................. 253
    Stalemate at Buna, Gona and Sanananda.................................... 253
    A costly victory ............................................................................... 254
Figuring Out Jungle Warfare ................................................................... 254
    Air power wins the battle at Wau................................................. 255
    Destroying enemy shipping in the Bismarck Sea....................... 256
    Closing in on Salamaua .................................................................. 257
Seizing the Enemy Base at Lae ............................................................... 258
    The preparation: Training and planning ..................................... 259
    Devastating air attacks on Wewak ............................................... 260
    Landing our troops near Lae ........................................................ 260
    Paratroops secure Nadzab ............................................................ 261
    Racing to take Lae .......................................................................... 261
Forcing the Enemy from the Huon Peninsula...................................... 262
    A close shave at Finschhafen ....................................................... 262
    Scaling the heights of Sattelberg.................................................. 263
    Stepping up the pace of the advance .......................................... 264
Into the Finisterre Range: The 7th Division's Offensive...................... 264
    Quick thinking captures Kaiapit.................................................... 265
    Chasing the Japanese through Death Valley .............................. 265
    A one-man front on Shaggy Ridge................................................ 265
    The final prize: Madang.................................................................. 266

## Chapter 16: Fighting to the Finish, 1944–45 .....................269
  With MacArthur to the Philippines ................................................. 270
    Our ships at Leyte: The greatest sea battle................................ 271
    Combating Kamikaze attacks at Lingayen Gulf ........................ 272
  Mopping Up in New Guinea and the Islands ................................. 273
    Resenting every death in Bougainville........................................ 275
    Keeping watch over Rabaul ........................................................ 276
    Slogging it out at Aitape and Wewak ......................................... 277
  Unnecessary Battles in Borneo........................................................ 277
    Seizing Tarakan for oil and airfields .......................................... 278
    Regaining British Borneo ........................................................... 280
    Against our wishes — fighting the last battle at Balikpapan........ 280
  Dealing with a Defeated Japan ....................................................... 281
    Joining the British Pacific Fleet in Japanese waters.................... 282
    Taking the Japanese surrender .................................................. 283
    Punishing the war criminals....................................................... 283

## Chapter 17: The Civilian Side of the War .....................285
  Governing the Nation during War................................................... 286
    Involving the Opposition ........................................................... 286
    Curtin and his War Cabinet........................................................ 287
    Conscription for overseas service............................................... 288
    Wartime politics ......................................................................... 289
  Cooperating with Allies................................................................... 290
    Handing control to MacArthur................................................... 290
    Balancing the war effort............................................................. 291
  Marshalling the Nation's Resources................................................ 292
    Building wartime industries ...................................................... 293
    Regulating all aspects of life ...................................................... 293
    Conscripting the workers .......................................................... 294
    Rationing and restricting ........................................................... 294
  Serving in Other Ways..................................................................... 296
    Lost at sea — our merchant navy's war...................................... 296
    Allowing women to do men's work............................................ 297
    Working for no pay: The volunteers .......................................... 299
  Reshaping the Nation...................................................................... 299
    Calculating the cost ................................................................... 299
    Opening our doors to migrants.................................................. 300

## Part VI: The Aussies Do Their Bit in the Cold War ...... 301

### Chapter 18: Taking up Arms for the United Nations in Korea, 1950–53 .................................................. 303

The Occupation of Japan .................................................. 304
    Signing on for more military service ............................. 304
    Living with the former enemy ...................................... 305
Seeking Future Security ................................................... 305
    Pinning our hopes on the United Nations ...................... 306
    Restructuring our defences ......................................... 306
    Responding to the Cold War ........................................ 307
    Breaking the Berlin Blockade ...................................... 307
The Korean War — The Cold War gets Hot .......................... 308
    Winning friends in Washington .................................... 309
    Sending our forces to Korea ........................................ 310
The Royal Australian Regiment's First War .......................... 310
    Advancing to the Yalu River ........................................ 312
    Retreating to Seoul .................................................... 312
    Kapyong — a remarkable achievement against great odds ........ 313
    Showing great skill and determination at Maryan San ........... 315
    Raiding, patrolling and probing on the Jamestown Line ......... 315
    Holding on at the Hook ............................................... 317
    Remembering the forgotten war .................................. 318
Cementing our Alliance with the United States .................... 318

### Chapter 19: Backing the Brits in Malaya and Borneo, 1950–66 ..... 321

The British Empire's Last Gasp ........................................... 322
    Defending the Middle East from Malta ......................... 322
    Protecting the countries to our north — ANZAM and SEATO ..... 323
Countering the 'CTs' in Malaya ........................................... 324
    The Malayan Emergency ............................................. 324
    Bombing the jungle .................................................... 325
Contributing to Malaya's Defences ..................................... 325
    Sending our soldiers to Malaya ................................... 326
    Tracking and ambushing in the jungle ......................... 328
    Maintaining our presence in Malaya ............................ 328
Avoiding Conflict with Our Indonesian Neighbours ............... 329
    Reluctantly edging into war ........................................ 330
    Patrolling the borders of Borneo .................................. 331
    The Special Air Service's secret missions ...................... 332
    Watching the waterways ............................................. 333
    Securing the peace ..................................................... 334

### Chapter 20: Fighting Alongside the Yanks in Vietnam, 1962–72 ... 335
- Advising and Training the South Vietnamese Army ... 336
  - The advisers take to the field ... 337
  - Commanding a Montagnard battalion ... 339
- Sending Combat Troops ... 339
  - A contentious decision ... 340
  - The first battalion ... 341
  - Dominating Phuoc Tuy Province ... 341
  - Building the Task Force base at Nui Dat ... 343
  - Desperate defence at Long Tan ... 344
  - The two-edged sword — the disastrous barrier minefield ... 345
- Our Contest with Victor Charlie ... 346
  - The grunts carry the load ... 346
  - Patrolling and ambushing ... 347
  - Search and destroy ... 348
  - Hitting the enemy hard — the guns in the jungle ... 349
  - Bushrangers and dust-offs — helicopters prove their worth ... 350
- Challenging the Enemy's Main Force — the Tet Offensives ... 351
  - Street fighting in Baria and Long Dien ... 351
  - Coral and Balmoral — the biggest battles ... 352
  - The enemy confronts our tanks at Binh Ba ... 353
- Striking the Enemy from Sea and Air ... 354
  - The Air Force's war ... 354
  - The Navy's war ... 354
- Protest and Dissent ... 355
  - Opposing conscription ... 355
  - The moratorium marches ... 356
  - Our troops go home ... 356

## Part VII: On Overseas Service ... 359

### Chapter 21: Peacekeeping Near and Far, 1947–2010 ... 361
- Observing and Reporting when the Fighting Stops ... 361
  - The first peacekeepers — the mission in Indonesia ... 362
  - In the mountains of Kashmir ... 363
  - Keeping the Arabs and the Israelis apart ... 363
  - Policing in Cyprus ... 364
  - Monitoring the ceasefire in Zimbabwe ... 365
  - Overseeing the end of the Iran–Iraq war ... 366
  - Hopes dashed in Western Sahara ... 367
  - Unarmed in Bougainville ... 368

Rebuilding Shattered Nations ........................................................369
    Supervising elections in Namibia ...................................369
    Resolving the conflict in Cambodia.................................370
    Clearing landmines in Afghanistan.................................371
Enforcing Peace ..............................................................................371
    Guarding aid workers in Somalia ....................................372
    Genocide in Rwanda..........................................................373
    Safeguarding the new nation of East Timor...................374
    Quelling unrest in the Solomon Islands.........................376

### Chapter 22: Flying the Flag in Iraq and Afghanistan, 1990–2010 ....377

Iraq Invades Kuwait — We Defend our Vital Interests............................378
    Reaffirming our friendship with the United States.......379
    Boarding and searching — our ships in the Gulf of Oman ...........380
    A small part in the Gulf War............................................381
Twisting Saddam Hussein's Arm...................................................382
    Humanitarian relief in Kurdistan....................................382
    Disarming Iraq — sanctions and weapons inspection.................383
Terror Attacks in the United States: the Start of a New War.................385
    Joining the Americans in Afghanistan............................386
    Invading Iraq......................................................................387
    Dealing with the insurgency in Iraq...............................390
    Returning to the enduring war in Afghanistan..............390

## Part VIII: The Part of Tens ................................................ 393

### Chapter 23: Ten Top Australian Military Leaders ................395

Field Marshal Sir Thomas Blamey (1884–1951).......................396
General Sir Harry Chauvel (1865–1945)....................................397
Vice-Admiral Sir John Collins (1899–1989)...............................397
General Peter Cosgrove (1947–).................................................398
Lieutenant General Sir Talbot Hobbs (1864–1938)..................399
General Sir John Monash (1865–1931).......................................400
Lieutenant General Sir Leslie Morshead (1889–1959).............401
Air Chief Marshal Sir Frederick Scherger (1904–84) ..............401
Major General George Vasey (1895–1945)................................402
General Sir John Wilton (1910–81).............................................403

### Chapter 24: Ten Famous Australian Battles......................405

The Landing at Gallipoli...............................................................405
Beersheba.......................................................................................406
Villers-Bretonneux........................................................................406
Mont St Quentin............................................................................407

Sinking the *Bartolomeo Colleoni* ................................................................ 408
Kokoda ............................................................................................................ 408
El Alamein ...................................................................................................... 409
Bismarck Sea .................................................................................................. 409
Kapyong .......................................................................................................... 410
Long Tan ......................................................................................................... 411

## Chapter 25: Ten Myths of Australian Military History ............. 413
The Aborigines Didn't Resist White Invasion ............................................ 413
Breaker Morant Wasn't a War Criminal ..................................................... 414
Incompetent British Generals Recklessly Sacrificed
   First World War Diggers .......................................................................... 415
Monash Could've Commanded the British Army on
   the Western Front ..................................................................................... 415
Curtin Demanded that Churchill Return Our Troops
   from the Middle East ................................................................................ 416
HMAS *Sydney* was Sunk by a Submarine .................................................. 417
The Battle of the Coral Sea Stopped the Japanese from
   Invading Australia ..................................................................................... 417
The Kokoda Battles Saved Australia ........................................................... 418
The Menzies Government Planned to Defend Australia
   from the Brisbane Line ............................................................................. 419
The Whitlam Government Withdrew the Troops from Vietnam ............ 419

# Index ............................................................................. 421

# Foreword

It has been very pleasing over the past decade to see greater interest in Australian military history. During this time, attendance of Australians at Anzac Day services, Remembrance Day events, and individual war and battle commemorations has risen. Additionally, increasing numbers of books, television programs and movies have chronicled some of our most important and iconic battles. I consider this to be vitally important, because sadly, as the years go by, we are losing our direct link to our past. Already gone are our Veterans from the First World War and the number of Second World War, Korea and Vietnam Veterans diminishes every year. As the experience of these wars continues to recede, it is essential that we remember and honour these major aspects of our military history which saw the tragic loss of more than 100,000 Australian men and women. This is a debt we owe to all those who have sacrificed their life for our nation.

Additionally, as the Chief of the Defence Force, I am very happy that our increased commitments over the past decade have meant that we are currently enjoying a rejuvenated interest in the Australian Defence Force (ADF), our people and our operations. I firmly believe that Australia's armed forces are more professional, more capable and more ready to respond to unexpected demands than at any time in our history.

In the first decade of the 21st century the ADF has once again been at war. Following the 2001 terrorist attacks in New York and Washington, Australian Special Forces took part in a 12-month deployment to Afghanistan in order to deny the country as a safe haven for terrorists. In support of this operation, other units, including ships and aircraft, went to nearby areas in the Persian Gulf. In 2005, ADF men and women went back to Afghanistan and since then our people have made contributions to international campaigns against terrorism, countering piracy in the Gulf of Aden and maritime security in the Middle East Area of Operations. Additionally, in 2003, Australian forces also took part in one of the most complex operations ever undertaken by the ADF — Operation CATALYST. During the course of this six-year operation, thousands of Australian servicemen and women were instrumental in developing a secure and stable Iraq.

We have also had an increased commitment to peacekeeping and humanitarian operations. Over the past two decades Australia has been involved in more than two dozen other peacekeeping missions. Our largest was in 1999, when the ADF led the International Force for East Timor, which was our most significant military undertaking since the Second World War. We have also contributed to many humanitarian emergency relief operations both here at home and around the world. In 2009 alone, we assisted with the Victorian Bushfires, the Samoan earthquake, the Tongan Ferry Sinking, a plane accident in Papua New Guinea and the earthquake in Padang, Indonesia.

In all manner of operations our men and women in uniform have been at the forefront of Australia's engagement with the world. When I visit our people on operations I am struck by their courage, professionalism, dedication and pride in serving the nation. They are conscious of our military history and want to uphold the high standards of those who have served before them.

In this book David Horner, Professor of Australian Defence History at the Australian National University, provides a comprehensive but accessible guide to Australian military history. He has undertaken a significant service in explaining how the Australian military has served the nation in war and peace for more than two centuries. He explains what it means to serve in the military and chronicles Australia's role in all our wars and campaigns. I am particularly pleased that he has included vivid and detailed accounts of Australia's most recent operations. This is a scholarly book written by a highly skilled and knowledgeable author. Those familiar with the ADF and our operations will delight in the detail and insight Professor Horner provides.

Equally important though, is that his easy-to-read style and detailed narrative ensures that this book will also appeal to readers without any background knowledge or military experience. The hallmark of the *For Dummies* books is that they are written by experts. I am delighted that the publishers have seen fit to include Australian military history among their list of publications, thus making this aspect of Australian history more accessible to all Australians.

I commend this book to all readers. I consider it to be vitally important that all Australians understand and appreciate the role of the men and women of the ADF — both past and present — in keeping our nation and our national interests secure. I am immensely proud of every one of them, and the people of Australia should be too.

*A G Houston, AC, AFC*
*Air Chief Marshal*
*Chief of the Defence Force*
*June 2010*

# Introduction

Few countries celebrate their military history with as much enthusiasm as Australia. Most Australians possess at least a vague knowledge of the landing at Gallipoli in 1915 and the fighting on the Kokoda Trail in 1942. If you have ever glanced at television on Anzac Day you would be aware of some of the great iconic names of Australian military history. But for the average Australian the details of their military history can be daunting. And this is a shame, because Australians know that their military history is important.

Sure, plenty of good books are available to read, but most tell the story of just one aspect. The real challenge is to grasp the broad sweep of Australian military history — to understand why the nation went to war, why Australians were willing to sacrifice their lives, and how Australia's involvement in war has helped shape and form our society.

I have a passion for Australian military history, which is just as well because I earn my living writing books about it. But I enjoy it not because it pays the bills. I would write about Australian military history even if I were not paid (but don't tell my publishers). I'm enthralled by Australian military history because in the most dramatic and exciting manner it tells the story of who we are as Australians. There is nothing like the stress of battle to bring out the true character of a person, just as there is nothing like a war for survival to test the mettle of a nation.

## About This Book

The essence of writing history is to decide what to leave out. Obviously I cannot include every battle or issue in this book. However, the story of Australia's experience of war is not as extensive as, say, Britain, France or the United States. Australia was settled by Europeans not quite two and a quarter centuries ago. Australia has never had a civil war like the United States, nor has it been invaded like France, or fought numerous colonial wars like Britain. So with judicious selection I am able to include every war and military campaign conducted by the Australian armed forces, even though it might be mentioned only briefly. If you have heard of a particular large battle or campaign you will probably find it mentioned in this book, and you will be able to see where it fits in the bigger picture. In other words, this book is a 'one-stop shop' for military history. If you don't know much about Australian military history, this is the place to start.

Military history is not just about dates and names of units. To understand why military history is important we need to answer some questions:

- Why did Australia become involved in a particular war?
- Why was the campaign or battle conducted in a particular way?
- What are the connections between the different battles and campaigns?
- How did a particular battle affect the soldiers?
- What did a battle or campaign achieve?
- What effect did a battle, campaign or war have on the development of Australia?

To answer these questions I have focused on the how and the why. You might not always agree with my conclusions, but they will at least provide a starting point for debate.

## Conventions Used in This Book

Military history is full of its own peculiar conventions. For example, military units — squadrons, battalions, brigades, divisions, fleets — are usually described in particular ways. I have used these conventions, but you don't need to know them. (I explain what all these units mean in Chapter 2.) However, some conventions in writing military history make sense. Certain facts about a battle need to be explained before we can answer some of the questions posed in the preceding section. These include:

- What was the battle trying to achieve?
- What military units were involved?
- Who was in charge?
- What actually happened during the battle?
- How many casualties did our forces suffer?

In describing most of the battles mentioned in this book I have tried briefly to set out the answers to these basic questions before I get on to the more interesting issues of how and why things turned out the way they did.

## What You're Not to Read

If you really want to understand exactly how a campaign or battle was fought you need a list of the units that took part and their assigned missions. But such detail is not really necessary if you just want to get a feel for the battle and to appreciate what it was like and how it influenced other battles. I have put icons called Technical Stuff beside those passages that describe the details of units or command structures, indicating that you can easily jump over them and still pick up the general story.

Australian military history is full of interesting people and incidents that are not crucial to the overall story, but which I can't resist including. You'll find them in the sidebars — the shaded bits that appear here and there. You can skip the sidebars and not lose something from the main story.

## Foolish Assumptions

Although Australian military history is a relatively small subject by the standards of countries such as the United States or major European nations, it's still not that small. Huge numbers of books are available in bookshops and libraries, which is an indication of the subject's popularity. New books appear each week and no-one can possibly keep up with it all. Because you picked up this book I assume that one or more of the following is true:

- You want a general overview of Australian military history that deals with the major issues of who, what, where, why, when and how.
- You want a quick reference book so that you can quickly locate and place some battle or campaign in the broader story of Australian military history.
- You're interested in discovering how war and the military have shaped Australia as a nation.
- You want to brush up on your knowledge of Australian military history without needing to wade through heavy academic books, or consult unreliable websites, or try to decipher a whole lot of impenetrable military jargon.

# How This Book Is Organised

I have organised this book into eight parts, which cover either a specific topic or deal chronologically with a particular period of Australian military history.

## Part I: The Essentials of Australian Military History

In this part I give you some of the basic information that will help you make sense of the rest of the book. I explain some of the key questions, such as why Australia has gone to war and why Australians are fascinated by their military history. I introduce you to the mysterious world of the military, with its different weapons, ranks, uniforms, medals and its very own language.

## Part II: The Wars of Colonial Australia

Many people think that Australia's military history began with the Gallipoli landing in 1915. But it really began more than a century before, with the arrival of the First Fleet in 1788. In this part I explain how the 19th century Australian colonies had their own military history, ranging from the frontier wars with the Aborigines and the activities of the British garrisons, to the despatch of volunteers to fight in New Zealand, Sudan, China and South Africa as part of the contribution to the defence of the Empire.

## Part III: The First World War: Australia's Greatest Tragedy

The First World War is remembered because of the landing at Gallipoli on 25 April 1915 and because of the huge numbers of Australian casualties suffered there and on the Western Front. From a population of fewer than 5 million, Australia lost almost 60,000 killed. But the war involved more than just Gallipoli and the casualties. In this part I describe the whole Gallipoli campaign, the many battles in France and Belgium culminating in the war-winning offensive of 1918, and the fighting by the Light Horse in the Middle East.

## Part IV: The Second World War: The Empire Beckons

The Second World War began in September 1939 and ended in September 1945. Until Japan entered the war in December 1941 Australia sent forces to help the British Empire in the war against Germany and Italy. In this part I describe the role of the Navy, Army and Air Force in the Middle East and Europe. I discuss the Army's part in the campaigns in North Africa, including the battles of Bardia, Tobruk and El Alamein, and in Greece, Crete and Syria. I also describe the Air Force's part in the bombing offensive over Germany, which resulted in some of Australia's heaviest casualties of the war.

## Part V: Our War in the Pacific

Once Japan joined the war in December 1941 Australia put most of its effort into fighting in the Pacific. For the first time since white settlement Australia faced the possibility of invasion. In this part, I describe how Australian troops suffered heavily in the early stages of the Pacific War. They provided the majority of American General Douglas MacArthur's land forces in 1942–43; halted the Japanese advance in New Guinea; and led the counteroffensive in 1943. The Pacific War became Australia's largest ever military undertaking and decisively influenced the nation's development for the next half-century.

## Part VI: The Aussies Do Their Bit in the Cold War

The Cold War between the American-led Western Alliance and the Soviet bloc lasted from soon after the Second World War in 1946 until the collapse of the Berlin Wall in 1989. As a member of the Western Alliance, Australia played its part in the Cold War, deploying troops to the Korean War (1950–53), the Malayan Emergency (1950–60) and the Vietnam War (1962–72). Australia also helped Britain deal with Indonesia's Confrontation with the new nation of Malaysia. Australia's commitment to these wars was part of a policy known as 'Forward Defence'.

### Part VII: On Overseas Service

Australia's involvement in international peacekeeping activities began in 1947, but became larger and more frequent in the late 1980s and during the 1990s. Ignored in earlier histories, peacekeeping missions are now seen as a legitimate part of Australian military history. After the Vietnam War it seemed that Australia would never again send forces overseas to take part in foreign wars, but in 1991 Australian ships served in the Gulf War. In 2001 Australian troops began operations in Afghanistan, and troops were still serving there in 2010. In 2003 Australia joined the invasion of Iraq, and troops withdrew from Iraq in 2009. The new millennium heralded another phase in Australian military history.

### Part VIII: The Part of Tens

In this part, I provide lists of ten top military leaders, ten famous battles and ten myths about Australian military history. Lists are fun because they're always open to debate. But this part also offers a chance to look across two centuries of history, and to highlight some important people and incidents. You could read this part for entertainment, or you could read it first to gain a taste of what appears in the other parts of the book.

## Icons Used in This Book

To help you get your mind around the diverse aspects of Australian military history I have added icons, or little pictures, beside some paragraphs to draw attention to four different themes. The icons are easy to identity:

This icon focuses on how military campaigns were planned and how battles were fought, and indicates where the hottest action took place.

Military history is replete with curious incidents or interesting comments that illuminate the nature of the campaign or the character of the people involved.

 At various points I describe how the forces were organised, or who was commanding the units, or the command structure, or which units were designated to take part in a battle. I have called this technical stuff. You can skip the technical stuff information if you want to move quickly through the story, but you may want to study it further if you have the time.

 Every now and again I describe some key decision or activity that had a long-term effect on Australian military history, or some battle or incident that shows something special about the Australian military.

# Where To Go from Here

I have written each part so that it makes sense without having to read the other parts. All you need to do is consult the Table of Contents. So if you want to find out why Australia has gone to war, and what its armed forces consist of, you can get the information from Part I. If you're particularly interested in Australia's part in the First World War, consult Part III.

Within each part, the chapters generally follow the story chronologically, although a few chapters, such as Chapter 13, which deals with the Royal Australian Air Force's war in Europe, and Chapter 17, which summarises the home front in the Second World War, are thematic. If your father or uncle served in the Vietnam War you can find out the sort of experiences he might have had from Chapter 20. You can, of course, read the whole book as one amazing story of Australia at war. It's up to you.

# Part I
# The Essentials of Australian Military History

*An arsenal of Aussies*

## In this part ...

Australian military history is the story of Australians fighting to defend the nation. It includes wonderful stories of bravery, inspiring stories of triumph over tragedy, and some less edifying accounts of blunders and even dark deeds. But if you're really going to understand Australian military history you need to get your mind around some of the nuts and bolts of the military.

In this part I explore why and how Australians have gone to war, and explain why Australians think their military history's important. I then introduce the strange and mysterious world of the military. With this background you'll be better able to appreciate the finer points of our two centuries of military history as you work your way through the remainder of the book, or even if you just want to dip into one or two chapters.

# Chapter 1

# Exploring Why Australia Goes to War

*In This Chapter*
- Discovering where Australians have fought
- Finding out why Australians have fought
- Remembering the sacrifice of our troops

Walk into any bookshop in Australia and you'll realise that military history excites the interest of many Australians. History helps us understand who we are as a people, and most Australians understand that the experience of war has been a major factor in making the nation what it is today.

Yet many other countries have been affected by war to a much greater degree than Australia. The United States, for example, fought a war of independence with Britain and endured a dreadful civil war. Most countries of Europe have been invaded. Even Britain, which was last invaded by the Normans in 1066 and fought its last civil war in the 17th century, had its cities flattened in a prolonged German bombing campaign in 1940 and 1941. Elsewhere, countries have fought wars for independence or wars of national liberation.

By contrast with those other countries, since white settlement Australia has never been invaded by a foreign power. The Australian colonies didn't need to fight Britain to win their independence. Modern Australia has never been wracked by civil war. Ethnic conflict in Australia has never led to savage fighting such as we have seen in places like Bosnia, Rwanda or Sri Lanka in recent years. Contests between competing ideologies, such as occurred during the Korean War in the early 1950s, have never touched Australian shores.

In this chapter I explain why Australia has gone to war and how it has helped shape Australia. I then describe the part played by historians, and why Australians continue to be fascinated and inspired by the Anzac legend.

# Where Australians Have Fought

Apart from the conflicts with the Aborigines, all of Australia's wars have been fought overseas. In this book I tell of Australia's involvement in 14 wars. These are:

- **New Zealand, 1863–64.** Australian volunteers served in locally raised British units (see Chapter 3).
- **Sudan, 1885.** A New South Wales contingent assisted British forces (see Chapter 3).
- **South Africa, 1899–1902.** The colonies and later the new Commonwealth of Australia sent contingents to assist the British (see Chapter 4).
- **First World War, 1914–18.** Australia sent troops and ships to assist the Empire (see chapters 5 to 9).
- **Second World War, 1939–45.** Australia sent military forces to assist the Empire in Europe and the Middle East (see chapters 10 to 13), and then fought with the allies in the Pacific (see chapters 14 to 17).
- **Korean War, 1950–53.** Australian forces fought with the United Nations (see Chapter 18).
- **Malaya, 1950–60.** Australia sent military units to assist Britain and the Malayan Government in the Malayan Emergency (see Chapter 19).
- **Malaysia, 1964–66.** Australian forces assisted Britain and Malaysia in countering Indonesia's 'Confrontation' with Malaysia (see Chapter 19).
- **South Vietnam, 1962–72.** Australian forces assisted South Vietnam and the United States (see Chapter 20).
- **Gulf War, 1991.** Australian ships assisted the US-led coalition (see Chapter 22).
- **Afghanistan, 2001–02.** Australian forces assisted the United States (see Chapter 22).
- **Iraq War 2003.** Australian forces assisted the US-led coalition (see Chapter 22).
- **Iraq 2005–09.** Australian forces assisted the US-led coalition (see Chapter 22).
- **Afghanistan, 2005–.** Australia sent units to assist the force organised by the North Atlantic Treaty Organization (see Chapter 22).

# Why Australians Have Fought

The big question in Australian military history is why the nation has fought in so many wars. The short answer is that Australians, like all peoples, crave security. People feel secure if they believe that they're unlikely to be invaded, and people feel safe if they can go about their lives without fear of starving or of being mistreated. The great paradox is that while Australians have fought in 14 wars in the last 150 years, for most of that time Australia has been one of the most secure lands on Earth. In this regard, Australia has been the lucky country, and there are a variety of reasons for this.

- Australia is an island continent and any potential enemy needs to cross the oceans before it can mount an attack.
- Apart from the Aborigines, for most of its modern history Australia has been relatively free from ethnic and racial conflict. (I discuss conflict with the Aborigines in Chapter 3.)
- Australia has always been largely self-sufficient in food, so Australians knew that whatever might happen elsewhere they would not starve.
- Australians have always been ruled by democratic governments. With minor exceptions, such as at the Eureka Stockade in 1854 (see Chapter 3), Australians have never felt that they needed to take up arms against the government.
- Australia has no natural or historical enemies in the way that Koreans hate the Japanese, or in past centuries, the way Britain and France were enemies.
- Australia was part of the most powerful empire in the world, the British Empire. Then Australia became allied with the United States. Having powerful friends in a dangerous world is very comforting.

Some of the attributes that made Australia secure could also work to make Australians feel insecure. For example, if an enemy turned up unexpectedly Australia was a long way from its friends. And while Australia seemed remote from the wars in Europe, even just rumours of wars could cause concern. Clinging precariously to a foothold on a vast continent across the other side of the world from Britain, the early settlers, who were few in number, knew that their security and safety could be affected by conflicts elsewhere. The colonists feared that foreign warships would suddenly appear and threaten to bombard their cities. With the rise of Japan at the end of the 19th century, Australians feared that if Britain was preoccupied in Europe Australia might be exposed to attack by Japan.

Just as people in the community feel safe if they see the police walking the beat, a nation feels more secure if its armed forces have the ability to defeat the enemy. If the nation is small and its armed forces are weak, the next best way to feel secure is to have some reliable friends. The young Australian colonies expected to gain security through their membership of the British Empire. They hoped that Britain's Royal Navy would keep enemy fleets away from Australia and would protect their seaborne commerce. In return, and to a very limited degree, the colonies thought that they should help pull their weight in defending the Empire.

So volunteers went off to fight in New Zealand, and soldiers went to Sudan, and in larger numbers to South Africa. Australia continued to seek security by supporting its great and powerful friends in wars overseas, hoping that they would help Australia in time of need.

## *Australianists and Imperialists*

After Federation in 1901 the new nation's politicians and military leaders needed to consider how they would go about defending Australia. They broadly divided into two camps, the Australianists and the Imperialists.

- The **Australianists** believed that Australia should look after its own defence. Australia should form its own Navy and should possess a large Army made up of compulsorily enlisted part-time soldiers. The Army should not be permitted to serve overseas, but should be kept in Australia for home defence.
- The **Imperialists** believed that Australia couldn't defend itself alone and that Australia was best defended by cooperating with other British Empire countries. If the Empire were threatened elsewhere, then Australia should send troops overseas and Australian ships should operate as part of Britain's Royal Navy.

These apparently opposing views were not held in absolute terms. Australian ships could serve near home and across the world. People who believed in home defence could also see the value of working with the British Empire. Most Australians accepted that it was better to fight enemies far from Australia than to wait until they drew closer.

The Australianist and Imperialist approaches to Australian defence still exist, although with different names. After the Second World War the Imperialists became supporters of the Western Alliance. They believed that Australia needed to cooperate with its allies around the world. On the other hand, following the philosophy of the earlier Australianists, many Australians were still wary of sending forces overseas. As recently as 2007 the Howard Liberal–National Party Government argued that troops needed to serve in Iraq in support of the US-led coalition, while the Labor Party Opposition, led by Kevin Rudd, vowed to withdraw the troops if they won the 2007 election. Labor won and withdrew the troops.

But the reasons for supporting allies are more complex than simply paying an insurance premium on future security. Australia has been willing to lend its support to defeating evil regimes. The First World War was fought to defeat Prussian militarism. In the Second World War Australian servicemen fought to destroy the evils of Nazism, Fascism and Japanese barbarism. They truly felt that they were fighting in a noble cause. The clichés that we hear on Anzac Day, such as 'they gave their lives to keep us free', have a large measure of truth. In later wars Australians have fought communism and jihadism. (The *jihadists* are Muslims who believe in fighting a holy war.)

## Global conflicts that shaped the nation

Without question, the two world wars were the largest and most costly wars that Australians have been involved in, and they shaped the new nation. From a population of fewer than five million people, in the First World War Australia sent more than 300,000 soldiers to fight overseas and about 60,000 of them were killed. Few families in Australia were untouched in some way.

The men who fought at Gallipoli in 1915 were known as Anzacs because they served in the Australian and New Zealand Army Corps (ANZAC). Their achievement at Gallipoli, with its mateship, courage and endurance, became immortalised as the 'Anzac legend'. The new nation of Australia found its identity on the slopes of Gallipoli. The soldiers, sailors and airmen who served in later wars were seen as upholding the Anzac legend or demonstrating the Anzac spirit. (For the story of the Anzac Corps and the Anzac legend see chapters 5 and 6.)

The Second World War shaped the nation perhaps even more. Around the world Australian servicemen reconfirmed the Anzac legend, but there were broader effects. The industrialisation of Australia began during the war. Threatened with invasion, Australians realised that in future they would need to look to their own security. As a result, the post-war government introduced a massive immigration scheme that helped build up the Australian economy.

Australians have rarely needed to fight in direct defence of Australia. The only major occasion was in 1941–42 when Japanese forces advanced through South-East Asia, bombed northern Australian towns, and actually ventured into Sydney Harbour in mini-submarines. The Australian troops serving in New Guinea felt that they were fighting to prevent a Japanese invasion.

## Supporting our friends

Since the Second World War Australia has been involved in nine wars in which the chief reason for becoming involved was to support our allies, Britain and particularly the United States. But often the support has also been for a UN mission. For example, the US-led operations in the Korean War and in the Gulf in 1991 were authorised by the United Nations.

Critics of Australia's involvement in these wars have usually claimed that Australia was unnecessarily subservient to Britain or the United States. In response the government has usually made three strong arguments:

- Australia's interests are served by strengthening its alliance with the United States, which is the most powerful factor in ensuring Australia's future security.
- Many of the wars, such as the Korean War, the 1991 Gulf War, Iraq in 2003–09 and Afghanistan, were supported by the wider international community.
- The wars conducted by Britain and the United States were fully justified and Australia supported their aims.

Large groups in the Australian community have disagreed vociferously with these arguments. In particular, many people opposed Australia's involvement in Vietnam in 1966 and Iraq in 1991 and 2003. But the decisions have generally been supported by the majority of Australians.

## Doing good in the world

Apart from being involved in wars, Australians have served overseas in many other circumstances. These include:

- Occupying an enemy country after a war, such as in Japan in 1946–50 (see Chapter 18).
- Contributing to United Nations peacekeeping missions (see Chapter 21).
- Contributing to regionally organised peacekeeping missions, such as in Bougainville and the Solomon Islands (see Chapter 21).
- Maintaining troops in a friendly country to assist with their security, such as in Malaysia (see Chapter 19).
- Training the armies of friendly countries in the aftermath of war, such as in Uganda, or helping countries to become more secure, such as in Papua New Guinea (see Chapter 21).

- Helping to rebuild countries after conflict, such as clearing land mines in Afghanistan, Mozambique and Cambodia (see Chapter 21).
- Providing humanitarian assistance after natural disasters, such as in Indonesia after the 2004 tsunami.

There are many reasons Australia has become involved in such activities. Obviously it's good for Australia if the world is a more peaceful place. But Australia is especially interested in trying to ensure that nearby countries don't become places that can harbour enemies, so Australia has put more emphasis on peacekeeping and assistance missions in these countries. Sometimes our allies have asked us to take part in certain operations. Usually Australia has sent forces overseas for a combination of reasons.

On occasions, however, Australia has been motivated simply by a desire to do good works. Australia's long-serving Foreign Minister Gareth Evans, declared that Australia was an 'international good citizen'. For the troops, some of the most satisfying missions have been when they've been able to ease pain and suffering, or help people to live more peacefully.

# Remembering Our Military History

Interest in Australian military history is strengthened because most Australians know that their troops have fought and sacrificed their lives for the defence and security of Australia. They also appreciate that most of the Australians who've been killed in war fought as volunteers and almost all of them died in distant lands.

Thousands of Australians now travel to foreign countries to see where their relatives fought. Perhaps they want to understand why so many of their forebears were willing to leave the relative comfort of home and to risk their lives fighting around the world.

## Revisiting the stories of Australia at war

Australian military history is obviously concerned with the experiences and exploits of Australia's armed forces in war. But military history comes in many forms, including:

- Comprehensive histories of Australia's involvement in major wars
- Studies of high-level policy making
- Histories of particular battles and military campaigns

- Biographies of military leaders
- Analyses of military tactics and techniques
- Personal memoirs and stories of the exploits of remarkable individuals
- Histories of military units and organisations
- Sociological studies of subjects such as morale and leadership
- Studies of how war has affected society

The stories of Australia's war experiences are told by all sorts of people, ranging from professional historians like me who work in universities, through to journalists, former military people and enthusiastic (but often very talented) amateurs.

Australia's most famous military historian was the journalist Charles Bean, who accompanied the Australian troops in the First World War and wrote most of the 12-volume official history of the war. Bean told the story of ordinary Australians and he emphasised the war's role in helping to give Australians a sense of belonging to one nation. The official historians of the later wars followed Bean's model. Few Australians have read the official histories — they're too long and detailed — but they've become the starting point for almost all other writings on the major Australian wars.

Australian military history has been told in feature films. Charles Chauvel's *Forty Thousand Horsemen* (1940) portrays the Australian Light Horse in the First World War. Bruce Beresford's *Breaker Morant* (1980) is set in the Boer War and Peter Weir's *Gallipoli* (1981) focuses on the Gallipoli campaign. Military history also appears in television documentaries and dramas.

The stories of Australians at war can be found in thousands of books and magazine articles. Hundreds of television documentaries have been produced. No one organisation or group of people can own Australian military history. Anyone who wishes to take the time and effort can have his or her say. Most historians try to be accurate and factual, but history is always open to interpretation and argument.

## *Honouring the Anzac legend*

Australians continue to be fascinated with and inspired by the Anzac legend and they honour it by keeping the story alive. Beyond books and films, Australians are made aware of their military history through commemorative activities. The most obvious example takes place on Anzac Day (25 April) when men and women who have served in the armed forces march through the nation's cities and towns, and lay wreaths at war memorials.

## Chapter 1: Exploring Why Australia Goes to War

The government and private citizens continue to find more ways to honour the Anzacs. In the past, memorials were constructed in France, Belgium and at Gallipoli. In recent years the government has built memorials in places such as Isurava on the Kokoda Trail in Papua New Guinea, at Hellfire Pass on the notorious Thai-Burma Railway in Thailand and at Le Hamel in northern France.

In 1995 the Commonwealth Government organised the 'Australia Remembers' year to mark the fiftieth anniversary of the end of the Second World War. More controversially, in 2008 the government announced that the first Wednesday in September would become 'Battle of Australia' Day to commemorate the defence of Australia in the Second World War. Many historians have pointed out that there was never an actual battle of Australia.

An entire industry has now been built on honouring the Anzac legend. Whether prime ministers and governments have fostered this industry for political purposes (because they know that it strikes a chord in the community) or whether governments have merely responded to a mood from within the community is hard to determine. Whatever the answer might be, there is no doubt that Australians have an abiding interest in their military history.

# Chapter 2

# Coming to Grips with the Military

## In This Chapter

▶ Discerning an Australian way of war
▶ Sorting out the differences between the Navy, the Army and the Air Force
▶ Putting our Australian Diggers on parade

*I*f you've never served in the military, then its ranks, organisation and special ways of doing things can be a bit of a mystery. Even the word 'military' can be confusing. In past centuries the term referred to the members of the army, but these days it usually includes members of all the armed forces.

Actually, understanding the military is not all that hard. The armed forces of most countries are structured in the same way. They have a navy, which consists of ships (unless the country is landlocked and doesn't have a coastline), an army, which does the fighting on land, and an air force, which naturally contains the military aircraft. Even military ranks are similar. Most armies have sergeants, captains, majors and colonels. I give more information on what the ranks mean later in this chapter.

While basic structures are similar, each country's armed forces have their own special characteristics, which are determined by their circumstances. Some countries have large armies and small navies; a few countries have the opposite. In many countries young people are compelled to serve; other countries rely on volunteers. Nations also use their armed forces in different ways.

In this chapter I describe how, except in the war against the Aborigines, we have always fought overseas and alongside allies, and I explain why it is that politicians, rather than military leaders make the decisions about how our forces are used. I describe the components of our armed forces — the navy, army, air force and the more recently formed Australian Defence Force. You'll learn that the Australian military has included part-time and citizen soldiers, conscripts and regulars, and that surprisingly only a few — the infantry, pilots and sailors — actually do the front-line fighting.

# How Do We Fight?

Nations fight their wars in different ways, reflecting their history, geography and form of government. Some are willing to accept heavy casualties. Others plan to conduct a guerrilla war if they're invaded.

- Vulnerable countries like Israel prefer to get in first and strike their enemies if they think they're about to be attacked. The military call this a pre-emptive strike.
- Countries with long land borders and open plains, such as Germany in the Second World War and Iraq in the 1980s and 1990s, usually deploy large armies with armoured vehicles supported by aircraft in an attempt to overwhelm their enemies quickly. The military call this a blitzkrieg (lightning war).

Australia does none of these things. It prefers to fight overseas alongside allies to ensure that an enemy doesn't come near to the homeland. In the First and Second World Wars Australia sent large numbers of troops overseas, but after dreadful casualties Australia was less inclined to commit many troops in later wars. Instead, Australia sent relatively small numbers of troops overseas to show that it supported its allies, but not to risk heavy losses.

## Fighting alongside allies

Fighting alongside larger allies (military people call this *coalition warfare*) creates special problems. Australia's political leaders have always struggled to influence the way its larger allies have conducted the war. In the First World War the Australian Government accepted that Britain was running the war and it only learned that its troops had landed at Gallipoli some days after the event. In the Vietnam War the Australian Government had no say in the conduct of the war, even though its troops were involved.

## Chapter 2: Coming to Grips with the Military

> ## Military speak
>
> The armed forces speak a separate language, which at times is incomprehensible to ordinary people. In battle, military officers need to write orders very quickly and the military has developed a sort of shorthand, which all military people have to learn. Ordinary words are shortened. For example, the enemy becomes the 'en' and location becomes 'loc'. A 'locstat' is a statement of where a unit is located. The infantry are the 'inf' and the artillery are the 'arty'. The names of organisations, commanders and weapons are shortened by acronyms. One of the best known is the Australian and New Zealand Army Corps, which became ANZAC, and is now recognised by most Australians. The Australian Imperial Force (AIF) is also well known. But some acronyms can seem quite bizarre. For instance a Combined Special Operations Task Force is known as a 'CSOTF' and in conversation it is pronounced 'ca-sot-if'. Military abbreviations and acronyms are so numerous and confusing that the military list them in a special book. I've tried to keep military speak to a minimum in this *For Dummies* book.

On the battlefield, Australian military units have often served under British or American commanders. In the First World War Australian generals learnt to scrutinise carefully the plans prepared by their British superiors. After that, all Australian commanders were given the right to refuse a foreign commander's orders and to appeal to the Australian Government if they believed that their troops were being placed in an unnecessarily risky position, or were being ordered to do something that was contrary to Australian policy. In the Second World War in 1940, the British commander in the Middle East, General Wavell, ordered the Australian commander, General Blamey, to send part of his force from Palestine to Egypt. Blamey refused because the Australian Government required him to keep his force together as one organisation.

## *The pollies are in charge*

Australia is a democracy and its armed forces (the *Australian Defence Force* — the ADF) exist to serve the people of Australia. The armed forces are not allowed to carry out any activity, except for their normal training, without the permission of the government. Politicians rather than military leaders decide whether the armed forces are to be deployed overseas to take part in a peacekeeping mission or a war. During the Vietnam War some anti-war protesters abused our troops for serving in Vietnam. Such abuse was very unfair because the troops were acting at the direction of the government. It's illegal for troops to refuse to carry out orders from the government.

The ADF comes under the direction of the Minister for Defence. But important decisions such as to send troops overseas or to purchase expensive equipment are approved by the Federal Cabinet. The Defence Minister gives his orders to the Chief of the Defence Force (CDF). If the CDF does not agree with the government's decision, he has only two choices: He must either obey his orders or he must resign. When the Howard Government wanted to send troops to take part in the invasion of Iraq in 2003 it directed the CDF, General Peter Cosgrove, to make the appropriate plans and to send the troops.

## Her Majesty's Forces Down Under

Australian servicepeople serve the nation and they normally have the word 'Australia' sewn on the shoulders of their uniforms. Because Australia is a monarchy they are considered to serve the Queen, and her representative, the Governor General, is the Commander-in-Chief of the ADF.

The Governor General can't issue orders directly to the ADF; it receives its orders from the government. But recognising that the ADF acts on behalf of the Queen of Australia, its elements usually have Royal in their title. The Royal Australian Navy's ships have the title Her Majesty's Australian Ship (HMAS). The Army does not have the royal title but generally its components each have the Royal title; for example, the Royal Australian Armoured Corps.

## Royal Australian Navy

Following British tradition, the Royal Australian Navy (RAN) is called the senior service and is always listed first. The role of the Navy is to protect Australia by patrolling the seas and to fight naval battles if necessary. Australian ships might also be sent to work with Allied navies or to support Australian forces serving overseas.

Since Federation, the Navy's ships have come in all shapes and sizes, and warships are given different names, depending on their size and function. The biggest and most powerful warships in the First World War were the *battleships*, which were fast, well armoured and carried numerous high-powered, long-range guns. Australia has never possessed battleships. Slightly smaller ships were called *cruisers*, and the RAN possessed several of them in the First and Second World Wars. The best known was HMAS *Sydney*, which sank an Italian cruiser in 1940 and was itself sunk off the coast of Western Australia (see Chapter 10). Smaller than the cruisers were the *destroyers*, which were fast and manoeuvrable and were often used to help protect battleships from a sneak attack by small craft carrying torpedoes. Smaller warships include sloops, frigates, corvettes and patrol boats. The RAN's main combat ship is now the *frigate*, but it also has patrol boats and supply ships.

Australia had a few submarines during the First World War, but they weren't reintroduced into the RAN until the 1960s. After the Second World War the RAN obtained two aircraft carriers, *Sydney* and *Melbourne,* which served until 1973 and 1982 respectively. During the world wars the RAN also had armed merchant cruisers; that is, merchant ships that were equipped with guns.

Although the Navy's ships have generally been getting smaller, they have been equipped with increasingly powerful weapons. Ships still carry guns, but their main weapons include guided missiles, which can be used to shoot down aircraft and strike other ships, and they carry helicopters.

When a navy deploys a large number of ships at sea they're usually called a *fleet*. But because the RAN has always been fairly small, it has never had more than one fleet, and all the ships of the RAN are known as the Fleet. Smaller groups of ships are called squadrons or flotillas. When ships are brought together for specific tasks they form task forces or task groups.

The Navy consists of a relatively small number of ships, but each ship is generally self-contained. Each ship includes guns and gunners, communications equipment and technicians to maintain it, engineers to keep the engines running, cooks and supplies of food, supply staff, medical personnel, and helicopters with their crews and technicians. A well-maintained Navy ship can be deployed at quite short notice.

## *Australian Army*

The Army is structured in a completely different way to the Navy. Soldiers are grouped in organisations that reflect their jobs. For example, infantry soldiers are in the Royal Australian Infantry Corps. Transport drivers serve in the Royal Australian Corps of Transport. When the Army needs to undertake a task it draws on the personnel from the different corps to form temporary organisations.

Over the past century the basic fighting unit in the Australian Army has been the infantry battalion. In the First World War an infantry battalion had about 1,000 soldiers, but it now has about 700. For more than half a century an infantry battalion has generally consisted of four rifle companies, a support company and an administrative company. The infantry use rifles, machine guns and small support weapons.

Army organisations are fairly standard around the world and are built up incrementally as shown in Table 2-1.

| Table 2-1 | Army organisations | |
|---|---|---|
| **Organisation** | **Consists of** | **Commanded by** |
| Infantry battalion | Four rifle companies and support troops (700–1,000 troops) | Lieutenant colonel |
| Brigade | Three infantry battalions and support troops (3,000–4,000 troops) | Brigadier |
| Division | Three brigades and support troops (12,000–20,000 troops) | Major general |
| Corps | Two or three divisions and support troops (30,000–60,000 troops) | Lieutenant general |
| Army | Two or three corps and support troops (100,000 plus troops) | General |

The Army makes things confusing by using the same names for different purposes. The Infantry Corps is a management grouping that looks after all the Army's infantrymen, but the corps in Table 2-1 is a fighting organisation. The Australian Army contains all Australia's soldiers, but the army in Table 2-1 is a fighting organisation. So in the Second World War the Australian Army (the big national organisation) included the First and Second Australian Armies. That is the only time that the Australian Army has been large enough to put separate armies in the field.

Army units are numbered; for example, 1st, 2nd Battalion and so on. In the Second World War units in the 2nd Australian Imperial Force (see Chapter 10) were given the prefix '2'; for example, the 2/3rd Australian Anti-Tank Regiment.

As well as the infantry, fighting is also done by the cavalry. In the old days, cavalry on horses roamed far and wide seeking the enemy. In the First World War the Australian cavalry was provided by units called the Light Horse. These days the cavalry use armoured vehicles.

Sometimes television reporters inaccurately describe any armoured vehicle with caterpillar tracks as a tank. Proper tanks have very thick armour to protect the crews. They fire large calibre guns with explosive shells and are used to attack enemy positions or to deal with enemy tanks. Australian tanks supported the Australian infantry in New Guinea and Bougainville in the Second World War, and in South Vietnam. By contrast, armoured personnel carriers (APCs) have much thinner armour, which affords protection from rifle and machine gun fire but not from enemy tank fire. APCs are normally only armed with machine guns. APCs can carry up to ten infantry soldiers onto the battlefield, but aren't generally used for direct attacks on enemy positions.

> **Supporting and protecting the infantry**
>
> When infantry fight they're generally supported by artillery units, which fire the very big guns. The artillery helps the infantry by pounding enemy positions or by destroying enemy fighters who are attacking the infantry. Artillery guns come in different sizes. While guns used to be named after the weight of the shells they fired they're now known by the diameter of their barrel (the calibre). The 18-pounder gun used in the First World War had a range of six kilometres. The 155 mm howitzer (gun) presently in use can fire up to 30 kilometres with a rocket-assisted shell. The gunners are so far away from their targets that they need to do mathematical calculations (nowadays done by computers) to make the shells land and explode in the right place.

## *Royal Australian Air Force*

The RAAF was formed in 1921 and first went to war in the Second World War. Since then the RAAF has flown four general categories of aircraft on operations:

- **Fighters.** These are relatively small aircraft, usually with one pilot, and are designed to engage and shoot down enemy aircraft. The famous Spitfire, flown by Australian pilots in the Second World War, fired machine guns and cannon. Modern fighters, such as the F/A-18 Hornet, fire air-to-air and air-to-surface missiles, guided electronically.

- **Bombers.** These are larger aircraft which drop bombs on enemy positions, factories and transport centres. The Second World War Lancaster bomber had a crew of seven airmen. Australia's F-111 strike aircraft, which the RAAF first started operating in the early 1970s and has used for some four decades, has a crew of only a pilot and a navigator. It can drop laser-guided bombs.

- **Maritime patrol aircraft.** These aircraft carry out long-range reconnaissance patrols at sea to detect enemy ships or civilian vessels. In the Second World War, RAAF squadrons based in England flew Sunderland flying boats. The RAAF presently flies the AP3-C Orion aircraft, which has a crew of 12 airmen, most of whom are electronics analysts.

- **Transport aircraft.** In the Second World War, and in the following decade, the RAAF flew the Dakota DC3 transport aircraft. This was succeeded by the C-130 Hercules, and these have been replaced several times with newer models. The RAAF has also flown smaller transport aircraft such as the DHC-4 Caribou.

The basic fighting unit in the Royal Australian Air Force (RAAF) is the *squadron*, which normally contains 12 to 24 aircraft divided into three or four flights, and is commanded by a wing commander. Like Army units, the squadrons are numbered; for example, No 3 Squadron. Three or more squadrons form a *wing*, and two or three wings form a *group*. In the Second World War the RAAF formed the 1st Tactical Air Force with several groups.

## *Forming the Australian Defence Force*

Anyone with even a passing knowledge of the Australian military knows that it's called the Australian Defence Force (ADF). However, most people are unaware that the ADF didn't exist before 1976. From the First World War to the Vietnam War the three Australian Services — the RAN, the Australian Army and the RAAF — tended to operate separately. For example, in 1941 in the Second World War the RAAF's bomber squadrons were serving in England, the Australian Army's units were operating alongside the British Army in North Africa, and Australian ships were serving under British command in the Mediterranean. Even in the Vietnam War in the late 1960s the three Services generally worked separately under American commanders, except for the RAAF helicopters, which assisted the army. When they needed to, the Services worked together through cooperative arrangements.

After the Vietnam War, Australian political and military leaders realised that if the Services were to defend Australia they would need to be able to operate together. In 1973 the Navy, Army and Air Departments, which had existed since 1939 with their own ministers, were abolished and absorbed into the Department of Defence. In 1976 General Sir Francis Hassett took over as Chief of the Defence Force Staff, with command authority over the three Services, and a new organisation, the ADF, came into being.

Over the following decades arrangements were instituted to make it easier for the Services to work together in operations. These included:

- The Chief of Defence Force Staff changed his title to Chief of the Defence Force (CDF) to emphasise that he commanded all the ADF.
- Officer cadets from the three Services received their education together at the new Australian Defence Force Academy in Canberra.
- The Services logistic support organisations were brought together under one ADF Joint Logistics Command.

- The Services operational commands — Maritime, Land and Air Commands — were deemed to be 'joint' and came under the command of the CDF for operations.
- A Chief of Joint Operations was appointed to command all ADF operations on behalf of the CDF.
- When the three Services operated overseas in the same location they were placed under the command of a single ADF officer. It did not matter whether he was a Navy, Army or Air Force officer, he commanded all three Services in the area.

The three Services still exist and they have their own identities, but they know that they're all part of the one ADF.

## Chief of the chiefs

The Chief of the Defence Force (CDF) commands all the ADF, but he is assisted by the Chiefs of the Navy, Army and Air Force. (The CDF was originally called Chief of Defence Force Staff, but he fulfilled the same role.) The CDF commands the ADF's operations through the Chief of Joint Operations. Before the position of CDF was established in 1976 the Service chiefs dealt directly with the Minister for their Service. Since the appointment began, the following officers have commanded the ADF.

**Chief of Defence Force Staff**

General Sir Francis Hassett, 1976–77
General Sir Arthur MacDonald, 1977–79
Admiral Sir Anthony Synnot, 1979–82
Air Chief Marshal Sir Neville McNamara, 1982–84
General Sir Phillip Bennett, 1984–86

**Chief of the Defence Force**

General Sir Phillip Bennett, 1986–87
General Peter Gration, 1987–93
Admiral Alan Beaumont, 1993–95
General John Baker, 1995–98
Admiral Chris Barrie, 1998–2002
General Peter Cosgrove, 2002–05
Air Chief Marshal Angus Houston, 2005–

## The Diggers

The real heroes of Australian military history are the Diggers. Originally the term referred to Australian soldiers, but is now often extended to cover sailors and airmen as well.

Two aspects of military service make it completely different from any other activity in society — killing and dying. The purposes of military service are noble — protecting the country, or protecting other countries from aggression, or peacekeeping missions. But the means of achieving these purposes are nasty and brutal; ultimately it involves killing as effectively as possible. Soldiers don't join the Army to kill people, but they can only be successful if they're good at killing. Many military people are severely traumatised by their military service because by instinct, as well as belief in the sanctity of life, they're not killers.

Military service is different from any other profession or calling in that its members can be ordered to die. In the First World War one in five Australian soldiers on the Western Front died on active service. Fortunately military personnel no longer face odds like these. But we still expect our armed forces to achieve their missions even if it means our servicepeople have to die.

Until the Second World War the only women in the armed forces were nurses, but in that war the Services enlisted women to undertake non-combatant tasks (see Chapter 17). In the 1980s the Services began opening up jobs to women in combat and combat-related positions. Women can now fly combat aircraft, serve in Navy ships and work in Army jobs where they may become engaged in combat. But women are still prevented from working in Army units such as the infantry, which have the prime role of engaging in direct combat.

## Amateurs, Regulars and Nashos

The Australian Army in the First World War was unique in that everyone serving overseas was a volunteer, and many had no previous military service. The senior officers were drawn from Australia's tiny regular army and from the larger part-time militia forces. The militia, which included compulsorily enlisted soldiers, was not allowed to serve outside Australia, although its members could volunteer to join the specially raised force (the Australian Imperial Force) that deployed overseas.

Much the same thing happened in the Second World War, but as the war came closer to Australia the militia were called up to full-time service. They served in Papua and New Guinea, which were Australian territories, where they fought side-by-side with volunteers.

After the Second World War Australia formed a Regular Army, but also retained the part-time Citizen Military Forces (CMF). Only Regular soldiers served in the Korean War and in Malaya. In the 1960s the government reintroduced compulsory service, and national servicemen (Nashos) along with Regular soldiers served in Vietnam. Since Vietnam, most of the burden of Australia's overseas operations has been borne by the Regular Army, although part-time soldiers (now called Reservists because they're in the Army Reserve), are used to bolster their numbers. Over the past century, Australian soldiers have served in action on operations in one of four capacities:

- Regular and part-time (amateur) soldiers who volunteered to serve overseas.
- Ordinary citizens, with no prior military training, who voluntarily enlisted to serve overseas.
- Ordinary Australians who were conscripted into the army; they were known as conscripts or national servicemen.
- Regular soldiers who served overseas as part of their normal employment.

Regular Navy personnel were always required to serve overseas, although in the world wars their numbers were bolstered by Reservists and by sailors who joined just for the war. A similar situation applied to the Air Force.

## On the front-line: Those doing the fighting

Everyone in the armed forces, except for medical personnel and chaplains, can be required to fight. They all receive basic military training and learn how to use their weapons. But not everyone is required to engage the enemy in the normal course of their duties. In the Army, the soldiers whose main job is to fight the enemy at close range are called the *infantry*, sometimes called the PBI — the *poor bloody infantry* — because they end up doing the hardest work and take the most casualties. Other soldiers engage the enemy with longer-range weapons. These include soldiers in armoured vehicles, or helicopters, or those firing long-range guns.

Many more soldiers are needed to support the combat soldiers. These include communicators, intelligence analysts, drivers, engineers, supply troops, medical personnel, cooks, clerks, repairers, trainers and military police. Generally, the Army's support personnel are further away from the front-line than the infantry, but they can still be required to serve in the front-line, and wherever they serve in an operational area they are vulnerable to attack. In the military, administrative support is called logistics.

In the Navy the fighting is undertaken by ships, and within a ship only a small number of sailors actually fire the weapons. But everyone on a ship — the gunners, missile operators, communicators, engineers, medical personnel, cooks and supply clerks — are equally at risk if the ship is attacked. Indeed if the ship is sunk the engineers, deep in the bowels of a ship, are perhaps in more danger than the sailors on deck. On the other hand, the people serving in the Naval bases are often well way from the combat area.

In the Air Force the fighting is undertaken by the aircraft, so the only people to engage in combat are the aircrew. In the Second World War the aircrews in the bombing campaigns over Germany suffered heavy casualties. It was more dangerous to serve in a bomber crew than in the infantry. Fighter aircraft generally have only one pilot. Larger aircraft have several crewmen, including pilots, navigators, bomb-aimers and radio operators. But vast numbers of people in the Air Force — weapons fitters, maintenance crews, refuellers, intelligence analysts, radar operators, supply personnel, medical staff and so on — work at air bases that can be hundreds of kilometres from the combat area.

## Not avoiding the fighting

By pointing out that not everyone faces the same level of exposure to combat I don't intend to demean those in the less risky jobs. Everyone in the armed forces knows that they're part of one team. The fighter pilot's life depends on the skill of his or her maintenance crew. The vagaries of war are such that support troops can find themselves under fire. During the siege of Tobruk in North Africa in 1941 the troops who were unloading ships in the port, under constant enemy air attack, were in just as much danger as the infantry in their trenches. In Vietnam I knew a soldier in an infantry platoon who asked to be moved out because infantry work in the jungle was too dangerous. He was given the job of driving the vehicle used by the Salvation Army representative. He soon found himself driving alone with the 'Salvo' through Viet Cong-dominated villages and along lonely jungle tracks on frightening journeys to bring a cup of tea and a biscuit to the infantry.

## Knowing when to salute

The armed forces are built around a hierarchy of ranks. At the bottom are the sailors, soldiers and airmen. At the top are the admirals, generals and air marshals. Military personnel are divided into commissioned officers and 'other ranks'. Officers are given a commission (a piece of paper giving them command authority) by the Governor General on behalf of the Queen. The officers are the leaders and managers.

The sailors, soldiers and airmen who form the other ranks do the real work. Among the other ranks, some soldiers have positions with authority. They're called *non-commissioned officers* (NCOs). A sergeant is a senior NCO and sergeants are usually described as 'the backbone of the army'. Some soldiers are given extra authority and called warrant officers. To recognise the special authority of commissioned officers, the other ranks are required to salute them. A junior commissioned officer is also required to salute a more senior officer.

The top military officers — the admiral, generals and air marshals — are colloquially known as 'the top brass' or 'brass hats'. In the old days military people wore brass buckles and badges.

Military ranks are very important because officers have the authority to issue legal orders that might result in killing the enemy or in the death of their own troops. Failure to obey a legal command can result in punishment, including imprisonment (in the old days a person disobeying a legal command could be flogged). The ranks in the three services have different names, but are generally equivalent, as shown in Table 2-2, going from the most junior to the most senior.

| Table 2-2 | Ranks in the Royal Australian Navy, Australian Army and Royal Australian Air Force | |
|---|---|---|
| *Navy* | *Army* | *Air Force* |
| Seaman | Private | Aircraftman/woman |
| Able Seaman | Private (Proficient) | Leading aircraftman/woman |
| — | Lance Corporal | — |
| Leading Seaman | Corporal | Corporal |
| Petty Officer | Sergeant | Sergeant |
| — | Staff Sergeant | Flight Sergeant |

*(continued)*

### Table 2-2 *(continued)*

| Navy | Army | Air Force |
|---|---|---|
| Chief Petty Officer | Warrant Officer Class 2 | – |
| Warrant Officer | Warrant Officer Class 1 | Warrant Officer |
| – | Second Lieutenant | Pilot Officer |
| Sub-Lieutenant | Lieutenant | Flying Officer |
| Lieutenant | Captain | Flight Lieutenant |
| Lieutenant Commander | Major | Squadron Leader |
| Commander | Lieutenant Colonel | Wing Commander |
| Captain | Colonel | Group Captain |
| Commodore | Brigadier | Air Commodore |
| Rear Admiral | Major General | Air Vice-Marshal |
| Vice-Admiral | Lieutenant General | Air Marshal |
| Admiral | General | Air Chief Marshal |

## *Honouring the brave*

Military personnel are awarded medals to recognise their service. Until the 1970s, they were awarded British, or more strictly Imperial Medals, because they were awarded throughout the British Empire. After that, Australia began issuing its own medals (the Australian honours system). Generally medals are awarded for three categories of military service:

- **Campaign or service medals.** These medals recognise operational service overseas. If a military campaign is particularly noteworthy a separate medal might be awarded. Service in the Second World War resulted in the award of the 1939–45 Star, while servicemen who served in North Africa received the Africa Star as well. Under the Australian system, servicepeople on warlike operations presently receive the Australian Active Service Medal. Those who served in Iraq also received the Iraq Medal.

- **Medals for good work.** These medals recognise exceptional work either in peace or war. Under the Imperial system a serviceperson may be made a Member of the Order of the British Empire (MBE). Under the Australian system, he or she may be made a Companion or Member of the Order of Australia (AC or AM), or be awarded a special Defence Force medal, such as a Conspicuous Service Medal (CSM).

- **Medals for bravery.** The most highly prized medals are those awarded for bravery in battle, or for distinguished command in battle. Under the Imperial system a brave officer may be awarded a Military Cross (MC), while under the Australian system a similar officer would be awarded the Medal for Gallantry (MG). Under the Imperial system a commanding officer who led his troops in a successful battle might be awarded a Distinguished Service Order (DSO), while under the Australian system he would receive a Distinguished Service Cross (DSC). The most coveted medal, awarded for valour 'in the presence of the enemy' is the Victoria Cross (VC). Under the Australian system it is called the Victoria Cross for Australia. To date, 97 Australians have been awarded the VC, including the VC for Australia earned by Trooper Mark Donaldson for service in Afghanistan in 2008 (see Chapter 22).

Servicepeople who are awarded medals in the latter two categories are generally permitted to place letters after their names, indicating their awards. The Chief of the Defence Force from 2002 to 2005 was General Peter Cosgrove AC, MC. He was made a Companion of the Order of Australia (AC) for commanding the Australian force in East Timor in 1999–2000, and was awarded the Military Cross (MC) for bravery while commanding an infantry platoon in Vietnam in 1969.

If a soldier is awarded a medal twice (for instance, he might have demonstrated bravery on two quite separate occasions) he is not given two medals, but is permitted to place a rosette on the medal's ribbon. In that case he is described as having been awarded a Bar; for example, a Military Cross and Bar. No Australian has ever been awarded a Victoria Cross and Bar.

# Part II
# The Wars of Colonial Australia

'Personally, I'd like to declare war on whoever designed these heavy woollen uniforms'

## In this part ...

Many people think that Australia's military history began with the landing at Gallipoli in 1915. But it really began with the arrival of the First Fleet in 1788, more than a century before, and continued throughout the 19th century. The Australian colonists associated themselves with the exploits of the British Army, the units of which garrisoned and helped develop the infant colonies. The legacy can be seen in the barracks and forts still existing in modern Australia, as well as in the names of towns and roads.

In this part I explain how colonial Australia developed its own military history. Not fully recognised at the time, and dismissed for generations, the frontier wars between the Aborigines and the whites deserve a significant place in any account of Australians at war. Also, by the middle of the 19th century the Australian colonists were seeing themselves as a separate people, although still part of the Empire. Colonial volunteers then fought in New Zealand, Sudan, China and South Africa.

Despite this background, as Australia approached Federation in 1901 military history did not figure prominently in national consciousnesses. The Redcoats had long departed. The war against the Aborigines continued only in the remote parts of the continent. Except for the 16,000 volunteers who set sail for South Africa, few white Australians had any experience of true warfare.

# Chapter 3

# Colonial Conflicts

*In This Chapter*
- Struggling for survival at Sydney Cove
- Driving the Aborigines from their land
- Sending volunteers to help the Empire

Australian folklore has it that the nation was founded when Britain set up a new colony in New South Wales (NSW) in 1788 as a place to dump its convicts. The United States had recently won its independence and Britain could no longer send convicts, who were overcrowding its prisons, to that part of North America. Certainly, convicts played a large part in the European settlement of early Australia, with more than 165,000 of them arriving during the next 80 years.

But Britain also established its colony in Australia for other reasons. Britain wanted another port to improve its trade in the East Indies (now Indonesia) and China. In addition, Britain needed a naval base to resupply its warships, in case of war with the French, Dutch or Spanish, and a new British colony would prevent these countries from gaining a foothold in the recently discovered continent. Convicts conveniently provided Britain with an expendable source of labour. So, as part of Britain's strategy to maintain its empire, the NSW colony had a military dimension.

In this chapter I describe the period from the arrival of the First Fleet in Sydney in 1788 through to Federation in 1901. I explain the role of the British Army in defending the colony, the establishment of other colonies to forestall France, the use of troops to maintain order, the wars with the Aborigines, the raising of volunteers to serve the empire in New Zealand, Sudan and China, and the role of defence in encouraging Federation.

## Garrisoning the Colonial Outpost

White settlement in Australia began when Captain Arthur Phillip of the Royal Navy arrived in Port Jackson, now Sydney Harbour, with a fleet of 11 ships on 26 January 1788. He planted the British flag and took possession of what became the British Colony of NSW. Aboard the fleet were more than 700 convicts, transported across the world for a range of criminal offences. Also aboard were some 200 Marines, commanded by Major Robert Ross.

Marines were Royal Navy soldiers who spent much of their time aboard ships, ready for short-term operations ashore. At Port Jackson, the Marines were supposed to supervise the convicts, guard prisoners and provide protection from Aborigines. But the Marines disliked their service in Sydney and refused to supervise the convicts. Food was of poor quality and in short supply, and in 1790 the colony almost starved.

In 1790 an infantry battalion, the NSW Corps, arrived from Britain to relieve the Marines, who were glad to depart. Under Major Francis Gose, the Corps had been specially enlisted in Britain for service in the colony. Some soldiers had been in prison in England and discipline was poor. In Sydney the Corps officers took over the running of the colony, when Governor Phillip returned home sick. Officers received large land grants and developed a monopoly on the trading of goods, including spirits. The Corps became known as the Rum Corps, and one historian described the officers as 'haughty and arrogant to all outside their class . . . They were ruthless and vindictive to all those who interfered with the source of their wealth'. But some companies of the Corps were more disciplined and professional than their reputation has suggested, as illustrated when dealing with Irish rebels.

## The Battle of Vinegar Hill

After the Irish rebellion of 1798, political prisoners began arriving in Sydney from Ireland. In March 1804, a convict, Phillip Cunningham, roused 200 mostly Irish convicts working under light guard at a government farm at Castle Hill near Parramatta, the colony's second-largest town, inland from Sydney. The convicts seized weapons and, joined by more rebels, planned to seize Parramatta and then advance to Sydney, hoping to capture a ship and sail to freedom.

About 50 members of the NSW Corps under Major George Johnston hurried to Parramatta to join 60 soldiers there. North-west of Parramatta, near Rouse Hill, Johnston and about 30 men were confronted by 300 rebels. Cunningham came forward to negotiate, declaring 'Death or Liberty'. 'You scoundrel. I'll liberate you', replied Johnston, who pointed his pistol and promptly arrested him. The soldiers gave the rebels a volley of fire and then charged. The rebels fled, leaving 12 dead and 6 wounded, and were later rounded up. The skirmish, called the Battle of Vinegar Hill after a similar bloodier defeat in Ireland a few years earlier, was an extremely minor action, but it was significant as the first conflict between government troops and rebels in Australia.

## The Rum Rebellion

Despite their good performance in dealing with Irish rebels, the officers and soldiers of the NSW Corps were soon in conflict with the new Governor, Captain William Bligh. A strict disciplinarian, Bligh had been commander of HMS *Bounty* when his men had mutinied in 1789. Determined to control the trading of rum, he came up against a former Corps officer, Captain John Macarthur, who had extensive pastoral and commercial interests and was the colony's wealthiest and most powerful citizen. When Bligh attempted to prosecute Macarthur in the courts, Major Johnston gathered his troops on 26 January 1808, and with the band playing 'The British Grenadiers', marched on Government House and arrested Bligh. The incident became known as the Rum Rebellion.

Johnston set himself up as Lieutenant Governor and he and other officers governed the colony ineffectively, but to their own advantage, until Colonel Lachlan Macquarie arrived on the last day of 1809 as the new Governor. A regular English infantry battalion, Macquarie's own 73rd Regiment, took over from the NSW Corps, which returned to Britain. By this stage one in ten of Sydney's population was a soldier. For the next 60 years British infantry units would serve in Australia.

## Defending Sydney

While the infantry could adequately protect the colony from threat on land, successive colonial Governors, who were all military men, realised that if war broke out in Europe, the first they would know about it was when an enemy warship sailed into Sydney Harbour. Between 1793 and 1815 Britain was sporadically at war with France, there were frequent rumours of wars with Spain and Holland, and an actual war with the United States in 1812.

With this threat in mind, the first Governor, Arthur Phillip, instructed Lieutenant William Dawes of the Marines to construct gun emplacements around Sydney Cove. Two iron 6-pounder guns from HMS *Sirius* were landed on the eastern side of Sydney Cove, now Bennelong Point, the site of the Opera House, and a further eight guns were landed on the western side to form the nucleus of the Sydney defences. Gradually the defences were extended with guns from naval ships being brought ashore to be manned by the Marines, and then by the infantry. Batteries were installed at Dawes Point, near the southern end of the present Sydney Harbour Bridge, and at Bennelong Point. In 1801 work started on another position at George's Head to command the entrance to Sydney Harbour. Britain sent more guns and gradually the defences of Sydney Harbour were strengthened.

The Army did not just build forts. British Army engineers supervised the construction of barracks, public buildings, bridges and other facilities, and those that still exist provide a visible legacy of the impact of the British Army in Australia.

## Securing the vast continent

Defending Sydney was one challenge, but how could Britain secure the vast continent? The initial step was to prevent an enemy such as the French from establishing rival colonies, and this meant that Britain needed to establish settlements at key points around the continent, which could also become naval bases for ships of the Royal Navy.

The first major new settlement, at Hobart in Van Diemen's Land (Tasmania), was formed in 1804 with convicts sent from Sydney. It became a colony in its own right in 1825. A small British settlement was established near present-day Albany in Western Australia in 1827 to deter the French. Two years later Britain established another settlement on the Swan River (now Perth). Free settlers began arriving in South Australia in 1836. British immigrants to Port Phillip Bay, Victoria, arrived in 1839, and the colony separated from NSW in 1851. Queensland was settled by graziers who travelled north from NSW, and the colony was formally proclaimed in 1859.

From the mid-1820s to the early 1830s four British infantry regiments served in the Australian colonies, with the number rising to five in the late 1830s and 1840s. At its peak in 1847, more than 5,300 British infantry soldiers were serving in Australia. With the cessation of the transportation of convicts and the arrival of large numbers of free settlers, the infantry units were able to concentrate on dealing with bushrangers and Aborigines, for which the Colonial governments also formed groups of mounted police troopers.

## Soldiers versus miners — the Eureka Stockade

As every Australian schoolchild has learned, the discovery of gold in Victoria in 1851 brought huge numbers of immigrants from around the world, seeking their fortune. It also resulted in the famous battle at the

Eureka stockade near Ballarat on 3 December 1854. Miners had become discontented about the mining licence fee and police harassment, and groups of up to 10,000 miners demonstrated against the authorities. A smaller, more militant group formed a loose military organisation, burned their licences, unfurled the Eureka Flag (based on the Southern Cross) and vowed to defend themselves from licence hunts and harassment. The leader of the miners was 25-year-old Irishman Peter Lalor.

On 2 December, about 1,500 men were training with weapons in and around a roughly fortified area, known as the stockade. Only about 150 miners remained at the stockade overnight, and next morning a government force of 276, made up of soldiers from the 12th and 40th Regiments and police, attacked the stockade. In a battle lasting about fifteen minutes the troops overwhelmed the miners, some of whom were bayoneted as they surrendered. Between 20 and 30 miners were killed, along with an army officer and five soldiers.

Although it was only a small skirmish, it was one of the few instances of organised conflict between whites in Australia. Australian nationalists and some elements of the labour movement have seen the battle and the Eureka Flag as a symbol of the fight of the workers against tyranny. However, the miners might equally be considered small businessmen resisting over-regulation; they were recent arrivals in Australia and some had previous military service and knew how to use weapons. The Victorian Colonial Government could have handled the matter better, but needed to keep order on the goldfields.

## *Raising volunteers*

After 1850 the development of Australian colonial defences were affected by three events:

- The discovery of gold in NSW in 1851, followed by even larger discoveries in Victoria. The young colonies now would have sufficient funds to pay for their own defences, while at the same time presenting a more lucrative prize for enemy raiders.

- The institution of self-government in the colonies of NSW, Victoria, South Australia and Tasmania by 1860. The colonies were now required to take some responsibility for their own defences.

- The outbreak of the Crimean War in 1854 between Russia and Turkey, supported by Britain and France. Russian warships may arrive unexpectedly in Australian waters and British troops may be withdrawn; already the Maori Wars in New Zealand in the late 1840s had forced the transfer of some British units.

These events did not have a uniform effect in all colonies, but generally speaking the colonies raised volunteer units to help repel raiders and to fill the gaps that might occur with the withdrawal of British units.

The last British troops departed in September 1870, which *The Sydney Morning Herald* saw as Australia's 'first step toward nationality'. The colonies now relied even more on their own volunteer units, although New South Wales formed a permanent paid defence force with a battery of artillery and two infantry companies. By the 1880s many colonies were paying some of their volunteers to undergo training. These paid volunteer units were known as *militia*. In 1885 the volunteer and militia units in Australia had a strength of almost 21,000 men, or about one in every 43 men of military age.

## Building forts

Despite the completion of a telegraph cable from London in 1872, distant wars posed the danger of raiders appearing unexpectedly at the colonial capitals. In response, the colonies began constructing defences at the major ports. More than 100 guns were mounted in forts that still exist around the coast in locations such as Queenscliff in Victoria, Sydney Heads, Fort Scratchley, Newcastle, and Fort Lytton near Brisbane.

Any successful enemy attack against a city would have to have sufficient strength to deal with the forts, so small field forces comprising infantry, artillery, engineers and cavalry were needed to defend against such enemy landings. These forces were provided by part-time soldiers. But permanent staff were needed to care for the complicated machinery in the forts and to ensure that the guns were ready to repel an enemy raider at short notice. Permanent artillery units were therefore established in four colonies and these became the nucleus of the permanent Australian Army after Federation in 1901.

# Skirmishes and Massacres — the Frontier Wars

When Captain Arthur Phillip arrived in Sydney Cove in 1788 he had orders to protect his party from attacks by the natives, while at the same time attempting to establish some sort of friendly relationship with them. But the British had no concept of Aboriginal society. They did not know that as many as 700 distinct Aboriginal nations, each with its own systems of government, languages, cultural practices, religions and traditions, existed in the continent. No single Aboriginal leader was available with whom the early colonists could make a treaty.

The Sydney colonists soon were in conflict with the local Aborigines, and even Captain Phillip was wounded by a spear in one encounter. Much of the conflict arose out of confusion and suspicion. The Aborigines resented the colonists clearing land and taking fish. The conflict was to continue across much of the continent until well into the 20th century, but until more recent times it was not generally described as a war. Now it is clear that the Aborigines tried to resist the white invasion in their own ways, fighting the British soldiers, colonial police and settlers for control of the continent.

## Aboriginal warfare

While Aboriginal nations lived in their own areas and occasionally fought over women or property, they did not seize land from each other. They considered that they belonged to the land, rather than that they owned the land. Nations could move through others' lands under certain conditions and they could be guilty of unauthorised incursions.

Traditionally, the Aborigines fought four types of warfare:

- **Formal battles.** Fought to settle grievances and halted after a few participants had been killed or wounded.
- **Ritual trials.** Acts of punishment in which someone who had committed a crime such as murder or assault was required to stand his ground and accept any wounds he might receive.
- **Raids for women.** Women gathered food and bore children, so they were considered to be an economic resource that could be seized in a raid.
- **Revenge attacks.** Sometimes carried out stealthily at night, and conducted in revenge for a death through violence, or because it was presumed that one group had used sorcery to bring about someone's death.

The traditional weapons were spears and clubs. Short spears were for thrusting, while long spears were thrown accurately up to 100 metres. In battles with the whites, the Aborigines used their traditional weapons and methods. With their multitude of languages and small tribal groups they were not able to combine to fight the invaders, and generally fought on their own.

Initially the Aborigines did not understand that the Europeans intended to take their land. Some historians believe that certain Aboriginal tribes didn't even bother to attack whites because they weren't Aborigines.

Once they saw whites as a threat, the Aborigines tended to use their usual tactics of ambushes and light skirmishes. But they also found a way of conducting a form of economic warfare. When the settlers cleared land, established farms, grew crops and grazed their animals, the Aborigines saw that their land was being taken, and they burnt fences and farmhouses, took the crops, and killed and maimed the sheep and cattle.

Sometimes this halted the advance of the whites, but only temporarily. For example, in mid-1839 the Wiradjuri people of south-west NSW killed or stole so many cattle along the Murrumbidgee River that the settlers abandoned the area for a year, before returning in force, killing many Aborigines and re-imposing control.

## Settler, military and police methods

War against the Aborigines was conducted by settlers — either directly defending their farms or carrying out punishment raids — by British soldiers, and increasingly by mounted colonial police. The colonial authorities saw attacks by Aborigines as criminal acts rather than as part of a war, and hence when military units were sent to deal with the Aborigines, magistrates often accompanied them to provide the troops with some legal authority.

Initially the troops did not have it all their own way. The Aborigines understood the country and mounted ambushes in heavily wooded areas. Until about 1850 the soldiers used the muzzle-loaded Brown Bess flintlock musket. While the musket was deadly at short ranges, it was inaccurate as the range approached 100 metres, it was slow to reload and it often misfired. The Aborigines knew that once the soldiers had fired a volley it would be perhaps 20 seconds before they could fire again, and in that time the Aborigines could approach the soldiers and let fly with their deadly spears. The Aborigines seldom obtained and used muskets themselves.

When the soldiers and police troopers got breach and magazine-loading rifles and carbines in the mid-19th century they had superior firepower. Also, once the whites were mounted on horses, they had greater mobility. Well-armed stockmen on horseback were often able to deal successfully with local Aboriginal attacks, and the military or the police were usually only called in when the threat was considered more substantial. If a settler killed an Aborigine he could be tried for murder, but the settlers were seldom brought to account. Many colonies raised Native Police units specifically to fight the war against the Aborigines. Colonial administrators thought that raising Native Police was a means of civilising the indigenous peoples while making use of their bushcraft and tracking skills.

One of the settlers' most potent weapons was disease, and the Aborigines were devastated by smallpox, measles, influenza, tuberculosis and sexually transmitted disease. Some historians have claimed that without these diseases the Europeans would have been confronted by as many as four times the number of Aboriginal fighters in south-eastern Australia.

## Pacifying the frontier — 130 years of warfare

Fighting between whites and blacks generally took place on the frontiers of white settlement, as the colonists pushed inland from the towns in search of land for farms and grazing. The first war was fought around the Hawkesbury River, west of Sydney, against the Darug people, who attacked the settlers' farms. In one incident in 1816, soldiers from the 46th Regiment killed 14 Aborigines in a night-time attack on their camp.

As the settlers crossed the Blue Mountains and moved north beyond the Hunter River the local Aborigines again resisted the encroachment on their land. The Governor, Sir Thomas Brisbane, then raised the NSW Mounted Police to operate in these frontier areas. Major James Nunn led a police punitive expedition in northern NSW, in January 1838. At Waterloo Creek, south-west of Moree, the police came across a black camp and in the ensuing fight killed probably between 60 and 70 Aborigines, although the numbers claimed to be killed vary between 10 and 300. The outcome, in which no action was taken against the police, is often contrasted with that at Myall Creek a few months later (see the next section).

In a bitter conflict in Van Diemen's Land (Tasmania), the Aborigines conducted their most successful resistance. Finally, farmers, soldiers and police formed a line 200 kilometres long and marched across the settled districts, in an operation known as the Black Line, in a futile attempt to clear Tasmania of all Aborigines. Only two Aborigines were shot. In fact by this time few Aborigines were left in Tasmania and, un-nerved by the extent of the military campaign, most of these agreed to go to Flinders Island.

Frontier wars continued in the south-west of Western Australia, where the best known incident was the so-called Pinjarra massacre of October 1833, in which about 30 Aborigines were killed. In the second half of the 19th century conflict moved to western and northern Queensland and northern Western Australia. In Queensland the war was mostly carried out by the 200-strong Native Police. After 1860 the Aborigines were responsible for about 470 deaths, two-thirds of them whites, in Queensland, but at least 4,000 Aborigines were killed by Europeans and the Native Police.

Just as the whites perpetrated massacres, such as at Myall Creek, Aborigines also massacred isolated groups of whites. For example, in 1861 the Kairi battered and speared to death 19 whites, including women and children, 70 kilometres south of Emerald in Queensland. Punitive raids followed.

The frontier conflict continued into the 20th century in northern Western Australia and in the Northern Territory. Twenty-two whites were killed in the western part of the Northern Territory between 1921 and 1926. A police punitive raid against the Warlpiri people in 1928 resulted in an official death toll of 31, although other estimates put the number at 70.

## *The massacre at Myall Creek*

On 9 June 1838 eleven convict settlers and one free man at Myall Creek Station, 40 kilometres west of Inverell in northern NSW, claiming that some Aborigines had stolen cattle, set out to round up any Aborigines they could find. They gathered 28 Wirrayaraay people, including women and children, camping in the area, brutally killed them, and burnt the bodies.

News reached the Governor, George Gipps, who sent a group of mounted police under Captain Edward Day to investigate. Day found the massacre site, and returned to Sydney in September with the eleven convicts.

When the case went to court in November all eleven men were found innocent. One of the jury told a newspaper that he considered the men guilty of murder, but he thought blacks were 'a set of monkeys and the sooner they are exterminated from the face of the earth the better ... I would never see a white man hanged for killing a black'. The Attorney General ordered a new trial. Seven men were found guilty and hanged.

In 2000 a memorial stone was unveiled on the site of the massacre, and a ceremony is held each year on 10 June to commemorate the victims. On 7 June 2008 the Commonwealth Heritage Minister, Peter Garrett, announced the inclusion of the site on the National Heritage List.

## The great Australian silence

British military units, quasi-military mounted police and civilian settlers conducted an unofficial war against the Aborigines, who theoretically were British citizens with equal rights to the protection of the law. It was a sporadic, brutal, bloody and sustained confrontation, in which the Aborigines fought a guerrilla war, without the clear lines and battles of traditional Western warfare.

Total casualties are difficult to determine and numbers have been contested, although historians have suggested that the Aboriginal death toll from conflict, not disease, was in the order of 20,000. Almost 2,000 Europeans died — four times the fatal Australian casualties in the Boer War and the Vietnam War.

Until more recent times the magnitude of the conflict and the fact the Aborigines actively resisted the white invasion was ignored or even denied by historians. The eminent anthropologist, W E H Stanner, described the way this conflict had been written out of Australian history as 'the Great Australian Silence'. Some critics have argued that certain historians have deliberately inflated the extent of Aboriginal deaths. Several have claimed that the British consciously conducted a campaign of genocide (for which there is little evidence). But few now claim that there was no conflict.

Like others, the historian Richard Broome has argued that both Europeans and Aborigines need to acknowledge the violence they perpetrated. Broome feels that both whites and Aborigines should recognise past violence 'and become co-existing white and black Australians'.

## Responding to the Call of Empire

The Australian colonists were part of the British Empire. Unless they were convicts or Irish, or especially both, the colonists looked upon the British regiments in Australia as their own regiments. Some colonists actually joined the British Army and served elsewhere in the Empire. Many British soldiers remained in Australia after completing their time. Certainly, the soldiers were disliked by elements of the community, especially the miners. But nonetheless, the British Army was Australia's Army, and citizens were proud of its achievements on the battlefield. British victories and battles such as Waterloo, Alma and Balaclava, and military heroes such as Wellington and Picton (one of Wellington's generals) are still commemorated in the names of towns, roads and hotels around Australia.

As the Australian colonies became more populous and wealthy, the British Government in London began to see them as a source of assistance when imperial interests were threatened. Apart from the Crimean War (1854–56), Britain fought no major wars in Europe for almost a century after defeating Napoleon at Waterloo in 1815. But the British Army was almost constantly at war in some corner of the Empire, such as India, Burma, China and Africa, maintaining control over its scattered and valuable colonies. In the last 40 years of the 19th century the Australian colonies sent men to fight in the imperial cause in New Zealand, Sudan, South Africa and China. Except in the latter stages of the South African War (as described in Chapter 4), none of these soldiers fought as part of an Australian Army, but once they arrived overseas they often considered themselves to be Australians.

## To New Zealand, for Empire and a farm

While the Australian colonists continued their almost casual invasion of the continent, things were quite different across the Tasman Sea. The indigenous people of New Zealand, the Maori, signed a treaty with the British in 1840, which purported to protect their rights and land. But before long, some Maori groups considered, quite correctly, that they were losing control of their lands. When war broke out in 1845 detachments of the 58th Regiment, on garrison duty in NSW, sailed for Auckland, New Zealand.

Fighting ended in 1847 but erupted again in 1860 near New Plymouth on the east coast of the North Island. At the request of the Imperial authorities, the Victorian Government despatched its 500-ton steam corvette, Her Majesty's Colonial Ship *Victoria*, to the area, where it provided a useful means of transporting troops and supplies during the year-long conflict. The *Victoria* could hardly be described as a proper warship, and the Victorian Government had previously used her for police duties.

The theatre of war now moved to the Taranaki area, along the Waikato River, south of Auckland. In 1863 Major General Duncan Cameron, a veteran of the Crimean War, commanded the British force that included six British battalions. He sought volunteers from NSW and Victoria and eventually more than 2,500 men joined four battalions of the Waikato Militia Regiment, comprising about a quarter of his force. The Australians joined for pay, for adventure and for the promise of land. The Maori, who had obtained guns, fought stubbornly from well-defended villages, known as *pa*, but the British eventually prevailed in 1864. Although the Australians, who suffered only light casualties (perhaps 20 were killed), were part of a British force, they thought of themselves as Australians. Some remained in New Zealand, but most returned to Australia. For the first time, Australians had volunteered to serve overseas at the request of the Imperial government.

## Soldiering in Sudan

Australia's tradition of despatching formed military units beyond its shores (known as *expeditionary forces*) began in February 1885 when news arrived that General Charles Gordon, the revered Imperial hero and British Governor-General at Khartoum in Sudan, had been killed by rebels under a religious pretender known as the Mahdi.

Inspired by news that British forces were to march on Khartoum from the Red Sea port of Suakin, the Premier of NSW, William Dalley, immediately offered a battalion of infantry volunteers and two batteries of the permanent artillery. Victoria, Queensland, South Australia and New Zealand also offered contingents, but the British Government accepted only the NSW offer, although it wanted only one artillery battery, which it undertook to equip with six 9-pounder guns and ammunition on arrival at Suakin. Assembled and equipped in an impressively short period, the NSW force of 770 men was commanded by Colonel John Richardson, Commandant of the NSW forces, who had served in the Crimean War and New Zealand.

A crowd of over 200,000 Sydneysiders farewelled the expedition when it sailed from Circular Quay on 3 March. In the New Zealand wars Australian volunteers had joined their units in New Zealand; that is, the Australian colonies didn't raise and form units to serve overseas. The Sudan force was the first formed unit of volunteer soldiers to fight overseas.

By the time the NSW contingent arrived at Suakin on 29 March most of the fighting was over. While the British commander, Lord Wolseley, prepared to advance up the Nile River from Egypt, the force at Suakin, under Major General Sir Gerald Graham, was required to clear a route and build a railway from the coast to the Nile. Battling heat and thirst, the NSW infantry took part in a minor skirmish in which three men were wounded, but the artillery missed the action.

Meanwhile, concerned by a Russian threat in Afghanistan, the British Government withdrew the force at Suakin. On 23 June 1885 the troops arrived back in Sydney to be met by large crowds and pouring rain. None of the contingent had been killed in battle, but half a dozen had died of disease. Corporal Alfred Bennett of the infantry, who later served with distinction in South Africa and at Gallipoli, thought there had been 'much sweat but little glory'.

Captain Henry Airey of the contingent's artillery was given leave to serve with British forces in Burma in 1886, and he came back with a Distinguished Service Order for 'coolness under fire and marked gallantry'.

## Getting ready for Federation

The requirement to defend the vast continent provided some early impetus for Federation — the bringing together of the Australian colonies as one nation. The British Government saw great advantage in coordinating the colonial defence forces, as they might then be able to contribute to the defence of the Empire elsewhere. The commandants of the colonial defence forces, all British officers, also knew that they would need to cooperate to defend the continent.

Eventually the drive for Federation became more broadly based, to the extent that the defence issue became subsidiary. Nonetheless, the commandants met on several occasions in an attempt to establish a federal military organisation, and in July 1899 the permanent artillery units of NSW, Victoria and Queensland became regiments of the Royal Australian Artillery — the tentative beginnings of an Australian army.

By this time the colonial defence forces had become more substantial; Victoria even had a Defence Department. The existence of paid part-time forces meant that they could be used by the colonial governments for various activities. For example, in 1890 the Victorian government deployed the militia during a maritime strike. Major Tom Price was alleged to have advised his troops to 'fire low and lay the bastards out'. In Queensland troops were used to break the shearers' strike in 1891. Such actions persuaded the labour movement to look warily on the notion of raising a permanent army.

The colonial defence forces also raised volunteer units to serve in South Africa in 1899 (as described in Chapter 4), but the despatch of such forces raised questions as to whether the new nation should have a permanent army, and if so whether it should be permitted to serve overseas.

## Beating the Boxers at Beijing

The last expedition to be despatched by the Australian colonies was to northern China during 1900. Britain, with its colony at Hong Kong, as well as France, Germany, Russia and the United States, had established trading ports along the Chinese coast, and had demanded increasing concessions, which the Chinese were unable to resist. To arrest this foreign encroachment, the Chinese established militant societies, which campaigned against Westerners and Westernised Chinese, killing civilians and destroying property. One such society was called the Righteous and Harmonious Fists, dubbed 'Boxers' by Western correspondents.

## Chapter 3: Colonial Conflicts

In June 1900 the Boxers laid siege to the compound in Beijing containing the residences of the foreign *legations* (diplomats) and a sprinkling of naval troops from the countries involved. The siege became the subject of the 1963 movie *55 Days at Peking*. A second international force, from eight nations, landed on the coast in early June 1900 to march on Beijing. When it was held up by strong resistance, a larger force was formed under a British general. It began its campaign in mid-June and occupied Beijing on 14 August.

The British Government sought help from the Australian colonies at the end of June 1900. The British cruiser HMS *Wallaroo* was specifically allocated for the defence of Australia, but with the agreement of the colonial governments she sailed for north China early in July, along with two other British ships in Australian waters. With their shallow draughts they were suitable for river operations. The following month the South Australian colony's gunboat *Protector* headed to China, where it patrolled the Gulf of Pecheli (part of the Yellow Sea closest to Beijing).

Meanwhile, 260 men from NSW and 200 from Victoria formed a naval brigade consisting mainly of sailors acting as soldiers (known as bluejackets). They set sail on 8 August. The NSW contingent included soldiers who were titled the NSW Marine Light Infantry. The contingents arrived too late to take part in the advance on Beijing. They spent most of their time on routine guard and police duties, but were involved in some punitive expeditions. They left China in March 1901, having lost six of their number to disease.

Many of the soldiers and sailors who served in China felt that no-one knew or cared about their efforts. That's because the country's attention was on South Africa, where thousands more Australians were fighting. For more on that conflict, turn to Chapter 4.

# Chapter 4

# Battling the Boers, 1899–1902

### In This Chapter

- Understanding why the Boers went to war
- Joining the British Army's advance to Pretoria
- Tangling with the Boer commandos
- Confronting the cruelty of guerrilla warfare

The South African War or Boer War (1899–1902) was the longest, bloodiest and costliest of the British Empire's conflicts in the century before the First World War. It was also the first war in which British self-governing colonies made major contributions.

The enemy were the Dutch settlers who had arrived in southern Africa in the 17th century and had formed a distinctive society. The British later took over and established the Cape Colony. The Dutch, known as Afrikaners or Boers (farmers), migrated north in the Great Trek and founded the Orange Free State and the South African Republic (Transvaal). Many Afrikaners, however, remained in the Cape Colony. Meanwhile, the British gained the coastal colony of Natal, next to Portuguese East Africa. With Rhodesia established as a British colony to the north, and British Bechuanaland to the west, the Boer republics were cut off from the sea and surrounded. During the war the Boers won some impressive early victories, but ultimately they could not resist the might of the British Empire.

As many as 20,000 Australians fought in the bitter conflict as part of the British Army. In this chapter I describe the causes of the war, the initial British defeats and the decision by the Australian colonies to send volunteers. I outline the course of the war, including the British invasion of the Boer republics and the subsequent guerrilla campaigns. I highlight the role played by the Australian contingents, who made their mark, establishing a place in Australian military history. In South Africa the colonial troops thought of themselves as Australians. This was just as well, as Federation occurred soon after the war began and before the end of the war the new Commonwealth had sent a contingent.

## Sending Colonial Volunteers

The British and the Boers had been in conflict long before the outbreak of war in 1899. British empire-builders wanted to take over the Boer republics, thereby consolidating all of southern Africa under British rule. When the British tried to take over the Boer republics by military force in 1880 a brief war (known as the First Boer War) ensued, in which the Boers defeated the British Army. The British Government then granted the Boer republics a limited form of independence.

The discovery of gold in Transvaal in 1886 upset the fragile Boer–British relationship. English-speaking Uitlanders (foreigners), including Australians, flocked to the goldfields, where they built the city of Johannesburg and eventually outnumbered the Boers. The Transvaal Government taxed the Uitlanders but denied them civil rights, causing tensions with Britain. Walter Karri Davies, an Australian businessman, was a key Uitlander spokesman.

The Boers saw that if they allowed the Uitlanders citizenship they would lose control over their republic and ultimately over their way of life. Supported by large mining syndicates, British colonial leaders hoped to control all southern Africa and demanded rights for the Uitlanders. In 1895 the colonial leaders encouraged the Uitlanders to mount an uprising. If the Boers reacted the British Government would be forced to intervene. The uprising didn't take place, but a British adventurer, Dr Leander Jameson, with a small private army, crossed the border, where the raiders were rounded up by the Boers. Britain repudiated the action and sent the raiders to gaol, but the raid further inflamed relations.

After lengthy negotiations, in September 1899 the British Colonial Secretary, Joseph Chamberlain, demanded full equality for Transvaal's Uitlanders and Britain moved its garrison troops closer to the eastern border of Transvaal. President Paul Kruger of Transvaal, supported by President Martinus Steyn of the Orange Free State, gave the British 48 hours to withdraw their troops from their borders. If the troops weren't withdrawn the Boers would go to war. Britain rejected this demand and the Boer republics declared war on 11 October 1899.

## The Black Week of the British Empire

The Boer republics had only a tiny force of permanent artillery, but their farmers were skilled horsemen and hunters. Having fought African tribes and the British Army for control of their farmlands, the Boers had standing arrangements whereby in times of danger people of each district formed armed mounted units, called commandos, under elected leaders.

On the outbreak of war the Boer commandos conducted raids across their borders, besieging British forces in towns such as Mafeking, Kimberley and Ladysmith (refer to Figure 4-1). Initially the British Army in South Africa numbered about 10,000, but at the end of October the British 1st Army Corps with 40,000 troops, under General Sir Redvers Buller, arrived from Britain.

The British then mounted counterattacks in three locations during what became known as the Black Week:

- **10 December 1899:** A British infantry division, under Major General William Gatacre, tried to recapture Stormberg, south of the Orange River in eastern Cape Colony. The Boers defeated the British, inflicting 135 casualties and taking more than 600 prisoners.

- **11 December 1899:** Lieutenant General Lord Methuen, with 14,000 British troops, tried to relieve Kimberley. They were defeated in the Battle of Magersfontein, suffering more than 800 casualties.

- **15 December 1899:** General Buller himself led a British force of 21,000 troops in an effort to relieve Ladysmith. In the Battle of Colenso 8,000 Boers under General Louis Botha skilfully repelled the British attack, inflicting more than 300 casualties and causing the British to retreat.

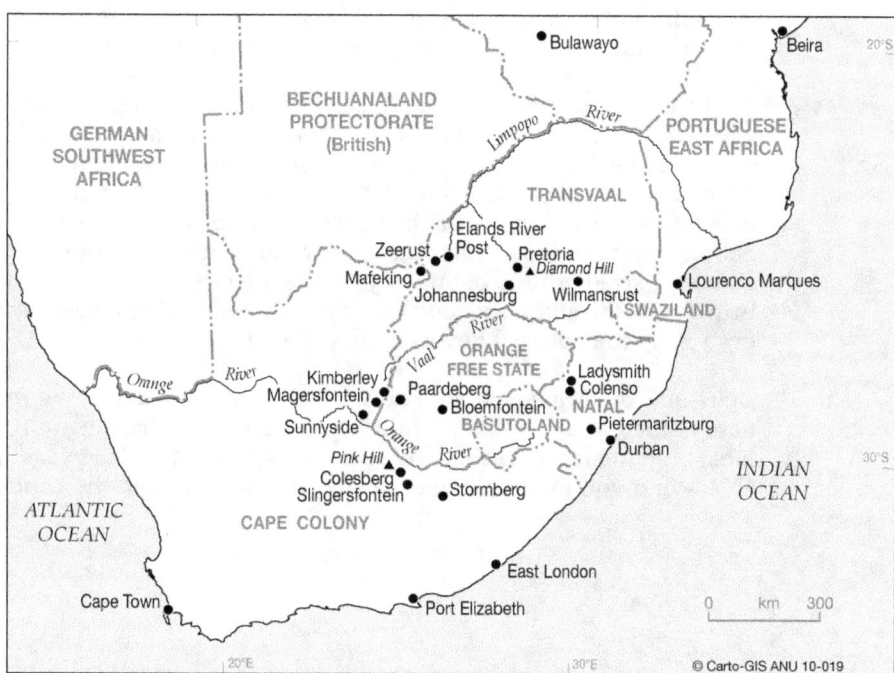

**Figure 4-1:** Southern Africa, 1895–1902.

Fortunately for the British, while their generals did not know how to win a victory, the Boer generals did not know how to take advantage of one. They could have used the momentum of their early victories to press their attacks further into British territory, but instead they stayed put in their defences. This gave the British time to reassess their conduct of the war.

While Sir 'Reverse' Buller (as he was now nicknamed) remained in command in Natal, where he managed more bloody defeats before eventually relieving Ladysmith at the end of February 1900, Field Marshal Lord Roberts arrived in January 1900 to succeed Buller as Commander-in-Chief. Britain sent two more divisions, as well as colonial volunteers, including contingents from Australia, bringing the force's strength to about 180,000. Roberts now planned a major offensive north from Cape Colony.

## Asking and offering: The colonies come to the party

Early in July 1899, well before the outbreak of hostilities, the British Government asked Canada, Victoria and New South Wales (NSW) for troops to join in a 'military demonstration' against Transvaal. Britain's claim that it was not seeking volunteers but a 'spontaneous offer' of assistance indicated that the colonial troops were for political purposes rather than for their military value. The colonies gave a lukewarm response and only Queensland, which had not been asked, offered 250 mounted infantry.

As the situation in South Africa became more unstable, the colonies debated whether to send troops, with some more eager than others. While the commandants made plans to raise a combined force, numerous volunteers from the militia, keen to show their military worth, offered their services. Finally, on 3 October the British Government again cabled, thanking the people of Australia for 'offering to serve in South Africa' and suggesting that company-sized groups of infantry — 125 men — that could slot easily into British units would do nicely. The commandants were eager to comply and eventually the colonial governments agreed.

Units quickly formed, though only a few embarked before the requested date of the end of October. The NSW Lancers were training in Britain and most volunteered to disembark in South Africa on their voyage home. In all, NSW's first contingent numbered 467 troops, including the Lancers, three squadrons of mounted rifles and members of the NSW Medical Corps. Victoria's first contingent numbered 250, Queensland's 262, South Australia's 127, Western Australia's 130 and Tasmania's 131.

## Questioning our involvement

Opponents of Australia's involvement in South Africa were always well in the minority but certainly existed. Members of the military establishment, the commandants and the part-time officers and soldiers of the militia, saw an opportunity to test and develop their skills. Not all officers and soldiers, however, were convinced.

At least four of the senior Australian militiamen who declined to serve in South Africa — Talbot Hobbs, James McCay, John Monash and Charles Rosenthal — became prominent generals in the First World War.

Many Australians claimed to be outraged by the treatment of the Uitlanders, a good number of whom were Australians. The Melbourne newspaper *The Age* in June 1899 referred to the Boers as 'a tyrannous little minority' who were taxing and impoverishing the majority Uitlanders 'while denying them the rights of citizens'. Others noted that the real issue was British prestige.

All the colonial parliaments voted to send volunteers, but only narrowly in some cases, with members from the labour movement opposing it. W M (Billy) Hughes, who later became prime minister, suggested that the Uitlanders had to accept the laws of the country to which they had gone voluntarily. If Transvaal did not fight, he said, it would be 'blotted out of the map of Africa by the slow and insidious process of political reform'.

Support for the British Empire rose considerably after the British Army's disastrous defeats in December 1899. Former opponents fell in behind the war effort. The Empire's prestige was at stake and if Britain appeared to be losing, European enemies such as Germany might come to the aid of the Boers. During December the colonies therefore raised more contingents, maintaining a pattern that continued throughout the war. Most Australians agreed that they needed to support the Empire, right or wrong.

## Arriving in South Africa

Australians took part in the early fighting. In Durban, the Uitlanders formed irregular units. One of those units, the Imperial Light Horse, consisted mainly of Australians and was co-founded by Walter Davies, the same Australian businessman who had served as an Uitlander spokesman before the war. Davies rose to the rank of major and was, according to one historian, 'probably the most influential Australian in the war'. The Imperial Light Horse formed the backbone of the defence of Ladysmith, which held up the Boers in their advance towards Durban.

The first Australians to arrive from overseas were the NSW Lancers who had sailed from England and reached Cape Town on 2 November 1899. The British Army equipped them with horses and, as happened with many of the Australian contingents, split them up and allocated them to different units. Twenty-nine Lancers went to General Methuen's force, which was preparing to relieve Kimberley, while 45 joined Major General John French's cavalry brigade in the Colesberg area. The Lancers with Methuen were the first Australians to see action on the Modder River shortly before the defeat at Magersfontein.

When the infantry units from Victoria, South Australia, Western Australia and Tasmania arrived at Cape Town on 26 November 1899 the local British commander formed them into a single unit known as the Australian Regiment. They were later joined by a NSW contingent. The commander of the Australian Regiment was Colonel John Hoad, a Victorian permanent soldier, who later became Chief of the General Staff and an advocate of a nationalist approach to Australian defence. Although the contingents' officers bickered over the regiment's management, as the first 'Australian', rather than colonial unit, it was a forerunner of the Australian Army.

## Skirmishing at Sunnyside

While the British leadership was in transition from Buller to Roberts, 200 troopers of the Queensland Mounted Infantry under Lieutenant Colonel Percy Ricardo joined a column led by British Lieutenant Colonel Thomas Pilcher, who was ordered to clear *Cape rebels* — Boers from the Cape Colony — from an area west of the railway leading to Kimberley. Pilcher's column also included 100 Canadian infantry, 40 British mounted infantry, a battery of horse artillery and a detachment of the NSW Medical Corps.

On 1 January 1900 the column approached a Boer camp on Sunnyside Hill. Pilcher ordered an attack, deploying the Canadians and the artillery on one flank while the Queenslanders blocked escape routes. As the Boers tried to break out they struck the Queenslanders. Two Australians were killed, the first to die in South Africa in Australian uniform. Forty Boers surrendered while the remainder withdrew, pursued by Pilcher's column.

Although a minor skirmish, the attack at Sunnyside Hill raised the morale of the British army and reassured the local residents that they could be protected from the Boers. The Australians formed the majority of the British column engaged, one of the few times this occurred during the war.

## *Advancing to Pretoria*

By February, Lord Roberts, the new British Commander-in-Chief, had completed his plans for his counteroffensive. He made the capture of Pretoria, the Transvaal capital, the ultimate goal, but along the way planned to relieve the siege of Kimberley, capture the capital of the Orange Free State, Bloemfontein, and capture Johannesburg.

Roberts now had a force of 40,000 men, including many more mounted troops than before. These included the NSW Lancers, a squadron of the Australian Horse from NSW, the Queensland Mounted Infantry, the NSW Mounted Rifles, as well as the NSW Medical Corps. There were about 600 Australians.

The increase in the number of mounted troops was a deliberate attempt by Roberts to learn from his adversaries and make his force more mobile. This also affected the soldiers of the Australian Regiment, who were given horses and retrained as mounted infantry. As mounted infantry, they could range far and wide as cavalry, but could dismount and fight as traditional infantry units when engaged.

The Australian Regiment served on the central front around Colesberg and when the second contingent arrived the Victorians and Tasmanians also went to this area, forming part of the Hanover Road Field Force, under Colonel Tom Price of the Victorian Mounted Rifles. Price was the only Australian to receive an independent command during the war, although it lasted for only a brief period. Even though the Australians in the Colesberg area were not part of Roberts's main thrust, they were to be tested quite severely.

## Almost like home

In the advance to Pretoria, the Australians traversed land that had many similarities with their own. The grassy plains (the *veldt*), the stony hills (*kopjes*), the eucalypt trees and the hard blue sky were all familiar. The Australians were acclimatised to the hot summer and many were good horsemen. Of course there were differences, including the African huts (*kraals*) and the exotic wildlife. But the Australians had little trouble mastering the elements and soon made their mark as soldiers.

## *Winning respect at Colesberg*

As Roberts made his main thrust towards Kimberley, he withdrew French's cavalry brigade from Colesberg, leaving the remaining forces there on the defensive. The Boers decided to test the defences and on 9 February 1900, 300 or 400 of them swung around the eastern end of the British line. A squadron of British cavalry held up the main attack at Slingersfontein, south-east of Colesberg, but the Boers pressed further south. At a place later known as Australian Hill, hundreds of Boers were held off by a troop of 20 Western Australian Mounted Infantry commanded by Major Hatherly Moor until darkness stopped the action. Had the Boers been able to force Moor's position they would have been able to compel the British cavalry to surrender.

A few days later the Boers tried again, this time attacking the other end of the British line, north-west of Colesberg. A breakthrough would have enabled the Boers to swarm into the rear of the main British defences, causing the whole front to collapse. Major George Eddy of the Victorian Mounted Rifles commanded a force, including 75 Victorians, 25 South Australians and 100 British troops, that held up the attack on Pink Hill for most of the day. Finally, with his position almost surrounded, Eddy ordered a withdrawal just before he was shot and killed. His leaderless force withdrew, but it was too late in the day for the Boers to continue their advance. The Australians had 8 killed and 33 wounded, but Eddy had bought enough time for the main British force to begin an orderly withdrawal.

By this time the Boer higher command realised that Roberts was invading the Orange Free State from the direction of Kimberley and they called off their offensive. In the battles around Colesberg the Australians had won the respect of their regular British Army comrades.

## Marching hard to Bloemfontein

By 10 February 1900 Roberts's column, now with 30,000 troops, began marching north along the railway line, still more than 100 kilometres from the besieged Kimberley. Major General French's 5,000-strong cavalry division, including 500 Australian Horse, NSW Lancers, Queensland Mounted Infantry and a detachment of the NSW Medical Corps, made a daring 120-kilometre sweep around the defenders and relieved Kimberley on 16 February. Although huge numbers of his horses were dying from exhaustion and lack of water, Roberts urged his horsemen to chase General Piet Cronje and his Boers towards Bloemfontein, capital of the Orange Free State.

Roberts caught Cronje at Paardberg on the Modder River. Headed off by French's cavalry, the Boers were trapped in the river gorge. Surrounded by a superior force Cronje held out for 11 days, hammered by artillery, until forced to surrender with 4,000 men on 28 February.

Roberts entered Bloemfontein on 13 March. The Australian Regiment and the Hanover Field Force advanced from Colesberg and joined their Australian comrades in early April in Bloemfontein, where the units were disbanded in preparation for Roberts's advance to Johannesburg. More than 3,000 Australians were now serving with Roberts's army.

## Riding with Hutton's mounted brigade

Roberts now prepared to knock Transvaal out of the war and he reorganised his mounted troops. French's cavalry division included the NSW Lancers and the Australian Horse. Major General Ian Hamilton was given command of a mounted division of two brigades and one of the brigades went to Brigadier General Edward Hutton, a mounted infantry specialist who had been commandant in NSW in 1893–96. Hutton's brigade had four mounted infantry corps. The first corps consisted of Canadian and British mounted infantry; the second the NSW Mounted Rifles and the Western Australian Mounted Infantry; the third included the Queensland and New Zealand Mounted Infantry; while the fourth had Victorians, South Australians and Tasmanians.

One-third of Hutton's 6,000 men were Australians and they wore a stylised A on their helmets. Half of Hutton's headquarters staff officers were Australians, including Colonels John Hoad and Joseph Gordon, both later to become Chiefs of the General Staff in the Australian Army. To the annoyance of the Australians, all four of the corps commands went to British regular officers.

Roberts began his advance to Johannesburg on 3 May 1900, with the Australians playing an important role as part of a larger British force. The Boers engaged in hit-and-run tactics, attempting to delay the advance, but on 31 May the British entered Johannesburg. With barely a pause the troops continued the pursuit. The first to reach Pretoria was Hamilton's mounted division and on 4 June Lieutenant William Watson, a young Sydney dentist in the NSW Mounted Rifles, rode into the capital under a flag of truce to demand its surrender. The city surrendered the next day.

The Boer army under General Botha did not surrender and began withdrawing along the Delgoa railway towards Portuguese East Africa. On 12 June the NSW Mounted Rifles distinguished themselves in the Battle of Diamond Hill, near Pretoria, when they conducted a daring, successful attack on foot. In these initial campaigns the Australians won praise from British generals. They looked after themselves in the bush, were good horsemen and showed reckless courage in a number of minor engagements.

## Australia's First Victoria Cross

The British Empire's highest award for gallantry, the Victoria Cross, had first been awarded during the Crimean War (1854–56), but never to an Australian before the Boer War.

Lieutenant Neville Howse was a British-born surgeon who had migrated to NSW in 1889. By February 1900, aged 37, he was serving in South Africa with the NSW Medical Corps and in July he was attached to a mounted infantry brigade that was heavily engaged by a Boer commando.

On 24 July British horsemen charged a Boer position but were halted by heavy fire. When a bugler rose to sound the retreat he fell wounded. Howse rode out under fire and although his horse was shot, Howse reached the bugler, bandaged his wounds and carried him to safety. He became the first Australian to be awarded the Victoria Cross. Five other Australians were awarded the decoration for similar acts of bravery in South Africa.

Howse later commanded the Australian Army's medical services at Gallipoli and on the Western Front in the First World War, reaching the position of Director General of Medical Services with the rank of major general. Knighted in 1917, in the 1920s he was a Commonwealth minister for defence and minister for health.

## Countering the Boer Raids

In December 1899 Britain asked the colonies for more volunteers, adding that while they had to be good shots and competent riders they need not necessarily be members of any regular trained force. The colonies raised units of bushmen, with much of the money for their pay and equipment being raised privately and by public subscription. Most soldiers were indeed bushmen with no military training, although some officers had previous military experience. The Citizen Bushmen, as they were known, embarked in March 1900.

Meanwhile, the British South Africa Company became concerned over the security of Rhodesia, fearing an African uprising as well as a Boer invasion. The British Government decided to divert the Australian bushmen to Rhodesia. It also sought another contingent of bushmen and agreed to pay all expenses. Many men volunteered and in April the fourth contingent, known as Imperial Bushmen, sailed from the various colonies, bound for Rhodesia.

## Enter the Bushmen

The Citizen Bushmen landed at Beira in Portuguese East Africa in April 1900 and made their way through fever-ridden country to join Major General Sir Frederick Carrington's Rhodesian Field Force at Bulawayo. The Imperial Bushmen joined them within two months, making the Australians, with about 3,000 of Carrington's 5,000 troops, the most numerous component of his force. The Bushmen's first action involved 100 dismounted Queenslanders who took part in the relief of Mafeking on 18 May.

After the loss of Pretoria the main Boer Army withdrew toward Portuguese East Africa, but other commandos dispersed into western Transvaal to attack outposts and carry out harassing raids. Carrington's Rhodesian Field Force helped hunt and counter the Boer commandos operating there.

## Learning a lesson at Koster River

By mid-1900 Boer commandos were menacing British supply lines in western Transvaal. On 22 July a patrol of 300 Australian Bushmen, in about equal numbers from NSW, Victoria, Queensland and Western Australia, was escorting a supply convoy when it blundered into an ambush. From hills overlooking the Koster River, near Zeerust, a Boer force of 400, soon to grow to 1,000, poured intense fire onto the Australians, who had dismounted.

*MILITARY STRATEGY*

Because the Boers were reluctant to leave their positions on the hills to attack, Australian casualties were relatively light, but many horses were shot or dispersed. The Australian commander, Lieutenant Colonel Henry Airey, a former British officer who had served with the NSW contingent in Sudan in 1885, seemed paralysed with indecision. But Major Harry Vials of the Western Australians got together a group of Bushmen to mount a counterattack against the nearest hill, coolly observing that it was 'very warm work'.

The Boers evacuated the hill, but then a small group of Australians in the valley raised a white flag to surrender and Airey thought he was honour-bound to surrender his whole force. At Vials's direction the other Australians refused to comply.

After eight hours of fighting, British reinforcements arrived and the Boers withdrew. Having lost many horses the Australians had to walk to the nearest town. Airey never again commanded in the field. Most of the Australians had fought well under punishing fire. They lost 6 killed and 22 wounded. And they learned hard lessons, especially the need to send scouts well ahead of the main force.

## Defending Eland's River

With the Boers raiding British outposts in western Transvaal, Lord Roberts ordered a small force to guard the Elands River Post, a supply dump with valuable stores and ammunition about 35 kilometres west of Pretoria. The task went to Lieutenant Colonel Charles Hore, a British officer commanding 300 Australian Bushmen from NSW, Queensland, Victoria and Western Australia, and 200 Rhodesians.

The Boer general, Koos de la Rey, with 2,000 to 3,000 troops and artillery, surrounded the exposed Elands River position on 4 August 1900 and pounded it with deadly artillery fire. The defenders were in a desperate situation. Caught in the open they improvised their defences. Even their water supply was 800 metres away across exposed ground.

Twice de la Rey offered Hore the opportunity either to surrender his garrison with honour, retaining their arms and being escorted to safety, or to suffer destruction by artillery. Hore refused to surrender and the shelling resumed. By this time, however, Hore was sick and Major Walter Tunbridge of the Queensland Mounted Infantry was effectively in command.

A British column under General Lord Kitchener relieved the defenders on 16 August. He reportedly told the Australians and Rhodesians that they had conducted a 'remarkable defence. Only Colonials could have held out and survived in such impossible circumstances'. The defenders' casualties had been astonishingly light: 36 were wounded and 12 were killed.

The siege became regarded as the most famous single exploit by Australians in the war, with some accounts describing in glowing terms how the Australians raided the Boer gun positions. No evidence supports these accounts and by the second week of the siege the Boers were melting away while it seems the Australians were 'either too inexperienced or timid to act', as one historian noted. Some defenders had become drunk on the supplies of rum. According to Craig Wilcox, 'Australia had lost eight men defending a mountain of beef, jam and rum'.

## Patrolling the Veldt

In mid-1900 the set-piece battles of the first phase of the conflict gave way to a mobile guerrilla war. When in September 1900 a Boer army of 2,000 crossed the border and surrendered to Portuguese authorities, Lord Roberts considered that he had won the war, and next month Britain annexed Transvaal. Roberts went home, leaving Lord Kitchener to tidy up. Although President Kruger departed and eventually reached Europe, the remaining Boer leaders did not accept defeat. Most of the Boer fighters had not been captured and large groups now roamed the veldt, attacking isolated British units. Others returned to their home districts where their families could assist them and from which they raided British bases, supply depots and communications.

The British tried to counter the Boer guerrilla campaign in three ways:

- The British formed mobile forces to patrol the veldt and to defeat and capture the Boers. Mounted units from Australia and others raised specially in South Africa played a key role in these operations.
- The British built 8,000 blockhouse (fortified buildings) along their supply routes to protect their communications and supplies.
- Finally the British sought to deny support to the Boer guerrillas by applying a scorched earth policy. They constructed barbed wire fences to hinder the Boer raiding parties, destroyed Boer crops and burnt homesteads. Then they rounded up civilians, including women and children, and interred them in concentration camps, where they suffered terribly from disease.

## Continuing the commitment

In December 1900 Kitchener asked for another Australian contingent and between February and April 1901 almost 5,000 Australians departed for South Africa. During the war, the various colonies sent between four and seven contingents, each serving for about a year.

By this time in the war there was little glory to be won but only hard riding, cold nights, uncooked meals and grim tasks. Captain David Ham of the Victorian Bushmen was ordered to turn women and children out of their farms and destroy their property. 'I pitied the women and children who knelt before us and begged and prayed that their houses and food might not be destroyed', he wrote, 'but it was an order, and my finer and humanitarian instincts had to be sacrificed'.

## Pursuing General de Wet

One of the most formidable and elusive Boer leaders was General Christian de Wet of the Orange Free State, who launched daring raids into western Transvaal. A British column caught up with him at Bothaville, near the Vaal River, on 6 October 1900. Troopers of the NSW Mounted Rifles, under Lieutenant Colonel Guy Knight, and the Western Australian Mounted Infantry, commanded by Lieutenant Herbert Darling, took part in the attack on de Wet's camp. De Wet and President Steyn escaped but lost their guns.

In January 1901 de Wet invaded the Cape Colony hoping to encourage the Cape Boers to join the fight. A column of Imperial Bushmen, Queensland Mounted Infantry and British cavalry under a British officer, Colonel Herbert Plumer, later to command the Australians at Messines in the First World War, chased de Wet across northern Cape Colony. For a week the two weary little armies, through rain and hail, chased each other across the veldt, until the Free Staters were halted by the flooded Orange River. Plumer struck again and took 100 prisoners, but de Wet eventually crossed the river with about 1,000 horses and 300 men, although without his guns.

## Humiliation at Wilmansrust

In June 1901 a British officer, Major General Stuart Beatson, was commanding a force operating in eastern Transvaal that included the 5th Victorian Mounted Rifles. Beatson divided the Victorians into two units, one of which consisted of 350 Victorians and two light guns, known as pom-poms, and was commanded by a British officer, Major Morris.

On 12 June this unit camped for the night near the Wilmansrust farm. Soon after dark 120 Boers, who had earlier reconnoitred the position, attacked the Victorians. Caught unawares, the Victorians lost 18 killed and 42 wounded. Some escaped in the dark but the remainder were captured, although subsequently released by the Boers. The Boers also killed, dispersed or captured all the Victorians' horses as well as seizing the pom-pom guns. It was a humiliating defeat, highlighting the Victorians' lack of experience.

Apparently Morris had followed Beatson's orders for the deployment of sentries and he had selected an inappropriate site. Nonetheless, Beatson described the Victorians as a 'useless crowd of wasters'. The Melbourne *Punch* responded that much of the blame could be attributed to British officers who were 'no more fit to handle a body of irregulars than a mule is fit to command eagles'.

The 5th Victorian Mounted Rifles later performed well and one of their number, Lieutenant Leslie Maygar, won the Victoria Cross for rescuing a soldier, whose horse had been shot, while under heavy fire.

## *Breaker Morant breaks the law*

By the last year of the war the British had raised irregular units in South Africa to counter the guerrilla campaign conducted by the Boers. One such irregular unit was the Bushveldt Carbineers, which included men who had previously served in regular units.

Harry 'Breaker' Morant was a well-known Queensland horse-breaker and bush balladeer who had been a lance corporal in the second South Australian contingent during 1900. In March 1901 he became a lieutenant in the Bushveldt Carbineers.

In August 1901 he was patrolling in northern Transvaal when one of his unit's officers was killed and mutilated, perhaps by Boers, but probably by native Africans. Morant then led a series of savage raids in which Boer prisoners were summarily shot. When a group of Boers tried to surrender to a patrol led by Morant and another Australian, Lieutenant Peter Handcock, Morant had them killed. A passing missionary, who saw the bodies, was later found shot.

Morant and Handcock were court martialled, found guilty of murder and executed by a firing party on 27 February 1902. Morant and Handcock claimed that they had been ordered to take no prisoners. The 1980 film *Breaker Morant* and several books have suggested that the British authorities made the Australians scapegoats and that they were wrongly executed. In truth, Morant and Handcock were guilty of war crimes. The savagery of a guerrilla war conducted by ruthless insurgents often provokes equal savagery by those charged with countering them. The Morant incident highlights the danger of entrusting these campaigns to ill-disciplined irregular troops.

## Australian Commonwealth Horse

After Federation in January 1901, the new Commonwealth Government had little capacity for raising military forces as it had not yet established a Defence department. In December 1901, however, Britain asked Australian Prime Minister Edmund Barton for another contingent and the government agreed. The state commandants cooperated and raised eight battalions of the Australian Commonwealth Horse. Many of the officers and men had previously served in South Africa.

More than 4,000 men of the Commonwealth Horse embarked, but only the first two battalions arrived in time to see any action. Both sides were tired of war and after long drawn-out negotiations they signed a peace treaty on 31 May 1902. The Boers were promised eventual self-government, but in the meantime, they reluctantly became British subjects.

## Counting the Cost

More than 16,000 Australians embarked for service in South Africa, but as some went twice, probably about 15,000 actually served there. Of these, 251 were killed in action and a further 267 died of disease. About 7,000 Australians served in irregular units raised in South Africa. Many had been living there, but the units also included men who had previously served in one of the Australian contingents. During the war NSW sent six contingents, Victoria five, Queensland seven, South Australia and Western Australia each six, and Tasmania four.

The Australians learned much about warfare in the Boer War. Individually they proved to be competent soldiers. They were good horsemen, even though they needed to take better care of their horses while on operations. Unfortunately no Australians commanded large bodies of men in action. The British Army used the Australian contingents as it saw fit and the colonies never insisted that their units fight as one body. The war did, however, provide valuable experience for officers who would rise to higher command in the Australian Army in the First World War.

# Part III
# The First World War: Australia's Greatest Tragedy

'Why can't they ever pick a nice spot for a war?'

## In this part ...

The First World War (1914–18) was Australia's greatest tragedy. From a population of less than five million, 330,000 Australians served overseas, almost 60,000 were killed, and thousands more were wounded, maimed and psychologically scarred. Few families were untouched by the war. The First World War shaped Australia for generations and, as the nation approaches the war's hundredth anniversary, the effects of the war are still evident.

Australia played only a relatively small part in this global conflict that involved Germany, Austria-Hungary, Bulgaria and Turkey on the one side, and Belgium, the British Empire, France, Italy, Romania, Russia, Serbia and later the United States, and other minor allies, on the other. The war was fought in Europe, the Middle East, Africa and briefly China and the Pacific Islands, as well as on and under the oceans. About 8.5 million soldiers were killed, and military casualties — killed, wounded and missing — were more than 37 million. Perhaps 13 million civilians died.

Yet Australia's contribution should not be discounted. In this part I describe how Australia's forces played significant roles at Gallipoli, in the Middle East, and in France and Flanders. Importantly, through their performance on the battlefield, Australia's soldiers helped define Australia as a nation and established the Anzac legend. The sacrifices have resonated with Australians through to the present day.

# Chapter 5

# Australia Goes to War, 1914

*In This Chapter*
▶ Deciding how to defend the new nation
▶ Laying the foundation of Australia's wartime commitment
▶ Taking on the Germans in our near region
▶ Volunteering and preparing to fight for the Empire

*I*n 1914 Australia was a self-governing country (called a *dominion*) within the British Empire, but the Commonwealth Government had no proper department of foreign affairs — it had no diplomats, and foreign policy was conducted by the British Government. Britain was Australia's main trading partner and, most importantly, the people of Australia still considered themselves to be British.

So when war clouds gathered following the assassination of the heir apparent to the Austro-Hungarian throne by a Serbian extremist on 28 June 1914, it was of little surprise that Australians showed that if war came, they firmly supported Britain. Indeed, many citizens thought that war would be a means of demonstrating the mettle of the new nation.

However, the manner in which Australia committed forces to war needs to be seen in the context of the developments of the previous dozen or so years. The Australian Imperial Force (AIF) of 1914 couldn't have been formed without the existence of the part-time citizen force that was created in the years after Federation in 1901 and became increasingly capable following the introduction of universal service in 1911. Similarly, the Australian warships that helped capture the Pacific colonies in August–September 1914 and escorted the first convoy safely through the Indian Ocean in November 1914 were part of the Royal Australian Navy that had been created in the five years before the war.

In this chapter I explain why Australia did not have a permanent army before the war and therefore needed to raise the AIF for service in the war. I also examine how the new nation formed its own navy and was therefore able to mount an expedition to seize German New Guinea. I recount the battle in which the Australian cruiser *Sydney* sank the German raider *Emden* while protecting the convoy of troops on the way to the Middle East. Finally, I tell how, after the troops arrived in Egypt, they formed the famous Anzac Corps as they prepared for their first combat, the landing at Gallipoli.

# Defending the Commonwealth

When Australia went to war in August 1914 the new Commonwealth had been in existence for less than 14 years. After Federation on 1 January 1901 and the federal election in March of that year, the Commonwealth Government, led by Edmund Barton, declared that 'as soon as possible' it would take measures 'for the judicious strengthening of the defence of the Commonwealth', relying heavily on 'our citizen soldiers'. Defence, however, did not initially have a high priority, as the government struggled to introduce new administrative structures.

The Commonwealth's defence forces were established formally on 1 March 1901, when the existing colonial forces were placed under Commonwealth control, but the new Commonwealth Department of Defence did not come into existence until 1 July, when the 12 members of the Victorian Defence Department took over this new responsibility. The military forces consisted of just 1,800 permanent officers and soldiers, 16,000 partially paid militiamen and 11,000 volunteers. The naval forces were considerably smaller. Only Victoria, Queensland and South Australia had naval forces, and these consisted of Victoria's 30-year old *Cerberus* (a slow ironclad ship with big guns); South Australia's gunboat, *Protector*, which had served in China in 1900; and eight other small gunboats and torpedo boats. Naval personnel numbered about 1,500, of whom only 250 were permanent officers and sailors.

## An Army for a nation

The colonial military commandants had always been British officers and the Commonwealth Government now sought a British officer to command the Commonwealth Military Forces. In January 1902 Major General Sir Edward 'Curly' Hutton arrived as the General Officer Commanding. He had previously been commandant of the NSW Colonial Forces and the Canadian militia, and recently had commanded a mounted brigade, including Australians, in South Africa.

Hutton's first task was to reorganise the army on a national basis and he proposed two forces:

- **The Garrison Force**, which would guard important ports. With a strength of 16,000 men, the Garrison Force would consist mainly of volunteers, who would man the guns in the forts and provide a small field force to protect the forts.
- **The Field Force**, which would have the highest level of training and would consist of 14,000 partly paid militia organised into six light horse brigades and three infantry brigades. The Field Force would conduct mobile operations wherever necessary in Australia.

Apart from the high cost of such a scheme, the Defence Minister, Sir John Forrest, and many in the government were suspicious that Hutton really wanted the field force to be available to the Empire for use anywhere in the world. Many politicians also did not want a permanent standing army because they feared it might be used to suppress the workers. The memory of the militia being used to deal with striking workers in the 1890s (see Chapter 3) was still fresh.

Hutton and Forrest struggled to agree on the conditions of the Defence Act to determine the legal basis and administrative structure for the Commonwealth forces. Parliament approved the Act in October 1903 and it was proclaimed on 1 March 1904. The government generally accepted Hutton's proposed structure, but did not provide sufficient funds to allow the structure to be formed properly. The government rejected any idea that the forces could be deployed overseas.

The Defence Act declared that no permanent forces were to be raised except those necessary to maintain the coast guns in the forts, and to train and administer the part-time militia. Further, the militia was not permitted to serve overseas. The Defence Act was of fundamental importance in shaping the Australia's defences for more than four decades, as the nation would need to raise special, separate forces to serve in the two world wars.

Hutton upset the politicians and other military officers by his forthright approach. When he completed his term, he was replaced by a committee of three military officers and two civilians called the Military Board. This structure continued for decades.

## Compulsory service for boy soldiers

Japan's defeat of Russia in the Russo–Japanese war of 1904–05 and Australia's insistence on the White Australia Policy by which it excluded non-Europeans, and especially Chinese and Japanese, from entering Australia, raised fears of a possible Japanese attack. Both the conservative government, led by Alfred Deakin, and the Labor Party Opposition favoured the introduction of compulsory service in the part-time militia.

Before the scheme was introduced, however, the government sought advice from British Field Marshal Lord Kitchener, who visited Australia in 1909–10. Acting on his advice, on 1 January 1911 Australian introduced a scheme of compulsory military training (known as universal training) for cadets between the ages of 12 and 17. At the completion of this training they would then serve in the citizen force until the age of 26. After seven years, according to the plan, the military forces would number 80,000 men.

The government also established the Royal Military College at Duntroon, near the site of the proposed capital at Canberra, to provide regular army staff officers for the much expanded citizen force. The college, with its four-year course, opened in 1911.

Despite the provisions of the Defence Act, the British Government did not give up hope that the Australian Army might be able to serve overseas in time of war, and the British ensured that the units and headquarters of the Australian Army were organised along the same lines as the British Army. Permanent Australian Army officers attended British training schools and officers were exchanged between the two armies. Indeed, the Committee of Imperial Defence, the body set up in London to coordinate defence arrangements in the Empire, included the Australian forces in its calculations, and the head of the Australian Army was called the Chief of the Australian Section of the Imperial General Staff.

While these events took place, the disagreement over the role of the Army continued — even within the Army itself. In the decade or more before the First World War, the Army included officers with two opposing ideas about the defence of Australia:

- **The Australianists.** Officers such as Major General John Hoad (Chief of the General Staff 1909–11) and Colonel James Legge (who drafted Australia's universal training scheme) considered that Australia should prepare an Army for the defence of the continent and should be wary of sending forces overseas on British imperial adventures.

- **The Imperialists.** Major General Hutton wanted the Australian Army to be available to serve the Empire. After he left Australia, his ideas were maintained by disciples such Brigadier General William Bridges (Chief of the General Staff in 1909 and first commandant of the Royal Military College) and Major Cyril Brudenell White, who planned the expeditionary force for the First World War. They believed that Australia was best protected by contributing to the broader defence of the British Empire.

At the 1911 Imperial conference, at the request of Britain, Australia agreed to prepare plans to send an expeditionary force overseas in case of war. Of course, the preparation of plans did not mean that the government had actually committed the force.

By the outbreak of the First World War, Australia had a substantial part-time army. Together, the permanent army and the citizen force numbered 45,645 men and while this was still considerably short of the planned figure, more than 100,000 youths were also undergoing military training.

## A Navy of our own

From the time of the First Fleet the Australian colonies had relied on the ships of the Royal Navy to protect the sea routes around the continent. Towards the end of the 19th century a British admiral was based in Sydney as Commander-in-Chief of the Australia Station.

At Federation, naval defence was provided by three groups of ships:

- **Royal Navy.** The Royal Navy was the most powerful navy in the world. One of its squadrons, the Australian Squadron, usually with one first-class and several second-class cruisers, was based permanently in Australian waters.
- **Royal Navy Auxiliary Squadron.** Seven third-class cruisers and gunboats were provided by Britain to serve in the Australia Station and were partly paid for by the colonies. They could serve away from Australia only if the colonial governments agreed.
- **Colonial naval forces.** Some of the colonies had purchased and manned obsolete ships and gunboats.

After Federation the colonial naval forces combined to form the Commonwealth Naval Forces and in 1903 the Auxiliary Squadron was abolished as a separate unit. The Commonwealth Government contributed to the upkeep of the British ships of the Australian Squadron and the Royal Navy allowed some Australians to be trained as officers.

Japan's victory in the Russo–Japanese War in 1905 brought the spectre of possible war with Japan. This fear was exacerbated when Britain, concerned about the rise of German naval power in European waters, withdrew its battleships from the Pacific and replaced some warships assigned to the Australia Station with inferior ships.

The two most influential advocates for an Australian navy were Captain William Creswell, Director of the Commonwealth Naval Forces, and the Prime Minister, Alfred Deakin, even though at times they proposed the purchase of different sorts of vessels. Deakin helped engender enthusiasm when, without consulting Britain, he arranged for the American Great White Fleet of 16 battleships and auxiliary vessels to visit Melbourne and Sydney during their tour of the Pacific in 1908.

Initially the British Government opposed the idea of Australia forming its own navy, preferring to keep existing arrangements, but eventually conceded to the Australians' desire to purchase destroyers. Further, in 1909 Britain, worried about the expansion of the German Navy, agreed to help Australia obtain and man a fleet unit consisting of a battle cruiser, three light cruisers, six destroyers and three submarines. In return, Britain ensured that the Australian ships would be suitable to play a role as part of the Royal Navy; that is, they were designed for operations around the world, rather than for the coastal defence of Australia.

Australia's first destroyers were commissioned in 1910 and in July 1911 the Commonwealth Naval Forces became the Royal Australian Navy (RAN). Britain and Australia concluded arrangements by which Australian sailors would be trained by the Royal Navy. Also, subject to Commonwealth Government approval, the ships of the RAN would come under British Admiralty control in time of war. The Navy established a training depot for general entry recruits and then opened the RAN College at Geelong, Victoria, in 1913 to train Australian naval officers.

The RAN's battle cruiser *Australia* was commissioned in June 1913 and, with Rear Admiral Sir George Patey of the Royal Navy, the Flag Officer Commanding the Australian Fleet, aboard, steamed into Sydney Harbour in October 1913. Accompanying *Australia* were the two light cruisers, *Melbourne* and *Sydney*, and three destroyers. The arrival of the Australian fleet was a source of immense national pride. By the outbreak of the First World War, the Navy also included two submarines, another light cruiser, *Encounter*, on loan from the Royal Navy, and a small cruiser, *Pioneer*, given by Britain. About half of the ships' companies were Australians, the others being British. The formation of the RAN in four years was a remarkable achievement, although not possible without the support of Britain.

# Joining the Empire's War — To the Last Shilling

In the last days of peace, Australia was in the midst of an election campaign. On 31 July the Prime Minister, Joseph Cook, affirmed that 'all our resources in Australia are in the Empire and for the empire'. Similarly, the leader of the Labor Opposition, Andrew Fisher — who became Prime Minister after the election on 5 September — declared that Australians would stand with Britain to 'the last man and last shilling'.

Warned from Britain about possible war, on 3 August the Australian Cabinet agreed to make two offers to Britain, which Britain later accepted:

- to place the Navy under control of the British Admiralty
- to despatch a military force of 20,000 men to serve wherever Britain thought useful

After the news arrived that Britain had declared war, there were scenes of wild enthusiasm from citizens who had no concept of the horror of modern war. While raising the military force would take a while, the naval ships could be deployed straightaway. That was convenient, because German forces weren't far away.

## A fight worth fighting

Some critics have claimed that Australia should not have taken part in the First World War and that it did so because of an ingrained obedience to Britain. Such a view does not do justice to the Australian politicians of the era.

Alfred Deakin, prime minister three times between 1903 and 1910, knew that Australia would need to look out for its own security, especially after the Russo–Japanese War. Along with the Labor Party stalwart, W M (Billy) Hughes, Deakin advocated conscription so that Australia would have an army to deter invaders. Japan might have been Britain's ally, but if Britain were defeated in Europe, Japan would be free to exercise greater power in the Pacific.

If Germany were to win the war, it too would have been able to operate more freely in the Pacific, where it possessed colonies, including north-east New Guinea. Before the war the German East Asia Cruiser Squadron developed plans to attack Australian shipping. Australia's political leaders understood that it was not in the national interest for a militaristic Germany to defeat Britain and to dominate Europe.

## Looking After our Backyard

One of the major threats to Australia at the outbreak of war was the German naval squadron based at Tsingtao in China. Under Vice Admiral Maximillian Graf von Spee, the squadron included two powerful armoured cruisers, *Scharnhorst* and *Gneisenau*. Spee's squadron sailed shortly before war was declared, but RAN wireless operators detected his signals that suggested he was in the Pacific, about 300 miles north-east of New Guinea. Until the German ships could be located they would be free to attack British shipping.

Rear Admiral Patey, commander of the Australian Naval Squadron, set out to find whether the German ships were at Rabaul, capital of German New Guinea, at the northern end of New Britain. After dark on 11 August he sent the light cruiser *Sydney* and three destroyers into Simpson Harbour, while he remained outside in his flagship, the battle cruiser *Australia*. The night was so dark that the destroyer *Warrego* reached the dock before realising that the German ships were not present. The Australians withdrew. The operation showed that the RAN had already reached a high level of proficiency.

Actually von Spee was heading across the Pacific, towards South America, where he would fight several battles with British ships, winning at first but eventually being defeated near the Falklands Islands. He left behind his newest light cruiser, *Emden*, which conducted a daring and successful campaign, capturing and destroying Allied merchantmen in the Indian Ocean. The British Government now asked Australia and New Zealand to mount expeditions to seize the German colonies in New Guinea and Samoa, and to destroy their wireless stations.

## Mounting the first expedition

Colonel James Legge, Chief of the General Staff, was given the task of preparing Australia's first overseas military expedition. The Australian Naval and Military Expeditionary Force, as it was known, consisted of a 1,000-strong battalion of infantry, specially enlisted in Sydney, and a smaller battalion of naval reservists and ex-seamen who were to serve as infantry. The force was also to include 500 young volunteers from a north Queensland citizen force battalion, the Kennedy Regiment, which had already been sent in the coastal liner *Kanowna* to Thursday Island to protect this remote area from possible attack. Colonel William Holmes, a militia officer who had served in South Africa, commanded all the troops.

## Chapter 5: Australia Goes to War, 1914

### Firing the first shot

After warnings from London, on 2 August the permanent gunners manning the forts at the main Australian ports went to war stations. When war was declared at 11.00 pm on 4 August (9.00 am on 5 August Melbourne time) the gunners were ready, at their posts.

At 7.45 am on 5 August the German cargo ship SS *Pfalz* steamed out of Port Melbourne and headed slowly down Port Phillip Bay. By about 10.00 am it had reached Portsea, where an officer of the Examination Service checked the ship's papers and allowed it to proceed. The ship had just got underway when Lieutenant Colonel Augustus Sandford, commanding the coast defences at Port Phillip Heads from Fort Queenscliff, received orders by telephone to stop the ship.

Already, the *Pfalz* was increasing speed. Sandford ordered Captain Moreton Williams, at the Fort Nepean Battery, to act immediately. Williams ordered the signal 'stop instantly' to be hoisted on the signal staff at the Fort, while his gunners loaded a 6-inch gun with a 100-pound projectile. The ship's pilot, Captain Robinson, failed to see the signal and the *Pfalz* continued on her course towards the Heads. The roar of the gun at close range and the scream of the shell as it crossed the bows drew Robinson's attention to the signal flying at Fort Nepean.

The gunners loaded another round, but it did not prove necessary. On the bridge of the *Pfalz* there was a short struggle between Robinson and the ship's master, Captain Kuhiken, before the ship turned around and steamed back to Portsea. With a change of name the *Pfalz* was used by the Australians for the remainder of the war.

The Australian gunners probably fired the first shot by British armies in the war. But the Royal Navy was in action even earlier. HMS *Lance* sank a German mine-layer off the Suffolk coast at midnight on 4 August 1914, three-quarters of an hour before the Nepean battery opened fire.

Towards the end of August, Patey, with *Australia*, *Melbourne* and a French cruiser, escorted a New Zealand contingent that occupied Samoa. By this time the Australian troops had departed from Sydney in the liner *Berrima* and had sailed up the coast to Palm Island, near Townsville, where they underwent further training. Continuing to Port Moresby with the cruisers *Sydney* and *Encounter*, they met up with the Kennedy Regiment in *Kanowna*, but Holmes doubted whether the young citizen soldiers had sufficient training or equipment for the task in New Guinea. He reluctantly allowed the ship to join the expedition but later the stokers on board refused to work, claiming that they had not expected to go to war. The Kennedy Regiment was therefore left behind. Off the eastern end of New Guinea, Patey in *Australia* joined the convoy and took command of the expedition.

## Seizing German New Guinea — No more 'Um Kaiser. God save 'Um King

Rabaul was defended by a small number of German Army reservists and locally enlisted natives. At daybreak on 11 September 1914 Patey and his ships entered Blanche Bay, east of Rabaul. He ordered a small group of naval reservists and soldiers to land at Herbertshohe and Kabakaul, on the southern shores of Blanche Bay about 30 kilometres south east of Rabaul, to destroy wireless stations in the area, before he proceeded further into Simpson Harbour and disembarked the main body of troops at Rabaul.

The party pushed inland from Kabakaul along jungle tracks until it was halted by German and native troops. In the first engagement in this area several Australians were killed or wounded, including naval reservists Able Seamen John Courtney and Bill Williams, who became Australia's first deaths of the war, and Captain Brian Pockley, the first Australian medical officer to be killed. He had given his Red Cross brassard, indicating he was a medical officer, to a wounded sailor so that he would be protected from fire. The Australians then told the German commander that 800 troops had been landed, and he surrendered his force of six Germans and 20 natives. During the afternoon Colonel Holmes landed half his infantry force, intending to mount a major attack the next day.

That evening the Germans advised Patey that Herbertshohe and Rabaul were unprotected and next day the Australians occupied the towns. In the afternoon of 13 September the British flag was formally raised in Rabaul and the occupation of New Britain was proclaimed. A translator told the natives: 'You savvy big master he come now, he new feller master ... No more 'Um Kaiser. God save 'Um King'.

Some fighting continued nearby, in which *Encounter* shelled the German defenders, and on 21 September 40 German white soldiers and 110 natives surrendered. Colonel Holmes became the military administrator of the newly captured territory. He sent forces to occupy the German colonies south of the equator and by Christmas had taken over New Ireland, the Admiralty Islands, the New Guinea mainland, Bougainville and Nauru. These areas remained under Australian control until seized by Japan in 1942. Only six Australians had been killed in the fighting. But on 14 September the Australian submarine *AE1*, with two officers and 32 sailors, half British and half Australian, was patrolling near Rabaul. The submarine was presumably lost; it was never heard of again.

## Falling In with Britain

While Colonel Legge was raising the expeditionary force to go to German New Guinea, and while the RAN's ships were searching for von Spee's squadron, the government turned its energies to raising the promised 20,000 men to serve wherever Britain thought they would be useful. The government appointed Brigadier General William Bridges, the first commandant of the Royal Military College and now Inspector General of the Commonwealth Military Forces, to command the force, which Bridges called the Australian Imperial Force (AIF). As the Defence Act did not permit existing forces to be sent overseas, a new force needed to be raised from volunteers.

## Raising the Australian Imperial Force

The eight-month delay between the beginning of the war in August 1914 and the landing of Australian troops at Gallipoli in April 1915 was extremely important in Australia's military history, even though few of its troops saw any military action during this time. Most soldiers of the newly formed Australian Imperial Force (AIF) spent these months training and preparing for war in Australia and Egypt. Military structures were fixed and attitudes were developed that were to shape the Australian Army for the remainder of the war and beyond. The concept of a volunteer force that could fight as a division under its own commanders was established.

At the same time, the government accepted that the AIF would serve under British command and would be deployed as the Imperial authorities in London saw fit. The AIF therefore reflected Australia's status as a self-governing dominion within the British Empire, one in which its people lived comfortably as both Australians and British subjects.

Planning for the force owed much to the brilliant staff work of Lieutenant Colonel Brudenell White, who became Bridges's chief of staff. The headquarters included a senior medical officer, Colonel Neville Howse, who had won the Victoria Cross in South Africa, and staff officers such as Major Thomas Blamey, a regular officer who joined in Egypt, and Captain John Gellibrand, a former British officer who was growing apples in Tasmania. There were plentiful volunteers for the ranks, many coming from the militia, but about a third had no military experience. Young men were eager to join for many reasons, including pay (they received six shillings per day and were called 'six-bob-a-day tourists'), adventure and support for the Empire.

At the outset the AIF consisted of just the 1st Division, with the following structure:

- **1st Infantry Brigade.** This brigade consisted of four infantry battalions, recruited from NSW, and was commanded by Colonel Henry MacLaurin, a young Sydney barrister and militia officer. (An infantry battalion had about 1,000 men.)

- **2nd Infantry Brigade.** This brigade's four battalions were raised from Victoria and it was commanded by Colonel James Whiteside McCay. He too was a lawyer and militia officer, and had also been Minister for Defence in an earlier government.

- **3rd Infantry Brigade.** The four battalions in the 3rd Brigade were raised from Queensland, South Australia, Western Australia and Tasmania. It was commanded by Colonel Ewen Sinclair-MacLagan, a British regular army officer then serving at Duntroon.

- **1st Light Horse Brigade.** Consisting of three light horse regiments, one raised in NSW, one in Queensland and one from South Australia and Tasmania, the 1st Light Horse Brigade's commander was Colonel Harry Chauvel, an Australian regular officer who had served in the Boer War. A light horse regiment was smaller than an infantry battalion and numbered about 550 men.

- **1st Division Artillery.** Three field artillery brigades (which artillery regiments were called at that time), each with 12, 18-pounder, field guns and about 650 men, made up the 1st Division Artillery. The commander of the division's artillery was Colonel J J Talbot Hobbs, a Perth architect with considerable militia experience. He had attended military schools in Britain at his own expense.

- **Supporting units.** These included an additional light horse regiment, engineers, field ambulances (medical units) and horse transport.

Later divisions were to have a similar structure. All the officers mentioned above in both the headquarters and in the brigades were to become generals, except for MacLaurin, who was killed at Gallipoli.

The troops began training, expecting to be sent overseas at the end of September. However, German cruisers were operating in the Pacific, and until these could be located the government was unwilling to risk despatching the troops. Eventually, at the end of October a large convoy with the complete Australian division gathered at King George's Sound, at Albany, Western Australia. Another convoy carrying New Zealand troops joined them and together they set sail on 1 November 1914. Raising such a force in less than three months had been an outstanding effort, but the troops would still need a lot more training before they were ready for combat.

## Shaping the future Australian Army

Major General Sir William Throsby Bridges did more than most officers to shape the future Australian Army. Born in Canada in 1861, he entered the Canadian military college, but did not complete the course as he followed his parents to Australia. Receiving a commission in the NSW permanent artillery, he served with the British Army in the Boer War.

Identified by Major General Hutton, first commander of the Commonwealth Military Forces, as a promising officer, he became the Army's chief of intelligence, and in 1909 became the army's first Chief of the General Staff. He was an advocate of greater professionalism and, following his mentor Hutton, saw the Australian Army as an integral part of the Empire's forces.

After serving in London as the Australian representative on the Imperial General Staff, Bridges returned as the first commandant of the Royal Military College, when it opened at Duntroon in June 1911. He was responsible for designing Duntroon's four-year course, with its balance of military and academic studies. He created the college's ethos, and cadets who entered during his tenure went on to lead the Australian Army.

He became the Army's Inspector General in mid-1914, just before the beginning of the First World War, and was then given command of the expeditionary force that he named the Australian Imperial Force (AIF). When the British Government suggested a slightly smaller force that could be incorporated more easily into a British formation, Bridges insisted on the larger force. As the Official Historian, Charles Bean, wrote, this stand 'taken by the far-sighted, sardonic soldier-statesman was the first and greatest step towards setting the character which the expeditionary force was destined to assume — that of a national Australian Army'.

Bridges was the first Australian to command an Australian division in action when it landed at Gallipoli in April 1915. Naturally taciturn, he was never seen as a charismatic leader, but more as a thinker and staff officer. One of his staff, Major Tom Blamey, later to become Australia's only field marshal, said of him, 'Never have I admired and disliked a man so much'. At Gallipoli, however, he won respect by sharing the hardships and dangers with his men. Wounded by a sniper, he died on 18 May 1915. An imperialist, rather than an Australian nationalist, he never led Australian troops to great victories, but he was responsible for forming the AIF, which set the standards for the Australian Army for future generations.

## *Sydney versus Emden* — 'Beached and done for'

In the first week of November 1914 a huge convoy of 38 transport ships was ploughing through the Indian Ocean carrying 20,000 Australian and New Zealand troops to the Middle East. In the previous three months, daring German raiders had hunted in the Indian and Pacific Oceans, and the most famous, the 3,500 tonne light cruiser *Emden*, had sunk or captured 25 Allied merchantmen and two warships. The *Emden*'s captain, Karl von Muller, had received word of a possible convoy and he envisaged steaming among the transports, doing as much damage as his ten 105-mm guns and two torpedo tubes could manage. In anticipation of such a threat, however, four cruisers — one British, one Japanese, and two Australian, *Melbourne* and *Sydney* — were escorting the convoy.

In the evening of 8 November *Emden* arrived near the Cocos Islands, oblivious to the convoy approaching from the south. Next morning *Emden* put a landing party ashore to destroy the cable and wireless station. The telegraph company operator sent an urgent message, 'Strange warship approaching', and then an even quicker SOS and a message that a warship was landing a party in boats, followed by silence as the Germans entered the radio room. Alerted by the message, the commander of the convoy, which was only 50 miles from the islands, ordered *Sydney* to investigate.

Sighting *Sydney*'s smoke, Captain Muller thought it was his collier, *Buresk*, which he was expecting. Too late, he realised that the Australian warship was closing fast. He abandoned his landing party and steamed out to engage. His guns had a greater range than *Sydney*'s captain, John Glossop, expected, and *Emden*'s shells struck the Australian ship, causing some damage. But Glossop's vessel was larger (5,400 tonnes) and faster, and his eight 6-inch (150-mm) guns were more powerful. Moving out of *Emden*'s range, *Sydney* pounded the German ship for 25 minutes, causing fearful destruction.

Muller realised that all was lost and ran his ship onto a coral reef. Glossop sent his famous signal, '*Emden* beached and done for'. He then set out after the *Buresk*, which its crew scuttled by opening the seacocks and allowing it to sink as *Sydney* approached. Returning to the Cocos Islands, Glossop opened fire again until Muller similarly scuttled his ship, the *Emden*, and surrendered. The *Emden* lost 145 of its crew killed, against *Sydney*'s four fatal casualties. Australia's young navy had won its first victory.

*Emden*'s landing party of about 50 sailors, under Lieutenant Helmuth von Mucke, commandeered a small schooner. Picked up by a German steamer, they sailed to Yemen, in the Arabian Peninsula, travelled along the coast, eventually met up with the Turkish Army and then continued by train to Germany, arriving in May 1915. Mucke later became a pacifist and was twice briefly imprisoned in a Nazi concentration camp for political dissent.

## Anzacs in Egypt — desert marches and pyramids

While the convoy with the Australian troops crossed the Indian Ocean, the Ottoman Empire joined the war on Germany's side. The Ottoman Empire was centred on Turkey but stretched into Syria, Palestine, Arabia and Mesopotamia. The British authorities now decided that rather than continue to Britain, where it was cold and wet, the Australians and New Zealanders should disembark in Egypt to strengthen its defences against the Turks. The first troops began arriving on 3 December and established a tented camp near the pyramids, just outside Cairo. The troops began vigorous training with long marches through the desert. But the division never trained as a complete formation.

On Good Friday a small number of men ransacked the Wassa district in Cairo, claiming that the prostitutes and brothel owners there had been dishonest and caused them to contract venereal disease. Apart from this hooliganism, the troops also began exhibiting characteristics that were to persist throughout the war. They still considered themselves to be citizens in uniform and railed against what they thought was pointless military discipline.

Meanwhile, as Australians continued to volunteer, the government raised the 4th Infantry Brigade, commanded by Colonel John Monash, a Victorian engineer and militia officer, and the 2nd Light Horse Brigade, commanded by Colonel Granville Ryrie, a NSW pastoralist and politician, who had served in the Boer War. They began to arrive in Egypt on 1 February 1915.

Field Marshal Lord Kitchener, the British Secretary of War, placed the Australians and New Zealanders in Egypt under the command of Major General Sir William Birdwood, a British officer who had served with Kitchener in South Africa and India. Birdwood formed an army corps, called the Australian and New Zealand Army Corps. The initials of the corps were ANZAC, but after a while the corps became known as the Anzac Corps, thus beginning the use of a term that has become famous for describing any Australian and New Zealand force, and also to refer to the spirit engendered by the Australians and New Zealanders when they later served at Gallipoli.

The Anzac corps consisted of:

- The 1st Australian Division, commanded by Major General Bridges, consisted of the 1st, 2nd and 3rd Australian Infantry Brigades, its artillery and support troops.

- The New Zealand and Australian Division, commanded by Major General Alexander Godley, a British officer who had been serving in New Zealand and who was commander of the New Zealand contingent. It included:
  - New Zealand Infantry Brigade
  - 4th Australian Infantry Brigade
  - 1st Australian Light Horse Brigade
  - New Zealand Mounted Rifles Brigade

- Corps troops, which included the 2nd Australian Light Horse Brigade.

While training in Egypt, on 20 February the Australians were excited to learn that British and French ships had bombarded the Turkish forts guarding the Dardanelles Strait. Winston Churchill, British First Lord of the Admiralty, had persuaded the British Government that the Royal Navy should attempt to fight its way through the Dardanelles and then attack the Turkish capital, Constantinople, to knock Turkey out of the war and to open a passage through to Russia.

Unfortunately the British and French ships were stopped by mines in the first half of March, with the loss of half a dozen old battleships. The British now decided to land troops on the Gallipoli Peninsula and the landing force was to include the men of the Anzac Corps. Eight months after their enlistment, the Australians were about to see their first action.

# Chapter 6

# Creating the Anzac Legend at Gallipoli, 1915

### In This Chapter
- Gaining a foothold at Gallipoli
- Defending the ridges and gullies
- Fighting valiantly in futile attacks
- Withdrawing reluctantly after a costly campaign
- Cementing a reputation for courage and mateship

The Gallipoli campaign, which began with the landing of British, French, Australian and New Zealand troops on 25 April 1915, holds endless fascination for historians. Strategists have considered it to be a sideshow, in that ultimately the war needed to be won in France where British and French armies were confronting the might of the German Army. Even if, by some miracle, the allied forces captured the Gallipoli Peninsula, and if by another miracle British ships reached Constantinople, and even if Turkey then surrendered, they argue that Germany, undaunted, would still have fought on in France.

The campaign's intrinsic interest lies in the imaginative plan to land thousands of troops on a foreign shore in what military experts consider to be the hardest military action of all — an amphibious operation. The campaign was, however, one of the most mismanaged in history. For success, it needed surprise, careful preparation, well-trained troops, decisive leadership, a weak enemy and luck. Unfortunately, none of these qualities were present.

For Australians, however, the campaign marked the beginning of the Anzac legend. By their dash and courage on the first day, the Australian troops made the world aware of this new nation on the other side of the world. The troops' exploits became a source of pride at home, and their conduct during the long, gruelling campaign came to represent what was later called the Anzac spirit, embodying attributes of courage, mateship and endurance.

This recognition was earned at great cost and, tragically, in a cause that appeared lost from the first day.

In this chapter I tell the dramatic story of the Australian landing at Gallipoli. I deal with the troops' achievements, explain what it was like to serve there, discuss the reasons for some of the disasters and assess the campaign's place in Australian history.

# Landing at Anzac Cove

The Gallipoli Peninsula runs along the north-west shores of the Dardanelles, a narrow strait that connects the Aegean Sea to the Sea of Marmara and separates Europe and Asia (refer to Figure 6-1). General Sir Ian Hamilton, commander of the Mediterranean Expeditionary Force, planned to land the 29th British Division at Cape Helles, at the tip of the peninsula, while French troops landed on the Asiatic shore to create a diversion. Meanwhile, General Birdwood's Anzac Corps would land 20 kilometres along the coast where the peninsula was just over six kilometres wide. The Anzacs would thrust inland, secure the high ground, cut the road communications to Cape Helles, and together with the British would then clear the end of the peninsula.

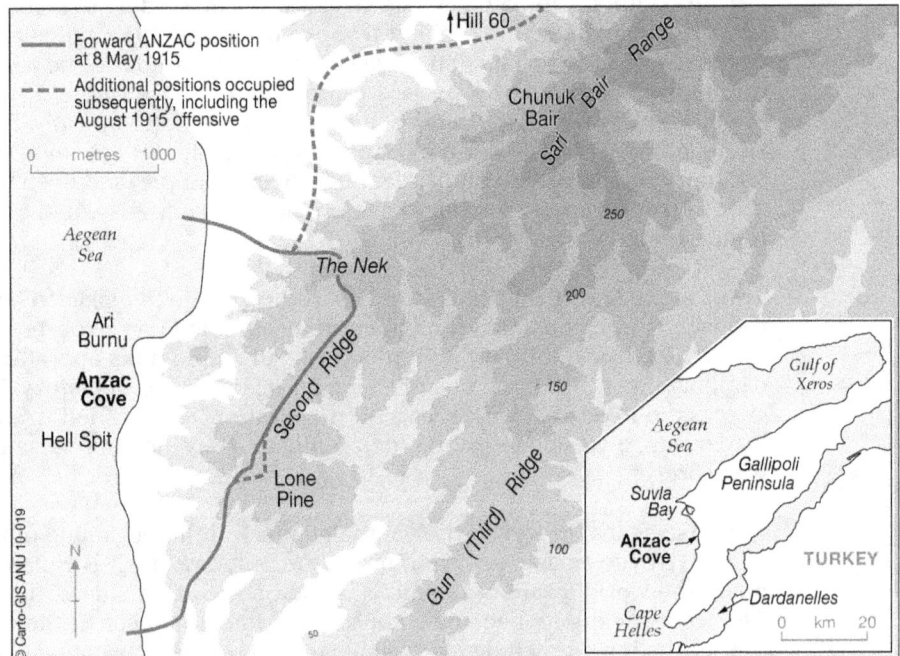

Figure 6-1: The Gallipoli Peninsula.

## Chapter 6: Creating the Anzac Legend at Gallipoli, 1915

The simple plan disguised myriad problems. The Allies had lost all element of surprise and the Turkish Army, commanded by German General Otto Liman von Sanders, with 40,000 determined troops, was expecting an attack. The British Army had no reliable maps of the peninsula and did not realise that its central spine consisted of steep ridges, with deep gullies running down to the sea. Hamilton's army went into battle with inadequate artillery, and it lacked sufficient supplies and medical support.

For his part of the operation, Birdwood decided that Major General William Bridges's 1st Australian Division would land first, to be followed later by Major General Alexander Godley's New Zealand and Australian Division. The first troops ashore would be the four battalions of Colonel Ewen Sinclair-MacLagan's 3rd Brigade, which were to seize a position known as Gun Ridge. The 2nd Brigade would then secure the heights of the Sari Bair Range. For inexperienced troops, with no specific training for such difficult manoeuvres, except for what they could complete on the Greek island of Lemnos, 100 kilometres from Gallipoli, the operation would be a major challenge.

## *Clambering ashore under fire — the stuff of legend*

In the dark of the early hours of 25 April rowing boats, towed in groups of three by small steamboats, approached the Turkish coast. Then, at about 4.30 am, as the dark sky lightened, the boats hit the gravel of the beach. The first troops were starting to wade ashore when the Turkish fire began. Men were struck and tumbled into the water as others scrambled onto the beach, expecting to find a gentle slope. Instead they came up against a precipitous 100-metre high hill that dominated the landing site. 'Explain to the colonel that the damned fools have taken us a mile too far north,' called a naval officer in charge of the boats.

Actually, the first troops had landed broadly within the intended area. Nonetheless, the reason for going too far north has been debated for decades. Although the shift was probably due to navigation error by the boat commanders, it saved the lives of countless Australian soldiers. Had they landed on the low beach further south they would have been cut down by Turkish machine-gun fire. The steep slope of the landing place partly protected the troops from enemy fire. But they had to clamber up cliffs, ridges and gullies through thick undergrowth as the Turks fired at them from above.

The Turkish division in this area called for reinforcements. The Turkish reserve division was commanded by Lieutenant Colonel Mustafa Kemal, who appreciated that the Turkish defenders were facing a major offensive and ordered a complete regiment to the battle area, with himself in the lead. 'I do not order you to attack; I order you to die', he said. 'In the time that passes until we die other troops and commanders can take our place.' Mustafa Kemal would make his name at Gallipoli and would eventually become the first president of Turkey.

## Thrusting inland: The confusing first day

Birdwood had told the troops, 'Keep going at all costs! Go as fast as you can!' So in small parties, often without orders or leaders, the Australians forced their way up the slopes and through the heath-like scrub, clearing the groups of Turks who were trying to form a defensive line. But many of the troops feared that they would become separated from their mates and would find themselves surrounded.

Colonel Sinclair-MacLagan had similar fears and, not knowing that some adventurous soldiers had actually reached the Third Ridge (Gun Ridge), ordered his men to halt and dig defences on the Second Ridge. By around 8.00 am about 8,000 Australian troops had landed. The Turkish defenders numbered only about 500, although Mustafa Kemal's regiment was approaching.

The 2nd Brigade was supposed to seize the higher ground of Sari Bair, overlooking the Australians on the left, but Sinclair-MacLagan was concerned about his right flank. He therefore persuaded the 2nd Brigade commander, Colonel James McCay, once he arrived, to deploy his men to the right flank, rather than to the left. It proved to be a fateful decision. Mustafa Kemal led his troops onto the higher ground, and mounted a counterattack later in the day on the left flank of the Australian position. In the next nine months of the campaign the Anzacs never reached the Third Ridge nor secured Sari Bair.

More Australians, followed by New Zealanders, came ashore until by late afternoon they numbered 16,000, and were in sufficient numbers to at least hold the Turkish attacks. On balance, the Anzacs had done well.

## Digging in for life

As night approached on the first day the Anzac position seemed precarious. Australian and New Zealand units were mixed up, many leaders had become casualties, and some troops were straggling back to the beach, where chaos reigned. Casualties numbered more than 2,000, and the wounded were lying on the beach, waiting to be taken to the ships offshore.

# Chapter 6: Creating the Anzac Legend at Gallipoli, 1915

## Diggers

Australian soldiers have been called *Diggers* since the First World War, but there is no evidence that the term derived from Hamilton's famous order. Before the war, miners in both Australia and New Zealand were called diggers, and by 1916 the term applied to soldiers from both countries. On the Western Front, as at Gallipoli, the troops were constantly digging, either to improve their trenches, or to construct tunnels under enemy positions. By 1918 the Australians were referring to themselves as Diggers, and the term still denotes an Australian soldier.

General Bridges, who had landed with his staff at about 7.30 am, knew that he had not achieved his objectives, feared that he might not be able to hold a Turkish attack the next day, and wondered whether it might be better to withdraw the force to reinforce the British at Cape Helles, which, so far as he knew, was doing better. Bridges and Godley worked themselves into a state of anxiety and recommended to Birdwood that he evacuate the force.

Birdwood was shocked but agreed to refer the decision to General Hamilton, aboard the battleship *Queen Elizabeth*. Admiral Cecil Thursby, in charge of the landing, advised that insufficient boats were available to evacuate the force. Then Hamilton received news that the Australian submarine *AE2* had torpedoed a Turkish gunboat in the narrowest part of the Dardanelles. He therefore ordered Birdwood and his troops to stick it out: 'You have got through the difficult business, now you have only to dig, dig, dig, until you are safe'. The Australians and New Zealanders would remain at the place now called Anzac Cove.

## *Our daring submariners — entering the Sea of Marmara*

The *AE2* was one of the RAN's two submarines, the other having been lost without trace off New Guinea in September 1914 (refer to Chapter 5). Commanded by Lieutenant Commander Henry Stoker of the Royal Navy, and with a mixed British and Australian crew of 31 officers and sailors, by January 1915 the submarine was serving in the Mediterranean.

When the British and French battleships failed to force their way through the Dardanelles, two British submarines tried and were lost. Stoker was determined to attempt the hazardous passage, and the British naval commander told him that if he succeeded he might do 'more to finish the war than any other act'. Stoker's first attempt on 24 April failed due to mechanical failure.

Next morning Stoker tried again, and in the strait sank a large Turkish gunboat. It was the news of this success which, along with other considerations, persuaded Hamilton that the Anzac troops shouldn't evacuate their foothold on the peninsula. The British naval commander hoped that the *AE2* would prevent the Turks from sending troops and supplies to Gallipoli by ship. A Turkish battleship, firing over the peninsula at the allied landings, stopped and retreated to safety after it spotted the *AE2*'s periscope. Trying to avoid being rammed by a Turkish destroyer the *AE2* ran aground directly in front of a Turkish fort, but escaped, and then endured 16 hours on the sea floor.

After reaching the Sea of Marmara, Stoker spent five days attempting to 'run amok' (as he had been ordered), but mechanical faults in his craft prevented further success. One of these faults caused the *AE2* to surface only a mile from a Turkish torpedo boat, which opened fire and damaged the submarine. Stoker had no choice but to scuttle his boat. He and his crew went into captivity, during which three died. Encouraged by the *AE2*'s success, other British submarines followed and disrupted the Turkish sea communications.

In 1998 Turkish and Australian divers located the submarine lying in 72 metres of water. In 2007 an Australian not-for-profit company began trying to determine how the wrecked submarine could be protected and preserved.

## Holding On

The Anzacs expected another attack on 26 April, but, like them, the Turks were exhausted; they had incurred 2,000 casualties the previous day. Both sides now started to dig the line of trenches around the perimeter — 2.5 kilometres long and no more than 1.5 kilometres deep — that was to remain mainly unchanged until the August offensive. From the high ground the Turks dominated the Anzac positions, which they shelled intermittently. Snipers were a particular danger and Colonel MacLaurin, commander of the 1st Brigade, was killed on the third day. On 2 May Monash's 4th Brigade and the New Zealand Brigade attempted to enlarge the perimeter, but were beaten back with heavy casualties.

At Cape Helles the British had been a little more successful. They had been met by murderous Turkish fire at some beaches, but elsewhere had got safely ashore. Observing from his battleship, Hamilton noticed that one landing was relatively unopposed and suggested to Major General Aylmer Hunter-Weston, commander of the 29th Division, that he reinforce it. Self-important and vain, 'Hunter-Bunter' declined because it would upset the landing plan, and Hamilton, displaying the lack of drive and determination that marred his command, politely refrained from pressing the issue.

The French met much less opposition on the Asiatic shore, but because they were only conducting a diversion they withdrew and joined the British at Helles. There the British and French advanced inland over open fields and through olive groves for about five kilometres before being halted by Turkish defences.

## Charging the Turkish line at Helles

Hamilton considered the attack at Helles to be his main effort, and wanted to seize the high ground at Achi Baba that dominated the plain. He therefore brought Colonel McCay's 2nd Brigade and the New Zealand Brigade by ships around to Helles. They arrived on 6 May and, along with troops of the 29th Division, the British Naval Division and the French, they conducted several unsuccessful attacks.

Late in the afternoon of 8 May, at short notice, Hamilton ordered the Australians to undertake a poorly planned assault. Two Australian battalions attacked side-by-side in extended line through flowery fields, with the other two battalions following, towards the small village of Krithia, at the base of Achi Baba. After advancing through intense Turkish artillery and machine-gun fire, the men tumbled into a trench to gather their breath. McCay jumped onto the parapet and called, 'Now then, Australians ... Come on, Australians!' The men rose and charged another 500 metres through a screaming hail of bullets, but they could not reach Krithia. McCay was wounded in the early hours of the next day while supervising the evacuation of the wounded. Having started the battle with 2,900 men, the brigade lost 1,000 men in an hour. The survivors returned to Anzac Cove two weeks later.

## Repelling the Turkish attack at Anzac

The troops at Anzac endured constant shelling and sniping, while they launched small raids and attacks. On 15 May a Turkish sniper wounded Major General Bridges, and he was carried aboard a hospital ship. 'Anyhow', he said, knowing he was dying, 'I have commanded an Australian division'.

Brigadier General Harold 'Hooky' Walker, a British officer of the Indian Army and Birdwood's chief of staff, took over the division.

In the weeks after the landing, the Turks brought forward two new divisions to join the two that had been manning the perimeter since the first day, for an all-out assault. The attack came before dawn on 19 May with the Turks yelling 'Allah, Allah!' The Australians were ready, responding with rifle fire, machine-guns, and in some places artillery. At Courtney's Post nine Turks entered an Australian fighting trench. Private Albert Jacka from Victoria leapt into the trench, shot five of the Turks and bayoneted two others. He was the first Australian to win the Victoria Cross in the war.

The Turkish army facing the Anzacs had numbered about 40,000. Of these about 10,000 became casualties, with about 3,000 being killed, an astonishing casualty rate for one day of fighting. The Australians lost 160 men killed and 468 wounded. The dead bodies, rotting in the sun, created such a health risk that the two sides arranged an armistice on 24 May to bury the bodies and to recover any wounded still lying between the lines. After this debacle the Turks reverted to trench warfare, strengthening their defences, while maintaining their shelling and sniper fire.

## *Surviving the worst conditions*

Conditions for the soldiers at Anzac were almost unbearable. Those in the trenches lived on the edge of their nerves, expecting a Turkish raid at any time. Turkish sniper fire was so accurate that the troops made periscopes to observe the areas in front of their trenches. Often the Turkish and Australian trenches were so close that they could throw grenades at each other, but the Anzacs were short of grenades and needed to improvise these out of jam tins.

No area within the Anzac perimeter was free from Turkish fire, and working parties, struggling up the hills from the beach, or staggering back down, carrying casualties, became casualties themselves. It was exhausting, heavy work, not helped by the monotonous diet. Rotting bodies bred flies and disease. Fit and healthy in April, the troops were soon gaunt and weak. The one relief was to swim at the beach, but even here they came under fire.

Trooper Ion Idriess described his experiences after opening a tin of jam: 'They swarmed that jam, all fighting amongst themselves. I wrapped my overcoat over the tin and gouged out the flies, then spread the biscuit, held my hand over it, and drew the biscuit out of the coat. But a lot of the flies flew into my mouth and beat about inside ... I nearly howled with rage ... Of all the bastards of places this is the greatest bastard in the world.'

## Chapter 6: Creating the Anzac Legend at Gallipoli, 1915

### The Man with the donkey

The exploits of John Simpson Kirkpatrick, better known as Simpson, or the 'man with the donkey', form one of the most celebrated stories of the Anzacs at Gallipoli. He was not actually an Australian, having been born in County Durham in 1892. While serving in a merchant ship he broke his contract in Australia and worked as an itinerant labourer before joining the AIF as a stretcher bearer in the Medical Corps in the hope of returning to Britain. Instead the AIF went to the Middle East.

Simpson landed on the first morning at Anzac and found himself to be the only survivor of his stretcher bearer section. Commandeering a donkey, for three and a half weeks he carried wounded soldiers down the hillsides and along Monash Valley to the dressing station near the beach. Few places at Anzac were safe from enemy fire, and on the morning of 19 May he was carrying two wounded soldiers down the valley when he was struck in the heart and killed.

Soon Simpson's story was seized upon by propagandists, and exaggerated accounts of his exploits appeared in Australian newspapers, followed by stories in books and eventually, in 1965, by a biography that promoted the myth of the folk hero.

The 'man with the donkey' became part of the Anzac legend and statues of them can be found in Durham, in Melbourne and at the Australian War Memorial in Canberra. He was mentioned in despatches for 'gallant and distinguished service in the field', but over the decades groups in Australia have sought the Victoria Cross for him. He was never recommended for one at the time, which is the first and overriding requirement. Undoubtedly he was a brave man who performed a valuable service, but so too did the other stretcher bearers who, unlike Simpson, ventured into no-man's land to retrieve the wounded.

The casualties from the fighting and disease severely reduced the strengths of the units. Monash's 4th Brigade landed late on 25 April more than 3,500 strong; eight days later his four battalions mustered 1,800. During May, light horsemen, without their horses, arrived to strengthen the defences. They were from Chauvel's 1st, Ryrie's 2nd, and Colonel Frederic Hughes's 3rd Light Horse Brigade, which had been raised in October 1914. The Anzacs were holding on, but neither they nor the British troops at Helles were making any progress. The campaign had reached a stalemate.

## *False Hope in the August Offensives*

To break the deadlock at Gallipoli the British Government sent Hamilton more troops and approved a new offensive. The Anzac Corps would make the main attack, and Birdwood planned an imaginative and daring operation, which would prove to be beyond the capacities of his tired men. Monash's

4th Brigade, the New Zealand Infantry Brigade, along with a British Army division and an Indian Army brigade, newly assigned to the corps, would move out of the perimeter at night near the coast, strike north through a tangle of gullies and ridges, and then turn east and make their way up towards the Sari Bair ridge to capture the high points, including Chunuk Bair.

Four subsidiary and successive operations would support the main offensive:

- The British 29th Division would attack at Helles to persuade the Turks to keep their forces there.

- The 1st Australian Division would attack and capture a position, known as Lone Pine, in the centre of the Anzac perimeter, to suck in Turkish reserves and divert attention from the main attack.

- Two Australian light horse brigades would then attack northwards to seize the high ground known as Baby 700, as part of a coordinated thrust towards Chunuk Bair by the New Zealanders approaching from the left flank.

- Hamilton had been given another British Army corps, the 9th, commanded by the elderly Lieutenant General Sir Frederick Stopford, brought out of retirement. Its two divisions would land at Suvla Bay, capture hills overlooking the area, provide a firm base, and protect the left flank of Birdwood's advance

## Seizing Lone Pine for no advantage

Lone Pine was a strong Turkish position on a small hill just beyond the Australian perimeter along the Second Ridge. Major General Harold Walker, commander of the 1st Division, did not like the idea of capturing it, but tried to minimise casualties by careful planning. The Australians dug tunnels underneath no-man's land and placed explosive charges in them to be detonated just as they attacked. For several days before the battle Australian artillery and naval guns pounded the area to cut the Turkish barbed wire, although with little success.

The attack began late in the afternoon of 6 August, when the explosive were ignited and troops of the 1st Brigade charged across no-man's land and flung themselves at the Turkish defences. The Turks had covered their trenches with pine logs, making it difficult for the Australians to enter. A vicious battle with bayonets and grenades ensued in the trenches and tunnels as the Turks mounted local counterattacks. At one stage, Major Iven Mackay of the 4th Battalion defended a trench alone with his rifle and bayonet. He rose to command all of the Australian Army forces in New Guinea in the Second World War.

The savage battle raged for five days, with most of Walker's division joining in. By the time it finished, the Australians possessed Lone Pine, but had suffered more than 2,200 casualties. Seven Australians had won the Victoria Cross. The Turks were thought to have lost 5,000. Initially they rushed troops to the area, but realising it was a diversion some went instead to Chunuk Bair where they stopped the main Anzac attack. The Turks had also figured out that the extremely costly British attacks at Helles were a feint.

## Dying at the Nek for no purpose

The Nek was the narrow saddle between the Anzac trenches at Russell's Top and the Turkish position at Baby 700. The opposing trenches were between 20 and 60 metres apart and the Nek was only about 80 metres wide. Brigadier General Hughes's 3rd Light Horse Brigade was to seize Baby 700 in an attack that would coincide with one by the New Zealanders, farther north against Chunuk Bair. Because of the narrowness of the area, the first assault would be by 150 men of the 8th Light Horse Regiment, followed two minutes later by another wave of 150 men. The 10th Light Horse would then send two similar waves.

Before the attack, scheduled to begin at 4.30 am on 7 August, the artillery laid down a terrific bombardment on Baby 700, but missed the forward Turkish trench, and because of poor synchronisation of timing, the guns stopped seven minutes before the Australians were due to leave their trenches. The expected New Zealander attack against Chunuk Bair had not eventuated. Nonetheless, the Australian assault went ahead.

Led by Lieutenant Colonel Alexander White, the first wave of light horsemen leapt over the parapet and was immediately cut down by a torrent of fire. The second wave followed without hesitation and met the same fate. Realising the futility of the attack, Lieutenant Colonel Noel Brazier of the 10th Light Horse tried to have the third wave cancelled, claiming that 'the whole thing was nothing but bloody murder'. Hughes's brigade major, Lieutenant Colonel John Antill, was incensed at Brazier's impertinence. 'Push on', he roared. Brazier returned to his men: 'Sorry lads', he said, 'but the order is to go'. Trooper Harold Rush knew that the order meant death. He farewelled his mate with the sombre words, 'Goodbye cobber. God bless you', before they 'hopped the bags' and charged into the firestorm. The 10th Light Horse's first wave was similarly slaughtered, after which the attack was called off.

In an area little bigger than a tennis court the 600 attackers lost 234 killed and 138 wounded. The Turks lost eight killed. The battle has become well known through Peter Weir's 1981 movie, *Gallipoli,* which inaccurately portrays the assault as a diversion to assist the British landing at Suvla Bay, rather than part of the coordinated strike against Chunuk Bair.

Fortunately, Brigadier General Chauvel, commanding the 1st Light Horse Brigade, had enough sense to call off his simultaneous attack at Quinn's Post when he saw that it would incur excessive casualties but gain nothing.

## Climbing Chunuk Bair for no gain

The main offensive began in the evening of 6 August, when two brigades cleared the way on the left flank and four more brigades trudged northwards through the dark before turning east. The assault on the Sari Bair ridge was to be conducted by two columns — the New Zealanders would lead the right column and Monash's 4th Brigade the left.

The otherwise imaginative plan had many weaknesses:

- ✔ The command arrangements were hopelessly inadequate. Major General Godley commanded the troops conducting the offensive but he had too many brigades to control and insufficient staff to help him. As Birdwood was in overall command he must accept the blame for the command muddle.
- ✔ The terrain north of Anzac was a maze of gullies and ridges that were almost impossible to navigate during the day, let alone at night.
- ✔ The Anzac troops were extremely tired and weak, having already spent more than three months at Anzac Cove, while the British troops were completely inexperienced.
- ✔ Even if the troops secured Sari Bair, the Turks would be able to concentrate their forces there faster than the British troops could be reinforced and supplied, especially with water and ammunition.

After moving north out of the Anzac perimeter Monash's brigade became lost, although he actually performed better than some critics have suggested. The following day the brigade encountered Turks on the left flank, became involved in a battle near Hill 60, and was never able to advance to Sari Bair.

With great gallantry, the New Zealanders eventually reached the crest at Chunuk Bair on 8 August and held off Turkish counterattacks before being joined by a few British troops. General Liman von Sanders, commanding the Turkish Army, gave the defence of the area to his most reliable commander, Mustafa Kemal, who brought in reinforcements. Kemal personally led his troops in the attack that forced the New Zealanders and British from the heights.

Elsewhere, on 9 August Gurkhas from the Indian brigade managed to reach the crest farther north. There they were mistakenly shelled by British naval guns and, already exhausted, couldn't hold out against a Turkish assault. By 10 August it was clear that the Anzac offensive had failed.

At Suvla Bay the British 9th Corps came ashore in the early hours of 7 August, but through the inability of the commander, General Stopford, and the inexperience of the troops, it did not push inland and drive the few Turkish defenders from the hills. Contrary to popular stories, however, the incompetence of the British force at Suvla Bay didn't alone cause the collapse of the offensive. The collapse had its roots in the complexity of the plan, its poor management by Birdwood and his subordinate commanders, and by the setting of impossible tasks. In four days Birdwood's force of British, Indians and Anzacs had lost 12,000 men. At first the Anzacs had been impressed by Birdwood's personal touch, but they later saw through the lack of substance in his pep talks, which they called 'Birdie's Bull'. And he was no great shakes as a planner.

## Sneaking Away

After the August offensive the Anzac perimeter was very much larger, eventually joining with the force at Suvla Bay. Although fighting continued around the Hill 60 position, however, the August attack was the end of offensive operations.

Birdwood's corps was reinforced by the arrival of the 2nd Australian Division. Its brigades, the 5th, the 6th and the 7th, had been raised in Australia in the first half of the year, and the division had been cobbled together in Egypt. Major General James Legge, who had been Chief of the General Staff, took command of the 2nd Division. Both the troops at Anzac and their commanders were tired and sick, and were occasionally withdrawn to the island of Lemnos for rest and recuperation.

### Reporting unpalatable truths to London

General Sir Ian Hamilton couldn't hide the failure of the August offensive from the British War Cabinet, but usually he refused to tell the truth about the progress of the campaign for fear of upsetting his masters. Then a young Australian journalist, Keith Murdoch, arrived on the scene. Murdoch didn't stay long; however, the respected British war correspondent Ellis Ashmead-Bartlett told him the campaign was a disaster, but that the correspondents, including the future Australian official historian, Charles Bean, were not permitted to say so.

Murdoch continued on to London where he wrote a lurid letter that reached British Prime Minister Herbert Asquith, a letter full of exaggerations and errors. The essence of the letter, however, was correct; Hamilton had lost control of the campaign, if he ever had it, and needed to be replaced. Meanwhile, Ashmead-Bartlett reached London with his own account. The government set up the Dardanelles Commission to enquire into the causes

of the disaster and sent General Sir Charles Monro from France to replace Hamilton. Monro believed that Britain should make its main effort in France. He took one look at Gallipoli and recommended withdrawal.

## Deciding to depart

Lord Kitchener, the British War Secretary, was shocked at Monro's message recommending evacuation, and travelled out to Gallipoli to see for himself. He agreed with Monro and returned to London to persuade the War Cabinet. He struggled to persuade the optimists, who amazingly now thought that the Navy could smash through the Dardanelles, but finally on 7 December the War Cabinet ordered the withdrawal.

In their trenches and dugouts on the peninsula the Anzacs had no idea of the impending withdrawal, but they knew that the approaching winter would bring more misery. In mid-October moderate seas smashed the pier at Anzac Cove, making it difficult it bring in supplies. Bad weather continued until a blizzard on 27 November covered the trenches with snow.

By this time Monro had been appointed commander of all the British forces in the eastern Mediterranean and Birdwood was given command of the army on the Gallipoli peninsula. Godley took over the Anzac Corps and would be responsible for its evacuation.

## Tricking the Turks

After the disaster of the August offensive Colonel Cyril Brudenell White became chief of staff of the Anzac Corps, and it fell to him to plan the Anzac evacuation, having been warned about it on 22 November. White knew that if the Turks realised that the Anzac forces were being gradually withdrawn they would attack the remaining, weakened forces, with disastrous consequences. White therefore set out to accustom the Turks to long periods of quiet, in which no shots or shells were fired or bombs were thrown. When the curious Turks approached the Anzac lines they were then suddenly shot down. Every night the Anzacs maintained periods of silence until the Turks became used to them. The ruse was known as 'The Silent Stunt'.

The next step was to reduce the numbers of troops at Anzac. Each night boats came into the beachhead to evacuate troops quietly, while the Turks were permitted to see the arrival of small numbers of other troops during the day. The forward positions were still occupied at the normal strength.

By the time of the formal evacuation order on 8 December the force at Anzac had been reduced to 36,000 men.

The troops weren't told of the evacuation plan until as late as possible and many were dismayed to be leaving their dead. 'I hope *they* won't hear us marching back to the beach', said one as he passed a cemetery. The final withdrawal took place on the nights of 18 and 19 December, with 10,000 men being evacuated on each night. On the final night the last troops filed down from their forward positions, their boots wrapped in sandbags to muffle the sound. Rifles had been left behind to fire automatically, triggered by water dripping into cans. Explosive charges in the forward trenches were detonated according to a timed program. The last boat departed at 4.00 am on 20 December.

General Hamilton had thought that the force would incur 50 per cent casualties in an evacuation. The Anzac Corps evacuation, brilliant managed by White, achieved the task for the loss of two men, one struck by a Turkish bullet as the last boats pulled away. When the Turks attacked the Anzac position at 7.15 am they found no defenders. The British force at Helles was evacuated early in January.

# Reassessing and Remembering

Gallipoli holds such an iconic place in Australian history that it's sometimes forgotten that other nations were involved. About 50,000 Australians served at Gallipoli and about half, more than 26,000, became casualties, of whom about 8,100 died. Proportionally, the New Zealanders lost even more: 2,700 died and 4,750 were wounded of the 8,556 who fought there. The British had about 74,000 casualties and the Turks about 250,000, including 86,000 dead. French casualties were about the same as the Australians, 27,000. The Indian Army had about 4,800 casualties and Newfoundland, 142.

Historians have argued about Gallipoli for almost a century. It's generally agreed that the campaign was ill-conceived and even if it had been successful it's doubtful the results would have met expectations. Countless studies have examined the bungled planning and the poor performance of the commanders.

From an Australian point of view, the campaign showed more about the character of the men, who demonstrated the 'spirit of Anzac', than the expertise of their officers. The Australians too had incompetent officers; it was just that they were not holding the high ranks of the British commanders.

Some critics have lamented that the Australians were sacrificed by Britain, while the Australian Government had no say over the conduct of the campaign. In truth, the British Government and its military leaders were just as willing to sacrifice their own men. The campaign caused the Australians to start to realise that they should control how and where their forces should fight, although this was not easy to achieve in a war conducted by the Empire.

For the Australian public, Gallipoli is important for its perceived role in giving the nation a sense of identity. The reverence for Anzac has not died as the decades have passed, and Anzac Day remains, or even continues to grow, as a time of national reflection. Each year, thousands of Australians make the pilgrimage to this distant battlefield to gain an appreciation of the sacrifices made by their forebears.

For the men of the AIF, Gallipoli had been a terrible ordeal. Never again would they need to endure such a prolonged and sustained period of privation and danger. But the actual battles on the Western Front would prove to be even more horrific and murderous.

# Chapter 7

# Enduring the Horrors of the Western Front, 1916–17

## In This Chapter

▶ Building on the Gallipoli experience
▶ Fighting in France
▶ Surviving a journey through hell
▶ Struggling to Passchendaele
▶ Understanding modern industrial warfare

At the beginning of 1916 the Australian battalions that had fought at Gallipoli were recovering in Egypt. They had been spared from serving in France in 1915, but that would soon end. For the remainder of the war, eventually five Australian infantry divisions would endure the horrors of trench warfare on the Western Front in France and Belgium.

Gallipoli (see Chapter 6) was a sideshow, as the war was always going to be decided in France. Although the Australian soldiers, the Diggers, established their reputation for courage, endurance and mateship at Gallipoli, many more of them served on the Western Front, where names such as Fromelles, Pozières, Bullecourt, Messines, Ypres, Menin Road and Passchendaele became engraved in Australian military history. Here, after bitter lessons, they built up their expertise and technical proficiency, without which they couldn't succeed.

In this chapter I relate how, after Gallipoli, Australia's expanded infantry force moved to France and took part in the dreadful battles in the Somme offensive of 1916. The Australians then followed up the German withdrawal in 1917, before being repulsed at Bullecourt. Fighting then switched to Flanders in Belgium where, after initial successes, the attacks foundered in mud and rain. Finally, I explain some of the techniques and technology of trench warfare and what it meant for the soldiers who were exposed to this new form of industrial warfare.

## Adapting to a New Theatre

In August 1914 the German Army invaded France in a great turning movement that took it through neutral Belgium and then in a southerly sweep towards Paris. The British Expeditionary Force and the French Army eventually halted the German offensive before it reached Paris. Both sides then constructed a line of trenches which, by November 1914, stretched nearly 800 kilometres from the Swiss border, through France to the Belgian coast. The French Army occupied 600 kilometres of the line in the east, the British Expeditionary Force held 130 kilometres from the Somme River to Ypres in Belgium, and Belgian and French troops then held the remaining front through to the sea.

The British Expeditionary Force had expanded during the first year of the war and by April 1916 consisted of 44 infantry and 5 cavalry divisions, organised in four armies under the command of General Sir Douglas Haig. The BEF numbered about 1.263 million troops.

## Enlarging the AIF

After the fighting at Gallipoli and the terrible list of casualties, so many patriotic volunteers crowded into the Australian recruiting depots that by the end of 1915 the government decided to form additional infantry divisions. Already, more than 30,000 Australian reinforcements had arrived in Egypt. Lieutenant General Sir William Birdwood, who had assumed command of the Australian Imperial Force (AIF) after the death of Major General William Bridges (see Chapter 6), and Lieutenant General Alexandar Godley, commander of the Anzac Corps, decided to enlarge the AIF by splitting the 16 battalions of the original first four brigades in half to become the nucleus of 32 new battalions, which would then be brought up to full strength with reinforcements.

### Dreading the Western Front

The term Western Front was coined by the Germans, who needed to prosecute a 'two-front' war, one on the Eastern Front against Russia and the other on the Western Front against France. As the horrors of trench warfare became known, the Western Front came to represent not just a location, but the image of a dreaded experience. *All Quiet on the Western Front* by the German author Erich Maria Remarque, published in 1929, became one of the great anti-war novels.

## Chapter 7: Enduring the Horrors of the Western Front, 1916–17

By February 1916 the new divisions were as follows:

- **1st Division.** Major General Harold Walker, who had succeeded Bridges, remained in command. 1st Division consisted of the original 1st, 2nd, and 3rd Brigades, which needed to be rebuilt after giving up troops to the other brigades.

- **2nd Division.** Major General James Legge, who had led the division at Gallipoli, was still in command. Its original brigades, the 5th, 6th and 7th, remained untouched as they had arrived much more recently from Australia.

- **3rd Division.** Still being raised in Australia, 3rd Division consisted of the 9th, 10th and 11th Brigades. Brigadier General John Monash, who had commanded the 4th Brigade at Gallipoli, was slated to take command once the division reached England.

- **4th Division.** Major General Herbert Cox, a British officer who had commanded an Indian brigade at Gallipoli, was appointed commander. The 4th Division consisted of the 4th Brigade, which had fought at Gallipoli, and two newly formed brigades, the 14th and 15th.

- **5th Division.** Major General James McCay, who had recovered from wounds received while commanding the 2nd Brigade at Gallipoli, was appointed commander. The division consisted of the 8th Brigade, which had arrived in Egypt too late to serve at Gallipoli, and two newly formed brigades, the 12th and 13th.

- **Anzac Mounted Division.** Major General Harry Chauvel, who had commanded the 1st Light Horse Brigade at Gallipoli, was appointed commander. The division consisted of the 1st, 2nd and 3rd Australian Light Horse Brigades and the New Zealand Mounted Rifles Brigade, and was placed directly under the British Commander-in Chief in Egypt. The Anzac Mounted Division's story is told in Chapter 8.

While the formation of new infantry divisions was a major undertaking, expanding the AIF artillery was an even bigger task. Only the 1st Division's artillery had been formed in Australia and the artillery in Egypt needed to expand from 18 to 60 batteries to take account of the additional guns that would be necessary on the Western Front. Each division had its own artillery, commanded by a brigadier general, consisting of 12 batteries of 18-pounder field guns and three batteries of 4.5 inch howitzers.

The new infantry divisions were organised into corps as follows:

- **1st Anzac Corps.** Commanded by Lieutenant General Birdwood, the 1st Anzac Corps consisted of the 1st and 2nd Australian Infantry Divisions and the New Zealand Division.
- **2nd Anzac Corps.** Commanded by Lieutenant General Godley, the 2nd Anzac Corps consisted of the 4th and 5th Australian Infantry divisions. The 3rd Division would join in December 1916.

# Deploying to France

Because the 1st Anzac Corps' reformed units were based on existing units, that corps completed its reorganisation first. In mid-March 1916, the troops began sailing across the Mediterranean to Marseilles in southern France. Then, in a new, exciting experience for many, they travelled north by train through the French countryside.

The 1st Anzac Corps was allocated a quiet sector of the British front known as 'the nursery' near the town of Armentières (see Figure 7-1). The troops were issued with steel helmets, which they had not worn at Gallipoli, and they learned how to call for artillery support and to maintain and improve their trenches. The troops also began to appreciate some of the differences between serving in France and in the Middle East, such as going on periodic leave to Britain.

Back in France the Australian battalions began raiding the German lines to gain experience in trench warfare. They also helped repulse some minor German attacks. Towards the end of June the 2nd Anzac Corps started to arrive from Egypt. The 1st and 2nd Divisions withdrew from the front and General Godley assumed responsibility for the sector, with the 4th and 5th Divisions and the New Zealand Division.

While the Australians conducted minor operations in their quiet sector, elsewhere the Germans and French were locked in a desperate battle. In February the German Army began a major offensive against the French Army at Verdun in eastern France, believing that for reasons of national pride the French would be unwilling to surrender the strategically important city and would fight to retain it despite heavy losses. If they could destroy the French Army, the Germans would be close to winning the war. The Germans crushed the French defences with artillery and then advanced position by position. The battle, which was to continue through 1916 with great loss of life, helped shape the operations on the Western Front.

## Chapter 7: Enduring the Horrors of the Western Front, 1916–17

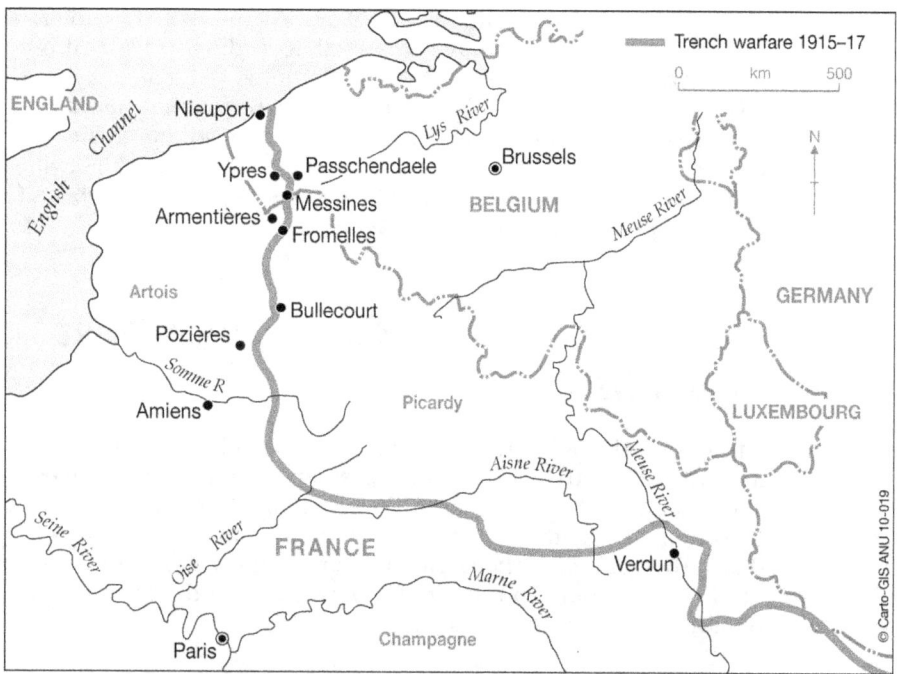

**Figure 7-1:** The Western Front, 1916–17.

# Attacking Under Fire

Under great strain at Verdun, the French commander-in-chief, General Joseph Joffre, persuaded General Haig to undertake an offensive elsewhere to force the Germans to ease their attacks at Verdun. As a result, on 1 July 1916 the British Army began a huge offensive north of the Somme River, while the French joined in by attacking south of the river. The British fired over 1.5 million shells, more than had been fired by the British Army in the first 12 months of the war, and detonated 17 mines in tunnels they had dug under the German frontline trenches and strong points. The attack was made by 13 British divisions, mostly from General Sir Henry Rawlinson's Fourth British Army. The first day of the Somme battle has become notorious as the bloodiest day in the history of the British Army, when 57,470 men became casualties, of which 19,240 were killed or died of wounds.

Despite the casualties, the British made some minor gains, so Haig resumed the offensive on 14 July with another attack. Rawlinson used a new artillery concept, known as *creeping barrage*. Artillery fire smashed down on the front of the German defences, destroying barbed wire and keeping the defenders in their dugouts and bunkers. As the British soldiers advanced, the line of artillery fire moved forward according to a timed program, usually a hundred metres each three minutes. This meant that the British soldiers could reach the first line of German trenches just as the defenders stumbled dazed from their dugouts, while the British artillery now struck the second line of German trenches. Using these tactics, Rawlinson's Fourth British Army inched forward, until it was stopped by stubborn German defence around the village of Pozières.

## Australia's worst day: Tragedy at Fromelles

Success on the Western Front was always a relative term, being measured in hundreds of metres captured for the loss of thousands of lives. The British success on the Somme caused the Germans to move reinforcements to the threatened area and the British high command came up with the bright idea that if they attacked the German line near the village of Fromelles, just south of the French–Belgian border, the Germans would be prevented from sending reinforcements to the Somme.

The task went to a British corps commander, Lieutenant General Sir Richard Haking, who was given a British division and the nearby 5th Australian Division, which had only recently arrived in France. The front in the chosen area was dominated by a *salient* (a bulge in the front-line) known as the 'Sugar Loaf', where the Germans had constructed concrete bunkers from which they could direct machine-gun fire across the front of their trenches.

After seven hours of ineffective bombardment the attack began at 6.00 pm on 19 July. Diggers from the three brigades of the 5th Division, side by side, stumbled over the water-logged ground on the northern side of the Sugar Loaf, and some of the troops crossed no-man's land and entered the German trenches. The 15th Brigade was, however, caught in withering fire from the Sugar Loaf. Then the Germans counterattacked, ejecting the Australians from the trenches that they had just captured.

The battle resulted in the deaths of more Australians in 24 hours than in any other time in Australian history. The 5th Division had lost 5,533 men, of whom 1,917 were dead and a further 470 were prisoners, and was effectively finished as a fighting force for several months. The heaviest casualties were in the 15th Brigade, whose commander, Brigadier General Harold 'Pompey' Elliott, had predicted the outcome and had tried to prevent the attack. When the historian Charles Bean met Elliott after the battle he 'felt almost as if he were in the presence of a man who had just lost his wife. He looked down and could hardly speak'. Haking, who had commanded the botched effort, said that though the attack had failed, it had done 'both divisions a great deal of good'. Elliott thought that Haking's conclusion that such an experience would do the infantry some good was 'a unique conception'.

## *Attempting the impossible on the Somme*

On the Somme, the 1st Anzac Corps was now to take over the offensive under the direction of the commander of the British Reserve Army, General Sir Hubert Gough. In seven weeks of operations the 1st, 2nd and 4th Divisions were thrown into battle in succession, with each having two tours in the line; in all they conducted 19 attacks. The 1st Division was commanded by the capable Major General Walker, supported by a first-rate chief of staff, Colonel Thomas Blamey, and they resisted Gough's first direction, 'to attack Pozières tomorrow night'. They planned their attack carefully and although the division took considerable casualties it advanced 1,000 metres and captured most of the village, not that anyone would have recognised it as having previously been a village because it was so heavily damaged. The troops then endured a fearful bombardment and a German counterattack.

Next, the 2nd Division took over, but its attack on 28 July was a sad and bitter failure. Major General Legge and his inexperienced staff were hurried into the attack. Like their predecessors, the troops also had to endure fierce bombardments. The division lost 6,848 men in 12 days 'in the line'.

The 4th Division continued the fight, trying to capture the remains of Mouquet Farm, 1.5 km north-west of Pozières and lost 4,649 men until it was relieved by the 1st Division, which was followed by the 2nd Division, until the 4th returned for another effort. Each assault gained a little more ground, until the Australians were withdrawn on 5 September having lost 23,000 men. As the historian Charles Bean wrote, the Pozières ridge 'was more densely sown with Australian sacrifice than any other place on earth'.

The mere recitation of statistics does not adequately bring home the horror of the fighting. Men huddled in dugouts for hours as high explosives rained on their positions. Then they struggled though churned earth and mangled corpses and, somehow, were expected to attack under machine-gun fire. Lieutenant Alexander Raws, 23rd Battalion, was buried twice with the dead and dying. 'The ground was covered with bodies in all stages of decay and mutilation', he wrote. He picked up a body to pull him from the ground and found 'a decayed corpse. I pulled a head off — it was covered with blood'.

### Australia's most famous soldier

Albert Jacka was the most famous Australian soldier of the war. Born in Victoria in 1893 he was working as a labourer when he enlisted as a private in 1914. At Gallipoli on 19 May 1915 Jacka was helping to defend Courtney's Post when the Turks captured a section of trench. He leapt over the parapet, shot five Turks, bayoneted two and forced the remainder to retreat. The first Australian to be awarded the Victoria Cross (VC) in the war, he became a national hero.

By the time of the battle of the Somme, Jacka was a lieutenant, commanding an infantry platoon in his battalion. In the morning of 7 August Jacka and some of his men were in a dugout where they had endured a night of heavy bombardment when the Germans counterattacked and rolled a bomb into the doorway. Jacka and his men were stunned, but he reacted first, charged up the steps, killed the Germans there and gathered his group of seven or eight soldiers. Then he saw that the enemy had taken 40 Australians prisoner and were marching them to the rear.

With his small party Jacka charged the enemy. Wounded seven times, Jacka is thought to have accounted for a dozen Germans. The captured Australians then turned on their guards in a fierce hand-to-hand battle, while other Australians, seeing the melee, joined in. By the time it was over they had captured 50 Germans. Bean described Jacka's counter-attack as 'the most dramatic and effective act of individual audacity in the history of the AIF'. Jacka was awarded the Military Cross, but many thought that he should have been awarded a bar to his VC (equivalent to a second VC; see Chapter 2). Seven other Australians were awarded the VC in the fight for Pozières; but referring to Jacka's initiative, Bean thought 'no action ever performed in the AIF quite so thoroughly deserved the higher award'.

In April 1917 Jacka, now a captain, was awarded a Bar to his Military Cross, fighting near Bullecourt. While commanding his troops at Polygon Wood in September 1917, some thought he should have been awarded the Distinguished Service Order. He continued serving on the Western Front until he was badly gassed at Villers-Bretonneux in May 1918.

After the war he became a small businessman and for a while was mayor of St Kilda in Melbourne. In the Great Depression his business failed and he died of illness in 1932. One thousand former soldiers led the funeral procession and eight VC winners were pallbearers.

## *A nation divided: Voting for or against conscription*

If the huge numbers of casualties that the Australians incurred in the Somme were to continue, it was clear that the AIF would have insufficient reinforcements to maintain all five divisions unless recruiting, which had declined, was to increase substantially. Already the British Government had introduced conscription and it seemed that Australia would need to do likewise. The decision rested with the Prime Minister, William Morris (Billy) Hughes, who had succeeded Andrew Fisher in October 1915 when the latter resigned to become High Commissioner in London. Many in the Labor Government, however, opposed conscription for overseas service.

In October 1916 the government conducted a referendum in which conscription was defeated by 72,476 out of 2,247,590 formal votes. In the context of strife in Ireland between Britain and those seeking Irish independence, Daniel Mannix, the Irish-born Roman Catholic Archbishop of Melbourne, rallied his flock against the proposal. The conscription campaign became highly divisive in the community and in November the Labor Party split. The pro-conscription element, led by Hughes, joined with Opposition members to form a new Nationalist Party government. At the end of 1917 Hughes again conducted a referendum to introduce conscription. The campaign was as bitter as the first one and conscription was defeated again.

## The Coldest Winter

After their ordeal on the Somme the Australian divisions occupied a quiet area near Ypres until in October 1916 they returned grimly to the Somme, this time accompanied by the 5th Division. They were involved in some minor offensives, but generally manned the line as the chilling autumn rains turned the battlefield, ploughed by countless bombardments, into a cold, desolate swamp. Haig called off the battle, but the Australians remained in the line during a bitterly cold winter. Birdwood's chief of staff, Major General White, demonstrated his great organising ability when he had camps, huts, roads and railways built in the rear areas.

Winter saw changes in command. Many commanders had not been up to the task, or were exhausted or sick. Nevill Smyth, an officer of the British-Indian Army who had commanded the 1st Brigade since Gallipoli, took over the 2nd Division from Legge. William Holmes, who had commanded the 5th Brigade at Gallipoli and on the Somme, succeeded Cox as commander of the 4th Division. J J Talbot Hobbs, who had commanded the 1st Division's artillery since the beginning of the war, replaced McCay as commander of the 5th Division. Many other changes were made in the brigade commands.

## Advancing to the Hindenburg Line

Towards the end of February 1917 the German Army unexpectedly withdrew between 15 and 50 kilometres to a new defensive position known as the Hindenburg Line. By shortening their line the Germans would need fewer troops and they had constructed strong defensive positions during the winter. As they followed up the withdrawing Germans, the Australians were able to conduct the more mobile operations, or open warfare, for which they had yearned during the bleak trench warfare and grim battles of attrition of the previous ten months.

Paralysed by months of inactivity, the Australians initially failed to act quickly, but as they gained momentum they sometimes overstepped the mark and received sharp reverses from German rearguard units. By early April the Australians had reached the outposts of the Hindenburg Line and could advance no further without a major assault.

## Bungling and bravery in the Bullecourt battles

General Gough, commander of the now-renamed British Fifth Army, to which the Anzac troops were assigned, ordered the 4th Division to capture the French town of Bullecourt, which was part of the Hindenburg Line. Gough planned to use British tanks to support the attack, but for the first attack on 10 April the tanks never arrived and the 4th Division commander, Holmes, withdrew his troops. Against the advice of General Birdwood and his chief of staff, White, Gough ordered the attack the next day, and although the tanks arrived most broke down and didn't provide the vital support. The division lost 3,300 men and their faith in tanks.

On 3 May 'Butcher' Gough, as referred to by the Australian troops, tried again in exactly the same spot with the 2nd Division. After an initial success, in which a foothold was seized in the Hindenburg Line, the division was heavily counterattacked. The 6th Brigade, under Brigadier General John Gellibrand, took the brunt and stood firm until relieved by troops of the 1st Division. The 5th Division later relieved the 1st and maintained the line. One diarist envisaged the prospect of an 'almost endless vista of brigades put in to hold this impossible position'. The second battle of Bullecourt had cost the AIF 7,000 casualties. Gough had bungled both battles, but Birdwood's corps headquarters made mistakes also.

## Success Ends in Failure in Flanders

Sir Douglas Haig (now a field marshal) planned to switch the main area of his offensive to Flanders, attacking in front of the Belgium town of Ypres, and hoping to drive the Germans away from the coast. By this time the British generals had refined an attacking technique called 'bite and hold'. By massing a huge amount of artillery in one area they could destroy a section of the German trenches, thus allowing the advancing infantry to seize the trenches relatively easily. If, however, the infantry advanced further they would move beyond the range of their own artillery support, so the infantry would merely hold the area and repel all attacks. The British artillery could then move forward to new locations and the process could start all over again.

The offensive would include Major General John Monash's 3rd Division, which had spent the second half of 1916 training on the Salisbury Plain in England before travelling to France and joining Godley's 2nd Anzac Corps in a relatively quiet area around Armentières. The corps' other formations were the New Zealand Division and a British division.

## *Making their mark: The 3rd Division at Messines*

The first step in the offensive, to be conducted by General Sir Herbert Plumer's Second British Army, was to seize a salient south of Ypres dominated by the Messines ridge. Plumer was to attack with three army corps, the southernmost being the 2nd Anzac Corps, to which was added the 4th Australian Division to be kept in reserve.

Plumer planned the attack in meticulous detail and British engineers, including the 1st Australian Tunnelling Company, dug deep tunnels under the German frontline, which were than packed with high explosives. The artillery bombardment began on 31 May and continued until the early hours of 7 June, when the explosives in 19 tunnels were detonated with a noise that was reportedly heard in London. More than 10,000 German front-line troops were obliterated. Then the British infantry attacked against the stunned German defenders.

Like Plumer, Monash too was a careful planner and his division in its first major battle, along with the New Zealanders and the British, achieved an outstanding success. The 4th Division then came in to press the attack, before the whole advance halted in the face of German counterattacks. The Messines salient had been eliminated, although it had cost the 3rd Division 4,100 casualties and the 4th Division 2,700.

## *Side by side on the Menin Road*

All the Australians were now to be involved in the series of battles known as Third Ypres that took place along the axis of the road that ran from Ypres to Passchendaele. The battle began on 31 July and, except for their artillery, the AIF was not involved until September. It then conducted three attacks:

- 20 September, at Menin Road using the 1st and 2nd Divisions
- 26 September, at Polygon Wood, using the 4th and 5th Divisions
- 4 October, at Broodseinde, using the 1st and 2nd Divisions (1st Anzac Corps) and the 3rd Division and the New Zealanders (2nd Anzac Corps), in line together

The Australian attacks differed from those on the Somme in a number of respects:

- For the first time all the Australians were under the command of 'Dad' Plumer, the careful 60-year-old general who insisted on three weeks' preparation.
- Plumer applied the 'bite and hold' tactics, in which limited objectives were secured before the artillery moved forward to support the next assault.
- Unlike on the Somme, Plumer gave his corps commanders considerable freedom in preparing their plans.
- For the first time, two Australian divisions fought side by side, which increased the confidence of the troops.
- By now all the commanders and their men were experienced. The only new divisional commander was Sinclair-MacLagan, who had returned from his training post in England after Holmes of the 4th Division was killed by an artillery shell. Of the 15 brigade commanders, only two had not commanded their formations in battle.

All three attacks were resounding successes, with the Germans being driven back by relentless hammer blows. But AIF casualties had been heavy, numbering over 17,000.

## Struggling through the mud to Passchendaele

The rains, which had mercifully held off during September after a wet August, came again early in October. No longer could the artillery be moved forward quickly to support each attack. The fragile canal system was shattered by the artillery and the area turned into a sea of mud, in which whole wagons with their horses sunk without trace. Men who slipped off the duckboards drowned in the mud, weighed down by their weapons and equipment. In a much criticised decision Haig ordered the offensive to continue. The 2nd and 3rd Divisions took part in futile attacks. By the time Haig called a halt on 14 November he had lost 250,000 men, 38,000 of them Australians.

The Australian divisions were withdrawn to the Messines area to rest. On 1 November Haig agreed to bring all the Australian divisions together as the Australian Corps. General Birdwood became the commander, with Major General White as his chief of staff. The Australians had now endured almost two years of bloody warfare on the Western Front. At last, they hoped, they would be able to fight as one Australian force.

## *Modern Industrial Warfare*

To the casual reader, the First World War might be seen as some great primitive, deadly brawl in which countless numbers of men were slaughtered by unimaginative and incompetent commanders until both sides were too exhausted to continue. While there is some truth in this view, the war owes its character to the industrial revolution of the 19th century, which enabled the nations to raise armies that numbered in the millions, to transport them across the seas by ship and to the battlefront by railway, and to feed them and supply them with ammunition.

As well as enabling the nations to field huge forces, new technological innovations caused a transformation in the way the war was conducted on the battlefield and at sea. The list of new technology is long and includes the use of the internal combustion engine (tractors, trucks and tanks) and wireless telegraphy for military purposes, the introduction of undersea warfare (submarines), the role of aircraft, the appearance of chemical warfare and improvements to artillery.

The problem was that the new technology favoured the defenders rather than the attackers. Even before they began their assault, the attackers came under heavy artillery fire from high explosives and shrapnel. Then the attackers needed to advance over *no-man's land*, the area separating the two lines of the trenches, where they could be cut down by machine-gun fire. Although the defenders' positions were pounded by artillery, they were better protected in their trenches and dugouts than the exposed attackers.

As Germany occupied French territory, the Allies had more incentive to attack than the Germans, who merely had to maintain their position and hope to wear out the Allies. To win, the Allies had to drive the Germans out of France. During 1915 and 1916 both sides mounted offensives, but the Allies conducted more and lost more men, without making much difference to the situation.

## Living in the trenches

The Australian who served at Gallipoli experienced trench warfare, but soon learned that it was conducted at a more sophisticated level in France. The British defences consisted of several lines of deep fighting trenches connected by communication trenches. Soldiers lived in the trenches or in dugouts constructed into the sides of the trenches. Barbed wire entanglements were placed in front of their trenches to protect them from enemy infantry attacks. Machine-guns were built into strong points so that they could fire out across no-man's land. Telephones were installed so that when an enemy attacked, the forward troops could call the artillery batteries in the rear to bombard the attackers.

During battles, life in the trenches was one of misery, fear, exhaustion and death. But trench life was tolerable in the quiet sectors, although both sides still conducted raids. Thinking that the soldiers spent their whole time in the trenches is a mistake. Most soldiers spent about half a year in the trenches, and only about a third of that time was in the front-line; at other times they were further back in support or reserve trenches. They also were withdrawn from the line for periods of rest, when perhaps they could enjoy a beer or cheap wine in a French *estaminet*. And there were also times when they were on leave, on training courses, or recovering from wounds or illness.

## Dominating the battlefield: The big guns

The Australians quickly understood that artillery dominated the battlefield. As the distinguished historian John Terraine wrote: 'Artillery was the battle winner, artillery was what caused the greatest loss of life, the most dreadful wounds and the deepest fear'. A field gun fired with a relatively low trajectory, while a howitzer fired with a higher trajectory, so that its shells could reach behind steep hills or into trenches. The Australian artillery units were mainly equipped with 18-pounder field guns and 4.5-inch howitzers, each with a range of about 7,000 metres. Heavier guns, such as 60-pounders and 8-inch and 9.2-inch howitzers, could fire about 10,000 metres. The 12-inch rail howitzers fired a 750 pound shell 14,000 metres. The AIF had one 8-inch gun battery and one 9.2-inch howitzer battery.

Artillery techniques developed remarkably during the war. Initially, guns needed to register a target by firing single shots at a target until they got the exact range. Once the artillery started to register a target, defenders knew that they were soon to be bombarded. Eventually, however, survey maps were improved so that units could locate their positions accurately.

Then, with meteorological information and the knowledge of the wear of each individual gun's barrel, rounds could be fired accurately to a particular location simply by using maps; that is, without registration. Observers in aircraft or in balloons were used either to locate enemy gun positions or to watch the fall of shots of their own guns. The artillery fire could then be adjusted according to instructions sent using primitive wireless sets.

Guns were used either to neutralise enemy defences, to destroy the enemy as they attacked in the open, or to destroy or neutralise enemy artillery positions (known as counterbombardment). The gunners located enemy gun batteries by the use of sound-ranging equipment or the use of observers who watched for gun flashes. Enemy positions were also identified by aerial photography.

Sound ranging relied on placing microphones along a baseline and calculating the distance to the enemy guns from the interval of time it took for the sound to arrive at the different locations. A key figure among the scientists and British artillery officers who developed the technique was an Australian-born scientist, Second Lieutenant Lawrence Bragg. With his father he received the Nobel Prize for physics in 1915 for their work on X-rays and crystal structure.

By the last year of the war attacks were supported by complicated bombardment plans in which guns were switched from target to target according to timed programs. For the Australian Corps' attack on 8 August 1918 (refer to Chapter 9) the commander of the corps field artillery, Brigadier General Walter Coxen, commanded 550 artillery pieces. The attack began with no preliminary bombardment and the guns all opened fire, without registration, at exactly zero hour.

## *Gas, gas, gas!*

The Germans first used chlorine gas, dispensed from cylinders, in April 1915, but having started the chemical war they made one bad miscalculation: The prevailing winds came from the west, so they were just as likely to gas themselves as the Allies. After that, both sides began delivering gas by artillery shells. Chlorine was replaced by phosgene, which was harder to detect but still fatal. By 1917 mustard gas was being used; actually a liquid, it caused severe blistering to areas it touched, as well as pain to the head, eyes and throat. The armies responded by issuing the troops with primitive and then increasingly sophisticated gas masks (respirators). A gas attack was a terrifying experience, as often the troops couldn't don their respirators fast enough and even then they didn't always work properly.

Troops operated less effectively when wearing their gas masks, so for their attacks the British would mix small numbers of mustard gas shells with high explosive shells during the preparatory bombardments, to force the defenders to wear their gas marks. Then at some point the gas shells stopped, allowing the attackers to advance without their gas masks. The Australians were subject to attack with phosgene and tear gas at Pozières and Messines, and to mustard gas at Third Ypres and at Villers-Bretonneux (refer to Chapter 9).

In October 1917, the 4th Division artillery suffered badly from gas shelling. Major Jeremiah Selmes, 101st Howitzer Battery, recalled that 'the experiences were heart-rending, rain, mud, shells, gas — casualties coming faster and faster ... For 12 days we averaged 14 hours a day with gas masks on. Through the night sleep was out of the question'. Another officer lost his voice for a week. He sat 'up most every night with a map board and protractor on my knees with a couple of candles burning and a gas helmet on, working out barrages for a timetable for the stunt [attack] next day'.

## *Above the maelstrom: The air war*

The First World War saw the first large-scale use of aircraft for military purposes. Initially their main purpose was for reconnaissance, either to detect enemy movement or increasingly to provide spotters for the artillery. To counter the reconnaissance aircraft, each side developed fighter aircraft, which soon conducted 'dogfights' as they tried to protect the slower, less manoeuvrable reconnaissance aircraft. Above the trenches the pilots were free from the constant shelling and mud. But they could be quickly shot down in flames and casualty rates were high.

Aircraft were also used to bomb rear areas and to strafe the front lines with machine-gun fire, and as the war progressed aircraft dropped ammunition to advancing troops. By the end of the war aircraft had become an integral part of the land campaign. The experiences of the squadrons of the Australian Flying Corps are described in Chapter 9.

# Chapter 8

# Riding to Victory in Palestine, 1916–18

## In This Chapter
▶ Introducing the Light Horse
▶ Patrolling the desert
▶ Winning fame at Beersheba
▶ Pushing to the waters of Jordan
▶ Acting as cavalry to crush the Turks

Australians played a central role in two of the British Empire's three major campaigns against the Ottoman Empire in the First World War — Gallipoli and Palestine. The Ottoman Empire in 1914 covered not just present-day Turkey, but also Mesopotamia (now Iraq), Syria, Palestine and Arabia. Egypt was nominally part of the empire, but in the late 19th century it had come under British control. The Ottoman Turks hoped to recover Egypt, threatening Britain's sea communications through the Suez Canal.

The first troops of the Australian Imperial Force (AIF) were sent to Egypt in December 1914 partly to boost its defences against a Turkish attack. From there they embarked for Gallipoli, and after that disastrous expedition (as described in Chapter 6) they returned to Egypt in December 1915. Most of the Australian troops then redeployed to France, but the Light Horse remained in Egypt and formed a vital part of the British force that advanced through Sinai, Palestine and into Syria before the Turks surrendered in October 1918.

The third campaign was in Mesopotamia. Early in the war a small British-Indian army had occupied southern Mesopotamia to protect the oil supply from Persia. This limited military commitment developed into a poorly planned and inadequately supported campaign that ended in disaster with the surrender to the Turks at Kut in April 1916. Reinforcements arrived and British forces captured Baghdad the following year. Only a few Australian pilots and aircrew served in this campaign.

Britain needed to defend Egypt. The best form of defence is attack so, at the time, the Palestine campaign seemed justified. And Britain did not want to lose prestige in the Muslim world. But the advantage of hindsight suggests that none of these campaigns were necessary.

In this chapter, I describe Australia's key role in the second campaign, Palestine, but it is really the story of the famous Australian Light Horse. In it I tell how the troopers fought without their horses at Gallipoli, but then, mounted, provided the backbone of the British campaign that began with the defence of Egypt. The light horsemen won the battle of Romani, advanced through Sinai, conducted their renowned charge at Beersheba that opened the door to Palestine, and ended the war with the greatest cavalry feat in history — the advance to Damascus in September 1918.

# Our Light Horse Tradition

The light horseman occupies a romantic place in Australian military history. Astride his Australian-bred horse, the waler, with his rifle slung over his shoulder and an emu plume in his slouch hat, the light horsemen is seen as the epitome of the Australian bushman. Self-reliant, daring, independent, looking after his mates and his horse, he is the idealised image of the Australian soldier of the First World War. In fact, most Australians served in the infantry on the Western Front, trudging through mud, battered by artillery, gassed, attacking strongly held German positions, dying in their thousands, yet eventually prevailing against the enemy's main army in the main theatre of war. But the light horsemen's achievements were extraordinary.

The tradition of the Light Horse was born in the Boer War (refer to Chapter 4) when Australian mounted troops established their reputation. Major General Sir Edward Hutton commanded some of the Australians in South Africa, and after Federation he became the first commander of the Commonwealth Military Forces. He was an advocate of mounted troops and was instrumental in forming 23 Light Horse regiments in the new part-time military forces. The Light Horse regiments drew most of their recruits from country areas as they were expected to provide their own horses. Hutton saw the Light Horse as mounted troops who could conduct reconnaissance and scouting tasks, but who would also dismount and fight as infantry.

## Setting up the Light Horse

When the AIF was formed in August 1914 it consisted of the 1st Infantry Division with three infantry brigades and the 1st Light Horse Brigade. So many recruits came forward to join the Light Horse that the government approved the formation of a second and then a third Light Horse brigade.

A Light Horse brigade was much smaller than an infantry brigade. While an infantry brigade consisted of four infantry battalions of 1,000 men each, a Light Horse brigade had only three regiments of 500 men each, with each regiment formed into three squadrons. Each squadron was made up of four troops; a troop had eight sections, with four men in each section. In battle one man in each section would hold the section's horses, thereby reducing the number of soldiers available for fighting. Taking into account headquarters and other support staff, a Light Horse brigade put at most 800 men into the dismounted firing line, while a full strength infantry brigade deployed 3,500 men.

By the time all the Light Horse units assembled in Egypt in February 1915 they consisted of:

- 1st Light Horse Brigade. Commanded by Colonel Harry Chauvel. 1st, 2nd, 3rd Light Horse Regiments.
- 2nd Light Horse Brigade. Colonel Granville Ryrie. 5th, 6th, 7th Light Horse Regiments.
- 3rd Light Horse Brigade. Colonel Frederic Hughes. 8th, 9th, 10th Light Horse Regiments.
- 4th Light Horse Regiment. Assigned to the 1st Division as divisional cavalry.

## No place for horses at Gallipoli

The Light Horse regiments didn't take part in the landing at Gallipoli on 25 April, but when casualties mounted there they were a ready source of reinforcements. The light horsemen didn't want their units broken up, so the men of the three Light Horse brigades left their horses behind in Egypt and went to Gallipoli, where they occupied some key forward positions, such as Pope's, Quinn's, Courtney's and Steele's posts. The 1st Brigade helped repel the major Turkish attack on 19 May, while two regiments of the 3rd Light Horse Brigade suffered huge casualties in the pointless charge at the Nek during the August offensive (refer to Chapter 6). Despite their losses, the troopers learned much about combat, which stood them in good stead in later battles.

The Gallipoli experience provided a stern test for the commanders of all the Australian units. In the case of the Light Horse, Chauvel of the 1st Brigade proved to be a reliable commander, and by the end of the campaign was the acting commander of the 1st Division. Ryrie of the 2nd Brigade lacked Chauvel's professional military knowledge but was a charismatic and respected leader. The elderly Hughes of the 3rd Brigade was relieved by his brigade major, John Antill, the regular officer who had rigidly ordered the charge at the Nek to continue despite its obvious futility (see Chapter 6). Major Will Glasgow, who had served in the Boer War, was promoted to command the 2nd Light Horse Regiment in August 1915. On return to Egypt he took over an infantry brigade and ended the war commanding the 1st Division.

# Clearing the Turks from Sinai

The Turks first tried to seize the Suez Canal in February 1915, but were repulsed. When the Gallipoli campaign, which had absorbed most of their available troops, ended in January 1916, the Turks again set out to invade Egypt. To do so they would need to cross the formidable desert of the Sinai Peninsula. The British had plentiful troops in Egypt, but most, including the newly organised Australian infantry divisions, were earmarked for service in France or in northern Greece. The defence of Egypt therefore rested on several British infantry divisions and Australian, New Zealand and some British mounted units. The mounted troops had already shown their worth in dealing with rebellious Arabs in western and southern Egypt, and they were the only troops with the mobility to operate in the desert. General Sir Archibald Murray arrived from Britain to command the troops defending Egypt, known as the Egyptian Expeditionary Force.

## Reforming the mounted troops

The Australian Light Horse had initially arrived in Egypt as separate brigades, and in some cases as individual regiments. As part of the general expansion of the AIF (described in Chapter 7) the Anzac Mounted Division was created by combining the mounted units, consisting of:

- 1st Light Horse Brigade. Commanded by Brigadier General 'Fighting Charlie' Cox, who had led the 6th Light Horse Regiment at Gallipoli.
- 2nd Light Horse Brigade. Brigadier General Granville Ryrie.
- 3rd Light Horse Brigade. Brigadier General John 'Bullant' Antill.
- New Zealand Mounted Rifles Brigade. Brigadier General Edward Chaytor.

## Chapter 8: Riding to Victory in Palestine, 1916–18

The 50-year-old Chauvel, who by now had been promoted to major general, was appointed to command the division. Initially a volunteer officer, he had transferred to the Queensland Permanent Military Forces in 1896 and had seen extensive service with the Queensland Mounted Infantry in the Boer War. Shy and reserved, he led the 1st Light Horse Brigade successfully at Gallipoli, displaying coolness and courage in crucial battles. As a regular officer he understood the value of training and discipline.

## *A decisive victory at Romani*

General Murray deployed his forces beyond the canal in the Romani area, near the northern coast of the Sinai Peninsula, to prevent the Turks from attacking through this area (refer to Figure 8-1). In April 1916, however, the Turks successfully raided the British position, showing that they were a determined and capable foe. Throughout the hot summer months the Light Horse regiments patrolled the desert, denying water supplies to the Turks and keeping watch over their movements.

In August 1916 the Turks, guided by a German colonel, Freiherr Kress von Kressenstein, resumed their offensive with about 14,000 troops. British infantry were deployed near the coast with the Anzac Mounted Division on the inland flank. The Turks swept through the desert and in the early hours of 4 August attacked the 1st and 2nd Light Horse Brigades, which conducted a controlled and well-fought withdrawal.

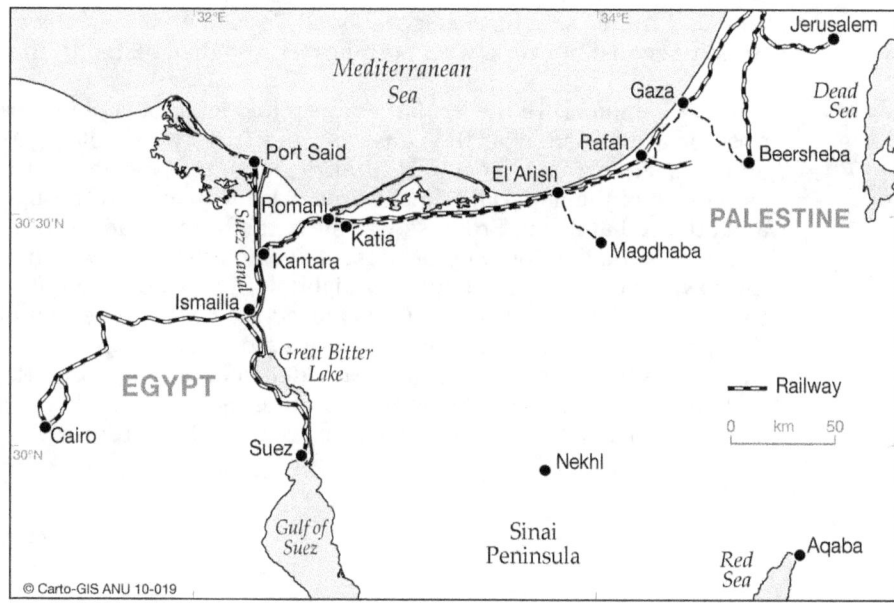

**Figure 8-1:** The Sinai Desert and southern Palestine, 1917–18.

Surprisingly, Brigadier General Ryrie, who was a federal politician, had headed off to London for a parliamentary conference, and his 2nd Brigade was led by Brigadier General 'Galloping Jack' Royston, a South African who had led Australians in the Boer War. Royston was an outstanding horseman and commander who, it's claimed, wore out 14 horses rallying his men during the Romani battle.

Chauvel coolly deployed his men, and then ordered a counterattack with the New Zealanders and a British mounted brigade. By the morning of 5 August the Turks were in retreat with the 3rd Light Horse Brigade in pursuit. The Turks lost about 5,000 killed and wounded and about 4,000 captured. Anzac casualties were about 900. Chauvel had not been in command of the whole British force, but under his direction the mounted troops had been the decisive factor and he was later knighted as reward. The battle was the turning point in the defence of Egypt. The Turks never again threatened the Canal.

## Marching across the desert to Magdhaba

Murray reinforced and reorganised his force in the desert, which would now be commanded by Lieutenant General Sir Charles Dobell. The advance troops, known as the Desert Column, would be commanded by Lieutenant General Sir Philip Chetwode, but Chauvel's Anzac Mounted Division remained the main striking force. The British advance was determined by the speed with which they could build a railway to transport infantry and supplies, and an accompanying water pipeline. In the meantime, Chauvel's mounted troops sought to seize isolated Turkish positions. It was hot, thirsty, exhausting work, with both horses and men tested to the limit.

By 22 December 1916 the British had reached an unoccupied Turkish position at El Arish, near the coast, but the Turks were holding Magdhaba, about 40 kilometres inland. Part of Anzac Mounted Division, with the assistance of the Imperial Camel Corps Brigade, marched through the night and attacked at dawn. Progress was slow, the horses had been without water for a long period, and because it seemed that they would not secure the town, with its water supply, by nightfall Chauvel ordered his brigades to withdraw. 'Fighting Charlie' Cox ignored the order. 'Take that damned thing away and let me see it for the first time in half an hour', he told the runner. His troopers rushed the enemy defences and captured the position. A similar raid by mounted troops on another isolated Turkish position at Rafah in January 1917 brought Eastern Force to the border with Palestine.

## A job for difficult men

In early 1916 a pro-Turkish Arab tribe, the Senussi, were posing a threat in western Egypt, so the British raised four companies to be mounted on camels that would be able to operate in the waterless desert. Insufficient volunteers could be found from the Australian infantry so commanders saw an opportunity to off-load their more difficult characters to the Camel Corps. Perversely, these men relished the challenge of working with their equally difficult beasts. The operations against the Senussi were so successful that the Camel Corps was expanded.

Lieutenant Colonel Clement Smith, a British officer who had served in the Boer War and had won the VC in Somalia in 1904, trained and formed the Imperial Camel Corps Brigade. It consisted of two Australian battalions, an Anzac battalion (with Australians and New Zealanders) and a battalion of British troops, along with an attached mountain battery. With 2,800 men it was about twice the strength of a Light Horse brigade. The Camel Corps' men were tough fighters. While defending a hill in April 1918 they ran out of grenades, but fought off the attacking Turks by hurling boulders at them. The camels could operate for up to five days without water and could remain in the desert for longer periods than the Light Horse, but the men were not mounted troops like the Light Horse. Dismounted, they fought as infantry and in greater strength than the Light Horse.

The brigade took part in the attack at Maghdaba and suffered heavy casualties during the second battle of Gaza in 1917. Once the British forces moved into the more fertile country of northern Palestine there was less need for the Camel Brigade and most of the units were disbanded. The Australians from the brigade then formed two more Light Horse regiments.

# *Third Time Lucky at Gaza*

The main approaches to Palestine were either through the town of Gaza on the coast, or through Beersheba, 45 kilometres inland. The Turks had developed defences at Gaza but did not hold the town in great strength. In preparation of the offensive, Murray increased the number of mounted troops. Earlier in the war Australia had formed a fourth Light Horse brigade, but it had been promptly disbanded and its regiments had been used for ad hoc tasks. The brigade was now reformed, and with the arrival of British mounted units Murray raised the Imperial Mounted Division.

With these changes the mounted forces consisted of:

- Anzac Mounted Division, Major General Harry Chauvel
  - 1st Light Horse Brigade, Brigadier General Charlie Cox
  - 2nd Light Horse Brigade, Brigadier General Granville Ryrie

- New Zealand Mounted Brigade, Brigadier General Edward Chaytor
- 22nd Yeomanry Brigade (*Yeomanry* was a fancy British name for part-time volunteer cavalry)
- Imperial Mounted Division, Major General Sir Henry Hodgson, a British cavalry officer.
- 3rd Light Horse Brigade, Brigadier General Jack Royston
- 4th Light Horse Brigade, Brigadier General John Meredith
- 5th and 6th Yeomanry Brigades

## Disappointment at the first battle of Gaza

To capture Gaza, General Dobell decided to send Chauvel's Anzac Mounted Division around the town to the north to cut it off from reinforcements. The rest of the mounted troops would fan out to prevent enemy reinforcements approaching from the east. The British 53rd Infantry Division, supported by the 54th Division, would attack the town from the south east.

The operation began on 26 March 1917 and Chauvel's troops were soon in position. But the infantry attack was delayed until nearly noon. Chauvel was now ordered to attack Gaza, which his dismounted troops promptly did, ducking through cactus bushes, and bayoneting and shooting the Turks at close range. The other mounted troops successfully held off Turkish reinforcements trying to reach the town. The British forces outnumbered the Turks and as night approached the infantry had advanced into the town.

To the astonishment of the fighting troops, Dobell and Chetwode, out of touch with the battle, and fearing the arrival of the Turkish reinforcements, suddenly ordered a withdrawal. Chauvel complained, 'But we have Gaza', but had to obey. British casualties, mostly in the infantry, numbered 3,500. The Turks had lost 2,500. Reporting to London, Murray praised 'a most successful operation' that had 'filled our troops with enthusiasm'. Trooper Ion Idriess, who had fought among the cactus bushes, exclaimed: 'How can we believe the news of our victories in France, when we read such lies as this!'

## The second battle of Gaza and the Desert Mounted Corps

The Turks were not stupid. Having held off the first attack, they strengthened their defences, brought in more troops and extended their line so that it would be harder for British mounted units to encircle them. The second battle of Gaza in April 1917 was even more disastrous than the first. British casualties numbered almost 6,500, 547 from the Imperial Mounted Division, and 345 from the cameleers (as the men of the Camel Corps were known).

After this second defeat, Chetwode replaced Dobell as commander of Eastern Force. Chauvel was promoted to lieutenant general and took command of the Desert Column, renamed the Desert Mounted Corps. Chauvel was the first Australian to command an army corps — not just an Anzac formation, but a British Empire corps with 34,000 men from Australia, New Zealand, Britain and India. The corps consisted of:

- Anzac Mounted Division, commanded by Major General Edward Chaytor, who had led the New Zealand Mounted Rifles Brigade since Gallipoli. 1st and 2nd Light Horse and the New Zealand Mounted Rifles Brigades.

- Australian Mounted Division, the renamed Imperial Mounted Division (much to the joy of the Australians). Major General Sir Henry Hodgson. 3rd and 4th Light Horse and 5th Yeomanry Brigades.

- Yeomanry Mounted Division. Major General Guy Barrow, a British-Indian Army officer. 6th, 8th and 22nd Yeomanry Brigades.

- Imperial Camel Corps Brigade, Brigadier General Clement Smith.

The most important change was the arrival of General Sir Edmund 'Bull' Allenby, who had commanded the Third Army in France, to succeed Murray as commander-in-chief of the Egyptian Expeditionary Force. The British Prime Minister, Lloyd George, told Allenby, 'Jerusalem by Christmas'. Fortunately for Allenby he was given more infantry divisions to help him complete the task, which was just as well, because the Turks were also sending more troops.

## Charging the enemy lines at Beersheba

Allenby left the luxury of his Cairo hotel and, unlike his predecessor, moved his headquarters forward to the desert. He also abolished Eastern Force and took direct command. With the arrival of more divisions, he now had seven infantry divisions, divided into two corps, plus Chauvel's Desert Mounted Corps. Allenby planned to attack Beersheba from the south-west with an infantry corps while Chauvel's mounted troops attacked from the east. The other corps would apply pressure at Gaza. Deception measures aimed to persuade the Turks that the main attack would still be at Gaza. The biggest problem was to find sufficient water to maintain the mounted troops in the Beersheba area.

The deception measures worked and the Turks expected the next attack at Gaza. At dawn on 31 October 1917 the artillery started to bombard the Turkish line west of Beersheba and the infantry divisions attacked, making steady progress. Chauvel's mounted troops circled the town from the south and approached from the east, but the attacking Anzac Mounted Division was held up by the defences. If the town was not taken by nightfall the mounted troops would need to withdraw due to lack of water. Part of the Australian Mounted Division had been kept in reserve, so Chauvel decided that the 4th Light Horse Brigade, now under Brigadier General William Grant, should attack a less well defended area south of the town on horseback. Chauvel's order was short and to the point: 'Put Grant straight at it'.

Two Light Horse regiments mounted the charge, trotting first, then at a gallop, over more than six kilometres of open ground, crossed by dry river beds. The soldiers were holding their bayonets like swords in the manner of cavalry. Surprised by the closing horsemen, the Turks' rifle fire was too high to stop the charging troopers, while the dust from the galloping hooves helped obscure them from view. The horses jumped the Turkish trenches and the men leapt at the defenders from the rear with their bayonets. Half an hour before nightfall the Australians had captured the town and the vital water supply.

The two regiments had sustained 67 casualties but had captured more than 1,000 Turks. A captured German staff officer said that they did not believe that the Australians would push the charge home: 'I have heard a great deal about the fighting qualities of the Australian soldiers. They are not soldiers at all; they are madmen.'

## Pausing for Breath in Palestine

Having captured Beersheba, Allenby now sent the mounted troops to cut off the Turkish defenders at Gaza from the rear, while his infantry attacked the town from the south, skilfully capturing it by 2 November. The confused Turks did not know whether the British planned to strike inland towards Jerusalem, or along the coastal plain. In 17 days the British forces advanced nearly 100 kilometres.

## Christmas in Jerusalem

By 24 November 1917 the British had advanced north of Jaffa along the coast, but had still not reached Jerusalem. Then the weather broke. In the cold and wet, British infantry with some support from mounted troops attacked towards Jerusalem, and entered the city on 9 December. For the first time since they had left Australia three years earlier, the troopers of the 10th Light Horse Regiment spent the night in houses. In contrast to the German Kaiser, who had ridden into the city, Allenby entered on foot through the narrow Jaffa gate. As Lloyd George had wished, Allenby had provided a 'Christmas present to the British nation'.

Allenby now consolidated his forces, bringing up supplies and giving some of the troops a well-earned rest. By February the infantry and the Anzac Mounted Division had captured Jericho. But before Allenby could advance further he needed to wait on the outcome of the great battles taking place in France. Meanwhile the Turks strengthened their defences in a line across northern Palestine from the coast to the Jordan River, north of Jericho.

## *The Australian Flying Corps over the desert*

Aircraft had more influence over the outcome of operations in the Middle East than on the Western Front. By contrast with France, the expanse of the desert allowed the armies to manoeuvre, and aircraft were vital for reconnaissance. The desert also provided few places to hide, so guns, horses and men were extremely vulnerable to air attack.

The 1st Squadron, Australian Flying Corps, was raised in Australia and arrived in Egypt in April 1916, but many of its reinforcements came from the Light Horse. Initially the squadron was equipped with two-seater BE2c aircraft that were outclassed by the German aircraft flown by their opponents. Nonetheless, the squadron, one of only two British squadrons in the Middle East, did good work on reconnaissance and bombing missions. In mid-1917 new aircraft began to arrive and the squadron flew the excellent two-seater Bristol Fighter, the RE8 reconnaissance aircraft and, at the end of the war, a Handley-Page bomber. Also, additional British units arrived, so that by mid-1918 the Australian squadron was just one among seven British squadrons in Palestine; but the British air commander considered the Australian squadron to be his best.

The squadron included some outstanding pilots. Richard Williams, an original graduate of the Australian Central Flying School, was a flight commander; by the end of the war he was commander of one of the wings of the Royal Air Force Palestine Brigade, with the rank of lieutenant colonel. He became the first and longest serving Chief of the Air Staff of the Royal Australian Air Force. Captain Ross Smith, who had been a sergeant in the Light Horse in the battle of Romani, was also an outstanding pilot. After the war he and his brother Keith were knighted for their flight from England to Australia. Lieutenant Frank McNamara was awarded the Victoria Cross for rescuing a fellow flyer.

## Raiding beyond the Jordan River

While Allenby's troops were advancing into Palestine, several British officers, led by Colonel T E Lawrence (later to win fame as Lawrence of Arabia), were assisting groups of tribesmen from Arabia to revolt against their Turkish rulers, and by early 1918 the Arabs were harassing the Turks along their railway line south of Amman. In March 1918 the Anzac Mounted Division conducted a raid towards Amman to assist the Arabs (refer to Figure 8-2). In cold driving rain the light horsemen were opposed by a strong Turkish force and were compelled to withdraw back to the Jordan Valley.

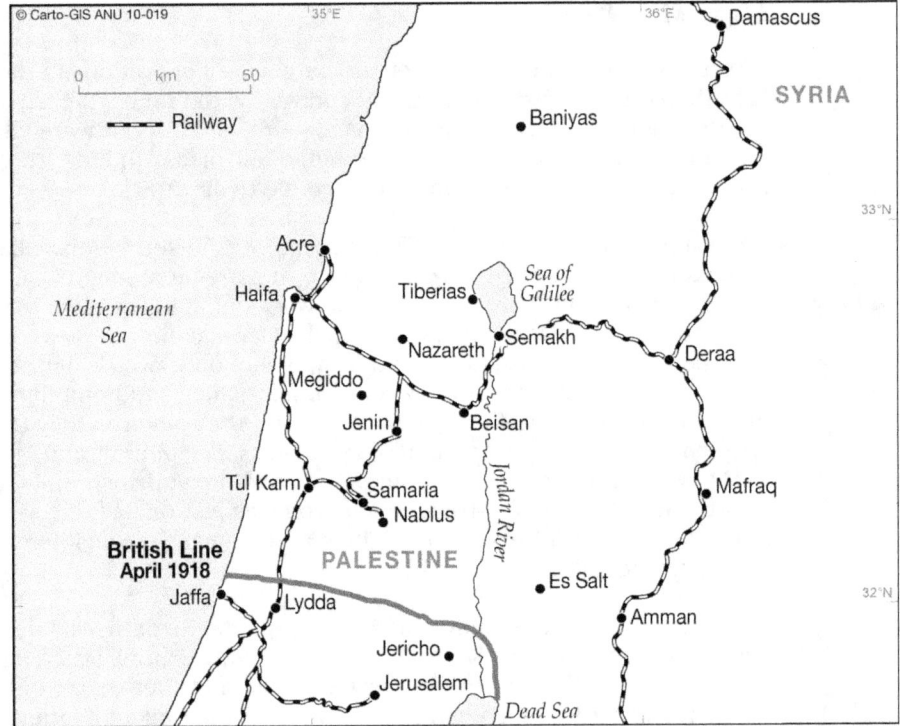

**Figure 8-2:** Northern Palestine and southern Syria, 1917–18.

At the end of April the Australian Mounted Division tried again to raid Amman. At first all went well and the horsemen captured Es Salt. The Turks counterattacked and almost cut off the whole division. The troopers conducted a desperate fighting withdrawal along narrow mountain tracks and eventually made their way back to the Jordan. Although both raids had ended in failure there was one favourable outcome: The Turks were falsely led to believe that Allenby planned to capture Amman as the next step in his advance. As a result, throughout the summer of 1918 the Turks continued their attacks against the light horsemen in the hot, steamy, malarial Jordan Valley, keeping many of their troops in this area rather than in northern Palestine, where Allenby was truly planning on attacking.

## A Perfect Victory

In March 1918 the German Army in France began a massive offensive to drive the British Army back to the Channel ports. (For Australia's role refer to Chapter 9.) In the emergency, Allenby was ordered to send two infantry divisions to France, as well as some of his Yeomanry regiments. In return he was given two Indian Army divisions that had previously served in Mesopotamia as well as Indian cavalry brigades.

Allenby was compelled to reorganise his army. His seven infantry divisions were divided into two corps that occupied the defensive line across central Palestine. As operations had moved away from the desert, the Imperial Camel Corps was broken up and the Australians in it retrained to help form the new 5th Light Horse Brigade.

The main striking force would be the mounted troops. Chaytor's Anzac Mounted Division remained in the Jordan Valley, but the rest were allocated to Chauvel's Desert Mounted Corps, which now consisted of the 4th and 5th Cavalry Divisions and Hodgson's Australian Mounted Division, with the following brigades:

- 3rd Light Horse Brigade, Brigadier General Lachlan Wilson
- 4th Light Horse Brigade, Brigadier General William Grant
- 5th Light Horse Brigade, Brigadier General George Macarthur Onslow

## Deceiving the Turks: Planning the breakthrough

General Otto Liman von Sanders, who'd defeated the allies at Gallipoli, assumed command of all the Turkish and German forces in Palestine, but he would not have the superiority he had enjoyed in the earlier campaign.

His force included 26,000 infantry and 2,000 mounted troops, compared with Allenby's 57,000 infantry and 12,000 mounted troops. Allenby would have a superiority of 6 to 1 in mounted troops and 2 to 1 in infantry.

But Allenby was not going to rely on just superior numbers. He planned to break the Turkish line near the coast. Then the Desert Mounted Corps would burst through the gap, ride quickly north and turn east towards the River Jordan, cutting the rear communications of the Turkish infantry holding the defensive line across northern Palestine. The plan relied on mobility, speed, secrecy and especially deceiving the Turks into believing that the main attack would come from the Jordan Valley. Chauvel's mounted troops in the valley sneaked away at night and hid among the orange and olive groves near the coast. There the troopers of the Australian Mounted Division were issued with cavalry swords and British cavalrymen trained the Australians in their use. The Light Horse had become cavalry.

Meanwhile, the men of the Anzac Mounted Division made thousands of dummy horses to fill the empty horse lines. Mules dragged branches along the tracks, throwing up dust as though from parties of mounted troops. A bridge was constructed over the River Jordan. Each day companies of infantry marched into the valley, and each evening lorries carried them out again, giving the impression that the infantry were being built up for the attack. And British aircraft, which now dominated the skies, ensured that German aircraft could not observe the preparations for the battle.

## *The greatest cavalry feat in history*

In the early hours of 19 September British guns started bombarding the Turkish defences near the coast, and after the infantry cut the Turkish line, the two cavalry divisions poured through the gap, heading north and then north-east towards the Sea of Galilee. By dawn next day British cavalry were trotting into Nazareth, where General Liman von Sanders had his headquarters. He escaped by car in his pyjamas.

The Australian Mounted Division followed through the gap and took a more easterly course. In the evening of 20 September the 3rd Light Horse Brigade swooped on the town of Jenin and by next morning had captured 8,000 prisoners. The 5th Light Horse Brigade, operating on the right of the advance, seized the key town of Samaria, behind the main Turkish line. British and Australian aircraft roamed behind the lines, disrupting Turkish communications and bombing concentrations of Turkish troops as they moved through narrow defiles.

By 22 September Chauvel's force had taken 15,000 prisoners. Completely disrupted by the enemy appearing in their rear, the Turks fell back, and von Sanders hoped to hold a line south of the Sea of Galilee. Before dawn on 25 September the 4th Light Horse Brigade conducted another mounted charge and seized the town of Semakh at the southern end of the lake.

Chauvel's sweep threatened the Turkish communications south of Damascus, and the Turks facing Chaytor's Anzac Mounted Division in the Jordan Valley now started to withdraw. Chaytor light horsemen followed closely and entered Amman on 25 September, cutting off the Turkish Army south of the city. Caught between the Arabs pressing from the south and the Anzac Mounted Division from the north, the Turkish Army surrendered. Chaytor's force took 10,300 prisoners.

## *Entering Damascus in triumph*

The Turkish armies south of Damascus were now completely broken, and the mounted troops thrust northwards towards the ancient city. Turkish infantry and German machine gunners tried to hold up the advance, but each time they struck the defences, the light horsemen used their superior mobility to sweep around the defenders and cut off their withdrawal routes. The light horsemen were tired and worn, but knew that if they kept up the pressure they could break the Turks. The 5th Light Horse Brigade by-passed Damascus and blocked a Turkish escape route from the city on the road through the Barada Gorge towards Beirut. The 3rd Light Horse Brigade pursued the Turks into the gorge where they trapped the jumble of men, horses, wagons and motor cars. Macarthur Onslow of the 5th Brigade wrote: 'I turned eight machine-guns and every rifle onto this mass of humanity — it was awful'.

More Turks were escaping from the city and Wilson of the 3rd Brigade was ordered to skirt the city to prevent their escape. Turkish control of the city was disintegrating and various Arab leaders were attempting to take over for their own political ends. Wilson took a chance and ordered the 10th Light Horse Regiment to gallop through the city in pursuit. So, on 1 October 1918, the Australian light horsemen became the first British troops to enter the city. Welcomed as victors, they were soon chasing the Turks north.

Chauvel and his light horsemen were now exhausted, although they still needed to keep order in the city. The British cavalry continued the pursuit into northern Syria. The Australian Mounted Division was on the road north when, on 31 October it learned that Turkey had signed an armistice, ending its war. In congratulating Chauvel, Allenby said that the performance of the mounted troops was 'the greatest cavalry feat the world has known'.

## Seeking vengeance at Surafend

Not everything that the Anzacs did deserves praise. After the armistice the horsemen withdrew to the coast to prepare to return to Australia. By December 1918 some soldiers of the Anzac Mounted Corps were becoming bitter at the loss of several of their number who had been shot by Arabs. In the Surafend area, near Jaffa, a New Zealander was shot and killed while chasing Arabs who he had caught robbing his tent. The New Zealanders, with some Australians, perhaps 200 in total, attacked the Bedouin camp, where the offending Arabs had stayed. They killed 20 Arabs (although one witness claimed to have counted 137) and burnt the camp.

General Allenby demanded that the culprits be punished, but when none could be found he punished the whole division by withholding awards and avoiding praising it in his official despatches. He addressed the division and, according to one trooper, told them: 'I was proud to command you, but now I'll have no more to do with you. You are cowards and murderers'. Allenby never apologised for his comments, but later wrote a letter praising the Australians in the campaign:

'The Australian Light horseman combines with a splendid physique a restless activity of mind. This mental quality renders him somewhat impatient of rigid and formal discipline, but it confers upon him the gift of adaptability, and this is the secret of much of his success mounted or on foot. In this dual role, on every variety of ground — mountain, plain, desert, swamp, or jungle — the Australian light horseman has proved himself equal to the best. He has earned the gratitude of the Empire and the admiration of the world.'

He did not excuse the actions of a few Anzacs; but nor should those actions tarnish the reputation of the whole force.

# Chapter 9

# Hammering the Huns, 1918

*In This Chapter*

▶ Gaining ascendancy over the Germans

▶ Advancing to the point of exhaustion

▶ Acknowledging Australia's air aces

▶ Maintaining command of the seas

▶ Tallying the butcher's bill

By the beginning of 1918, Germany was in a desperate situation. The German High Seas Fleet, despite a narrow tactical victory over the Royal Navy at Jutland in 1916, had been unable to break the British blockade against merchant ships entering or leaving German ports. Denied vital military and civilian supplies, including food, Germany was in danger of being starved out of the war. Equally bad for the Germans, the unrestricted submarine warfare they had unleashed as a response to the blockade had been one of the factors that had brought the United States into the war on the Allied side.

But General Erich Ludendorff, effectively the commander of the German Army, saw an opportunity to strike a winning blow. After Russia had collapsed into revolution, the Russian Army ceased to be a threat, enabling Ludendorff to transfer 33 divisions from the Eastern to the Western Front before the end of 1917. With those extra divisions, and with the severe challenges the British and French were having finding reinforcements while also having to bolster their Italian allies, for a short period in early 1918 the German Army had numerical superiority on the Western Front: 192 German divisions compared with 156 in the British and French armies. Ludendorff therefore planned a mighty offensive to drive the weakened British Army into the sea and cause the French to surrender before the Americans arrived in force and the German homeland succumbed to the effects of the blockade.

In this chapter, I describe how the Australian Corps of the Australian Imperial Force (AIF), its men well-trained and confident, rushed to help stop the German Army's dangerous March 1918 offensive and then how the

Australians played a leading role in the famous offensive of August 1918 that ended with the November armistice. The chapter also includes an account of the work of the Australian Flying Corps and tells the story of the Australian ships that helped the Royal Navy to maintain control of the seas. Finally, I briefly assess the cost and the legacy of the war for Australia.

# Crushing the German Offensive

By early in 1918 the British forces in France were having to take over areas held by the French in 1917. Ludendorff's so-called Michael Offensive began on 21 March, when 70 German divisions attacked the British Fifth Army's 15 divisions and part of the Third Army on its left (refer to Figure 9-1). The attack was preceded by a massive artillery bombardment by more than 6,000 guns and 3,000 mortars, and was led by specially trained German assault troops.

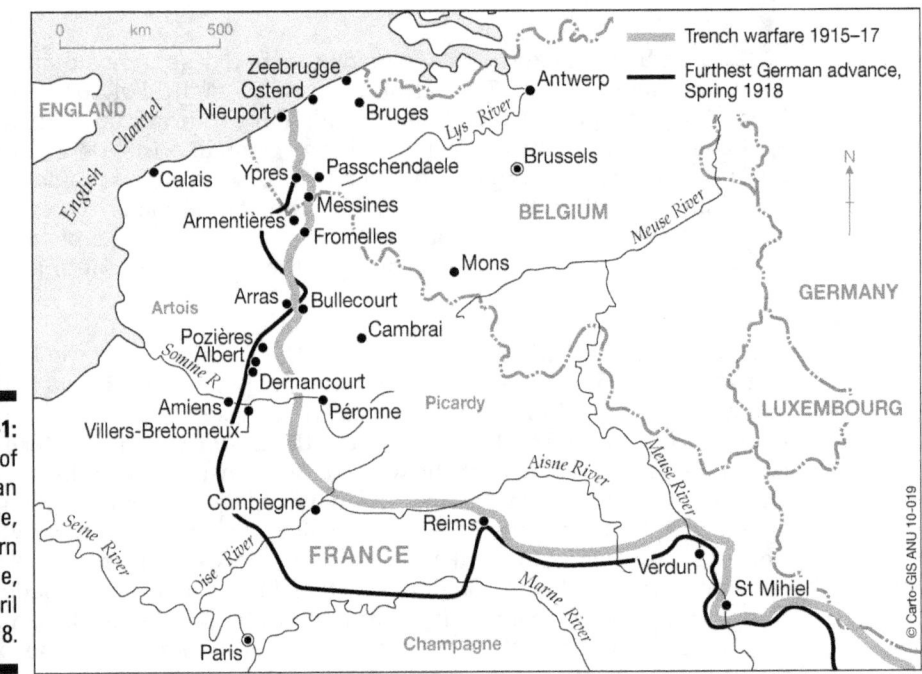

**Figure 9-1:** Area of German offensive, northern France, March–April 1918.

The British troops fell back before the onslaught, and by 26 March the Germans had not only captured the town of Albert, they had recovered all the ground given up when they had withdrawn to the Hindenburg Line in February 1917. It seemed that nothing would stop the Germans from taking the key transport centre at Amiens. British casualties numbered 38,000, and more worryingly, 21,000 of these were prisoners, indicating a breakdown in organisation and morale because the troops preferred to surrender rather than fight. The German success created the biggest British defensive crisis since 1914.

The 3rd and 4th Australian Divisions, resting out of the line near Messines, were immediately put on alert and Major General Ewen Sinclair-MacLagan's 4th Division headed south in long lines of motor lorries. As they passed the town of Hébuterne, the 4th Brigade was enlisted to help with the town's defence, a task the brigade undertook so successfully that the local British commander would not release it for a month.

The remainder of the division pressed on, and after a night march across the front of the Germans reached the area west of Albert, where they found the villagers fleeing and nervous, and tired British troops withdrawing. A British artillery brigadier told Colonel Lavarack, MacLagan's chief of staff, 'You Australians think you can do anything, but you haven't a chance of holding them'. Lavarack relied, 'Will you stay and support us if we do?' The brigadier agreed, adding his guns to the Australian artillery.

The 3rd Division arrived by train and its commander, Major General John Monash, began deploying his troops in relief of the exhausted British infantry. While the Australians didn't, by themselves, stop the German offensive, they closed the gaps and raised the morale of all with whom they came in contact. The Tommies (British soldiers) rallied and the French sent troops to assist.

## Determination at Dernancourt

Two brigades from the 4th Division, the 12th under Brigadier General John Gellibrand, and the 13th under Brigadier General William Glasgow, arrived just before midnight on 27 March at a railway embankment at Dernancourt, just south of Albert, and held off a German attack the next day. The Germans resumed their offensive on 4 April, attacking with 15 divisions on a front of 33 kilometres. Next day, at Dernancourt, three German divisions, with 25,000 troops, assaulted the two under-strength Australian brigades, numbering about 4,000 men, in what Bean called 'the strongest attack made against Australian troops in the war'.

Glasgow and Gellibrand were two of the AIF's most experienced brigade commanders and their men were well-trained and battle hardened. At times the forward infantry were compelled to withdraw, but the battalions mounted local counterattacks to keep the Germans off balance. The counterattack by Lieutenant Colonel Ray Leane's 45th Battalion was, according to an observer, 'one of the finest ever carried out by Australian troops'.

The Australian artillery was also involved, and at one time the infantry withdrew, streaming past a gun position. Horse teams arrived to withdraw the guns, but the gunners ordered them away. Nine members of the 43rd Battery alone were awarded Military Medals during this action. Sometimes only two men (rather than the usual ten) were on each gun, including officers. The enemy's bombardment was as heavy as they ever experienced. No batteries were silenced, even though the gun shields were the only protection for the gun crew; there had been insufficient time to dig emplacements.

The Australian infantry eventually held the line for the loss of 1,000 casualties. MacLagan thought that his two brigades could resist no longer, but the Germans didn't know this and called off the attack because they thought the Australian defences were too strong.

## Saving Hazebrouck

The 1st and 2nd Divisions hurried south to join their mates fighting in front of Amiens, and by 10 April the Diggers of the 1st Division were marching forward to relieve the 3rd Division. That evening the division was ordered to retrace its steps to Amiens where it was to entrain to return north. Ludendorff had begun another offensive on 9 April, and near Armentières had smashed through the Allied line held by dispirited Portuguese troops.

If the Germans could break through to the Channel ports they would split the British Army. On 11 April, Field Marshal Sir Douglas Haig, Commander-in-Chief of the British Army in France, issued his famous order: 'There is no other course open to us but to fight it out. Every position must be held to the last man: there must be no retirement. With our backs to the wall and believing in the justice of our cause each one of us must fight on to the end.' The 1st Division reached the line at Hazebrouck on 12 April, just in time to reinforce and relieve British troops who had been driven back and were exhausted. In a fortnight-long battle the Australians and British halted the German offensive.

## Valour at Villers-Bretonneux

During early April the Diggers were fighting defensive battles right across the front. While most of the 4th Division was in action at Dernancourt, its 4th Brigade was holding Hébuterne, and the 1st Division was defending the Channel ports at Hazebrouck. Monash's 3rd Division was covering Amiens and his 9th Brigade, commanded by Brigadier General Charles Rosenthal, helped British units defend the key town of Villers-Bretonneux. A spectacular charge by the brigade's 36th Battalion halted a German attack on 4 April.

## Lieutenant Bethune's Special Order

Frank Bethune was an Anglican minister from Tasmania who enlisted as a 37-year-old private in the 12th Battalion in 1915 and later became an officer. While travelling by ship across the Mediterranean in April 1916, in the absence of the chaplain, he preached to the troops. 'We are not heroes', he said, 'and we do not want to be called heroes ... We are on that great enterprise, with no thought of gain or conquest, but to help right a great wrong.'

In March 1918, when he was commanding No. 1 Section, 3rd Machine Gun Company, Bethune was ordered to defend an exposed position at Messines. Realising the danger, he asked for volunteers, and his whole section stepped forward. He wrote at the time: 'I am taking in three good men and three new ones, as I do not want too many of the old section to get scuppered if we get it in the neck, while at the same time we must be good enough to extract payment before we are blown out, and there are plenty of Mills grenades for the final flutter.' Bethune then issued his men with written orders:

*Special Orders to No 1 Section 13/3/18*

1. This position will be held and the section will remain here until relieved.
2. The enemy cannot be allowed to interfere with this programme.
3. If the section cannot remain here alive, it will remain here dead, but in any case it will remain here.
4. Should any man, through shell shock or other cause, attempt to surrender, he will remain here dead.
5. Should all guns be blown out, the section will use Mills grenades, and other novelties.
6. Finally, the position, as stated, will be held

F. P. Bethune, Lt
OC No 1 Section

Fortunately, in 18 days in the position Bethune's 'cheery section' encountered nothing worse than gas shelling. By the end of the war Bethune, now a captain, had been awarded the Military Cross for bravery in action.

When the Germans renewed their attack on Villers-Bretonneux on 17 and 18 April using mustard gas, the Australians lost 1,000 men, but held on until relieved by British troops. At dawn on 24 April, however, the Germans tried again with tanks and captured the town. To recover the town, two Australian brigades, the 13th, under the experienced and determined Will Glasgow, and the 15th, commanded by the brilliant but tempestuous Harold 'Pompey' Elliott, were loaned to the British corps commander in the area. He wanted the Australians to attack in daylight, with the 13th Brigade striking from the south and the 15th from the north. Major General Hobbs, commander of the 5th Division, and Glasgow insisted on an attack at night, from the east. 'If God Almighty gave the order, we couldn't do it by daylight', declared Glasgow. Eventually the British corps commander compromised and agreed to the 13th Brigade attacking at 10 pm. It still proved to be too early because the Germans saw the 13th Brigade moving into position before the attack.

Despite casualties caused by the 13th Brigade's early attack, the troops quickly closed in on the Germans. Attacking an hour later from the north the 15th Brigade's 59th Battalion conducted a wild bayonet charge. By dawn on the third Anzac Day of the war the Diggers were fighting from house to house, and by afternoon they had secured the town. General Monash thought that 'this counterattack, at night, without artillery support, is the finest thing yet done in the war, by Australians or any other troops'. British Brigadier General George Grogan VC, who saw it, called it 'perhaps the greatest individual feat of the war'. The battle marked the end of the German offensive to capture Amiens.

In the 1920s school children in Victoria donated money to build a primary school in Villers-Bretonneux. A notice on the school wall says that 1,200 Australian soldiers, 'the fathers and brothers of these children, gave their lives in the heroic recapture of this town from the invader on 24th April 1918 and are buried near this spot'. Above every blackboard in the school are the words 'N'oublions jamais l'Australie' — Never forget Australia.

## *The Counteroffensive that Won the War*

Except for the 1st Division, which was still in the north, the Australian Corps was at last all together under Lieutenant General Birdwood in the area between Villers-Bretonneux and Dernancourt. The confident Diggers now began a campaign of harassment, which they described as Peaceful Penetration, creeping forward to capture small groups of enemy, seizing outposts and conducting raids. Soon they had achieved complete dominance over their opponents. In one of the larger raids at Morlancourt the 7th Brigade captured 325 German prisoners. The German divisional commander reported that 'a complete battalion had been wiped out as with a sponge'.

In the midst of this campaign, at the end of May, Birdwood was appointed to command the British Fifth Army, and he took Major General White with him as chief of staff. Sir John Monash became the new commander of the Australian Corps. The appointment of Monash, who had been born in Australia of German-Jewish parents and was just short of his 53rd birthday, proved to be wise. An engineer and militia officer, he had led the 4th Brigade at Gallipoli and had commanded the 3rd Division at Messines and Third Ypres in 1917, and in the defence of Amiens in April 1918. Intelligent and articulate, he was a meticulous planner. Brigadier General Thomas Blamey, a brilliant staff officer and later Australia's first field marshal, became his chief of staff.

## The most decorated soldier

Henry 'Mad Harry' Murray received more decorations for bravery than anyone in the British forces in the First World War, but he rarely attended an Anzac Day march after the war. A modest man, he told his daughter, who had asked what he had done to earn the cross with the purple ribbon — the Victoria Cross — that he had fetched a bottle of rum for his commanding officer. Born in Tasmania in 1880, he left school early to help on the family farm, and later worked in Western Australia where he employed men cutting timber for the railways. He enlisted as a private in the 16th Battalion in 1914, landed at Gallipoli on 25 April 1915 and was wounded the next day. As a lance corporal he was awarded the Distinguished Conduct Medal for 'exceptional courage, energy and skill' during the fighting in May. He was wounded again, but was promoted to sergeant and was then commissioned in the field.

By the time of the Somme battles in mid-1916 he was a captain in the 13th Battalion, and was awarded the Distinguished Service Order (DSO) for leading his company while wounded twice. In February 1917 his company took part in an attack which secured its objective. The enemy conducted three intense counter-attacks and Murray's company suffered heavy casualties. He rallied his company, encouraging his men, heading bombing parties, leading bayonet charges and carrying wounded to safety. By his example he inspired his men to hold the position and was awarded the Victoria Cross.

In the first battle of Bullecourt he was awarded a Bar to his DSO (see Chapter 2 for further discussion of medals awarded during war). He was also promoted to major and became second-in-command of his battalion. In May 1918 he was promoted further to lieutenant colonel to command the 4th Machine Gun Battalion, remaining in command until the end of the war. Serving as an adviser to American troops in the breaking of the Hindenburg Line, he was recommended for an American Distinguished Service Medal. He was awarded the French Croix de Guerre, was made a Companion of the Order of St Michael and St George (CMG) and was Mentioned in Despatches four times.

After the war he became a grazier in Queensland. In the Second World War he commanded a militia battalion and later his local battalion in the Volunteer Defence Corps. He died in January 1966 after a car accident. The Official Historian Charles Bean called him 'the most distinguished fighting officer in the AIF'.

Three new divisional commanders were appointed, and the five divisional commanders were then:

- **1st Division: Major General William Glasgow.** A storekeeper, after serving with the light horse at Gallipoli he had commanded the 13th Brigade brilliantly since March 1916.

- **2nd Division: Major General Charles Rosenthal.** An architect, he commanded an artillery brigade at Gallipoli, the 4th Division artillery on the Somme and took command of the 9th Infantry Brigade in mid-1917.

- **3rd Division: Major General John Gellibrand.** Australian-born, he had served 20 years in the British Army before growing apples in Tasmania. A staff officer at Gallipoli, he commanded the 6th and 12th Brigades in France.

- **4th Division: Major General Ewen Sinclair-MacLagan.** Although a British officer, he had joined the AIF at its inception and had commanded the 3rd Brigade at Gallipoli and in France before assuming command of his division in mid-1917.

- **5th Division: Major General J J Talbot Hobbs.** An architect, he commanded the 1st Division artillery at Gallipoli and on the Somme, before taking command of his division from McCay in January 1917.

## Trying out new methods at Hamel

Gradually the Australians increased the scale of their raids, but to attack the village of Hamel, just north of Villers-Bretonneux (refer to Figure 9-2), Monash decided to try some new techniques in an effort to reduce casualties. Sinclair-MacLagan would command the assault, with brigades from four of the Australian divisions to gain experience. The attacking troops, only 7,000 in number, would come from the 4th and 11th Brigades with a feint by the 15th Brigade. The attack was to be mounted on a front of 700 metres with 60 of the new British Mark V tanks, and the troops would advance alongside the tanks, immediately behind an artillery barrage. Four companies of American infantry would accompany the Australians to gain experience. Before the attack, noise from the artillery and from low-flying aircraft would drown the sound of the approaching tanks.

The attack began at 3.10 am and was a brilliant success. Monash had planned on the operation taking 90 minutes; he miscalculated — it took 93 minutes. The tanks tore gaps in the wire, and their machine-guns provided excellent covering fire for the accompanying infantry. British and Australian aircraft dropped ammunition by parachute to the advancing infantry. The 15th Brigade's diversionary attack was also successful. In the two attacks the Australians lost 1,400 casualties. Perhaps 2,000 Germans were killed or wounded, while 1,500 were taken prisoner. The action at Hamel was on only a small scale, but it provided a model for using tanks in cooperation with the infantry in the future. Of the 60 tanks used in the attack, only three had been knocked out.

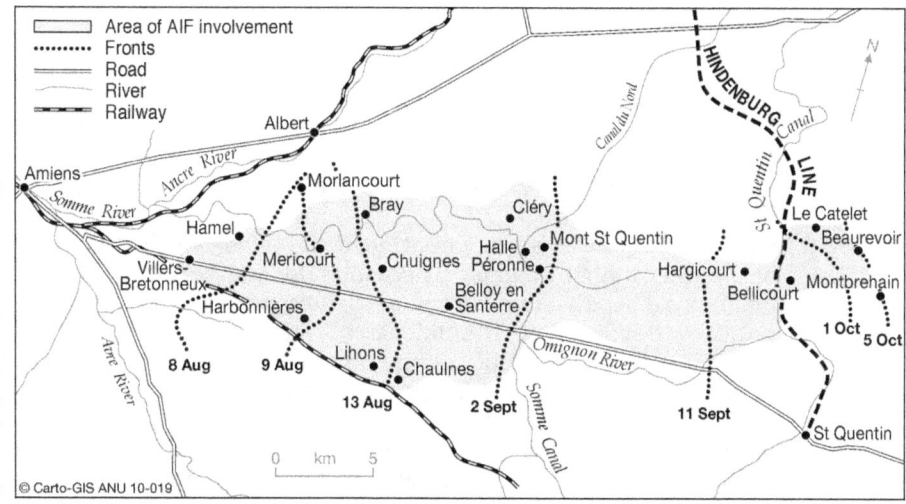

Figure 9-2: Australian Corps offensive, northern France, August–October 1918.

## Black day for the Germans at Amiens

The attack by the Australian Corps near Amiens on 8 August was part of the larger offensive by General Sir Henry Rawlinson's Fourth Army, which in turn was part of a wider Allied offensive. The Canadian and Australian Corps were, however, to spearhead the assault. The Australian Corps was to advance on a front of 7,000 metres and advance to a maximum depth of about 12,000 metres. In the first phase the 2nd and 3rd Divisions would attack side by side. Then the 4th and 5th Divisions would move through to continue the attack. The 1st Division, brought down from the north, was in reserve.

In effect, the Australians were to replay the Hamel battle, but on a larger scale, and the real story of the battle concerns the preparation beforehand. Each infantry division would be supported by 24 tanks, and aircraft would support the infantry by attacking enemy positions. The essence of the plan was secrecy, and the guns were not to undertake a preliminary bombardment but rather were to open fire, without registration, at exactly zero hour. All movement of guns and ammunition before the battle took place at night. Monash displayed his masterly grasp of detail in ensuring that each division knew exactly what was expected.

At 4.20 am on 8 August the Australian Corps' 550 guns opened fire and the attack began in a thick morning mist. Across the whole area the Germans were driven back, with the Australians advancing 10,000 metres. The Fourth

Army took 13,000 prisoners and over 200 guns. For the loss of 2,000 men the Australians captured 7,925 prisoners. After the war General Ludendorff wrote: 'August 8th was the black day of the German Army in this war'.

## Storming Mont St Quentin

Next day Rawlinson's army continued the offensive. For the first time in the war an Australian corps commander was required constantly to manoeuvre his divisions on the battlefield, occasionally pulling divisions out of battle for a rest. The units were under-strength, but the troops were experienced and confident, and the battalions now had a higher allocation of Lewis machine-guns. Most of the Australian divisions advanced on the southern side of the Somme River with some troops on the northern bank, but on 29 August the troops reached the town of Cléry, where the river takes a sharp bend to the south. Across the river loomed the heights of Mont St Quentin, held by one of the German Army's best divisions.

Monash ordered his divisions to rush across the river, hoping to catch the German defenders by surprise, but they failed. He then ordered Gellibrand's 3rd Division to move left to take Cléry on the north side of the river. Engineers bridged the river and the 3rd Division cleared Cléry just in time to allow Rosenthal's 2nd Division to pass through and thrust south-east towards Mont St Quentin. The 5th Brigade's three battalions each had only a pathetic 330 men available for the attack, which began at 5.00 am on 31 August. Cheering, the troops charged up the 90-metre-high hill, but were held just below the summit.

Next day the 6th Brigade reached the summit of Mont St Quentin, and the remainder of the division closed in on the nearby town of Péronne from the north. By this time the 5th Division had crossed the river and seized the rest of Péronne. General Rawlinson thought the victory was the finest feat of the war. Monash had manoeuvred his divisions well, but the credit belonged to the infantry of the 2nd Division who had taken the strongly held feature without tanks or a creeping barrage. Six Australians won Victoria Crosses on 1 September.

## Breaking the Hindenburg Line

The British Army advanced across the whole front, but the Australian Corps remained in the vanguard, pushing ahead, beyond the British corps on its flanks. The Allied advance now reached the Hindenburg Line, which had been strengthened even more since the Germans had occupied it in 1917, and Monash was given the task of breaking the German line. The Australians faced an area where the German line ran along the St Quentin Canal but then disappeared into a five-kilometre long tunnel. The ground above the tunnel was an obvious area for an attack and the Germans had thickened the defences there. The Australian divisions were so under-strength that only two of them, the 3rd and the 5th, were fit for action, so to make up for Monash's lack of troops, two American divisions were placed under his command. Monash planned to attack in the area above the tunnel using the American divisions. Then the Australians would move through to continue the advance.

The attack began at dawn on 29 September. Some American units were stopped by the Germans, but others seemed to make considerable progress. Unfortunately, the inexperienced Americans had left many German positions untouched and didn't reached their objectives. When the Australian divisions started to move forward they came under intense fire. The under-strength Australian battalions were now composed of skilful fighters and despite casualties, on 3 October they broke through the German defences. One of Monash's biographers attributed Monash's 'erratic handling of the battle' to tiredness. The same could be said for his troops. Meanwhile, a British corps had crossed the canal, south of the tunnel, in a brilliant operation, and it too was advancing. The 2nd Australian Division took over the advance and captured the town of Montbrehain on 5 October. It was the last battle fought by the Australian infantry in the war.

The Australian divisions were withdrawn for a rest, and were just moving forward to resume the advance when the armistice came into effect on 11 November. The advance of 60 kilometres by the Australian Corps, from the initial attack on 8 August until early October, made a significant contribution to the Allied victory. It had been a triumph for the morale and fighting ability of the Diggers, but also for Monash's skill as a commander. The Australian Corps' casualties had numbered more than 21,000, but it had captured 21,144 prisoners and 338 guns. The Australians had comprised about 8 per cent of the British Army in the line, but the prisoners and guns it captured represented about 22 per cent of those taken by the British Army in this last phase of the war on the Western Front.

# Gallant Airmen: The Australian Flying Corps

By comparison with the infantry, the aviators of the Australian Flying Corps made only a limited contribution to the war, but a contribution that was significant for several reasons. Australia was the only dominion to form its own flying corps, and it became the nucleus of the Royal Australian Air

Force (RAAF) that was formed in 1921. Prominent pilots and officers were later to become leaders of the RAAF in the Second World War. Australia began building its flying corps before the war, when the Central Flying School was established at Point Cook in Victoria in 1913, and the first pilots' course began in August 1914.

The first aviators to see action were the four pilots and 41 ground crew of the Half Flight that went to Mesopotamia in May 1915 to support the British-Indian army conducting operations against the Turkish Army. This small unit had a trying time and many were captured when the Turks forced the surrender of the British-Indian army at the battle of Kut in April 1916. For the exploits of the 1st Squadron, Australian Flying Corps, in Egypt and Palestine refer to Chapter 8.

The 2nd, 3rd and 4th Squadrons, each equipped with 18 aircraft, were raised partly in Australia and partly from volunteers from the AIF overseas. After limited training, No 3 Squadron went to France in September 1917 to support the Australian Corps, flying RE8 aircraft on reconnaissance and observation missions. The other two squadrons arrived a little later and flew fighters. The 4th Squadron flew the more advanced Sopwith Camel. A total of 57 Australian pilots became aces, meaning that they had destroyed at least five enemy aircraft. Captain Harry Cobby became the Flying Corps' leading ace and was accredited with destroying 29 enemy aircraft.

## Speaking Digger Lingo

Many Australian slang words that we use today came from the First World War. Some words applied only during the war and often were used by other British troops. Here are a few of them.

**Chats:** Lice, which infested all front-line soldiers

**Dinkum:** Authentic, genuine; a Gallipoli veteran was a 'dinkum'

**Furphy:** Rumour (soldiers gathered around water carts, made by J Furphy and Sons, to swap stories)

**Hop the bags:** Leave the trenches and 'go over the top' to attack the enemy

**Hun:** German serviceman; also Fritz

**Oil:** Information or news, such as 'the good oil'

**Plonk:** Wine, probably from the French 'blanc', as in vin blanc, or white wine

**Possie:** An individual soldier's place of shelter or firing position

**Six-bob-a-day tourist:** Australian soldier (Australian soldiers were paid six shillings per day)

**Stunt:** An attack, raid or action

The popular image of daring young pilots fighting a chivalrous and exciting war in the air, free from the mud and terror of the battlefield, is misleading. Casualty rates in the squadrons reached a peak at 88 per cent and averaged 50 per cent over the war. A total of 460 officers and 2,234 men served in the Australian Flying Corps during the war.

Australian pilots also flew with the Royal Flying Corps and the Royal Naval Air Service, which joined to form the Royal Air Force in April 1918. Captain Robert Little was rejected by the Central Flying School so made his way to England and joined the Royal Naval Air Service. With a tally of 47 enemy aircraft he became Australia's leading ace. He was killed in France in May 1918, aged 22. Major Stan Dallas also paid his own way to England and joined the Royal Naval Air Service. When he was shot down and killed in France in June 1918 his official tally was 39 aircraft destroyed.

# Sailing the Seas: The Navy's Experience

The First World War was fought primarily on land, so the contribution of the Royal Navy is sometimes overlooked. Nonetheless, by commanding the seas, ships of the Royal Navy ensured that the British Empire could conduct land campaigns around the world with little fear that they would be disrupted by hostile naval forces.

The Royal Navy's main tasks were:

- Attempt to break through to Constantinople and support the landing at Gallipoli in April 1915. (For a brief description refer to Chapter 6.)
- Clear the seas of German raiders, involving several significant actions early in the war. (See Chapter 5.)
- Prevent German merchant ships from leaving neutral ports as part of the blockade of Germany, requiring long patrols and the boarding and inspection of suspect vessels.
- Conduct a campaign against German submarines, especially by escorting convoys in the last years of the war
- Patrol the North Sea in force to ensure the German High Seas Fleet remained in port, a task interrupted by the Battle of Jutland in mid-1916.

Ships of the Royal Australian Navy (RAN) took part in all these activities, although generally as part of the Royal Navy. Australia was the only dominion to contribute a significant naval force, but it was still relatively small. At the outbreak of the war the RAN had a permanent strength of 3,800 officers and sailors, and by June 1919 this had risen to 5,250, with about 20 per cent coming from the Royal Navy. The RAN began the war with 16 vessels, including the battle cruiser *Australia*, the light cruisers *Melbourne*, *Sydney*, *Encounter* and *Pioneer*, and the small destroyers *Parramatta*, *Warrego* and *Yarra*. Additional ships commissioned during the war included the light cruiser *Brisbane*, and the destroyers *Torrens*, *Huon* and *Swan*.

Initially most of the ships patrolled the waters near Australia until the threat from German raiders declined. One raider, the 5,400-tonne cruiser *Königsberg*, took refuge in a river in German East Africa. The small Australian cruiser *Pioneer* joined the British naval force that patrolled the river mouth, and was part of the expedition to destroy the *Königsberg* in mid-1915. *Pioneer* remained off East Africa for another year and was engaged in more actual fighting — mainly gunfire support to land operations — than any other ship in the Australian fleet.

In August 1917, after patrol duties around the Dutch East Indies, Singapore, Thailand and Burma, the destroyers *Parramatta*, *Yarra*, *Huon*, *Swan*, *Warrego* and *Torrens* arrived in the Mediterranean to conduct anti-submarine escort duties for convoys. They then helped guard the mouth of the Adriatic Sea to prevent the Austrian Navy from venturing into the Mediterranean. *Torrens* was involved in an engagement when several Austrian ships tried to break into the Mediterranean.

After serving as flagship in home waters (see Chapter 5), the battle cruiser *Australia* joined the Royal Navy's Grand Fleet in the North Sea in 1915 and served there for most of the war as flagship of the 2nd Battle Cruiser Squadron, but she did not take part in the Battle of Jutland, as she was undergoing repairs at the time. In mid-1916 the light cruisers *Sydney* and *Melbourne* joined the Grand Fleet, serving as part of the 2nd Light Cruiser Squadron. Patrolling the North Sea involved long hours in trying conditions of weather and sea. In May 1917 *Sydney* had a running fight with a German Zeppelin (air ship) that dropped a dozen bombs while *Sydney* retaliated with anti-aircraft fire. No-one was hurt before the Zeppelin departed.

More Australian sailors died as a result of injury or illness than from enemy action. After the armistice the German High Seas Fleet was required to surrender in the Firth of Forth on the Scottish coast. *Australia* led the battle cruisers of the port line as the Grand Fleet sailed out to meet the German ships on 21 November 1918. The war gave the Australian officers and sailors valuable experience on which to build as the navy expanded in the years before the Second World War.

# Lest We Forget

The end of the war came quickly. By the end of October 1918 Bulgaria, Turkey and Austria-Hungary had sought an armistice and the crews of some German warships had mutinied. On the Western Front, the Germans were being driven back by relentless blows from British, French and American armies. Early in November an almost bloodless revolution in Germany forced the Kaiser to abdicate and the government of the new German Republic accepted the Fourteen Points proposed by the US President, Woodrow Wilson, as the conditions for peace. All operations ceased on the Western Front at 11.00 am on 11 November 1918. Some German military officers later claimed that they had been 'stabbed in the back' by politicians at home, but in truth the German Army had been completely defeated on the Western Front.

At the end of the war, 92,000 Australian troops were in France, 60,000 were in England and 17,000 were in the Middle East. General Monash was given the task of organising their repatriation and the Prime Minister, Billy Hughes, who was in England, helped find the shipping. All the troops were home by the end of 1919. The speed and efficiency of the repatriation could be attributed to Monash's brilliance as an organiser.

# Counting the casualties

At the outbreak of the First World War Australia had a population of 4.875 million, and 416,809 Australians served in the armed forces. Most of these, 331,781, served overseas; 59,342 were killed or died of wounds, 152,171 were wounded and 4,084 became prisoners.

By comparison with other countries in the British Empire, Britain and New Zealand proportionally put more troops in the field from their respective populations — 11.2 per cent from the United Kingdom, 8.9 per cent from New Zealand and 6.8 per cent from Australia. Unlike the other countries, however, Australia did not employ conscription — all its soldiers were volunteers.

New Zealand had the highest proportion of deaths from its population, with 1.514 per cent, and Australia was second with 1.217 per cent. But in comparison with troops deployed overseas, Australia had the highest percentage of total casualties — 64.8 per cent, compared with 58.6 per cent for New Zealand. The high proportion of casualties can be attributed partly to the fact that most Diggers were in combat rather than logistic units. The Australian Army needed fewer logistic units in France and Palestine because it relied heavily on the British Army for the supply of food and ammunition.

 The numbers didn't include the men who hadn't sought treatment after being gassed but then endured breathing difficulties for the rest of their lives. Nor did they include the thousands of ex-servicemen who suffered from what is now called post-traumatic stress disorder, but then went under various names such as war neurosis or shell shock. Some received treatment; others struggled to survive by themselves or had to be supported by their long-suffering families.

The effect of the casualties on the Australian community was immense. By 1931 the Department of Repatriation was providing 283,322 pensions, less than a third to ex-servicemen (not all of whom sought assistance) and more than two-thirds to widows, wives and children. Harder to quantify was the loss of some of the most talented young men who might have gone on to play leading roles in Australian society.

## *Reaping political benefits*

The Australian Prime Minister, William Morris (Billy) Hughes, was in England when the armistice was signed and doggedly persisted until he was permitted to attend the Paris peace conference, which began in January 1919, as the representative of an independent country, not as part of the British Empire delegation.

The various leaders had their own agendas. Georges Clemenceau of France wanted Germany to pay heavy reparations. David Lloyd George of Britain spoke in a tough-minded manner but was actually more moderate. Woodrow Wilson of the United States idealistically wanted a soft peace and the establishment of the League of Nations. Hughes was closer to the French position on reparations — he estimated that the war had cost Australia £364 million, but in the end asked for £100 million. By the time the payment of reparations ceased in 1932 Australia had received £5,571,720.

 Hughes had a bitter debate with Wilson over his desire for Australia to gain control of German New Guinea, which he saw as vital to the defence of Australia. Wilson was adamant that his Fourteen Points for peace did not permit annexation. When Wilson challenged Hughes's right to make the claim, Hughes said that he spoke for 60,000 dead, meaning Australia's deaths in the war. Wilson summed up Hughes's attitude, claiming that if he got his way the conference would break up, which would be 'disastrous to the future happiness of eighteen hundred millions of the human race, in order to satisfy the whim of five million people in the remote southern continent you claim to represent'. The pugnacious Hughes replied: 'Very well put, Mr President, you have guessed it. That's just so'. Hughes got his way and Australia took control of German New Guinea as a mandated territory of the League of Nations. Japan obtained a League of Nations mandate over the former German islands north of the equator.

Another issue was Japan's efforts to ensure 'equality of nations and of equal treatment of their nationals', which Hughes saw as a threat to the White Australia Policy (see Chapter 5). Hughes ensured that Japan's statement was not approved. Hughes and Sir Joseph Cook, the High Commissioner in London, signed the Versailles Treaty on behalf of Australia on 28 June 1919. Hughes had secured matters that he thought were vital to the security of Australia.

## *Commemorating the fallen*

Australians killed in the First World War were buried in cemeteries near the battlefields. The largest number of Australian war graves is found in France, where almost 26,000 Australians are buried in 39 cemeteries. In Belgium 8,587 Australians are buried in 12 cemeteries, and there are 2,848 war graves at Gallipoli. The Australian National Memorial at Villers-Bretonneux lists the names of 10,892 Australians who were killed in France but for whom there is no known grave. Similarly, the Lone Pine Memorial at Gallipoli lists the 3,268 Australians and 456 New Zealanders who fought there and have no known grave, and the 960 Australians and 252 New Zealanders who were buried at sea after evacuation. The cemeteries are administered by the Commonwealth War Graves Commission and contain headstones of a uniform design and the words 'Their Name Liveth For Evermore'.

First World War memorials can be found in most Australian country towns, many of them recording the names of the men who volunteered to serve overseas, as well as those who died. As the Australian dead were buried overseas, these local memorials gave families a place of focus in remembering the dead. The Australian War Memorial in Canberra, completed in 1941, combines the function of national memorial, museum and archive. The body of the Unknown Australian Soldier was interred in the memorial's Hall of Memory on 11 November 1993.

Anzac Day, 25 April, was first remembered by soldiers of the AIF in 1916, and has been commemorated officially in every Australian state since 1925. Although it initially applied specifically to the fallen from the First World War, it later became the day when Australia formally remembered those killed in all of its wars.

The day begins with a dawn service at the war memorials in capital and provincial cities and in small towns. Then later in the morning, former servicemen and women take part in a march that ends with a service at the town or city's war memorial. Hundreds of thousands of Australians attend the marches and ceremonies around the country. More recently, up to 20,000 young Australians travel across the world to attend the annual service at Gallipoli. Others attend a similar service at Villers-Bretonneux in France, as well as at significant locations elsewhere around the world.

# Part IV
# The Second World War: The Empire Beckons

## In this part ...

The Second World War (1939–45) was the biggest, most tragic and costliest war ever. More than 60 million people were killed and nations were shattered. The major warring countries deployed huge armies, navies and air forces. On one side were the Axis powers — Germany, Italy and Japan. On the other side were the Allies — Britain and its Empire, the United States of America, the Soviet Union, China, France and many smaller countries.

When compared with the commitment and losses suffered by many other countries, Australia's involvement appears relatively small. Nonetheless, as I describe in this part, the war made a tremendous impact on Australia, which in the first two years sent substantial forces to help Britain in Europe and the Middle East. It looked as though Australia was again responding to the demands of the British Empire. But Australia's leaders understood that it was in the nation's interest to help Britain survive and ultimately defeat Germany. As it turned out, Australian forces contributed decisively to the outcome of the war in the Middle East in 1941–42.

# Chapter 10

# Winning the First Battles, 1940–41

*In This Chapter*

▶ Hoping for the best between the wars
▶ Organising for war
▶ Contributing to British sea power around the world
▶ Overrunning the Italian Army in Libya

The Second World War began on 1 September 1939, when Germany, led by Adolf Hitler and his National Socialist (Nazi) Party, invaded Poland as part of its plan to dominate Europe. Britain and France, which had guaranteed Poland's sovereignty, declared war. Germany subsequently invaded Norway, the Netherlands, Belgium and France. Britain tried to defend Belgium and France, but the German Army prevailed, and by mid-1940 Britain and its Empire stood alone against all-conquering Germany, which had been joined by Italy. The war spread to northern Africa and the Balkans. Then in June 1941 Hitler took on the Soviet Union.

The war expanded further to the Pacific region in December 1941, when Japan, which was at war with China, attacked British, Dutch and American colonies in Asia, forcing the United States to join what became a global conflict. Eventually the Allies won. Germany surrendered in May 1945, and Japan in September that year.

During the war, Australian forces fought against Germans, Italians, French and Japanese, experiencing both defeat and victory. While the first 17 months of the war was a period of defeat for Britain, the Australians won their first battles in this time.

Australia was largely unprepared for the war. In this chapter, I explain why the nation neglected its defences before the war, and how, on the outbreak of war, it raised and trained a special expeditionary force for overseas service. I then describe how, by contrast with the other services, the Navy was ready and its ships were available to serve with the Royal Navy. Finally, I tell how the Army won it first battles in the Middle East.

# Australia Neglects Its Security

Australia's lack of preparation for war in 1939 was determined by its defence policies in the years between 1919 and 1939. With its small population, and located thousands of miles from Britain, Australia had an enduring fear of invasion from Japan. Before the First World War, Australian Defence planners had identified Japan as a possible enemy, and, although Japan had been an ally during that war, they still viewed Japan as a threat. This view was influenced by racial aspects. Many people feared the 'Yellow Peril' and earlier the government had introduced the notorious White Australia Policy to keep the Asians out. After the war, the League of Nations gave Japan responsibility for the former German islands north of the equator, while Australia retained control of north-east New Guinea, which it had captured from Germany in the war. In these waters to the north Japan and Australia were now neighbours.

With the Japanese threat in mind, in 1920 senior Australian Army generals recommended that Australia establish:

- A substantial naval force to help Britain's Royal Navy defend its possessions in the Far East.
- A large part-time militia force of two cavalry divisions and the equivalent of five infantry divisions (refer to Chapter 2).

## The war-weary nation

After the tragic losses of the First World War, the Australian public was understandably weary of war and many people believed that it was no longer necessary to keep large forces ready for another conflict. (For a description of the casualties refer to Chapter 9.) Scarce finances, they thought, should be used for national development, and successive governments sought ways to reduce expenditure on defence. As part of the international effort to prevent conflict, at the Washington Naval Conference in 1922, Britain, the United States and Japan agreed to limit their naval forces. Under the treaty, the Royal Australian Navy (RAN) was included as part of the Royal Navy, and the old battle cruiser HMAS *Australia* was scuttled off Sydney Heads. 'Strong men were wet-eyed,' observed one officer. 'It was a tragic blunder.'

Although the conservative Nationalist Party Government agreed to build up the militia, it failed to provide the necessary funds and the existing scheme for compulsory military service was watered down. The military chiefs had hoped that the militia would have a strength of 270,000 soldiers in time of war, but by 1922 it numbered only 37,000. Many officers in the tiny regular army were retrenched. It was impossible to conduct realistic training in units that often existed in name only. As one historian put it, 'Defence lay defenceless before the political onslaught'.

## Still tied to Britain

The dilemma was how to defend a small, economically weak, remote country against an enemy such as Japan. The solution was to secure protection from within the Empire. At an imperial conference in London in 1923, Britain proposed building a naval base at Singapore, to which it would send its main fleet in time of threat to deter the Japanese fleet.

This scheme, known as the Singapore Strategy, rested on several premises:

- The base could be built in time to be of use.
- Britain would be willing to send its main fleet in time of war.
- If the fleet did arrive it would be able to defeat the Japanese Navy.
- Singapore could hold out against attack until the main fleet arrived.

Much doubt was expressed about these premises. In particular, Japan was unlikely to strike unless Britain was preoccupied in Europe, and, in that case, Britain mightn't be able to spare its fleet to go to Singapore. This indeed eventuated in 1941–42 (see Chapter 14).

The Australian Government's blind optimism was demonstrated by Prime Minister Stanley Bruce's comments at the London conference: 'While I am not quite as clear as I should be as to how the protection of Singapore is to be assured, I am clear on this point, that apparently it can be done'. The falseness of this hope was similarly to be demonstrated in 1942.

Under the Singapore Strategy, Australia built up its Navy, but the Army, required merely to deal with small-scale raids against the Australian mainland, was starved of funds. Australian Army generals didn't agree with this strategy, but the RAN's chiefs supported it. When presented with conflicting views, the Australian Government sought advice from Britain, which naturally backed the Singapore Strategy.

## Penny-pinching depletes our defences

The Labor Government, led by James Scullin, came to power in 1929 and, in accordance with Labor Party policy, immediately suspended compulsory military service. The Army strength fell from 47,000 to 27,000. Soon the economic effects of the Great Depression were being felt. Some RAN ships were scrapped. In lean times the government was in a difficult position, but was unsympathetic towards the armed forces. In June 1930, Scullin declared, 'If this Government stands for anything, it is for general disarmament'.

At one stage, the Defence Minister considered handing over the Navy to Britain, and amalgamating the Army and the Air Force. Regular soldiers were required to work one day a week without pay.

In January 1932, the newly formed United Australia Party came to power with Joseph Lyons as Prime Minister, but, while anxious to build up the forces, it was still hampered by lack of funds.

## Belatedly re-arming

During the 1920s the democracies hoped to prevent future war by promoting disarmament agreements. But in the 1930s, authoritarian regimes in Germany, Italy and Japan built up their armed forces, and increasingly indicated, by their actions, that a major war was approaching:

- **1931:** Japan seizes Manchuria.
- **1933:** Adolf Hitler comes to power in Germany. Japan and Germany leave the League of Nations.
- **1936:** Germany reoccupies the demilitarised Rhineland and sends fighters to the Spanish Civil War. Italy seizes Abyssinia.
- **1937:** Japan goes to war against China.
- **1938:** Germany occupies Austria.
- **1939:** Germany takes over Czechoslovakia. Japan fights a short war with the Soviet Union in Mongolia.

Although constrained by the weak economy and the difficulty of purchasing armaments overseas, the Australian Government belatedly tried to build up its forces. Relying on the Singapore Strategy, it concentrated on modernising the Navy, which by mid-1939 had a strength of about 5,500 permanent officers and sailors.

## Chapter 10: Winning the First Battles, 1940–41

The envigorated Navy consisted of:

- Two heavy cruisers (*Australia* and *Canberra*), commissioned in 1928
- Three light cruisers (*Perth*, *Hobart* and *Sydney*), commissioned in 1935–39
- One old light cruiser (*Adelaide*), commissioned in 1922
- Five old destroyers (*Stuart*, *Waterhen*, *Vampire*, *Vendetta* and *Voyager*), commissioned in 1917–18, on loan from the Royal Navy
- Two sloops (*Yarra* and *Swan*), commissioned in 1935–36

As the Defence Act didn't allow for a large regular army, the government sought to boost the part-time militia, and by March 1939 it had a strength of 70,000. It was poorly trained and equipped, lacking tanks and modern artillery. The regular army was pathetically small — fewer than 4,000 in number.

By mid-1939, the Royal Australian Air Force (RAAF) had 12 squadrons and a Regular and Citizen Force strength of 3,600 personnel. Its newest aircraft were already obsolescent. Modern aircraft were on order, but the Wirraway, which was just arriving, was only a trainer, not a proper combat fighter. That Australian industry had the capacity to build the latest aircraft was doubtful.

Some historians have argued that with a weak and faltering economy the government had no option but to rely on Britain and the Singapore Strategy. To its credit, in the late 1930s the government started to manufacture munitions. But the permanent officers and soldiers felt badly treated by successive governments, and muddled thinking by government ministers abounded.

## Not Another War!

At 9.15 pm on Sunday 3 September 1939, Prime Minister Robert Menzies addressed the nation by radio: 'Fellow Australians, it is my melancholy duty to inform you officially that, in consequence of the persistence by Germany in her invasion of Poland, Great Britain has declared war upon her, and that, as a result, Australia is also at war'.

The First World War had ended just a little over 20 years earlier and most Australians appreciated the tragedy of war. They didn't want another. But they generally accepted that Hitler's Germany had to be opposed, and saw themselves as loyal members of the British Empire. The question was — how could Australia contribute?

Menzies wanted to aid Britain, as Australia had done in the First World War, but he knew that Australia's own defences were inadequate and he feared a possible attack from Japan. It was also, unclear what forces Britain would need. After overrunning Poland in September 1939 Germany began no further offensive operations during the northern winter of 1939–40. This period of inactivity was known as the *phoney war*.

## Gearing up

On the outbreak of war the Navy immediately went to a war footing, calling up reservists to bring its strength up to 10,000. Permanent soldiers manned the guns around the Australian coast, and groups of militia were called up to help guard important locations. But it was not until 1 January 1940 that the government introduced compulsory service in the militia. In an effort to maintain calm, the government called for 'business as usual', but this gave the impression of complacency.

### 'Pig-Iron Bob'

Robert Menzies became Prime Minister in April 1939, at the age of 44, soon after the death of Joe Lyons. He remained in power until August 1941, when he was overthrown in a party room ballot. A successful Melbourne barrister, he had served in the Victorian Government before moving to the federal parliament in 1934, becoming Attorney-General and Minister for Industry. In 1938, after challenging unionists who refused to load pig-iron bound for Japan, he was given the nickname 'Pig-Iron Bob'.

Menzies lacked knowledge of military affairs, and his failure to serve overseas in the First World War drew criticism. His great strength was his lawyer's ability to grasp the essentials of an issue and bring an argument to a logical conclusion. His apparent weakness was his failure to appreciate the sensitivities of his colleagues.

Paul Hasluck, who served as a minister under Menzies, thought that Menzies 'had the disadvantage of his own brilliance'. He wrote further: 'A man of fine presence, ease of manner, poise and style, he incurred the suspicion of being vain, of lacking sincerity, and of being aloof. A man of keen intellect, he inevitably had often made lesser men seem foolish'.

His government achieved much more in the first two years of the war than has been generally recognised, and he fought hard to ensure the security of Australia against the mounting Japanese threat.

One of the government's first acts was to establish a War Cabinet, which consisted of Prime Minister Menzies and five (later ten) senior ministers. Menzies also took on the job of Minister for Defence. The chiefs of the Navy, the Army and the Air Force often attended War Cabinet meetings to provide military advice to the ministers. The War Cabinet became the key decision-making body for the remainder of the war. Its early decisions were directed towards accelerating the production of ships, aircraft and munitions.

Frederick Shedden, Secretary of the Department of Defence and Secretary of the War Cabinet, became a highly influential figure as Menzies's principal adviser on the conduct of the war.

## Recruiting a new force

Under the Defence Act, the government was not permitted to send the militia overseas. It was not until 15 September 1939 that Menzies announced the raising of a special force of 20,000 troops for service at home or abroad, depending on the circumstances, soon to be known as the Second Australian Imperial Force (2nd AIF). The main part of the force was the 6th Division, so named because there were already five militia divisions. Lieutenant General Sir Thomas Blamey was selected to command both the 2nd AIF and the division. He had been chief of staff of the Australian Corps, under Monash, in the First World War, and had later commanded a militia division. He was to become Australia's top military leader during the war.

Menzies hoped to send an air expeditionary force overseas, but instead he accepted a British request to provide men for the Empire Air Training Scheme (see Chapter 13).

The 2nd AIF was recruited from the militia and from men from all walks of life. They were soon training in hastily constructed camps, often without uniforms or weapons. The division's commanders came from the militia, and most had served in the First World War. These appointments caused considerable resentment among senior permanent officers, who believed that they were entitled to be considered. For the remainder of the war, Australia had two armies: The militia, which was confined to Australia, and the volunteer AIF, which could serve overseas. This unfortunate two-army policy was to bedevil Australia's military effort.

Critics have claimed that Menzies was so anxious to please Britain, which he admired ardently, that he recklessly sent forces overseas, thereby exposing Australia to risk. In fact, he was reluctant to send the AIF overseas, for fear of Japan, and it was only after Britain assured him that it would defend Australia if a threat arose that he finally agreed to dispatch the AIF. The first brigade sailed for the Middle East in January 1940.

In February 1940, the War Cabinet decided to raise a second infantry division, to be known as the 7th. The two divisions would then form the 1st Australian Corps, with Blamey as commander. Major General Iven Mackay, a militia officer, took over the 6th Division, and Major General John Lavarack, a regular officer who had been Chief of the General Staff in the 1930s, was made commander of the 7th Division.

## Training in Palestine

The first units of the 2nd AIF went to Palestine to complete their training before confronting the Germans in Europe. But Germany's invasion of France in May 1940 changed these plans. Britain was driven out of France, many troops escaping in the famous evacuation at Dunkirk in late May and early June. When Italy entered the war on Germany's side in June (hoping for easy spoils), it posed a new threat in the Middle East. The Italian colony of Libya had a common border with Egypt, which was controlled by Britain. If Italy attacked Egypt it would threaten the Suez Canal, which provided the shortest route between Britain and the Far East. The Australian units therefore remained in Palestine.

In the meantime, at the height of the fighting in France, the convoy carrying the 18th Brigade of the 6th Division and other troops was diverted to Britain. The 6th Division in Palestine needed to be brought to full strength, and a brigade was transferred from the 7th Division, which began arriving in Palestine in November 1940. After the British disaster in France, volunteers continued to flock to Australian recruiting depots, and the War Cabinet raised yet another AIF division, the 8th, which remained in training in Australia.

Blamey arrived in Palestine in mid-1940 to take command, and gradually his troops were equipped with more modern British weapons. The troops were based at Gaza, which the Palestinians later occupied after the formation of Israel in 1948. Blamey strongly resisted pressure from the British Commander-in-Chief, General Sir Archibald Wavell, to commit the incompletely trained and equipped Australians to battle until he was satisfied that they were ready. For the rest of the war Australian commanders kept alert to ensure that their troops were not risked unnecessarily by British or American generals.

## Supporting the motherland

While the majority of the AIF troops were training in Palestine, the 18th Brigade and other troops arrived in England, where they prepared to repulse a German invasion. The additional troops formed a second brigade, and these two brigades became the nucleus of the 9th Division. Members of the RAAF were also serving in Britain (see Chapter 13). By the end of the year, once it was clear that Germany was not going to invade, the 9th Division set sail for the Middle East to join the rest of the AIF.

General Blamey now had a force of three infantry divisions — the 6th, 7th and 9th — at various stages of development and training. A tremendous effort had been employed to raise this force, which numbered at least 65,000 men. The Australian troops had the immense advantage of time. Unlike the British Army, which was thrown into combat in France in May 1940, the soldiers of the 6th Division were able to train for at least a year before their first battles in January 1941.

# Gaining Control of the Oceans

The British Empire's survival depended upon maintaining trade between Britain and its dominions. (In those days the self-governing countries of the Empire — Australia, Canada, New Zealand and South Africa — were known as dominions.) As might have been expected, then, the RAN was far more ready for war than the other services and most of its ships were available almost immediately. Initially they remained in home waters. Several passenger liners were converted to become armed merchant cruisers, trawlers became minesweepers, and destroyers and sloops began to be constructed. As the war situation became clearer, however, the Australian Government started to allow RAN vessels to serve overseas with the Royal Navy.

## Patrolling the coast at home

Balancing the demands at home and overseas was difficult. An important task was to escort the convoys of troops as they sailed to the Middle East during 1940, but an enduring priority was to protect Australian coastal trade from attack.

One early action arose after Italy entered the war on 10 June 1940, and two Italian liners, *Remo* and *Romolo*, were operating in Australian waters. *Remo* was seized in Fremantle harbour, but *Romolo* had already sailed from Brisbane. The newly converted armed merchant cruiser, HMAS *Manoora*, began a cat-and-mouse chase but couldn't act until war was formally declared. After seven days, *Manoora* caught *Romolo* about 350 kilometres south-west of Nauru, near the equator. The Italian captain scuttled his ship, and *Manoora* rescued its passengers and crew.

During the second half of 1940, three German armed merchant cruisers operating in Australian waters sunk several merchant ships by gunfire or by laying sea mines in shipping channels. The few remaining Australian naval vessels in home waters couldn't intercept the raiders, but, because the other ships serving in the Indian Ocean, the Mediterranean and the Atlantic were engaged on more important tasks, risks needed to be accepted at home.

## Contesting the Mediterranean

In December 1939, the five old Australian destroyers, *Stuart*, *Waterhen*, *Vampire*, *Vendetta* and *Voyager*, arrived in the Mediterranean, where they endured a cold winter on patrol. German propaganda derisively nicknamed the destroyers the 'scrap-iron flotilla', but the crews adopted the title enthusiastically.

Commander Hector Waller, captain of *Stuart*, commanded a flotilla with the five Australian vessels and four British destroyers. He and the Australians had already won the admiration of the famous commander of the British Mediterranean Fleet, Admiral Sir Andrew Cunningham.

When Italy entered the war in June 1940, the Mediterranean suddenly became a major theatre. The light cruiser HMAS *Sydney*, under Captain John Collins, had arrived in May. The French and British combined fleet in the Mediterranean was about the same size as the Italian Navy, but when the French withdrew from the war, Cunningham was outnumbered. He immediately took the initiative; he sank several Italian submarines and bombarded Italian positions along the coast of Libya.

## Sinking Italian ships

Later in June 1940, Cunningham's 7th Cruiser Squadron intercepted Italian destroyers trying to transport troops and supplies to Libya. *Sydney*'s guns sank the Italian destroyer *Espero*. *Voyager* was among the destroyers that sank an Italian submarine, *Uebi Scebeli*. The Australian ships were often attacked from the air.

On 19 July *Sydney* was protecting a division of destroyers on anti-submarine patrol off the western end of Crete. Two fast Italian cruisers attacked the destroyers, which withdrew hastily towards *Sydney* and another escorting destroyer. Maintaining radio silence, Collins turned towards the cruisers. As they came in sight, *Sydney* opened fire, putting the *Bartolomeo Colleoni* out of action, and then chased the other Italian cruiser, which was damaged but managed to escape. *Sydney*'s escorting destroyer torpedoed the *Colleoni*. 'We didn't feel sorry for the Italians, just elated,' said one sailor. It had been a brilliant victory.

## Helping out at Berbera

After Italy entered the war, it invaded British Somaliland from its colony in Abyssinia. The cruiser HMAS *Hobart*, under Captain Harry Howden, was part of a small British naval force supporting the British army as it attempted to defend the British colony. The British troops were driven back to the capital, Berbera, and Howden commanded the naval force — 11 ships, including 3 cruisers — that evacuated more than 7,000 British troops and civilians on 19 August 1940. Australian sailors went ashore to help with the evacuation, and *Hobart*'s guns bombarded the city as the ships withdrew.

## Fighting the French at Dakar

With the defeat of France, its colonies had to decide whether to continue the war on the side of the Allies, or to accept the authority of the new German-controlled government, located in the provincial town of Vichy. One such colony, which remained under Vichy control, was French West Africa. From the port of Dakar enemy ships could threaten British convoys. On 7 July 1940, British ships, including the heavy cruiser HMAS *Australia*, attacked and partly disabled the French battleship *Richelieu* at the port.

When the Vichy Government took over, General Charles de Gaulle, a French Cabinet member, escaped to Britain and established the Free French Forces. De Gaulle persuaded Winston Churchill, the British Prime Minister, to support a landing by Free French troops, who were thought could take over the city without bloodshed. *Australia* was part of the British naval force during the landing operation between 19 and 23 September 1940. The Vichy forces fought back strongly, and *Australia* found itself in a savage battle with French ships and shore batteries. Eventually the Free French troops withdrew and the ill-fated expedition was called off. *Australia* suffered only light damage, but its aircraft was shot down and its crew killed.

Churchill had ordered the operation without consulting the Australian Government, and Menzies complained that not being informed was 'humiliating'. It demonstrated the danger of handing forces over to another government. Britain, on the other hand, did not quite grasp that Australia was an independent country.

## Backing a coup in New Caledonia

Another French colony forced to decide its allegiance was New Caledonia, just 1,500 kilometres north-east of Brisbane. In July 1940, the French sloop *Dumont d'Urville* arrived at Noumea, the capital of New Caledonia, and a Vichy governor was installed. General de Gaulle sent the French commissioner in the New Hebrides, Henri Sautot, to regain New Caledonia. Sautot travelled in a Norwegian steamer escorted by the cruiser HMAS *Adelaide*. Although *Dumont d'Urville* and shore batteries threatened to fire, *Adelaide* showed that it was ready to respond, and safely landed Sautot on 19 September 1940. He then led local residents in a march on the governor's office and seized power. *Dumont d'Urville* departed and the Free French governed New Caledonia for the rest of the war.

# Upholding the Digger Legend in the Middle East

The vain Italian dictator, Benito Mussolini, wanted to emulate the conquests of his ally Adolf Hitler, and in September 1940 ordered the large Italian Army in Libya to invade Egypt. After advancing 110 kilometres, the Italians established a stronghold at the coastal town of Sidi Barrani (refer to Figure 10-1).

The British Commander-in-Chief, General Wavell, had formed the Western Desert Force, under Major General Richard O'Connor, to defend Egypt but, when the Italians halted, the British struck hard. On 9 December O'Connor's force, including the 7th Armoured Division (equipped with tanks) and the 4th Indian Division, attacked Sidi Barrani, captured 38,000 prisoners and drove the remaining Italians back to the Libyan frontier. There the Italians occupied strong defensive positions in the small port of Bardia.

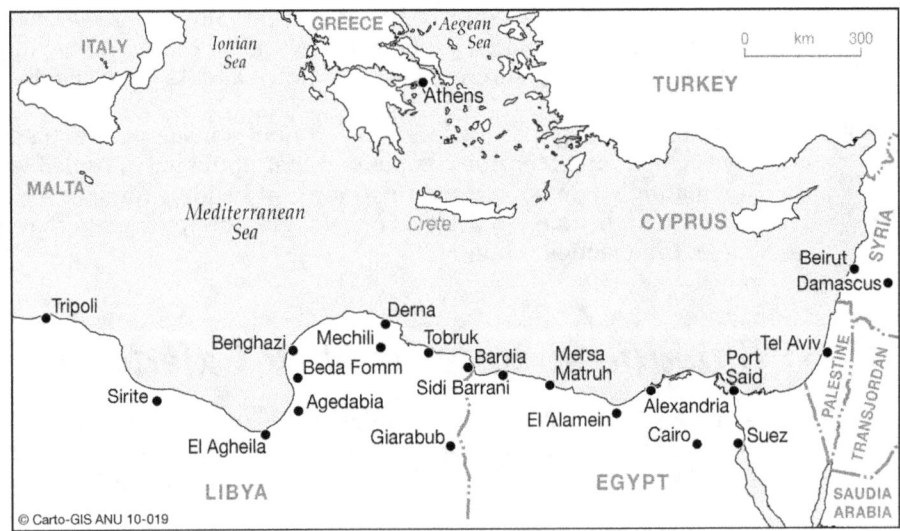

**Figure 10-1:** The Middle East theatre, 1940–41.

Wavell now sent the 4th Indian Division off to Sudan to take part in an invasion of Abyssinia. He then ordered the 6th Australian Division to relieve the Indians in the Western Desert Force and capture Bardia. After a year of solid training, testing themselves against British regulars in Palestine, the Australians were itching to join the battle. Many of their fathers and uncles had served in the First World War. They were conscious of the proud record of the 1st AIF and were eager to prove that they could uphold its traditions.

## Baptism of fire at Bardia

With one side facing the sea, Bardia was defended by a 29-kilometre arc of barbed wire, concrete strongholds, machine-guns and anti-tank ditches. It was defended by more than 45,000 Italian troops, although the Australians thought that there were only 23,000. The Australian attackers numbered 16,000. The Italian commander, General Annibale Bergonzoli, known as 'Electric Whiskers', told Mussolini that Bardia was impregnable.

Major General Iven Mackay, commander of the 6th Division, planned to attack with two of his brigades, Brigadier Arthur ('Tubby') Allen's 16th and Brigadier Stanley Savige's 17th, assisted by a regiment of British tanks, the full weight of artillery, and the fire of three battleships and seven destroyers. (For the role of tanks and artillery refer to Chapter 2.) With no scope for manoeuvring the Italians out of their defences, it was a careful, deliberate battle, similar to those conducted by Mackay and his brigade commanders as more junior officers in the First World War.

The 16th Brigade began the main attack against the western defences in the cold, early hours of 3 January 1941. Supported by tanks and artillery, the engineers were able to breach the barbed wire, and then the infantry and tanks made good progress. The Italian anti-tank guns couldn't penetrate the British Matilda tanks. The 17th Brigade was meant to conduct diversionary attacks from the south, but Savige pressed the assault, taking heavy and unnecessary casualties in deep, dry creek beds, known as wadis. Mackay now brought up his third brigade, the 19th, under Brigadier Horace ('Red Robbie') Robertson, which joined the fighting on 5 January. The battle was won that evening.

It was a battle of myths and legends. The widespread story that the Australians went into battle singing songs from *The Wizard of Oz* is not true. Some Italian soldiers apparently believed another myth — that the leather over-vests, known as jerkins and worn by the Aussies to keep out the cold, made them impervious to bullets.

The most enduring myth is that the Australians won because of their courage and tactical brilliance. In truth, the British tanks and guns were decisive. Some Italians had fought well, but their weapons were poor and their commanders proved to be inadequate.

Australian losses totalled 130 killed and 326 wounded, but the Aussies had captured about 38,000 prisoners as well as hundreds of guns, tanks and invaluable motor vehicles. Photographs show thousands of dispirited prisoners being guarded by lone Australians. It was a magnificent victory. Somehow 'Electric Whiskers' evaded capture and walked to Tobruk.

## Capturing the fortress at Tobruk

While the Australians rounded up the prisoners and counted their booty, O'Connor sent the 7th Armoured Division 120 kilometres along the coast to surround the next Italian fortress at the port of Tobruk. The Australian infantry was to attack against defences similar to those encountered at Bardia, and again the 16th Brigade was to lead the way.

The assault began before dawn on 21 January 1941, supported by artillery. Once the 16th Brigade, helped by the 17th Brigade, had breached the defences, the 19th Brigade charged through the gap and thrust north. Next morning the Italian resistance collapsed. The Australians had lost 49 killed and 306 wounded. Italian prisoners numbered 25,000. Quickly the British opened the port and began bringing forward the necessary supplies to sustain a further advance.

The flamboyant Brigadier Robertson took the surrender from the Italian fortress commander, a general, as well as from an admiral based in the town. When an Italian colonel tried to surrender, Robertson said: 'Throw him back. Nothing but generals and admirals for me today'.

## Outmanoeuvring the Italians

With the fall of Tobruk, O'Connor ordered Mackay to advance along the coast, while the 7th Armoured Division struck inland. Unfortunately, O'Connor's tanks couldn't move for lack of fuel, and on 25 January both the 17th and 19th Brigades attacked the Italian defences at Derna. The Australians slowly worked their way through a tangle of steep-sided wadis before the Italians began to withdraw on 2 February.

The best battle tactic is to outmanoeuvre the enemy rather than to conduct a head-on attack. At dawn on 4 February, O'Connor ordered his refuelled tanks to strike adventurously through the desert, bypassing the more populated and better defended coastal hills, to reach the sea, south of Benghazi (refer to Figure 10-1). At Beda Fomm, just off the coast road, they blocked the retreating Italians. After a bitter fight, the Italians surrendered early on 7 February. The British took more than 20,000 prisoners, including General Bergonzoli.

The leading troops of the 6th Division had entered Benghazi unopposed on 6 February. In two months, the Western Desert Force, with never more than two divisions, had destroyed an Italian army of ten divisions, and had driven the Italians out of the eastern part of Libya, known as Cyrenaica.

## *Sideshow at Giarabub*

During the fighting in northern Cyrenaica, the 6th Australian Cavalry Regiment, mounted in trucks, had been keeping watch over an Italian garrison at Giarabub, a desert oasis 230 kilometres south of Bardia. By mid-February about 1,500 Italians remained in well-defended positions, supported by artillery.

Brigadier George Wooten, commander of the 18th Brigade, was ordered to take one of his battalions in trucks to join the cavalrymen and to capture the oasis. Attacking in a dust storm from the south on 19 and 20 March, while the cavalry advanced from the north, the Australians overcame the defenders. In the big picture, this was a bit of a sideshow, but it was deadly serious for the 94 Australians who were killed. About 250 Italians were killed, and 1,300 surrendered.

For the moment, the Cyrenaica campaign was over. Earlier, on 11 February, Blamey and Menzies had visited Benghazi to congratulate the troops and to enjoy a victory dinner. Blamey and his staff was then given responsibility for the defence of Cyrenaica. But already Churchill was planning a campaign that was to lead to a bitter defeat for the Australians. And on 12 February the brilliant, charismatic German general Irwin Rommel arrived in north Africa to lead the German–Italian counteroffensive (see Chapter 12).

# Chapter 11

# New Theatres, New Allies and New Enemies, 1941

### In This Chapter

- Withdrawing through Greece
- Fighting valiantly in Crete
- Beating the Vichy French in Syria
- Anticipating the Japanese threat

By early 1941 the British Empire and the dominions stood almost alone against the Axis powers, Germany, Italy and their allies. Hitler's Germany had overrun most of northern Europe and had forced France to surrender. Italy, led by Benito Mussolini, joined the war just before the French surrender and then invaded Greece in October 1940. The following month Hungary, Romania and Slovakia joined the Axis. And with the troubles in Europe, the Japanese began acting a little more brashly in Asia.

In this chapter I describe Australia's contribution in the 1941 campaigns against German tanks in Greece, against German paratroopers in Crete, and against the French and their Foreign Legion in Syria. Australians also fought Iraqis and Persians. At the same time, politicians and military leaders at home started getting nervous about the Japanese threat and began making plans.

## Blitzkrieg and Bombing in Greece

At the beginning of 1941 Greece was Britain's only ally still fighting in Europe. The poorly equipped Greek army had successfully repulsed the incompetent Italians, but British intelligence warned that Hitler would come to the aid of Mussolini. Winston Churchill, the British Prime Minister, believed that Britain had a moral obligation to support Greece and that if it failed to do so its reputation would be damaged in the eyes of the United States and other neutrals. Churchill therefore ordered General Sir Archibald

Wavell, British Commander-in-Chief in the Middle East, to prepare to deploy forces to Greece. Wavell planned to send the 6th and 7th Australian Divisions and the New Zealand Division.

The decision to send troops to Greece is one of the most contentious in Australian military history. Not only did the campaign prove to be a disaster, but Britain forced Australia into approving it without allowing Australia access to all the relevant information. Attending the British War Cabinet in London, the Australian Prime Minister, Robert Menzies, had reservations about the project, arguing that if it 'was only a forlorn hope, it had better not be undertaken'. General Blamey, commander of the Australians in the Middle East, also had misgivings about the 'hazardous operation', but thought, erroneously, that Menzies had approved it. Believing that Blamey had agreed, Menzies reluctantly accepted Churchill's arguments. On Menzies' advice, the Australian War Cabinet approved the expedition on 26 February 1941.

## Reviving the Anzac Corps

The British force in Greece, known as Lustreforce, was commanded by Lieutenant General Maitland Wilson (known as 'Jumbo' because of his size) and was to defend northern Greece in cooperation with the Greek Army.

The troops began arriving in Greece and by 5 April Lustreforce consisted of:

- Headquarters 1st Australian Corps, Lieutenant General Sir Thomas Blamey
  - 6th Australian Division, Major General Sir Iven Mackay
  - New Zealand Division, Major General Sir Bernard Freyberg
- British 1st Armoured Brigade, Brigadier Harold Charrington

The 1st Australian Corps, about 30,000 strong, began deploying to the Olympus-Aliakmon Line ready to meet a probable German attack through Bulgaria. The New Zealand Division occupied a line with its right flank against the sea. In the 6th Division, Brigadier Arthur ('Tubby') Allen's 16th Brigade held the Veria Pass further left (refer to Figure 11-1). Brigadier George Vasey's 19th Brigade was moving to the front and Brigadier Stan Savige's 17th Brigade was still crossing the sea. The 7th Division had not even left Egypt.

Lustreforce was still moving into position when on 6 April the German Army invaded Greece and Yugoslavia. The Greeks began falling back, while the Germans quickly overran Yugoslavia. As the situation deteriorated Blamey renamed his command the Anzac Corps, to recognise its large component of New Zealanders and to revive the association from the First World War.

# Chapter 11: New Theatres, New Allies and New Enemies, 1941

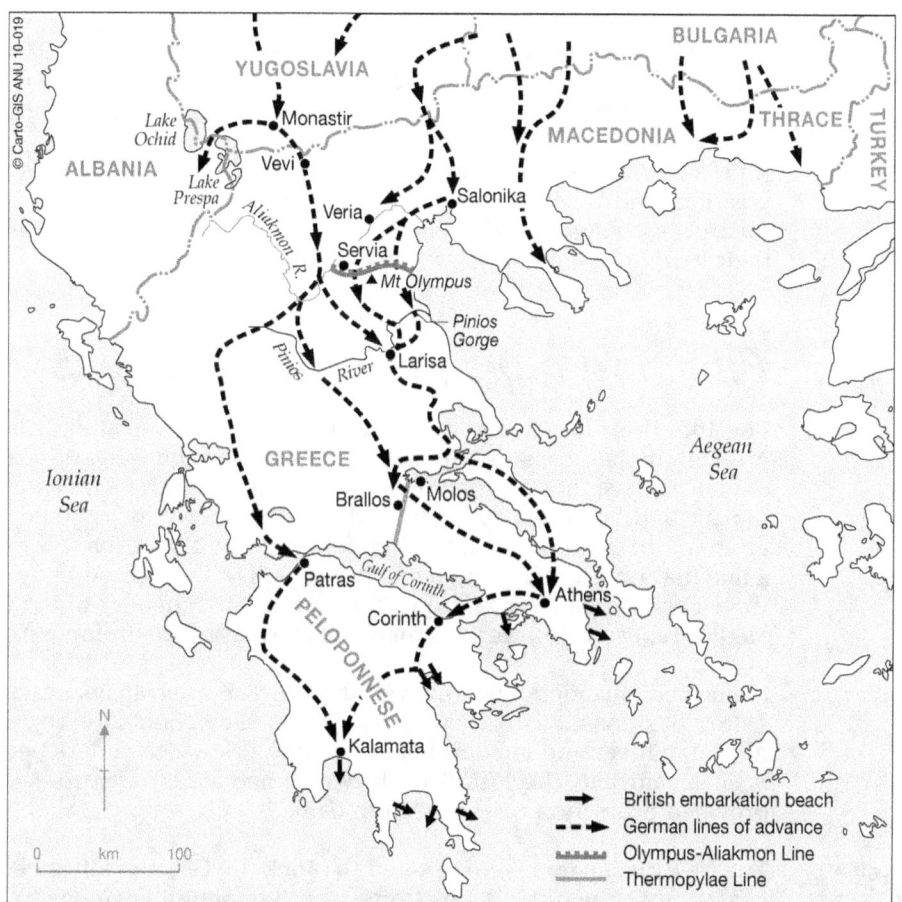

**Figure 11-1:** Allied withdrawal from Greece, April 1941.

## Meeting the German panzers at Vevi

While the Anzac Corps faced heavy pressure from the front, Wilson recognised that German units could advance through Yugoslavia and south through the Monastir Gap to strike his forces in the rear. To meet this danger, Wilson ordered Mackay to block the Monastir approach using the 19th Brigade and the 1st Armoured Brigade. This meant Vasey, who was given the task, had only two of his own infantry battalions and a British battalion to make a stand along a 16-kilometre front near Vevi.

The Australians met the full force of the German blitzkrieg. The German SS Adolf Hitler Division led the advance with *panzers* (tanks) and motorised infantry, supported by dive bombers. When the Germans reached Vasey's positions on 10 April they were hit by Australian artillery.

An Australian artillery observer ordered the guns to fire at extreme range. 'I brought up my glasses', he wrote, 'and the next instant a puff of dust and smoke appeared, as by magic, where the nearest lorry had been. A direct hit first round.' 'Out first ball', commented the cricket-loving General Mackay.

After a two-day battle German tanks rolled into the forward Australian positions and Vasey skilfully organised a night-time withdrawal. But an Australian company had been captured and some troops had thrown away their weapons while fleeing through the snow.

## Plugging gaps in northern Greece

The 19th Brigade rejoined the Anzac Corps, which was already being pressed by the Germans who had advanced through Bulgaria. Wilson did not believe that he could rely on the Greek divisions that were facing Albania and Yugoslavia and realised that the Anzac Corps could be cut off from the western flank. He therefore ordered the corps to withdraw to a line that ran from Thermopylae to the Gulf of Corinth. Already General Wavell and Admiral Sir Andrew Cunningham, commander of the British Mediterranean Fleet, were planning on evacuating Lustreforce from Greece.

Blamey commanded a fighting withdrawal. The Australians evacuated their hilltop positions, destroyed any equipment they couldn't carry, crossed the Aliakmon River and in coordination with the New Zealanders began moving back. Meanwhile, the 17th Brigade, which had at last arrived in Greece, provided protection on the western flank.

The New Zealanders were ordered to block the German advance along the coast and through the Pinios Gorge, south of Mount Olympus. When the Kiwis failed to stop the Germans, Blamey redeployed the 16th Brigade to prevent the Germans breaking into the plains. The main German attack was met by the 2/2nd Battalion, commanded by Sydney lawyer Lieutenant Colonel Fred Chilton. A fierce battle on 18 April allowed the remainder of Anzac Corps to withdraw. After holding the Germans all day, Chilton's battalion was forced to scatter, with small groups escaping at night through the hills.

Chilton led a small party who travelled on foot at night to the Greek coast and eventually managed to board a Greek fishing boat that took them to neutral Turkey. Chilton and his party, which had grown to more than 30, reached Egypt on 24 May 1941, five weeks after the battle.

## On the run

After the battle in the Pinios Gorge, the remains of the 16th Brigade fought a desperate rearguard action against the panzers. Lieutenant Colonel Jimmy Lamb of the 2/3rd Battalion ordered his men to lie on the ground wherever they were. Expecting to be overrun, one platoon commander tried to get his men together 'more for sentiment's sake than for usefulness'. He was gently chided by a decorated First World War veteran, Sergeant Arthur Carson. 'We're not platoons here', he said. 'We are the AIF'. Firing rifles and pistols, the infantry somehow held off the panzers in failing light.

The withdrawal down the Greek peninsula was a severe ordeal, as German aircraft patrolled the road, machine-gunning and bombing the convoys. South of Elasson the Australian artillery located a large supply of ammunition and knocked out tank after German tank with deadly shooting. By the time they withdrew, the gunners of the 2/3rd Field Regiment had fired 6,500 rounds and the paint on the gun barrels had been blistered by the heat.

## Last stand at Brallos

To defend the Thermopylae line Blamey deployed Freyberg's New Zealanders on the coastal plain, while Mackay's 6th Division was responsible for the inland area around Brallos Pass. Mackay gave the main task to Brigadier Vasey's 19th Brigade.

Vasey knew that he wouldn't be able to hold this new position against a sustained attack, but needed to defend it long enough for the evacuation to begin. He issued his orders: 'Here we bloody well are and here we bloody well stay'. Vasey was not known as Bloody George for nothing. His staff officer translated: 'The 19th Brigade will hold its present defensive position come what may'.

The battle for Brallos Pass began in the morning of 21 April when aircraft machine-gunned the Australian positions and German mountain troops began infiltrating the widely scattered infantry battalions. The Diggers repelled the assault during the day and into the next, when news came that they needed to hold on until the night of 24 April to allow for the evacuation. The forward troops withdrew step-by-step against strong German attacks, until at 10.15 pm on 24 April the last soldiers jumped in their trucks and escaped.

## Evacuation

Lustreforce troops were evacuated from beaches across southern Greece by Royal Navy warships and transports, while rearguards tried to hold off the Germans. Many ships were attacked by air as they sailed south, but only two destroyers and four transports were lost along with 500 troops. More than 50,000 troops were evacuated, but over 14,000 were captured. The Australians lost 320 killed, 494 wounded and 2,030 prisoners.

The Australians had generally fought well against a superior enemy but some troops were unnerved by the unequal fight. The Commonwealth forces lacked a strong air force of their own to counter the Luftwaffe's dive-bombers and they were overwhelmed by experienced German divisions with tanks and motorised infantry. The Greek high command proved irresolute and the Greek Army did not have sufficient modern equipment and logistic support to fight a modern war.

### Blamey loses respect

General Blamey's performance in Greece became the subject of much controversy. On the face of it, he commanded the Anzac Corps with skill and foresight. On arrival he reconnoitred southern Greece to identify the most suitable beaches for evacuation. The fighting withdrawal was masterful, as brigades were deployed to counter each panzer attack, while the remainder headed south along the one available road. Witnesses attested to his calm, measured demeanour. Brigadier Clive Steele, the chief engineer, thought that Blamey 'showed up best; for vigour, endurance, clarity of vision and power of sane decision'.

Others believe that Blamey lost his nerve. His chief of staff, Brigadier Sydney Rowell, described him as 'rather tired and distressed'; he 'seemed completely broken'. The skilful withdrawal has been attributed to Rowell and the decision to send the 16th Brigade to hold Pinios Gorge resulted from Rowell's quick-thinking. Senior officers in Greece were equally divided on the issue.

Shortly before the evacuation Wavell ordered Blamey, Mackay and Freyberg to fly back to Egypt. Blamey was to become Deputy Commander-in-Chief of the Middle East.

Blamey selected his key staff and, finding one extra seat on the aircraft, included his only surviving son, a major serving as a liaison officer. Even his most sympathetic biographer has described the decision as 'injudicious'. Vasey thought that 'Some excuses *might* be made for him, but to include the boy was just too terrible ... he has lost a lot of caste [social standing] on account of it'. Freyberg refused to obey the order to fly to Egypt and commanded his division until it was evacuated.

# Chapter 11: New Theatres, New Allies and New Enemies, 1941

## Desperate Defences in Crete

Having occupied mainland Greece, the Germans decided to seize the island of Crete to deny it to the Allies and to dominate the eastern Mediterranean. Anticipating this, Britain had started to garrison the island, but had made little progress before the Greek campaign. In the haste to evacuate Greece, however, many troops were taken to the island. Major General Freyberg was appointed commander of all the Commonwealth forces on Crete and was ordered to defend it against an expected German attack using airborne troops. By 17 May Freyberg's command included 15,000 British troops, 7,700 New Zealanders, 6,500 Australians and about 11,000 Greeks. Brigadier Vasey commanded all the Australians. Some battalions had arrived almost intact, but others had tumbled ashore in groups, and 1,500 men, who had survived the sinking of the transport ship *Costa Rica,* landed without arms, equipment and, in some cases, even without boots. Vasey formed ad hoc battalions from disparate groups of infantrymen and gunners (who no longer had their guns).

## Digging in with the Kiwis again

From his headquarters in Canea, Freyberg assessed that he needed to defend four key locations — Maleme airfield, the main port at Suda Bay, Retimo and Heraklion (refer to Figure 11-2).

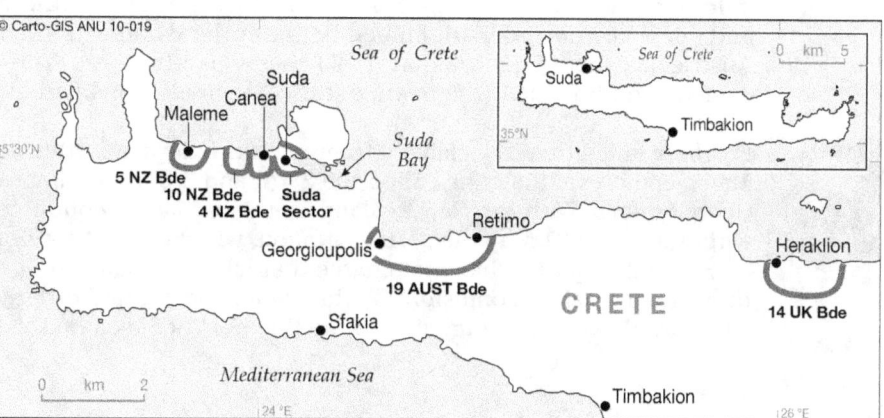

**Figure 11-2:** Crete, Allied dispositions, 19 May 1941.

Freyberg deployed his forces as follows:

- Maleme Sector, New Zealand Division (Brigadier Edward Puttick), two New Zealand brigades
- Suda Bay Sector, British Mobile Naval Base (Major General Eric Weston), the equivalent of three British battalions and two composite Australian battalions
- Force Reserve, near Suda Bay, one New Zealand brigade
- Georgioupolis–Retimo Sector (Brigadier George Vasey), 2/1st and 2/11th Australian Battalions at Retimo, and 2/7th and 2/8th Australian Battalions at Georgioupolis
- Heraklion, 14th British Brigade (Brigadier Brian Chappel), the equivalent of four British battalions and the 2/4th Australian Battalion

Greek battalions were attached to each of the sectors. All the British units lacked artillery, communications and transport, and most were below strength.

## Shooting German paratroopers

By mid-May Crete was under constant German air attack. Then on 20 May German paratroops and gliders landed at Maleme, Retimo and Heraklion. At the key position, Maleme, the battle raged for more than 24 hours before the Germans took control and the Kiwis began to withdraw towards Suda Bay. The defenders did much better at Heraklion with the British and Australians shooting more than 1,000 enemy paratroopers. The Germans gained a foothold near the town, but the defenders remained in control.

Freyberg failed to act decisively to prevent the Germans advancing from Maleme, but eventually he called the 2/7th and 2/8th Battalions from Georgioupolis. With the New Zealanders the battalions conducted a fighting withdrawal. On 27 May the 2/7th Battalion, with nearby New Zealanders, carried out a spirited bayonet charge that killed at least 200 Germans and threw them back in confusion. By this time Freyberg had ordered a general withdrawal over the mountains to the tiny port of Sfakia on the south coast.

## Futile defence at Retimo

At Retimo, Lieutenant Colonel Ian Campbell commanded both his own 2/1st Battalion and the 2/11th Battalion. The Australians took a heavy toll of the first wave of German paratroopers. Eventually the Germans established a foothold around one of the villages and the Australians counterattacked through olive groves and vineyards. Each time the isolated Australians gained the upper hand, more German reinforcements arrived.

Out of communication with Freyberg's headquarters, Campbell didn't know that an evacuation had been ordered, so his men fought on, short of ammunition and food, but still counterattacking. Finally on 30 May Campbell learned that strong German forces with tanks and light guns were advancing from the west, which was now obviously in German hands. Campbell therefore ordered his battalion to surrender. Major Ray Sandover, commanding officer of the 2/11th Battalion, told his men that they could try to escape in small parties into the mountains; most were captured but more than 50 eventually reached Egypt.

## Saved by the navy

While the Australians conducted their courageous defence at Retimo, the main force trudged over the mountains to Sfakia on the south coast. Vasey commanded the rearguard while the other troops were evacuated on the nights of 28, 29, 30 and 31 May.

On the final night the 2/7th Battalion had the task of holding off the Germans until the last minute, when it would march down the goat tracks to board the boats that were to take them out to the warships. Arriving in the dark they found that base troops had swarmed onto their allocated landing craft. The disciplined battalion stood on the shingle beach, 'quiet and orderly in its ranks'. Their commander, Lieutenant Colonel Theo Walker, had gone ahead to organise the evacuation and had boarded a landing craft believing his men were being evacuated. Realising that they hadn't made it, he stepped ashore so that he could lead them into captivity.

The Navy evacuated about 11,000 men from Sfakia. The Commonwealth force had lost 15,900 men, of whom 4,000 were killed and wounded. The Australians lost 274 killed, 507 wounded and 3,102 captured.

## Fierce battles at sea

The battle for Crete was fought at sea as well as on land. The Germans hoped to bring troops across from Greece on fishing boats and other assorted craft, escorted by Italian destroyers and patrol boats. Admiral Cunningham deployed his cruisers and destroyers, including several Australian vessels, that destroyed the flotillas carrying the German troops and successfully prevented them from reinforcing Crete. But his ships endured fierce attacks by Luftwaffe dive-bombers and lost two cruisers and four destroyers.

The evacuation was equally challenging. On the night of 28 May the Royal Navy evacuated 4,000 troops from Heraklion, but German aircraft sank two destroyers, damaged others and machine-gunned and bombed the survivors in the water. About 800 troops were killed, wounded or taken prisoner; 48 Australian soldiers were killed.

Despite serious losses, Cunningham was determined that the 'navy must not let the army down', declaring: 'It takes three years to build a ship. It will take 300 years to build a new tradition. The evacuation will continue.'

After withdrawing from Sfakia on the night of 29 May, the Australian cruiser *Perth,* with more than 1,100 troops aboard, was hit by a bomb and four sailors and nine soldiers were killed. Four Australian destroyers also took part. For example, *Napier* and *Nizam* were the only ships to arrive at Sfakia on 30 May; they took off about 1,500 troops. Next day a German bomb landed on *Napier*, slid under the rail and exploded alongside. *Napier* was briefly dead in the water before limping back to Egypt on one engine.

In the battle for Crete the Navy lost over 2,000 killed, more deaths than incurred by the Army ashore. Of the 54 warships that participated in the battle, only 20 were not lost or damaged.

# Invading Syria

When Germany defeated France in 1940 it set up a pliant French government at the provincial city of Vichy to administer the unoccupied areas of the country, known as Vichy France. The French colony of Syria remained under a pro-Nazi Vichy governor and was garrisoned by well-equipped French regular and Foreign Legion troops. During May 1941 German aircraft refuelled in Syria on the way to support nationalists in Iraq. Fearing that the Germans would establish a base in Syria, Churchill decided to invade Syria, hoping the Vichy French troops would offer only token resistance.

General Wavell put together a mixed force under Wilson. The main attacking troops would come from Major General John Lavarack's 7th Australian Division (21st and 25th Brigades), which had not yet been in action. The plan envisaged an advance from northern Palestine on three axes (refer to Figure 11-3):

- Along the coastal plain to Beirut. 21st Australian Brigade.
- Through Merjayoun and north to Rayak. 25th Australian Brigade.
- Inland towards Damascus. The 5th Indian Brigade and a Free French force.

# Chapter 11: New Theatres, New Allies and New Enemies, 1941

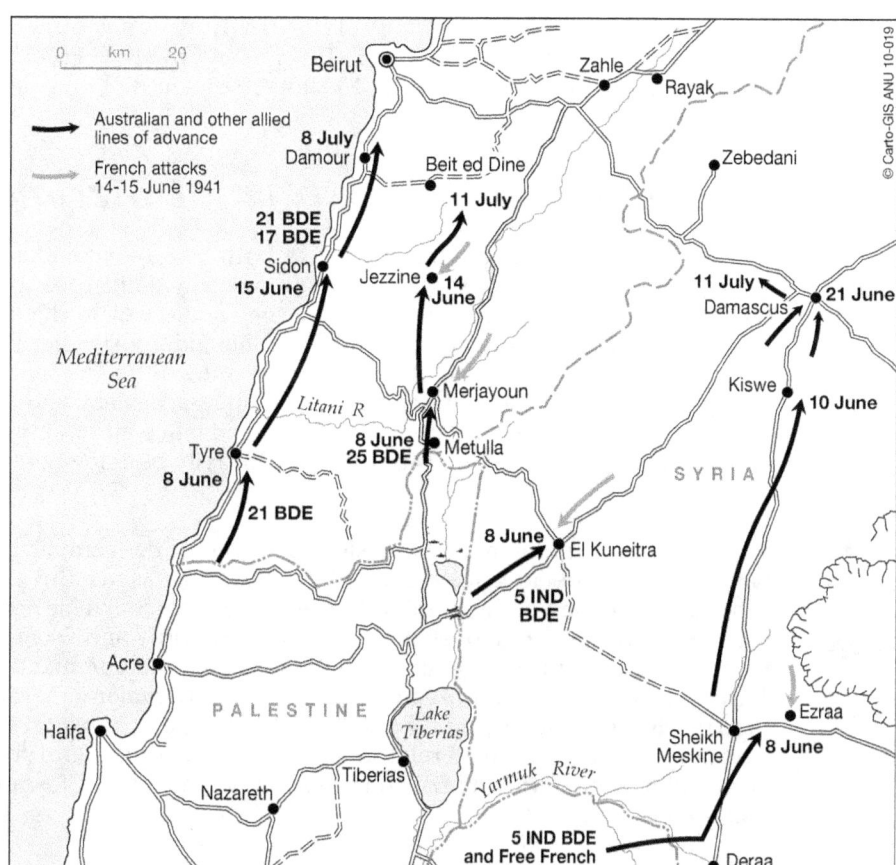

Figure 11-3: Allied invasion of Syria, June–July 1941.

## Crossing the frontier

Expecting the Vichy French to surrender quickly, some Australians thought that all they needed to do was wave their slouch hats to the French and walk in. The British high command severely misjudged the attitude of the Vichy French forces. When the invasion began on 8 June 1941 the Vichy French put up much stronger resistance than expected, aided by difficult terrain. The Diggers quickly donned their steel helmets. Along the coast the 21st Brigade crossed the Litani River and advanced slowly, capturing Sidon on 15 June.

On the central route, the Australians took two days to capture Merjayoun just north of the frontier. Lavarack now changed his plan. Instead of pushing north, he left a small force to protect Merjayoun, while most of the 25th Brigade thrust north-west, along mountain roads, to capture Jezzine, threaten Sidon and take advantage of the 21st Brigade's good work along the coast. On the inland route the Indian brigade and the Free French initially did well before being halted about 15 kilometres south of Damascus.

## The French counterattack at Merjayoun

On 15 June the French counterattacked at both Merjayoun and south of Damascus. The attack on Merjayoun was especially dangerous, because if the Vichy French could capture the town they could isolate the 25th Brigade at Jezzine. Lavarack ordered his artillery commander, Brigadier Frank Berryman, to take command of an ad hoc brigade in the Merjayoun area, named Berryforce, that included infantry, pioneers, cavalry and artillery. Australian artillery delayed the Vichy French advance and Berryman ordered a series of counterattacks that lost heavily but slowly regained the initiative.

Jumbo Wilson had planned to transfer command of the campaign to Lavarack when the advance reached Beirut and Damascus. But as his campaign had gone badly, Jumbo decided to let someone else sort out the mess. Lavarack took over the 1st Australian Corps and was given responsibility for the campaign. Tubby Allen, who had commanded the 16th Brigade in Libya and Greece, was promoted to major general to lead the 7th Division, which would now concentrate all its efforts on the coastal advance. Lavarack received reinforcements and Major General John Evetts of the 6th British Division arrived to look after the advance towards Damascus.

## Closing in on Damascus

In the advance to Damascus, Evetts was given an extra British brigade as well as the 2/3rd Australian Machine Gun Battalion and the 2/3rd Australian Infantry Battalion, which had been reformed after its ordeal in Greece. Normally the 2/3rd Infantry battalion had a strength of 800 men; it now numbered fewer than 400.

The 2/3rd Infantry Battalion was prominent in the attack on Damascus and a 90-man company, led by Captain Philip ('Punchy') Parbury, cut the road through the Barada Gorge to Beirut. Parbury intercepted and captured Vichy French troops, but exceeded his capabilities. He advised his superiors: 'A Company is astride Damascus–Beirut road at map reference 19831751. Water, rations and ammo almost exhausted. Enemy on high ground dominate this position from both sides of the road and at dawn position will become untenable. I intend to attack'. Fortunately another company of his battalion came to his assistance and they cleared the French defences.

Meanwhile, other troops had seized Damascus. Lieutenant Colonel Arthur Blackburn, VC, commanding officer of the 2/3rd Machine Gun Battalion, accepted the surrender on 21 June. Australians had also captured the ancient city in 1918 (refer to Chapter 8).

## *Victory at Damour*

Allen's 7th Division planned to conduct the main attack along the coast to take Damour. The 25th Brigade would hold Jezzine, the 21st Brigade would mount a frontal attack on Damour and the newly assigned 17th Brigade would sweep through the mountains to attack the city from the flank and rear. Brigadier Stan Savige had commanded the 17th Brigade in Libya and Greece, but after losses in Crete his brigade could muster only one battalion, so a pioneer battalion and the 2/3rd Battalion were added to it.

The attack began on the night of 5 July and after a four-day battle the Australians took the city. A captured French colonel said, 'Until I saw your infantry crossing the Damour River and fighting in the mountains, I believed that the Foreign Legion were the toughest troops in the world'. The Vichy French surrendered and an armistice was signed on 12 July. The Australians formed the majority of the Allied troops in the campaign and suffered the most casualties — 416 killed and 1,136 wounded. At the beginning of the campaign the Vichy French numbers roughly equalled those of the attackers; it had been a remarkable effort to defeat such a force in five weeks.

## *Watching over the Persian Gulf*

Britain had treaty arrangements with Iraq that allowed the use of airfields, but in March 1941 Iraqi nationalists deposed the pro-British regent. In May, British and Indian troops invaded Iraq and restored the regent. The Australian destroyer *Yarra* operated in Iraqi waterways at the head of the Persian Gulf to support the invasion.

After Germany invaded the Soviet Union in June 1941, Britain hoped to send supplies through Persia (Iran) to the Soviet Union. Britain also wanted to secure the Persian oilfields. When the Persians resisted requests to expel German advisers, the Soviet Union and Britain invaded on 25 August. *Yarra* and the Australian armed merchant cruiser *Kanimbla* helped secure the southern Persian ports.

*Kanimbla* led a daring attack to seize the port of Bandar Shapur and the eight enemy merchant vessels docked there. Some of *Kanimbla's* crew dressed as Arabs and sailed an Arab dhow (small boat) up the river approaches to clear the way for the small flotilla of assorted craft with Indian troops that successfully carried out the operation.

 The Australians were becoming multicultural. In the first eight months of 1941 they had fought Italians, Germans, Vichy French, the French Foreign Legion (including African troops), Iraqis and Persians. (They hadn't yet fought the Japanese, but would do so before the end of the year.) They had served alongside British, New Zealand, Greek, Free French and Indian troops.

## The Jitters Set in at Home

After the First World War the Australian Government decided to rely on the Singapore Strategy, by which Britain agreed to send its main fleet to Singapore in the event of war with Japan (refer to Chapter 10). The problem was that Britain would only be able to send the fleet if it wasn't under threat in Europe. So after the outbreak of war in September 1939, Prime Minister Menzies had been wary of sending troops overseas for fear of Japan and he only agreed to do so when Britain promised to help defend Australia if the threat materialised.

 Australia's security was affected by the course of the war in Europe, for if Britain were defeated by Germany, Japan would have a free hand in the Far East. The disastrous British campaigns in Greece, Crete and in northern Africa (refer to Chapter 12) in the first half of 1941, and the German invasion of Russia, caused Australian politicians and the public to look with anxiety at the growing evidence of Japan's ambitions.

### Recognising the Japanese threat

Germany's defeat of France gave Japan its opportunity and in September 1940 Japanese troops marched into French Indo-China. Britain, Australia, the Netherlands East Indies and the United States began planning how to deal with a Japanese attack. In December 1940 the Australian Government decided to deploy a brigade to Malaya to bolster the British forces there and to send Menzies to London to seek reinforcements for Malaya. Arriving in London in February 1941, Menzies took part in the decision to send troops to Greece, but was unable to persuade Churchill to reinforce Malaya.

 In February 1941 British and American military leaders met in Washington and agreed that in the event of war with Japan they would fight a 'holding war' in the Pacific and concentrate their forces on defeating Germany. This 'Beat Hitler First' strategy posed dangers to Australia. Increasingly nervous, Australia's political leaders decided to send additional forces to Malaya.

## Reinforcing Malaya

After the fall of France in mid-1940, the government formed two new infantry divisions, the 7th and the 8th. The 7th followed the 6th Division to Palestine, but as the threat from Japan developed, the 8th was retained in Australia. The division's 22nd Brigade went to Malaya in February 1941. Major General Henry Gordon Bennett, commander of the 8th Division, arrived at Singapore in August 1941, along with his headquarters and his 27th Brigade. His third brigade was retained at Darwin, although one of its battalions went to Rabaul in New Britain. Bennett's troops began jungle training in southern Malaya.

The British forces in Malaya and Singapore consisted mainly of troops from the British-Indian Army, and the air force included obsolescent aircraft, sent in the misguided belief that they would be adequate to deal with the Japanese air force. Churchill, however, agreed to send the modern battleship *Prince of Wales*, the battle cruiser *Repulse* and an aircraft carrier. Unfortunately, the aircraft carrier was damaged on a training cruise. The other two warships arrived at Singapore on 2 December.

## Changing our political leaders

Bob Menzies arrived back in Australia in May 1941 determined to improve the government's war management. But he also wanted to ensure that Australia's voice was heard in London and he thought that he was best suited to this task. While he had been away, however, some members of his own party doubted that he was showing sufficient leadership. Realising the party's mood, on 28 August Menzies resigned and Arthur Fadden, leader of the Country Party, took over as prime minister, but little else changed.

When the budget was presented in parliament two independents, who had previously supported the government, opposed the budget and Fadden resigned. The Labor Party came to power on 3 October 1941 with 51-year-old John Curtin as prime minister. Curtin had led the party since 1935 but had not previously served in government. Gaoled briefly for anti-conscription activities in the First World War, he had been editor of a union newspaper in Perth. His inexperienced government remained in power for the rest of the war.

## Kormoran sinks Sydney

During 1941 the Germans operated several converted merchant ships in the Pacific and Indian Oceans, laying mines and attacking Allied merchantmen. On 19 November, the cruiser *Sydney* was sailing off the Western Australian coast when she sighted a merchant ship that claimed to be a Dutch vessel. Under the command of Captain John Burnett, *Sydney* imprudently approached the ship, asking it to 'Show your secret sign'. The ship was the German raider *Kormoran,* which immediately opened fire on *Sydney*, causing tremendous damage. *Sydney's* guns returned fire, crippling *Kormoran* and setting her afire. At nightfall *Kormoran's* crew abandoned ship. *Sydney* was last seen on fire on the horizon; it's now known that she sank with the loss of all 645 crew members. *Kormoran's* survivors were picked up by other ships or made their way to the Australian coast where they became prisoners of war.

The loss of *Sydney* was a reminder that although the main battles to this time were being fought in Europe, the Middle East and the Atlantic, Australia was involved in a global conflict and was not immune from attack. The events after Japan entered the war in December 1941 were to drive home this point.

# Chapter 12

# Defeating the Afrika Korps, 1941–42

### In This Chapter
▶ Escaping the clutches of the Afrika Korps
▶ Thwarting Rommel at Tobruk
▶ Sending forces home to deal with the Japanese
▶ Halting the panzers at Tel el Eisa
▶ Helping Monty win at El Alamein

The North Africa campaign holds a curiously romantic place in the history of the Second World War. With no large cities, battles could be fought without causing widespread civilian misery. The desert's open spaces allowed the forces to manoeuvre, thus avoiding the murderous battles of attrition fought elsewhere. The German Africa Corps — the Deutsches Afrika Korps — that played the central role was largely free of the fanatical Waffen-SS troops and Gestapo found in German forces elsewhere, and it fought an honourable war. And the campaigns were dominated by charismatic military commanders such Germany's Erwin Rommel and Britain's Bernard Montgomery. Despite these characteristics, the campaigns were still hard-fought, bloody and costly.

The war in North Africa was governed by the demands of supply and transport. The British forces were supplied from the Nile Delta. As the British advanced across North Africa, the journey by their supply trucks along the single road grew longer as the advancing troops moved farther west. Similarly, the Axis (German and Italian) forces' supplies needed to be transported east from Tripoli in Libya. Fighting was easier when conducted closer to the supply base.

Hampered by the supply problem, for two years the opposing armies chased each other back and forth across North Africa. Finally, in November 1942 a British army under Montgomery won the battle of El Alamein and pursued the Axis army across North Africa to Tunisia.

Australians were involved in most campaigns up to and including El Alamein. I describe Australia's part in the first campaign in Chapter 10. In this chapter I tell the story of the 9th Division's battles with the Afrika Korps, including the siege of Tobruk in 1941, the defensive battles at El Alamein in July 1942, and the victory at El Alamein in October–November 1942.

# The Benghazi Handicap: Australia's Part in the Retreat

After crushing the Italian Army in Cyrenaica (eastern Libya) in January 1941 (see Chapter 10), General Sir Archibald Wavell, British Commander-in-Chief Middle East, prepared to send the 6th and 7th Australian Divisions to Greece. Wavell believed that if the Germans reinforced the Italians in Libya it would be months before the enemy could be ready for an offensive, so he defended Cyrenaica with the 2nd Armoured Division (minus one of its two armoured brigades, which had gone to Greece) and the 9th Australian Division, the least trained of the three Australian divisions in the Middle East.

Wavell had underestimated his foe. On 15 February the first troops of the Afrika Korps began to arrive in Tripoli. The Italian dictator, Mussolini, put his forces under German command, and Hitler selected Lieutenant General Erwin Rommel, who had led a panzer (tank) division in France with great daring and enterprise, for the task. Rommel immediately began probing the British positions at El Aghelia and discovered that they were held weakly. Hitler ordered Rommel not to attack but Rommel typically ignored the order and, although his main forces had still not arrived, began an offensive.

## Deploying to the desert

Wavell had hoped the 9th Division would have time to complete its training and equipping in the desert. The division's most experienced troops — the 18th and 25th Brigades, which had been part of the division from its formation in Britain a year earlier — had been transferred to the 7th Division and designated to go to Greece. The remaining brigades, the 20th, 24th and 26th, were the least trained and most poorly equipped of all the Australian brigades in the Middle East.

The division was without many essential weapons such as light machine-guns, mortars and anti-tank guns, and was short of transport and signals equipment. Because its artillery regiments lacked guns and its cavalry lacked armoured vehicles, only the infantry brigades and support units went to Cyrenaica. The troops arrived progressively and by mid-March Brigadier John Murray's 20th Brigade and Brigadier Ray Tovell's 26th Brigade were deployed south of Benghazi (refer to Figure 12-1). Brigadier Arthur Godfrey's 24th Brigade had not yet reached Tobruk.

One thing the 9th Division did have was capable leadership. Major General Leslie Morshead, who had earlier led the 18th Brigade from its formation in late 1939, was in command of the division as it deployed. Originally a school teacher, he had led a battalion in the First World War and later became a shipping executive. A strong disciplinarian, he was known to his men as 'Ming the Merciless' after a character in the 1930s Flash Gordon comics.

## *Falling back to Tobruk*

Towards the end of March 1941 Rommel attacked the British forces at El Aghelia and brushed aside the British tanks, which were no match for the Mark III and Mark IV panzers. While some of Rommel's forces swept across the desert towards Mechili, others advanced along the coast to meet the Australians south of Benghazi. Belatedly, Hitler approved Rommel's offensive.

On 4 April the Germans attacked the Australians along the coast with tanks and motorised infantry. The Diggers conducted a fighting withdrawal and then crammed into trucks to escape along the coast road. During the retreat, wryly called the 'Benghazi Handicap', the Germans captured two British generals. Despite harassment from German troops, tanks and planes, Morshead skilfully brought his two brigades back to Tobruk.

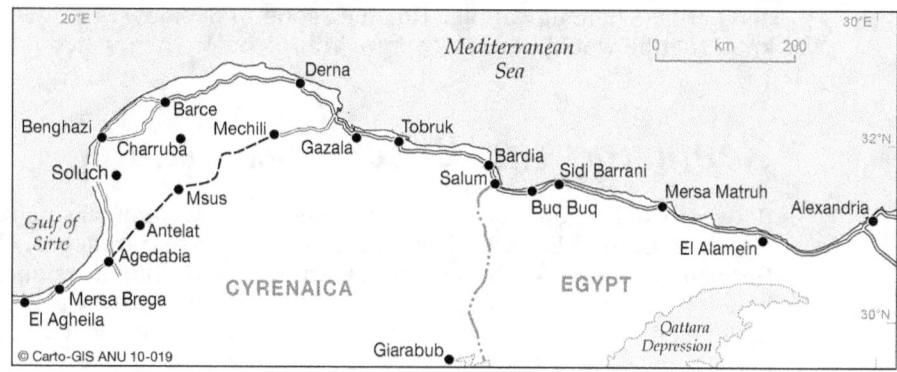

**Figure 12-1:** Cyrenaica and northern Egypt.

Meanwhile, German tanks dispersed the badly depleted 2nd Armoured Division and reached Mechili. Gunners of the 2/3rd Australian Anti-Tank Regiment helped defend Mechili while the other troops escaped, but their 2-pounder anti-tank guns couldn't hurt the panzers. By the time the battle ceased on 8 April the 2/3rd had lost 100, killed, wounded and captured.

## Surviving the Siege of Tobruk

While the main body of the 9th Division was withdrawing, its third brigade, the 24th, arrived at Tobruk, a port city the Australians had first captured from the Italians in January. There it was joined by Brigadier George Wootten's 18th Brigade, detached from the 7th Division, which, in the emergency, Wavell decided not to send to Greece. Major General John Lavarack of the 7th Division took command of the Tobruk defences, which included Morshead's 9th Division, some British artillery and a few British tanks.

With German troops approaching, the Australians laboured to improve the defences that stretched for 48 kilometres around the port in an arc. The defensive line included trenches, strong points, barbed wire, minefields and an anti-tank ditch. The 9th Division's brigades held the perimeter, while the 18th Brigade was kept centrally in reserve, and the artillery prepared to deal with the German tanks.

Morshead was adamant: 'We'll have no Dunkirk here [the British evacuation from a French port the previous year]. If we have to get out of here it will be down a road we have cleared for ourselves in battle, but there will be no surrender and no retreat'.

The Afrika Korps initially bypassed Tobruk and chased the remaining British units back to the Egyptian border, but Rommel feared to continue the advance while the 9th Division remained on his flank, ready to sally forth and cut his communications. Rommel, soon to be known as the 'Desert Fox', knew that he would have to capture Tobruk before he pushed into Egypt.

## Repulsing the Desert Fox's tanks

Between Good Friday, 11 April, and Easter Sunday, Rommel's panzers attacked the 20th Brigade. The Diggers stayed in their trenches, allowed the German tanks to pass through, and then dealt with the following German infantry. As the tanks pushed deeper, they were stopped by artillery and anti-tank fire. The Germans withdrew in disorder, having lost 17 tanks and more than 400 infantry.

A captured German officer struggled to explain how he found himself a prisoner: 'I cannot understand you Australians. In Poland, France and Belgium once the tanks got through the soldiers took it for granted they were beaten. But you are like demons. The tanks break through and your infantry keeps fighting'.

Lavarack returned to Egypt and Morshead took command of the whole fortress. After several more attacks Rommel's troops captured a salient, five kilometres deep, but could advance no further. He remarked on the courage of the Australian infantry: 'The enemy fought with remarkable tenacity. Even their wounded went on defending themselves with small arms fire and stayed in the fight to their last breath'.

To retain the initiative, during May Morshead ordered a series of counterattacks to recapture perimeter posts or to seize enemy vantage points. The attacks, which were repeated in August, were unsuccessful and because of the heavy casualties were perhaps unwise, but they showed Morshead's determination.

## *Patrolling the perimeter*

Repulsed with heavy losses, Rommel now resorted to a siege. The Australian positions in the desert were exposed to constant artillery fire, while dive-bombers attacked the port and any visible guns or transport. German aircraft dominated the skies and delivered air raids on every day except one of Morshead's period in command. The Australians didn't sit passively in their dugout and trenches, but maintained an active patrolling program, sometimes seeking to capture prisoners to obtain information about enemy intentions, and other times raiding the German and Italian lines to prevent Rommel from withdrawing troops that could be used on the Egyptian frontier.

Conditions were arduous in the extreme. In the heat of the North Africa summer the soldiers endured dust, flies and vermin. Water was in short supply and food was poor. During the day the soldiers hid in their dugouts and trenches to avoid enemy air attacks, while at night they ventured into no-man's land on reconnaissance and fighting patrols, or to improve their defences. For the first time since Gallipoli Australian soldiers spent month after month living in an area where they were under constant threat of attack.

### Rats of Tobruk

Failing to overcome the garrison, the Germans began a propaganda campaign, dropping leaflets to tell the Diggers that they couldn't escape and ought to surrender. A propaganda broadcaster from Germany, known by the British as Lord Haw Haw, sneered at the defenders as the 'poor desert rats of Tobruk', probably because of their use of tunnels for shelter. The propaganda backfired. When Radio Berlin described the Australians as 'caught like rats in a trap', they wryly called themselves 'the Rats of Tobruk'. The famous war correspondent Chester Wilmot thought that Berlin Radio had 'made a fatal mistake in trying to gibe and scare the Australian soldier into surrender. The longer the odds Lord Haw Haw offered against the Digger's chance of getting out, the more heavily the Digger backed himself'. The Australians even struck their own unofficial medal bearing the likeness of a rat, made of aluminium from a German bomber shot down by the Rats. After the war the survivors formed the Rats of Tobruk Association.

## *Running the gauntlet — our ships sustain the garrison*

The Tobruk garrison was sustained by the supplies, ammunition and fuel brought in by the ships of the so-called Tobruk Ferry. The ships departed Alexandria in the morning, made the final run into Tobruk at night, unloaded the supplies and departed, having taken wounded troops onboard, before dawn, for the 14-hour return journey. Throughout, they came under ferocious attack from German aircraft.

The Australian ships involved were the destroyers *Napier*, *Nestor*, *Nizam*, *Stuart*, *Vendetta*, *Voyager* and *Waterhen*, and the sloops *Parramatta* and *Yarra*, although not all of them operated all the time:

- In April dive-bombers severely damaged the British hospital ship *Vita*. *Waterhen* tried to tow her, but when that proved impossible, 437 patients and 53 medical staff were transferred to *Waterhen* by candlelight.

- On 29 July German dive-bombers attacked *Waterhen* and she sunk the next day. The British destroyer *Defender* took off her crew, but was herself sunk less than a fortnight later. *Vendetta* rescued the crew and the 275 troops aboard.

- *Parramatta* was sunk on 27 November with the loss of 147 lives.

Over a six-month period the Australian destroyers made a total of 139 runs, with *Vendetta* completing the most passages, 39. The ships were constantly damaged and repaired. They were 'literally falling to bits', said Admiral Cunningham, 'and were only kept running by the sheer grit and determination of the men of the engineering departments'.

## Demanding relief — Blamey becomes the most hated man in the Middle East

As the siege approached its fourth month General Sir Thomas Blamey, commander of the Australian army in the Middle East, became concerned that his troops were being worn out by their ordeal. He thought that the British Commander-in-Chief, General Sir Claude Auchinleck, who had replaced Wavell, wanted to leave the Australians at Tobruk, even though they were exhausted, so that fresh British troops could be used for an offensive.

A fierce dispute ensued between Blamey and Auchinleck, who feared troops would be lost in the journeys to and from Tobruk. Winston Churchill appealed to the Australian Government, which supported Blamey. At a high-level meeting Auchinleck stated that Tobruk couldn't be relieved. 'Gentlemen', said Blamey, 'I think you don't understand the position. If I were a French or an American commander making this demand what would you say about it?' 'But you're not', replied Auchinleck. 'That is where you are wrong', said Blamey. 'Australia is an independent nation. She came into the war under certain definite agreements. Now, gentlemen, in the name of my Government, I demand the relief of these troops.' Auchinleck shrugged and said: 'Well, if that's the way you put it, we have no alternative'. Blamey added later that he was now 'the most hated man in the Middle East'.

British and Polish troops relieved the garrison, and by the end of October only one Australian battalion remained, and that was because the ship sent to remove it was sunk approaching Tobruk. In the campaign the 9th Division had suffered 3,349 casualties, including 788 killed. By insisting on its relief Blamey ensured that the division would be ready for its next campaign.

## Scaling Down Australia's Forces in the Middle East

Morshead was a tough taskmaster. After almost eight months in combat he decided that his troops needed intensive training, which they began in Syria. Meanwhile, a counteroffensive by the British Eighth Army, in conjunction with a breakout by the Tobruk garrison, forced Rommel out of Cyrenaica. But as Rommel withdrew, the whole strategic situation changed when Japan entered the war by attacking Pearl Harbour on 7 December 1941.

Many Australian ships had already headed home for refit and the remainder now left the Mediterranean. Churchill suggested that the 1st Australian Corps, including the 6th and 7th Divisions, be transferred to the Far East and they began embarking at the end of January 1942. In March Blamey was recalled and Morshead took over as commander of the remaining Australians, including his 9th Division, still training in Syria. Australia's war effort was now concentrated in the Pacific (see chapters 14 to 17), but the 9th Division was to still play an heroic role in the desert campaign.

## Bitter Battles: Preventing the Germans from Reaching the Nile

Rommel received reinforcements and, ever-daring, in January 1942 mounted a counterattack that forced the British back to Gazala, just west of Tobruk. By May he had gathered sufficient strength for a major offensive. The battle swirled around Gazala for almost a month, but Rommel was the master of mobile warfare. His force, now called Panzer Army Africa, chased the British back to Egypt, while a South African division tried to emulate the Australian effort by holding Tobruk and was overwhelmed in a day.

While panicking British staff officers in Cairo burnt their papers, fearing they would fall into German hands, Auchinleck took personal control of the Eighth Army at El Alamein, an insignificant railway station just 100 kilometres west of Alexandria. He planned to defend a line that ran south from the coast for 64 kilometres to the Qattara Depression, an area that was impassable to vehicles (refer to Figure 12-2). At Alamein, Auchinleck fought a fine defensive battle, and Rommel's exhausted forces went on the defensive, digging in and laying minefields.

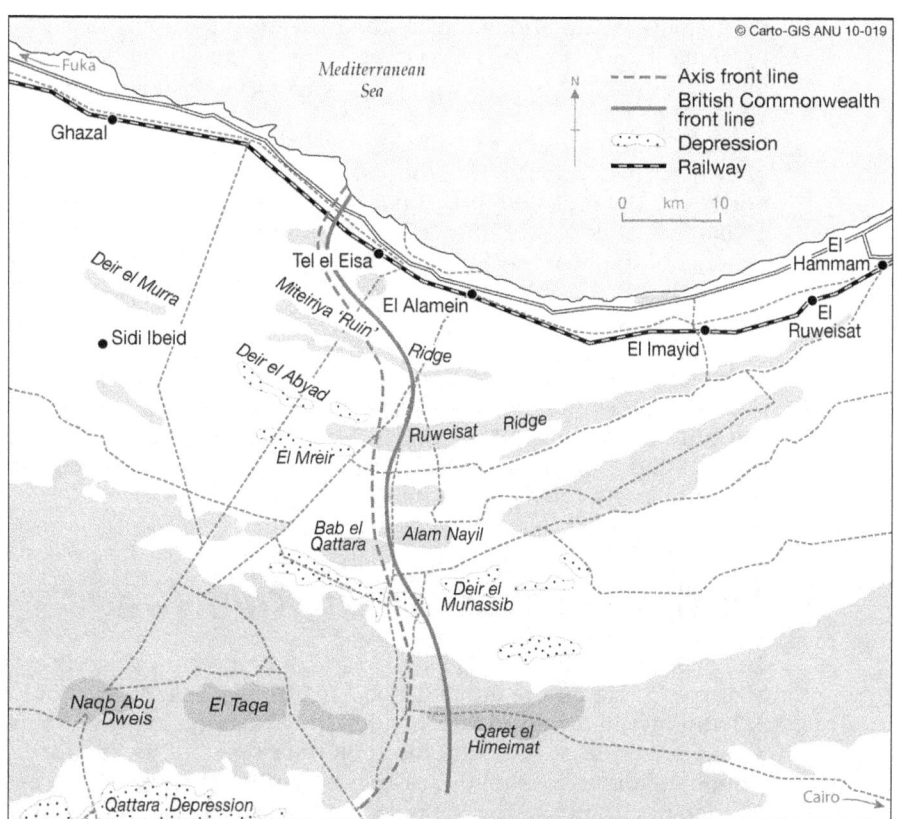

**Figure 12-2:** El Alamein area.

The 9th Division, complete, rested and retrained, was recalled from Syria. As his troops arrived Morshead received orders to break his division into smaller groups to be thrown into the battle. Morshead believed this was against the Australian Government's instructions to keep his force together. When Auchinleck demanded a brigade, Morshead refused, stating that it would fight with the rest of the division. In the emergency, Morshead eventually comprised and made the brigade available, but he had made an important point about the independence of Australian forces.

## Keeping the Germans off-balance at Tel el Eisa

The 26th Australian Brigade successfully seized part of Tel el Eisa Ridge, held by an Italian division, in a silent night attack on 10 July. The infantry of Lieutenant Colonel 'Tack' Hammer's 2/48th Battalion caught some of the Italians in bed and led away their commander in his brightly coloured pyjamas. The Australians also captured Rommel's main signals interception unit, thus denying this vital intelligence source to the Germans.

Rommel, newly promoted to field marshal, was just mounting a major offensive further south. He stopped his offensive and rushed his panzers north. For the first time, the Australians had the support of their full divisional artillery and they held off Rommel's tanks, destroying 18 of them, in some of the heaviest fighting the Australians ever experienced. After six days of battle the 9th Division had inflicted more than 2,000 casualties and had taken 3,708 prisoners.

To keep the Germans off-balance, Auchinleck now planned to break through the Axis line with a major series of coordinated attacks. The 26th Brigade was still holding part of the Tel el Eisa Ridge. On 22 July it tried to capture the remainder of the ridge but suffered more than 300 casualties and had to withdraw to its original positions.

## Losing a battalion at Ruin Ridge

As part of Auchinleck's offensive, on 17 July the 24th Brigade attacked Miteiriya Ridge on the 9th Division's southern flank. As part of the attack the 2/28th Battalion tried to take a subsidiary position known as Ruin Ridge. On its second attempt the battalion took the ridge, but its supporting vehicles were halted in a minefield. A British brigade was supposed to assist but was unable to do so. The tanks of the British 1st Armoured Division refused to advance until the gaps in the minefields were cleared. German panzers surrounded the Australian battalion, which surrendered on 27 July. In one of the 9th Division's darkest days the 2/28th Battalion lost 65 men killed and wounded and 489 missing or captured. The British 1st Armoured lost just three tanks.

The first battle of El Alamein was over. Rommel had been stopped, but the Commonwealth forces would need some retraining and reorganising before they would be ready to turn the tables on the Desert Fox.

## Australian airmen patrol in the desert

While Australian troops were making their presence felt on the ground in North Africa, Australian airmen were battling in the skies above the desert as well. The RAAF squadrons did not operate separately, but were an integral part of the British air force structure.

## Chapter 12: Defeating the Afrika Korps, 1941–42

HISTORICAL TRIVIA

### A 'Killer' named Caldwell

Australian airmen also served in British squadrons, gaining an excellent reputation for aggressive combat flying. One such pilot was Clive Caldwell, who served with the Royal Air Force's No. 250 Squadron.

A superb pilot, Caldwell became an excellent marksman thanks to a training technique he developed. By practice firing at the shadow of his aircraft as it flew across the desert, he became an expert at aiming in front of an aircraft to allow for its speed of movement.

In one remarkable action over Cyrenaica in December 1941 'Killer' Caldwell accounted for five enemy aircraft in 18 seconds of air combat. By the time he left the Middle East in mid-1942 he had 19 kills.

Caldwell was transferred to the Pacific Theatre to command an RAAF Spitfire wing against the Japanese. His total of kills rose to 28 and a half (he shared a kill with another pilot). He was Australia's leading air ace of the war.

No. 3 Squadron of the Royal Australian Air Force (RAAF) saw the most action. Equipped with Gloster Gladiator biplanes, No. 3 supported the 6th Australian Division during the first Cyrenaica campaign, fighting against the Italian air force.

When Rommel and the Afrika Korps arrived in North Africa in March 1941 they were joined by Luftwaffe squadrons that soon dominated the skies over the desert, but now with Hurricane fighters No. 3 Squadron ably supported the British army as it retreated into Egypt. During mid-1941, the RAAF squadron was re-equipped with Tomahawk fighters, and it then supported the Australian army in the Syrian campaign (see Chapter 11).

No. 3 Squadron returned to the Western Desert in December 1941 where, along with the RAAF's No. 450 Squadron (Desert Harassers), it was re-equipped with Kittyhawk fighters. During 1942 the Desert Air Force gained air control and thereafter provided strong support to the Commonwealth forces as they advanced from Egypt to Tunisia. Several RAAF bomber squadrons also operated in the Mediterranean on anti-submarine and maritime strike duties.

## *Winning at El Alamein*

During August 1942, General Sir Harold Alexander became Commander-in Chief in the Middle East and Lieutenant General Bernard Montgomery took over the Eighth Army in the field. A careful but confident commander, described as 'quick as a ferret, and about as likeable', Montgomery set about revitalising the army. Warned by intelligence reports that Rommel was going to attack the Alam Halfa Ridge in the southern part of the defensive line, Monty was ready, and although Rommel's tanks thrust into the British line they were forced to withdraw. The battle weakened Rommel's forces, raised British morale and gave Montgomery time to retrain the Eighth Army.

During the battle, the 20th Australian Brigade, led by Brigadier Victor Windeyer, who had commanded a battalion at Tobruk, mounted a diversionary attack in the north, known as Operation Bulimba. The Australians captured their objectives but their tank support wasn't coordinated properly and they had to withdraw.

## Plans and preparations

Montgomery prepared for the coming battle with meticulous attention to detail. Fresh units arrived, his armoured units were equipped with new American Sherman tanks, and he tried to improve the cooperation between tanks and infantry. By the time he was ready to strike, the Eighth Army had 220,000 men and 1,100 tanks, compared with Rommel's 115,000 men and 559 tanks. Montgomery's army was near to its supply base in the Nile Delta, while Rommel's supply route across the Mediterranean and along the coast road was attacked mercilessly by British aircraft.

Montgomery's Eighth Army, very much a Commonwealth and Imperial force, consisted of:

- 30th Corps, closest to the coast. In order from the north, it consisted of the 9th Australian, 51st Highland, 2nd New Zealand, 1st South African and 4th Indian Divisions.
- 13th Corps, at the south of the line. It included the 44th British and 7th Armoured Divisions.
- 10th Corps, held in reserve. It consisted of the 1st and 10th Armoured Divisions.

Montgomery's original plan didn't envisage the Australians playing a greater role than any of his other infantry divisions. On the night of 23 October the 9th Australian, the 51st Highland, the 2nd New Zealand and the 1st South African Divisions would attack side by side across a 12-kilometre front in the northern sector, force their way through the German minefield, and clear a corridor for the advance of the two armoured divisions of the 10th Corps. After that, the British tanks would hold off the German tanks while the British infantry destroyed the Axis infantry in what Montgomery called 'crumbling operations' or the 'dogfight'.

## Crossing the start line

Supported by a massive artillery barrage, on the first day of the attack the infantry achieved about 80 per cent of their objectives, but the Axis defences were stronger than expected and the armoured thrust didn't begin until the night of 24 October. Then Montgomery's plan began to unravel as the tanks came up against strong German and Italian resistance.

Fighting continued through 25 October, but the crumbling operations were proving costly, and the infantry divisions took considerable casualties. The 20th and 26th Australian Brigades had originally attacked the Axis line some four kilometres inland from the coast, and as they pushed through the enemy line they left a large pocket of enemy defences to the north of their positions. The exposed location of the brigades, however, offered the possibility of changing the direction of the attack. Seeking to surprise the enemy, Montgomery ordered the 9th Division to attack northwards towards the coast, while the 1st Armoured Division continued the offensive to the west along the original axis.

The new attacks began on the night of 25 October. The tanks failed to make progress, but supported by a huge concentration of artillery, Brigadier David Whitehead's 26th Brigade succeeded brilliantly. The Australian attack had a crucial effect on the final outcome of the battle. Thwarted elsewhere, Montgomery turned to the Australians to maintain the momentum, planning to launch his armoured forces once the Australians had cleared the way.

## Drawing in the German reserves

In the north the British forces faced constant attacks by German tanks, supported by artillery and infantry, but the Australian thrust worried Rommel. If the Australians broke through to the coast they would get behind his main defences and cut off the 164th German Division. He therefore launched the 90th Light Division against the exposed left flank of the Australians and ordered the 21st Panzer Division north from the southern front.

Despite the German counterattacks, on the night of 28 October the 20th Brigade struck north, supported by the fire of 360 guns. The 2/13th Battalion had been fighting for five days and nights and its companies had been reduced from 120 to barely 35 men, but again the Australians seized important German positions. Morshead kept up the pressure and passed the tired, understrength 26th Brigade through the 20th Brigade for another attack on the night of 30 October.

The next Australian attack was overambitious. Important ground was taken, but casualties were heavy. By the following night the 2/48th Battalion was down to 41 men, having begun the battle on 23 October with 30 officers and 656 other ranks. The brigade then consolidated in an area known as 'the saucer' as it held off determined German counterattacks with tanks.

That night Morshead ordered Brigadier Arthur Godfrey's 24th Brigade to relieve the 26th Brigade. Relief-in-place, at night, in the face of the enemy is one of the hardest military operations, but when dawn came fresh battalions were waiting to meet the German assault. That day the full might of the Afrika Korps hit the brigade. Godfrey was killed but the position held.

## Breaking through the line

The Australians had achieved their mission. They had drawn onto themselves the full force of the German reserves of tanks and mechanised infantry. Rommel had expended valuable fuel and tanks against the Australians. The way was clear for the major British armoured offensive, which Montgomery launched further south. Within days the British had broken through and the Germans and Italians were in retreat.

On 4 November, with victory assured, Montgomery went straight to Morshead's headquarters to thank him. Later Montgomery wrote: 'We could not have won the battle in 12 days without the magnificent Australian division'. When another British general congratulated the general known as 'Ming the Merciless' by his troops, Morshead's reply was a classic understatement. 'Thank you, General. The boys were interested.'

Total Eighth Army casualties were 13,650. The 9th Division alone accounted for 2,694. Forming perhaps one-tenth of the attacking force, the Australians suffered 22 per cent of the casualties.

## Heading home

Alamein was the beginning of the end of the war in North Africa. While the 9th Division played the crucial role, the hard fighting of the other divisions shouldn't be underplayed. Nonetheless, having incurred almost 6,000 casualties since July the division was in no shape to continue the advance. During the year, Blamey, now Commander-in-Chief in Australia, and General Douglas MacArthur, an American general commanding all the Allied forces in the Southwest Pacific Area, had pressed Prime Minister Curtin for the return of the division. Curtin asked Churchill to release the division from the Middle East and the British Prime Minister eventually agreed. The 9th Division had fought its last battle in North Africa. In February 1943 it arrived back in Australia.

# Chapter 13

# Our Airmen in Europe, 1939–45

*In This Chapter*
- Establishing the Royal Australian Air Force
- Joining the Empire's air force
- Defending Britain on land and at sea
- Hammering Germany in the strategic air offensive

The story of the Royal Australian Air Force (RAAF) in the Second World War's European Theatre is one of immense achievement, bravery and sacrifice, but a story that is often overlooked and has elements of disappointment. Even though the RAAF underwent a massive expansion during the war, increasing from a strength of about 3,500 officers and airmen in 1939 to more than 182,000 men and women in August 1944, most of those who served in Europe and the Middle East did so as part of British Royal Air Force (RAF) squadrons, and there were no obvious Australian air operations. But while some Australians were disappointed at not being able to serve in distinctly Australian units, they served with distinction. Our airmen in Bomber Command in both RAF and RAAF squadrons played a major role in defeating Germany and suffered the highest rate of casualties of any Australian servicemen in the war.

While large numbers of Australian airmen were serving in Europe and the Middle East, Australia formed almost a separate air force to defend the homeland and to support the campaigns conducted by Australian and American forces in the Southwest Pacific Area after Japan entered the war in December 1941. The squadrons that served in the Pacific were an integral part of the operations in which Australian naval and army units were important contributors. I tell their story in chapters 14, 15 and 16.

In this chapter I begin by explaining how the RAAF was formed and why this led to the formation of two separate air forces during the Second World War. I then tell the story of the Australian squadrons that served in Europe and the Middle East between 1940 and 1945. Except for a few squadrons that supported the Australian Army's campaigns in the Middle East in 1941 and 1942 (refer to Chapter 12), these squadrons conducted operations that had no relationship to the main Australian military campaigns.

## An Air Force of Our Own

At the beginning of the First World War aircraft were used primarily for reconnaissance tasks; that is, to locate the enemy and to warn commanders of enemy movements. In response, each side developed fighters to attack the reconnaissance aircraft. Seeking to gain control of the air above the battlefield, fighters fought each other in battles known as *dogfights*, and the pilots who shot down five or more enemy aircraft were known as *aces*. Aircraft also bombed and strafed enemy troops and guns, either in the rear areas, as they moved up to the front-line, or in the trenches themselves, and in so doing they were an integral part of the land operations.

Gradually, however, some commanders began to realise that aircraft could influence the outcome of the war by activities far beyond the land battlefield. For example, German Zeppelins (air ships) attacked British cities in 1915, in an attempt to undermine British morale and to damage the production of *war materiel* (arms and war equipment). The Royal Naval Air Service retaliated by bombing the Zeppelin factories and bases in Germany. Bombing attacks on Germany, by aircraft from the British Army's Royal Flying Corps and by the Royal Naval Air Service, increased as the war continued. The concept of using aircraft to attack the enemy's economic ability to wage war, rather than to destroy its land or naval forces, is known as *strategic bombing*.

Since strategic bombing can be conducted separately from land or naval campaigns, some argued that the air services should be removed from control by the Army or Navy. The South African general and politician General Jan Smuts headed a committee that recommended to the British Government that because of its potential for the 'devastation of enemy lands and the destruction of industrial and populous centres on a vast scale', a new air service should be formed on a level with the Royal Navy and the Army. As a result, on 1 April 1918 the Royal Flying Corps and the Royal Naval Air Service amalgamated to form a new service — the Royal Air Force (RAF), under the control of the new Air Ministry.

In the First World War, Australian airmen served in the Australian Flying Corps, but some also served in the Royal Naval Air Service (refer to Chapter 9). Many generals, such as Sir John Monash, who commanded the Australian Corps in France in 1918, and Sir Cyril Brudenell White, the senior staff officer of the Anzac Corps for much of the war, saw the immense value of aircraft, and they believed that as aircraft provided an important supporting arm for land operations, they were best commanded by the Army.

## Forming the Royal Australian Air Force

After the war, Australian senior officers debated whether to follow the British lead and form a separate air force. The Australian Prime Minister, Billy Hughes, supported the idea, but Navy and Army officers were concerned that if a separate air force were to be created, there would be no guarantee that aircraft would be available to support their operations. They preferred to retain separate air services, but as Australia couldn't afford two air forces they accepted the argument for a single air force, although they couldn't agree on who should control it. The government therefore formed an Air Council that included the Minister for Defence and the heads of the Navy and Army to provide high-level direction, while a subordinate Air Board, comprising senior air force officers, provided for day-to-day administration and control. The Australian Air Force, soon to be granted the Royal prefix, was formally established on 31 March 1921.

The fledgling RAAF had plentiful aircraft, a gift of surplus war equipment from Britain, but just 151 personnel. Most of the officers had served in the Australian Flying Corps but some had been in the Royal Naval Air Service. The first Chief of the Air Staff, Wing Commander Richard Williams, had served as a lieutenant colonel in the Australian Flying Corps in the Middle East. His deputy, Wing Commander Stanley Goble, had been a pilot in the Royal Naval Air Service until it became part of the RAF. These two officers ran the RAAF until the Second World War, with Williams serving as Chief of the Air Staff for 14½ years and Goble for 4½ years.

## Struggling for survival

The early leaders of the RAAF faced great challenges. As the original aircraft became obsolete they needed to be replaced, bases needed to be established around Australia, training schools needed to be formed, and the new service had to fight for status and recognition from the other two longer-established services. Eventually the Air Council was abolished and the Air Board ran the RAAF, just as the Naval and Military Boards ran their services. With the Great Depression, beginning in 1929, the Navy and Army suggested that they might dismember the RAAF and split it between them.

The RAAF didn't begin to grow until the mid-1930s when the government began to spend more money on defence. The problem was how to obtain aircraft. The British Government pressured Australia to purchase British aircraft, even though many aircraft being manufactured in the United States were more capable. Another alternative was to build aircraft in Australia, but that would be expensive, with no guarantee of producing better aircraft. Nonetheless, the Commonwealth Aircraft Corporation was formed to construct the American-designed Wirraway trainer. As war approached neither Britain nor the United States were willing to give Australia high priority for aircraft delivery.

In 1935 the permanent air force had a strength of less than 1,000; on the outbreak of war in 1939 it had grown to 310 officers and 3,179 airmen. The RAAF had 12 squadrons and 246 aircraft, but many were obsolete, with the most modern aircraft being 54 biplane Hawker Demon fighter-bombers, 21 Seagull amphibians and 82 Avro Anson bombers. Despite the efforts in the late 1930s, the RAAF was still very small and wasn't ready for war.

# A Last Call of Empire: The Empire Air Training Scheme

Soon after the outbreak of war in September 1939 the Australian Government offered to form an air expeditionary force of four bomber and two fighter squadrons to serve overseas. The following month, however, Australia agreed to join a scheme whereby the resources of Australia, Britain, Canada and New Zealand would be pooled to train 50,000 aircrew per year, who would then serve in the RAF as part of a 'unified Empire force'. Britain could train only 22,000 aircrew per year, so the remainder would come from the dominions. In effect, Britain would contribute the aircraft and the dominions the men. Canada would provide 56 per cent of the dominion allocation, Australia 36 per cent and New Zealand 8 per cent.

The details of the Empire Air Training Scheme (EATS), as it was known, were thrashed out at a conference in Ottawa in November–December 1939. About half of the Australians would be trained at home. Others would undertake elementary training in Australia and then complete their post-elementary training in Canada. The EATS — 'a last call of empire', as the historian John McCarthy called it — was a massive undertaking, and the RAAF, which had previously graduated about 50 pilots annually, now needed to train 10,478 aircrew a year for three years.

## Losing our identity

Under the initial EATS proposal the aircrew would all serve in the RAF, but Australia wanted the graduates to be associated with their respective dominions. Eventually Britain agreed that 18 RAF squadrons (allocated numbers 450 to 467) would be designated as Australian, and that they would formally become RAAF squadrons when the majority of their members were Australians. This arrangement was formalised under Article XV of the EATS agreement, and the squadrons formed by it were known as Article XV squadrons.

Despite these high ideals, in practice the Australians lost a large measure of national identity:

- Many of the ground staff in the squadrons were provided by the RAF, so it was hard for a squadron to reach a point where the majority of its personnel were from Australia.

- The British Air Ministry made little attempt to post Australian aircrew to Australian squadrons, while at the same time it was quite happy to send Australian aircrew to RAF squadrons, even when Article XV squadrons were understaffed with Australians. In January 1945, 1,453 Australian aircrew were serving in Article XV RAAF squadrons, forming 66 per cent of the squadrons' aircrew. By comparison, 2,621 Australian aircrew were serving in RAF squadrons.

- Only two Article XV squadrons, Nos 451 and 453, both fighter squadrons, ever achieved 100 per cent Australian aircrew staffing.

- Sometimes British officers were appointed to command RAAF squadrons, even though better-qualified Australians were available.

- When the Australian Air Board stated that it preferred its squadrons to be given general reconnaissance or bomber roles, the RAF replied that it alone would decide the roles.

- The Australian Government had absolutely no influence over how or where the Australian squadrons were used.

Many of the young EATS graduates who served in RAAF or RAF squadrons were not concerned by this matter of identity. As part of a bomber crew, the pilots, flight engineers, navigators, bomb aimers, wireless operators and gunners developed a camaraderie that transcended their place of origin. They all felt themselves to be part of the Empire. But from a wider perspective, their achievements, bravery and sacrifice could easily be overlooked. Further, few RAAF officers were able to gain experience in higher command positions that would have been valuable in the Pacific and in the post-war air force.

Apart from the EATS graduates, many other Australians served as members of the RAF. Before the war RAAF officers were seconded to the RAF and some transferred to the RAF where there were greater opportunities. Others travelled separately to Britain to join the RAF, or were in Britain at the beginning of the war and joined the RAF. In late 1939 about 450 Australians were in the RAF, and during the war at least half a dozen rose to high rank.

## The tools of trade

Australian airmen flew a wide variety of aircraft; some of the main ones are listed here:

**Avro Lancaster.** An excellent four-engine British heavy bomber, introduced into service late in 1941, with a crew of seven.

**Bristol Beaufighter.** A robust twin-engine British fighter-bomber used for maritime strike with a crew of two.

**Curtiss P-40 Kittyhawk.** A robust single-seat American fighter and fighter-bomber.

**De Haviland Mosquito.** A fast twin-engine British fighter-bomber and reconnaissance aircraft, with a crew of two.

**Handley Page Halifax.** A four-engine heavy bomber, introduced into service in 1940 with a crew of seven.

**Hawker Hurricane.** A capable British single-seat fighter, introduced into service in 1935.

**Short Stirling.** A four-engine British heavy bomber introduced into service in 1941, but withdrawn to secondary tasks in 1943. It had a crew of seven.

**Short Sunderland.** A four-engine British flying boat used for maritime patrol with a crew of up to 11.

**Supermarine Spitfire.** An excellent British single-seat fighter, introduced into service in 1938, but constantly improved and used throughout the war.

**Vickers Wellington.** A twin-engine British medium bomber introduced into service in 1938 with a crew of six.

## Training and serving around the world

The Empire Air Training Scheme gave thousands of young Australian men the opportunity to train and serve around the world. More than 10,000 aircrew completed their training in Canada (and some married Canadian women), while more than 600 Australians also completed their training in Rhodesia (now Zimbabwe).

A total of 17 (out of the allocated 18) Article XV squadrons were formed. In addition, two permanent RAAF squadrons also served in the Middle East–Europe theatre under British command. Of the 19 squadrons, seven were equipped with fighters, seven were bomber squadrons, two were light bomber squadrons and three were maritime patrol squadrons, although sometimes the roles changed. Some squadrons served in more than one theatre. In Britain, the Australian squadrons served as part of either Bomber, Coastal or Fighter Command. Table 13-1 lists the squadrons and where they were deployed.

## Table 13-1   RAAF Squadrons in Europe and the Middle East

### *Article XV squadrons*

| Squadron | Deployment |
| --- | --- |
| 450 Squadron | A ground-attack and fighter squadron, 450 Squadron was equipped with Kittyhawks. It served in North Africa in 1942–43 and in Italy in 1943–45. |
| 451 Squadron | An army cooperation squadron, it was equipped with Hawker Hurricanes and Westland Lysanders and served in the Middle East in 1941–43. Re-equipped with Spitfires, 451 Squadron served in France in 1944 and, based in Britain, operated over Germany in 1945. |
| 452 Squadron | A fighter squadron, 452 Squadron was equipped with Spitfires and served in Fighter Command in Britain in 1941–42. It redeployed to Australia and served in the Northern Territory in 1943–44, and at Morotai and Tarakan (Netherlands East Indies) in 1945. |
| 453 Squadron | A fighter squadron, it was equipped with obsolete Brewster Buffaloes and served in Malaya in 1941–42. Reformed and re-equipped with Spitfires, 453 Squadron served in Fighter Command in Britain in 1942–45. |
| 454 Squadron | A light bomber squadron, 454 Squadron was equipped with Blenheims and served in the Middle East in 1942. Re-equipped with Belmores, it operated as a maritime strike and ground support squadron in North Africa and Italy in 1943–45. |
| 455 Squadron | A bomber squadron, 455 Squadron was equipped with Hampden medium bombers and served in Britain in 1941–42. It transferred to Coastal Command as a torpedo bomber squadron, was later equipped with Beaufighters and served until 1945. |
| 456 Squadron | A night fighter squadron, 456 Squadron was equipped with Beaufighters and Mosquitoes and served in Fighter Command in Britain in 1941–45. |
| 457 Squadron | A fighter squadron, 457 Squadron was equipped with Spitfires and served in Britain in 1941–2. It returned to Australia and served in the Northern Territory in 1943–44, and at Morotai (Netherlands East Indies) and Labuan (Borneo) in 1945. |
| 458 Squadron | A bomber squadron equipped with Wellingtons, 458 Squadron served in Bomber Command in Britain in 1941. It then served as maritime strike squadron in the Mediterranean in 1942–45. |

*(continued)*

### Table 13-1 *(continued)*

| | ***Article XV squadrons*** |
|---|---|
| **Squadron** | **Deployment** |
| **459 Squadron** | A maritime patrol squadron equipped variously with Blenheims, Venturas, Wellingtons, Hudsons and Baltimores, 459 Squadron served in the Middle East in 1942–45. |
| **460 Squadron** | A bomber squadron equipped with Wellingtons and Lancasters, 460 Squadron served in Bomber Command in 1941–45 and flew the most bombing raids of any Australian squadron. Its 1,018 fatal casualties (589 Australians) were the highest of any of the Australian squadrons. |
| **461 Squadron** | A maritime patrol squadron, it was equipped with Sunderland flying boats and served in Coastal Command in Britain 1942–45. |
| **462 Squadron** | A bomber squadron, 462 Squadron was equipped with Halifaxes. It served in the Middle East in 1942–44, and in Bomber Command in Britain in 1944–45. |
| **463 Squadron** | A bomber squadron equipped with Lancasters, 463 Squadron served in Bomber Command in Britain in 1943–45. It had the highest percentage loss rate of any of the Australian bomber squadrons, losing 546 aircrew (225 Australians). |
| **464 Squadron** | A light bomber and then fighter bomber squadron, it was equipped with Venturas and Mosquitoes and served in Bomber and Fighter Commands in Britain in 1942–45. |
| **466 Squadron** | A bomber squadron, it was equipped with Wellingtons, Halifaxes and Liberators, and served in Bomber Command in 1942–45. |
| **467 Squadron** | A bomber squadron equipped with Lancasters, it served in Bomber Command in 1942–45. Its casualties, 760 (284 Australians), were the second highest of the Australian squadrons. |
| | ***Non-Article XV squadrons*** |
| **Squadron** | **Deployment** |
| **3 Squadron** | A permanent RAAF squadron, 3 Squadron was equipped with Gloster Gladiators, Tomahawks, Hurricanes, Kittyhawks and Mustangs. It served in army cooperation and fighter and fighter-bomber roles in the Middle East and Italy in 1940–45. |
| **10 Squadron** | A permanent RAAF maritime patrol squadron, it was equipped primarily with Sunderland flying boats and served in Coastal Command in Britain in 1940–45. |

The Australians in RAF squadrons operated in many parts of the world. For example, more than 1,000 Australians served in the Burma–India theatre of war in 60 RAF squadrons, flying fighters, bombers, transport and maritime patrol aircraft. Casualties were quite high and 242 died in the theatre. The most important categories in Europe and the Middle East were fighters, maritime patrol aircraft and bombers.

## Fighters and Flying Boats

The first Australians to serve in Europe were those already in the RAF. One of these Australians was Flying Officer Leslie Clisby, who fought in France before the British evacuation at Dunkirk in May 1940, tallied up 14 kills and became one of Australia's first aces. After shooting down an enemy bomber that landed in a field, Clisby landed nearby, chased one of the enemy crew that was making a run for it and brought him down with a rugby tackle. He was shot down and killed later that May.

### A few of the few: Our airmen in the Battle of Britain

In the second half of 1940 the RAF was engaged in a prolonged and famous campaign, known as the Battle of Britain, against German bombers, escorted by fighters, which attacked British radar installations, airfields, factories and cities. The British Prime Minister, Winston Churchill, praised the Battle of Britain pilots with the words: 'Never before in the field of human conflict has so much been owed by so many to so few'.

Thirty-five Australians served in the Battle of Britain, mainly pilots who had transferred from the RAAF before the war or Australians living in Britain who had enlisted on the outbreak of war. One such pilot was Pat Hughes, who transferred from the RAAF in 1937. Flying a Spitfire, between 8 July and 7 September 1940, when he was killed, he destroyed 15 enemy aircraft, making him the equal third-highest scoring ace in the Battle of Britain. He had insisted on wearing his worn-out dark blue RAAF uniform to the end.

### Finding tasks for the fighters

No 452 Squadron was the first Australian fighter squadron formed under the Article XV arrangements. Equipped with Spitfires, it began operations in May 1941. Based in England, 452 Squadron conducted sweeps over France and escorted bombers attacking Germany. As a new squadron, it was led by RAF officers, although its first commander, Squadron Leader Robert Bungey, was a regular RAAF officer who had transferred to the RAF and had already gained much combat experience. An Irish-born ace, Paddy Finucane, was also sent to the squadron because, as he was told, the Australians had 'never been in a scrap', and he was to teach them by example. He did so, adding ten more kills to his already impressive tally. Keith ('Bluey') Truscott, a well-known Victorian footballer, learned from Finucane and scored 16 kills. None of these three officers survived the war. In its first year, 452 Squadron became one of the most successful in Fighter Command, destroying 62 enemy aircraft.

Flying over France in 1941 and 1942, the fighter and fighter-bomber squadrons conducted two different forms of operations — Ramrod and Flying Circus. Ramrod operations aimed to destroy targets on the ground and were conducted by bombers alone or by cannon-firing fighters. In Flying Circus operations, aircraft attacked targets on the ground with the express purpose of enticing German fighters into aerial combat where they could be destroyed on the British fighters' terms.

Later in the war, 464 Squadron, equipped with Mosquito fighter bombers, conducted some interesting operations. In February 1944 it took part in a special precision bombing raid, Operation Jericho, on a Gestapo prison in Amiens to release members of the French Resistance held prisoner there. In July it raided German SS barracks in France and later attacked Gestapo headquarters in Denmark.

Nos 3 and 450 Squadrons, which served in North Africa, followed General Montgomery's Eighth Army to Italy in 1943. Equipped with Kittyhawks and, in the case of 3 Squadron, later with Mustangs, they supported the advance up the Italian peninsula, attacking bridges, enemy tanks, guns and shipping in the Adriatic Sea, until the German surrender in May 1945.

## *Searching the seas: Coastal Command protects the convoys*

When the war began, the nucleus of 10 Squadron, a permanent RAAF squadron, was in England preparing to take delivery of its Short Sunderland flying boats from an English factory. The squadron was brought to full strength and remained in Britain for the rest of the war, based initially at Pembroke in Wales, and later near Plymouth in south-east England.

As part of Coastal Command, the squadron's main task was to locate and destroy German submarines that were attacking merchant ships in the north-east Atlantic. Later its focus moved to the Bay of Biscay where it hunted submarines moving from bases in France to the Atlantic. The patrols were long and arduous, and although the squadron bombed and sunk only six submarines, it attacked many, forced them to submerge and generally interrupted their activities. In July 1942, 461 Squadron, also with Sunderlands, joined the operations and it too sank six submarines. Both squadrons conducted rescues at sea. The aircraft of Coastal Command played a vital role in the Battle of the Atlantic, in which German submarines attempted to destroy merchant ships bringing essential food and raw materials to sustain Britain's war effort.

Sometimes the Sunderlands found themselves in combat with German long-range maritime aircraft. In June 1943 eight Junkers Ju 88 (a capable twin engine torpedo bomber) attacked a Sunderland from 461 Squadron over the Bay of Biscay. With its bristling machine guns (it was known as the flying porcupine), the Sunderland destroyed three enemy aircraft, damaged another three and although damaged, limped back to England.

No. 455 Squadron also served in Coastal Command flying obsolete Hamden torpedo bombers in 1942–43, harassing German shipping off the Norwegian coast. Re-equipped with Beaufighters, the squadron joined with a New Zealand squadron to form the Anzac Wing, which attacked German vessels in the English Channel and along the Dutch and Norwegian coasts. The Beaufighters were required to fly through Norwegian fiords often only 200–300 metres wide with vertical sides, where they endured attacks by German anti-craft and machine-gun fire before they could strike at the German ships sheltering there.

# Bombing: The Deadliest of Jobs

Chased out of continental Europe in 1940, the only way that Britain could effectively attack Germany initially was by bombing industrial and transport centres. Many Australian crews took part in this campaign and helped support the troops on the ground when the Allies finally invaded France in 1944.

Although losses in some missions were very high, on average about 3 per cent of aircraft involved in a bombing mission were lost. Each aircrew member was expected to conduct 30 operations to complete a tour. So theoretically he had a 90 per cent chance of not surviving to the end of his tour. However, many of the replacements were killed, so in practice, an airman had about a 40 per cent chance of surviving his operational tour.

Some aircrew returned for a second tour, thereby increasing their chances of being killed. The airmen fatalistically accepted these odds, although all knew that each bombing mission might be their last. The bravery and devotion of the thousands of young Australians who served in Bomber Command need to be remembered alongside the better-known Australian battles at Gallipoli, Tobruk, Alamein and Kokoda.

## Night stalking

Early in the campaign, the British bombers, some of which were obsolete, were vulnerable to attack by German fighters, so the strategic bombing raids took place at night. One fact that became obvious as the campaign continued throughout 1941 was that the bombers couldn't deliver their bombs accurately on the factories, oil plants, train marshalling yards or docks. Indeed, in some raids bombs were scattered so widely that the Germans couldn't discern what targets had been attacked. With the aircraft and navigation equipment then available the smallest targets that might be hit with any confidence were whole towns. Britain now decided to attack German cities as area targets, believing that if it could 'de-house' the German civilian workforce it would reduce their morale and disrupt German war production.

At the beginning of 1942 a new British long-range heavy bomber, the Lancaster, started to enter service, and in February 1942 Air Chief Marshal Sir Arthur Harris took over Bomber Command. In May 1942 Harris organised a raid with 1,000 bombers over the city of Cologne, causing massive damage. He continued similar attacks against other cities. In July 1943 a fire bombing attack on Hamburg killed 40,000 people. Then in November 1943 Harris switched the target to Berlin. In these raids, Bomber Command suffered very heavy casualties and was not able to sustain the campaign.

## Bomber Command's war

Five RAAF squadrons served in Bomber Command, although two joined it later in the war. During 1943, three RAAF squadrons — 460, 466 and 467 — were heavily involved in the night bombing offensive over Germany. These squadrons were never manned fully by Australians, while many Australians served in RAF units. Australians were therefore found in all of Bomber Command's major operations and their aircraft ranged across Europe. Major cities and industrial centres in Germany were the prime targets, but bombers attacked Turin and Milan in Italy, and submarine pens along the French coast.

## Bravery above the clouds

Flight Sergeant Rawdon Middleton had worked as a jackeroo before he joined the RAAF and graduated from the Empire Air Training Scheme as a pilot. In February 1942 he began flying Stirling bombers in an RAF squadron in Bomber Command. By November that year he had completed 28 operational flights, when he conducted a bombing mission over the Italian city of Turin.

As Middleton and his crew began their attack, anti-aircraft fire struck the aircraft. A shell exploded in the cockpit, destroying Middleton's right eye and exposing the bone above it. He lost consciousness and the aircraft dived to just 800 feet before the second pilot, who along with the radio operator had also been wounded, brought it under control. When Middleton regained consciousness he took control, continued the bombing run and completed the attack.

He knew that his damaged aircraft had insufficient fuel to complete the journey home, but he rejected the idea of bailing out over German-occupied France, and in agony, barely able to see, and in further pain when he spoke, began the four-hour flight over the Alps towards England.

Over France they again came under anti-aircraft fire until they reached the English Channel with only five minutes of fuel left. On crossing the English coast Middleton ordered the crew to abandon the aircraft. Five of his crew bailed out, while two remained with him as he turned back towards the Channel to avoid crashing into a populated area. The two who remained behind parachuted into the sea and drowned. Middleton was too weak to leave and was killed when his aircraft crashed into the sea. He was posthumously awarded the Victoria Cross.

No. 460 Squadron suffered the heaviest casualties of the Australian squadrons with 1,018 deaths (589 Australians). This means that the squadron's aircrew was completely replaced five times. In total, 4,050 Australians were killed while serving in Bomber Command, and this comprised more than 10 per cent of all Australian fatal casualties in the war. By comparison, 3,552 Australian army personnel were killed in North Africa (including Tobruk and Alamein), Greece, Crete and Syria. Flying in Bomber Command was far more dangerous than fighting in the infantry.

One of Bomber Command's outstanding air commanders was an Australian, Group Captain Donald Bennett, who had joined the RAF before the war. He led the Pathfinder Force, which located enemy targets and dropped markers to illuminate them for following bombers.

## Surviving a sortie over Germany

No one bombing mission was the same, but they had similar patterns. On the afternoon of a mission the Lancaster crews would gather for a briefing. Final checks would be completed before the aircraft took off in the early evening. Even at this early stage, with the aircraft carrying 9,000 litres of fuel, more than eight tonnes of high explosives and 14,000 rounds of ammunition, a crash would result in almost certain death.

Once all the aircraft involved had reached the desired altitude, they gathered in a very loose formation and headed across the North Sea for the coast of Europe. As they crossed the coast of Holland they were likely to come under fire from anti-aircraft guns and this continued all the way to their target. Searchlights swept across the sky, hoping to pin a bomber so that it could be attacked more easily. German night fighters lurked ready to pounce. If they did so the bomber's gunners would return fire while the pilot took evasive action. Enemy fire was likely to be even heavier over the targets, but often bombers would press home their attacks even though the aircraft had been damaged and crew members wounded.

After the aircraft released their bomb loads they could turn for home. Without the weight of the bombs, and having used nearly half their fuel, the aircraft could climb higher and faster, but they were still susceptible to attack from night fighters and often they faced a head wind. If an aircraft had been damaged it had to be nursed home by pilots and flight engineers. Sometimes crews had to bail out over the sea, or aircraft crashed over England. Getting back to England before dawn was crucial, as the aircraft would become sitting ducks once daylight arrived. With the sun rising in the east over Europe, the aircraft flew west, 'chased by the sun' as they tried to reach home in the safety of darkness.

## Supporting the Normandy landing

In the midst of the strategic bombing campaign against Germany many bombers were diverted to prepare the way for the Allied invasion of Normandy in June 1944. Attacks on Germany continued to keep German fighters at home, while other bombers struck at major railway centres in France to isolate the coast and to prevent the Germans sending reinforcements there. As usual, Australian aircraft were involved. For example, in an attack near Paris in April, 463 and 467 Squadrons provided 37 of the 204 bombers that reached the target.

At that time, ten of the 292 British Commonwealth squadrons operating in Britain were Australian. Two were in Fighter Command, three were in Coastal Command, four were in Bomber Command and one fighter squadron was part of the Second Tactical Air Force, directly supporting the invasion. To support the landing, bombers struck at radar stations, gun batteries, military camps and munitions dumps. Maritime aircraft searched for German submarines and attacked German ships operating in the English Channel that might have interfered with the landing. Fighters patrolled the skies over France, while fighters and fighter-bombers tried to prevent German armoured vehicles and troops approaching the invasion area.

More than 200 Australian fighter pilots, in RAF and RAAF squadrons, took part in the effort to protect the Normandy landing. One such airman was Pilot Officer K E Martin, who was flying a British Typhoon. He disabled a German tank with his rockets and was turning to attack another at low level when his aircraft was struck and set on fire. His aircraft crashed but he escaped, badly burnt and with a broken leg. He evaded enemy patrols, was rescued by the French, and to avoid capture later posed as a deaf-mute who had been injured in a bombing raid.

## *Strategic bombing: Necessary evil?*

The Allied strategic air offensive against Germany has been the subject of much controversy, with a range of opinions about it. Consider:

- Except for some well-known instances, such the 'Dam Busters' raid of May 1943, aircraft were rarely able to deliver their bombs with any precision so inevitably they bombed civilian population centres.

- More than half a million Germans were killed by Allied bombing and some historians have condemned the attacks on the German civilian population as immoral. The February 1945 raids on Dresden, where evacuees were gathering, have been criticised as being unnecessary, cruel and even a war crime.

- Critics of strategic bombing have argued that it was ineffective because it didn't shake German morale and German war production increased as the war continued.

- However, the Nazi regime was barbaric and was killing millions in concentration camps. Many believe that every available means, including area bombing, needed to be used to bring about Germany's defeat.

- Detailed studies have shown that German war production was badly affected by the bombing. Huge numbers of German military personnel and large quantities of resources were diverted to defending the homeland, and by late 1944 German morale was becoming badly shaken, with absences from places of work. In effect, the bombing campaign brought Germany close to collapse and contributed substantially to the Allied victory.

The strategic air offensive cost the lives of about 50,000 British aircrew and similar numbers of Americans. A large proportion of British industrial resources, which could have been used for other purposes, were devoted to maintaining the bombing campaign.

---

### Completing the mission

Noble Frankland, an RAF navigator, recalled later in his book *History at War* (DLM) that on one of their early trips the pilot of an all-Australian crew decided that the aircraft was in such a bad way and the conditions so poor that he would abandon the trip. The pilot asked the navigator to give him a course for home, but the navigator, supported by the rest of the crew, refused. To resolve the impasse, one of the crew knocked out the pilot and restrained him. 'Flying the aircraft as best they could, this crew proceeded to the target, bombed it and returned to base. They then released the pilot and ordered him to land the aircraft, which none of them could have done. They told the pilot that if he promised never to turn back again, unless they all agreed to that course, they would say nothing about the incident... They flew a very successful tour of operations: the pilot was awarded the DFC and the rest of the crew received no recognition.'

# Part V
# Our War in the Pacific

*'That's far enough, sunshine ...'*

## In this part ...

The Pacific War (1941 to 1945) was the most significant event in the modern history of the Asia–Pacific region, and was both a part of the Second World War and a distinct entity within it. Although Japan was just one of the Axis powers, it played a singular role in the Pacific, and the other powers, Germany and Italy, were barely involved. Japan waged a pitiless war that left a legacy of bitterness across the whole region, changed national attitudes, and completely reshaped the political structure in Asia. By contrast, all the principal Allies — the United States, Britain, China, Australia and the Netherlands — were deeply engaged, and the Soviet Union joined the war near its end. The Pacific War became Australia's largest ever military undertaking and decisively influenced the nation's development for the next half century.

In this part I explain that Australia's contribution to the Pacific War was out of proportion to its size. With a population of a mere seven million, Australia put one million citizens in uniform. Australian troops suffered heavily in the early stages of the war: They provided the majority of American General Douglas MacArthur's land forces in 1942–43; they halted the Japanese advance in New Guinea; and they led the land counteroffensive in 1943. Australia also provided the main base for the Allied forces in the South West Pacific. Although Australia had fewer casualties than in the First World War, its war in the Pacific was still expensive in terms of human losses and expenditure of national treasure.

# Chapter 14

# The Japanese are Coming! 1941–42

### In This Chapter

▶ Trying to hold back the Japanese onslaught
▶ Marching into a grim and deadly captivity
▶ Anticipating and preparing for invasion at home
▶ Turning the tables on the Japanese in the Coral Sea and at Midway

The Pacific War began on 7–8 December 1941 when Japan attacked Pearl Harbor, Malaya and the Philippines. Japan claimed that after the United States applied crippling economic sanctions in July 1941 it had no alternative. But in truth, the war originated with Japanese expansionism and militarism during the half-century before 1941. Australians had long been concerned about the threat from Japan, whose earlier victories over China in 1895 and Russia in 1905 showed its willingness to use its growing military capability to seize overseas colonies. In 1931–32 Japan seized Manchuria and in 1937 it began hostilities against China.

As the Japanese threat increased in the 1930s Australia had a dilemma. With a small population and industrial base it couldn't defend its territory or trade routes, but Britain didn't seem to take the threat as seriously as Australia. When Britain went to war with Germany in 1939 Australian political leaders assessed that they needed to support Britain by sending military forces overseas, even if it denuded the home defences (refer to Chapter 10). And unless Japan attacked American territory there was no guarantee that the United States would be willing to come to Australia's aid.

Despite these fears, when Japan struck Pearl Harbor and Malaya, Australia's leaders were concerned, but initially not dismayed. As Japan swiftly conquered South-East Asia, however, concern turned to dismay and, in some quarters, to panic. For the first time since white settlement, Australia faced the prospect of invasion. A government propaganda poster summed up the mood by showing a Japanese soldier striding across Asia heading for Australia. 'He's coming south', declared the poster, 'It's fight, work or perish'.

In this chapter, which covers the six-month period from December 1941 to June 1942, I describe how initially the Japanese overwhelmed our forces. I then tell the story of how the Americans arrived in Australia and their carrier-borne aircraft won the Battle of the Coral Sea (with our help) and the Battle of Midway, which tipped the balance in our favour.

## Reeling from the Japanese Thrust

Most people have a vivid picture of the beginning of the Pacific War, especially if they have watched movies about the attack on Pearl Harbor on 7 December 1941 — a date which, as President Roosevelt said, 'will live in infamy'. The image is stark. Japanese dive bombers and fighters sit high above the hills of Oahu (Hawaii), and the Japanese airborne commander calls 'Tora, Tora, Tora' before, at 7.55 am, his aircraft swoop on the slumbering American warships.

But the Pacific War did not begin then. Ninety minutes earlier, just after midnight on 8 December local time, Japanese ships began shelling Kota Bharu in northern Malaya. In the first air attack against the Japanese in the war, Hudson bombers of No 1 RAAF Squadron struck the enemy convoy. By dawn, one Australian aircraft had been lost and a Japanese transport was sunk.

Why were Australian aircraft in Malaya? Before the war Britain had established a naval base at Singapore, planning to send its main fleet there if war with Japan appeared likely. Australia accepted this so-called Singapore Strategy (refer to Chapter 10) even when common sense indicated that Japan would probably go to war only when Britain was preoccupied in Europe and therefore unable to spare its ships for service in the Pacific. During 1940 Britain did what it could to build up its defences in Malaya and Singapore, and Australia sent forces to assist. By late 1941 the British land forces, under Lieutenant General Arthur Percival, numbered about 88,600, made up of 19,600 British, 15,200 Australian, 37,000 Indian and 16,800 Malay troops. There were at least six Indian brigades, each with one British and two Indian battalions. Two brigades of the 8th Australian Division, commanded by Major General Henry Gordon Bennett, were deployed in Johore state in southern Malaya. The British air force consisted of 12 squadrons of generally obsolete aircraft; three were from the RAAF, two flying Hudson bombers on reconnaissance missions and one flying outdated Buffalo fighters.

On 8 December 1941 Japanese troops landed at Kota Bharu and began advancing south, sweeping aside the Indian brigades and the Commonwealth air force squadrons (refer to Figure 14-1). Two days later Japanese aircraft sunk the British warships *Prince of Wales* and *Repulse* in the South China Sea, causing a devastating blow to British morale. For the next month the Japanese 25th Army, under Lieutenant General Yamashita Tomoyuki, pushed the British army south. The Japanese army's success was attributed to a variety of factors:

- The Indian troops had been enlisted only recently and weren't fully trained.

- The Japanese troops had fought in China and were hardened and experienced.

- The Japanese had superior aircraft and their pilots had fought in China. Stories that they were poor pilots because they wore 'Coke-bottle' glasses proved to be a myth.

- Cooperation between the British Army and the air force was poor.

- The Japanese overran the British airfields, denying them to the British and Australian air force units.

- The Japanese Army employed superior battle tactics, marching through the jungle to bypass British defensive positions, cutting their withdrawal routes and attacking from the rear.

- The Japanese employed light tanks along the good road network on the west coast of the peninsula; the British had none as they thought they wouldn't be suitable in the jungle.

- The British were so keen to save money that their commander in Singapore was ordered to hire the cheapest labour available. So the official photographer for the British naval base was a man who later turned out to be a Japanese army colonel. The Japanese therefore had excellent intelligence about the British defences.

- Percival was a weak commander who failed to take a strong grip on the fighting.

**Figure 14-1:** Malaya and Singapore, 1941–42.

## Jungle ambushes

As the Japanese pushed into southern Malaya General Sir Archibald Wavell, Commander-in-Chief of the American, British, Dutch, Australian (ABDA) Command, which covered the area from Malaya to Darwin, restructured the command arrangements in Malaya. On 10 January 1942 he gave Major General Bennett of the 8th Australian Division command of Westforce, consisting of the 27th Australian Brigade and three Indian brigades, and ordered him to halt the Japanese in northwestern Johore. Bennett was a citizen soldier, who had been a young brigade commander in the First World War. He was sarcastic and undiplomatically critical of the British and Indian troops, boasting that the Australians would at last stop the Japanese.

## Duelling with Japanese tanks

Lance Sergeant Kenneth Harrison commanded one of the anti-tank guns, which hit a Japanese troop carrier with its first round. As Harrison later described it in his book, *The Brave Japanese* (Rigby): 'Japs began pouring out, but as they were running in all directions our second shell crashed home, and the carrier rose in the air and toppled on its side. It lay there with men crawling out like wood bugs from a burning log'. Harrison's gunners found themselves in a fierce duel with three Japanese tanks, one of which they destroyed in flames. By this time the Australian gun detachment had been reduced to just Harrison and Gunner Joe Bull, the others having been killed or wounded.

Harrison recalled that he 'slammed another shell into the breech, tapped Joe on the shoulder, and then stood peering hopefully at the inferno up the road. Then there was a "whoomp" and a flash from the cutting, and something screamed by like an express train. This was followed by a deafening roar as Joe fired back at where a red flash had momentarily appeared amid the drifting pall of smoke; the breech flew open, hurling acrid cordite into our faces, and then the process started all over again ... after a while the fire died down. The last shot was fired at us; Joe fired back and did not miss. Either that, or they had had enough for one day. In any case, we were left in possession of the field. Our heads were ringing but unbowed, and we had exactly four shells'.

The 27th Brigade was placed astride the main road south at Gemas, with Lieutenant Colonel Frederick ('Black Jack') Galleghan's 2/30th Battalion in the forward position. On 14 January a Japanese battalion, riding bicycles, approached the Australians hiding in the jungle beyond a bridge over the Gemencheh River. After more than 1,000 Japanese had crossed, the Australians blew up the bridge and raked the Japanese column with machine guns, causing great slaughter. The battle continued for 24 hours. The Japanese brought forward tanks, which were temporarily halted by two Australian 2-pounder anti-tank guns, but the 2/30th Battalion withdrew.

## *Trapped at Parit Sulong*

Bennett deployed the 45th Indian Brigade to the Muar River, near the west coast, but the Japanese Imperial Guards Division bypassed them by moving along the coast in captured boats, attacked them from the rear and drove them back in disarray. Bennett sent the 2/29th, then the 2/19th Australian Battalion, as well as a gun battery, to assist, but the combined force of

Australians and Indians was compelled to withdraw along the road towards Parit Salong, now cut by the Japanese. By 20 January, the three Indian and two Australian battalions had been reduced to just five Australian companies and three demoralised Indian companies. The British brigade commander had been killed and Lieutenant Colonel Charles Anderson, commanding officer of the 2/19th Battalion, led the remnants.

The force was surrounded and the road was blocked by six Japanese machine-gun posts. Anderson ordered A Company to swing off the road and attack, urging them to sing to keep up their spirits. They sang 'Waltzing Matilda'. But the Japanese couldn't be moved, and artillery was falling on the column. Anderson moved to B Company and ordered another attack. The leading platoon was commanded by a corporal, so Anderson joined it. A month short of his 45th birthday, his eyes glinting behind his spectacles, Anderson led seven men in the attack. With grenades and his pistol he personally put two machine-gun posts out of action and then led the assault. Seeing this success, the whole company surged forward and overwhelmed the enemy position. Anderson then returned to command the brigade. The battalion swore that Anderson won his Victoria Cross five times over in that battle.

Anderson's force couldn't break through another roadblock and they were attacked repeatedly by Japanese tanks, artillery and aircraft. He had many wounded and had almost exhausted his artillery and mortar ammunition. Reluctantly, he left his wounded and ordered the fit men to try to escape through the jungle and swamps in small parties; about 500 Australians made it. The Japanese massacred the remaining 160 helpless, wounded Australian and Indian troops. After the war, a military court found the responsible Japanese officer guilty of war crimes and he was hanged.

## *The worst disaster: The fall of Singapore*

The Australians and Indians continued their fighting withdrawal and on 31 January crossed the causeway to the island of Singapore. Reinforcements had come from Britain and in smaller numbers from Australia. Percival now had about 85,000 troops, although 15,000 were base troops. He assessed that the Japanese were likely to attack the northern sector of the island across the Johore Strait and he placed his freshest troops there. General Bennett was made responsible for the western sector with his two battered Australian brigades, reformed after their losses in Johore, and an Indian brigade.

## Chapter 14: The Japanese are Coming! 1941–42

Percival had misjudged his enemy. The Japanese planned to strike in the west, not the north. After a heavy bombardment, in the evening of 8 February they crossed the straits in small boats and attacked the area held by the two Australian brigades. The Australian battalions were trying to hold too wide a front and, as the Japanese thrust between the companies, they were compelled to withdraw. Over several days, the Australians conducted a fighting withdrawal. Brigadier Harold Taylor of the 22nd Brigade misinterpreted his orders and pulled back prematurely. He had never worked amicably with Bennett and when he became exhausted Bennett relieved him of command.

The Japanese were now advancing on all fronts and when they seized the city's reservoir Percival saw no option but to surrender. In fact, Yamashita's forces had almost exhausted their ammunition and could barely have supported another assault. His supply system had broken down and his force could only continue operations for another three days. In a meeting in the afternoon of 15 February Yamashita demanded that Percival surrender by 8.30 pm. The Japanese had pulled off a brilliant victory. In 70 days they had travelled the entire length of Malaya — more than 700 kilometres as the crow flies — and had defeated a larger force.

During the campaign about 130,000 British, Indian and Australian troops became prisoners of war and about 8,000 were killed. By contrast, the Japanese lost about 10,000 killed and wounded. Proportionally, the Australians suffered the most. They formed about 13 per cent of the total force, but had about 20 per cent of the deaths. The British Prime Minister, Winston Churchill, called it 'the worst disaster and largest capitulation in British history'.

Shortly before the surrender Bennett handed command of the 8th Division to his artillery commander, Brigadier Cecil Callaghan, and escaped from the island, eventually reaching Australia. He claimed that he brought back valuable knowledge about jungle warfare, but others denounced him for deserting his troops. Although Bennett later commanded an army corps in Australia, he never again led troops in combat. A post-war investigation found that Bennett had relinquished his command without permission, but he received no punishment.

## Grim fate for Australian prisoners of war

With the fall of Singapore, 14,792 Australian troops became prisoners of war (POWs) and they were held, along with British and Indian prisoners, in the Selarang Barracks near Changi Gaol, on Singapore Island. A further 2,700 Australians, who had been captured in Java, eventually reached Changi. Conditions were harsh, and food and medicine was in short supply. The Japanese military code didn't include the possibility of surrender and anyone who surrendered was considered to have died. The Japanese therefore had no regard for Allied prisoners. Further, in the Japanese Army junior soldiers were beaten by their superiors, and prison guards had no compunction about thrashing prisoners for petty infringements of rules.

Initially the prisoners were employed in working parties on Singapore Island, but working parties were later sent further away. In mid-1942 the Japanese decided to build a railway from southern Thailand through mountainous jungle to Burma to transport supplies to the Japanese Army fighting on the Burma–India border. Large parties of British, Australian and Dutch POWs — the latter captured in the Netherlands East Indies — worked on the railway in appalling conditions. About 2,700 of the 13,000 Australians who worked there died from lack of food, overwork, tropical illness and maltreatment. In all, more than 12,000 Allied POWs died, or about one for every railway sleeper, before the railway was completed in October 1943. As many as 80,000 volunteer and conscripted Asian labourers also perished.

In addition to those seized in Malaya, Singapore and Java, the Japanese also captured Australians in Timor, Ambon and Rabaul, and prisoners were held in camps in Taiwan, Korea, Manchuria, Ambon, Hainan and Borneo. Those in Borneo had the worst experience. In January 1945 the prisoners at Sandakan, on the east coast, were ordered to march to Ranau, about 250 kilometres away. Many died from malnutrition, exhaustion, disease and ill-treatment, and once they arrived at Ranau the survivors were shot. Six, who managed to escape and were looked after by local people, were the only survivors of 2,500 Australian and British prisoners who set out on the march. All 292 prisoners who remained at Sandakan because they were too ill to march also died.

In total, about 22,400 Australians were captured by the Japanese during the war and of these 14,340 survived to return to Australia. The large numbers of Australian prisoners and their high death rate — almost one in five of all Australians to die in the war — became one of the defining features of Australia's experience in the Pacific War.

# Garrisoning the Islands to the North: Hostages to Fortune

In addition to fighting in Malaya, in the weeks after the outbreak of the war Japanese forces landed in the Philippines, seized Hong Kong, Guam and Wake Island, captured the oilfields of British Sarawak, and thrust into the

East Indies. As the enemy drew closer, Australia struggled to strengthen its defences. About 120,000 men were already overseas in the four divisions of the Australian Imperial Force (AIF) and 32,000 other AIF volunteers were training in Australia. The Labor Government, led by John Curtin, called up the part-time citizen force, bringing its seven divisions to full strength. But they would need more training and equipment before being ready for combat. The RAAF consisted of 53 Hudson reconnaissance aircraft, 101 Wirraway trainers to be used as fighters, a few flying boats and training aircraft.

To meet the threat, the government deployed what forces it had to the islands protecting the northern approaches. Late in 1941 a specially raised battalion had gone to Port Moresby in New Guinea and now two more were sent. An AIF battalion (from the 8th Division's brigade that had been withheld from Malaya) went to Rabaul on New Britain and the brigade's other two battalions deployed to the Netherlands East Indies islands of Ambon and Timor (refer to Figure 14-2). Independent companies went to Portuguese Timor, New Ireland and New Caledonia. RAAF squadrons with Hudsons and Wirraways joined the infantry at some of these forward locations, as well as at Darwin.

By deploying the battalions the government ensured that the Japanese would need to fight to take the islands, but the garrisons lacked sufficient strength to repulse a determined Japanese attack and were likely to be overwhelmed and lost. Although most of the ships of the Royal Australian Navy had returned to Australian waters, they didn't have the capability to intercept and destroy Japanese landing forces, which were usually protected by strong naval forces, including aircraft carriers.

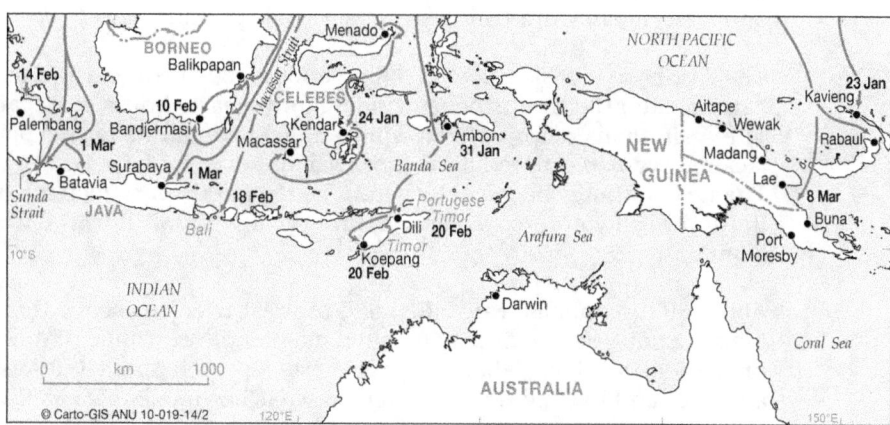

Figure 14-2: The northern approaches to Australia.

## The shock at Rabaul

Rabaul was the main town of New Britain in Australian-administered New Guinea and in February 1941 Australia agreed to send a small force there as the first step towards establishing an American base.

The Australian force at Rabaul, known as Lark Force, numbered about 1,400 troops, including the 2/22nd Battalion. Colonel Jack Scanlan, a First World War veteran, was in command. Four Hudson bombers and six Wirraway trainer aircraft were also located there. The Australian high command knew that this force couldn't adequately defend Rabaul against a large-scale attack, but thought the enemy should be made to fight for it.

Japanese and Allied strategists understood the strategic importance of Rabaul:

- Rabaul would provide the Americans with a link in any reinforcement route between mainland United States and the Philippines.
- Rabaul would give the Australians early warning of any thrust towards Australia.
- With its harbour and airfields, Rabaul would help the Japanese defend their Combined Fleet base at Truk in the Caroline Islands.

On 4 January 1942 Japanese aircraft from the Caroline Islands began air raids. The Wirraway fighters, really only trainer aircraft, were no match for the Japanese and were shot out of the sky. Wing Commander John Lerew sent a message to his superiors, 'Morituri vos salutamus' — the Roman gladiators' salute — 'We who are about to die salute you'. By 22 January only one Hudson and two Wirraways remained undamaged.

The Japanese invasion fleet included about 5,300 men and two aircraft carriers, and the troops began landing in the early hours of 23 January. The Australians put up a brief, spirited defence, but defensive plans were lacking. Scanlan ordered no withdrawal and everyone to fight to the death. Then when things became desperate he declared every man for himself. Both were silly orders. A planned, orderly, fighting withdrawal would have been best.

About 30 Australians were killed and the rest tried to escape through the jungle. About 400 eventually reached mainland New Guinea. At the Tol plantation, south of Rabaul, the Japanese captured about 160 Australians and shot and bayoneted all of them in what became known as the Tol massacre.

The Japanese transformed Rabaul into a massive sea and air base and also established a camp for civilian and military prisoners. In June 1942 more than 800 military prisoners and about 200 civilians embarked on the cargo ship *Montevideo Maru*, bound for China, but an American submarine sank it en route, unaware that prisoners were on board. With no known Australian survivors, it became the greatest single loss of Australian lives in the war. Out of 1,050 prisoners in Rabaul in 1942, only four were found alive there at the end of the war.

## *More troops are sacrificed: The loss of Ambon*

On the East Indies island of Ambon the 2/21st Battalion formed the main body of what was known as Gull Force, which, like Lark Force at Rabaul, was ordered to defend the island's airfield. After attacks from Japanese planes, the Australian aircraft withdrew and on the night of 30 January Japanese troops started landing. The battle continued for several days until on 3 February the Australian commander, Lieutenant Colonel Jack Scott (see the sidebar 'The Old Guard at war'), surrendered his force.

### The Old Guard at war

Jack Scott, aged 53, was the oldest Australian infantry battalion commander to see action in the Second World War. Decorated in the First World War, he was an insurance manager between the wars. In 1931 he was chief of staff of the 30,000 strong Old Guard, a secret army formed by citizens to keep law and order in New South Wales if civil government was overthrown by a socialist revolution.

Scott was friendly with Japanese businessmen, but after the outbreak of war he became a staff officer in Army Headquarters. When the commander of Gull Force complained that his force was inadequate for its task Scott volunteered to replace him. In captivity on Ambon and Hainan he handed Australian prisoners over to the Japanese for brutal punishment. He survived captivity, but most of his men despised him and he never attended a battalion reunion.

After the surrender, the Japanese massacred more than 200 Australians who had survived the battle for the airstrip, while 807 Australians went into captivity. A total of 49 Australians escaped and eventually reached Australia. About two-thirds of the prisoners remained on Ambon for the rest of the war and one-third went to Hainan off China. Suffering from malnutrition, disease and ill treatment, only 302 of the original force returned alive to Australia.

## Caught unawares in Darwin

By early 1942 Darwin, the closest Australian port to South-East Asia, was defended by almost 15,000 Australian troops, although most were militia units mobilised on the outbreak of the war with Japan. Some American troops had also arrived, hoping to go on to the Philippines. Darwin was poorly defended by the air force and only a few Hudson bombers and Wirraways were stationed there. However, a squadron of American P-40 Kittyhawks had recently arrived, expecting to deploy to Java.

In mid-February 1942, a Japanese fleet, with four aircraft carriers, sailed into the East Indies to support an attack on Timor. In the morning of 19 February, 188 Japanese aircraft from the carriers, led by Commander Mituso Fuchida, who had also led the raid on Pearl Harbor two months earlier, attacked the crowded harbour and town of Darwin. A Catholic missionary on Bathurst Island saw the aircraft heading for Darwin and radioed a warning, but this was not heeded and the Japanese aircraft caught Darwin's defenders by surprise. The American Kittyhawks, which were returning from an aborted flight to Java, were unaware of the approaching Japanese and were attacked as they tried to land. All but one were destroyed. Anti-aircraft gunners raced to their guns, but the Japanese had the initiative. About midday 54 Japanese bombers from bases in Ambon and Sulawesi conducted a high-level raid on Darwin airfield.

Ten ships were sunk in Darwin harbour, including an American destroyer and eight transport ships, while a further 25 ships were damaged during the two air raids. Twenty-three Allied aircraft and probably seven Japanese aircraft were destroyed. According to the official commission of enquiry, 243 military and civilian people were killed and about 350 wounded. Expecting an invasion, many civilians headed south and they were joined by some fleeing air force personnel.

The Japanese dropped more bombs on Darwin on 19 February than on Pearl Harbor, but because there were fewer warships at Darwin the attack was not quite as damaging. The attack was a considerable psychological blow to the Australian Government and the general population, although the extent of the damage was not publicised. The Army commander in Darwin was replaced and the town's defences were strengthened further. The attack was the first of almost 100 air raids against northern Australia during 1942–43.

## Guerrilla war in Timor

The Japanese air attack on Darwin coincided with their invasion of Timor. In December 1941 the 2/40th Battalion, commanded by Lieutenant Colonel William Leggatt, and support troops went to Koepang in Dutch (West) Timor, while the 2/2nd Independent Company, commanded by Major Alexander Spence, went to Dili in Portuguese (East) Timor. The Australian force in Timor was known as Sparrow Force and Brigadier William Veale took command of it in mid-February 1942.

The Japanese attack on Timor followed a similar pattern to the earlier attacks on Rabaul and Ambon. Air raids began towards the end of January and most of the RAAF aircraft were forced to withdraw to Australia. On 20 February Japanese troops landed near Koepang and Leggatt began withdrawing inland, heading for Portuguese Timor. His battalion was stopped by 500 Japanese paratroopers dug into a defensive position. After an Australian mortar barrage, Leggatt led his battalion in a bayonet charge, effectively destroying the paratroopers as a fighting force. The main Japanese force now arrived with tanks and on 23 February — with his men low in ammunition, hopelessly outnumbered, and without food or water — Leggatt surrendered his battalion.

The Japanese also landed at Dili and the 2/2nd Independent Company withdrew and began a guerilla campaign. Brigadier Veale and elements of Sparrow Force who hadn't surrendered made their way to Portuguese Timor where they joined up with the independent company. Sparrow Force lost contact with Australia for two months, but signallers built another radio and re-established communications, allowing the force to be supplied by air drops.

The year-long guerrilla campaign tied down large numbers of Japanese, but at considerable cost to the local East Timorese people; between 40,000 and 70,000 East Timorese died during the war. Veale was evacuated and Spence continued as Sparrow Force commander. In September 1942, the 2/4th Independent Company arrived to provide reinforcement. Most of the force was evacuated in December 1942.

Troops were ferried across from Darwin in corvettes under attack by Japanese aircraft. When the corvette HMAS *Armidale* was sunk by enemy aircraft on 1 December 1942, Ordinary Seaman Teddy Sheean disregarded the order to 'abandon ship' and although wounded, stayed at his post firing his Oerlikon gun to bring down an enemy bomber. He was still firing when the ship sank.

## Overpowered in the fight for Java

General Wavell established the headquarters of the American, British, Dutch, Australian (ABDA) Command on the island of Java and cobbled together Allied forces to defend the Netherlands East Indies. The 1st Australian Corps, consisting of the experienced 6th and 7th Divisions, had embarked from the Middle East to form the main land force in Java. In anticipation, the corps commander, Lieutenant General John Lavarack, flew ahead to Java. By the time the first ship, carrying two Australian battalions, arrived off Sumatra on 14 February, the Japanese were already preparing to invade. Lavarack therefore advised the Australian Government that the troops shouldn't disembark as they would be too weak to repel the Japanese and would probably be lost. The government accepted Wavell's contrary advice and the two battalions disembarked at Batavia, the capital and main port of Java.

With the surrender of Singapore on 15 February, and the fall of Timor and Ambon a few days later, ABDA Command was dissolved and Wavell and Lavarack flew out of Java. The Japanese now closed in. On 27 February a naval force with American, Australian, British and Dutch cruisers intercepted a Japanese invasion convoy, but the Japanese were too powerful and sank two Dutch cruisers. The remaining Allied cruisers then intercepted another Japanese convoy in the Sunda Strait. They sank or damaged a few Japanese transports, but the Australian cruiser *Perth,* the American cruiser *Houston* and the British cruiser *Exeter* were sunk.

After Lavarack departed, Brigadier Arthur Blackburn VC commanded the Australian troops in Java, known as Blackforce, and they formed an ad hoc brigade that included the 2/3rd Machine Gun and the 2/2nd Pioneer Battalions. The Japanese landed in Java on the night of 28 February and Blackforce deployed to halt the Japanese advancing from the west, while the Dutch covered other enemy approaches. Blackforce held up the Japanese advance for three days, but then Blackburn learned that the Dutch had surrendered. He hoped to fight on in the mountains but, unable to care for his wounded, on 11 March he reluctantly surrendered his force. Of the 2,920 Australians in Blackforce, 36 were killed and the remainder captured; about one-third of these men died in captivity.

## Curtin demands that our troops come home

In early February 1942 the remainder of the 1st Australian Corps was sailing across the Indian Ocean heading for Java, but when Singapore surrendered on 15 February General Lavarack in Java recommended that the troops not land there. Lieutenant General Vernon Sturdee, Chief of the General Staff, advised Prime Minister Curtin that the troops should be diverted to Australia, which would become the main Allied base for the counteroffensive against Japan. Curtin agreed and on 17 February he cabled the British Prime Minister, Winston Churchill, requesting the troops sail to Australia.

US President Franklin Roosevelt now decided to send an American division to Australia, suggesting that Australia could reciprocate by allowing one of its divisions to go to Burma to halt the Japanese advance there. Disregarding Curtin's request, in the evening of 20 February Churchill ordered the convoy carrying the leading Australian troops to change course and head for Rangoon in Burma. On Churchill's behalf, Roosevelt cabled Curtin seeking permission to use the Australians in Burma. Curtin and his government remained firm, and indeed Sturdee told the War Cabinet that he would resign if the troops didn't return to Australia. But when Curtin again told Churchill that the convoy should return to Australia, Churchill replied that the convoy was still proceeding to Burma and as it would need to refuel before changing course to Australia, the Australian Government would have a few days to reconsider.

The Australian ministers were confused and angry. Curtin, who was 'greatly shocked', went for a long walk around the hills near Canberra before returning to his office late on 23 February to send a cable to Churchill reiterating his original request. Churchill had no option but to comply. Curtin made one concession; he allowed two brigades of the 6th Division to help garrison Ceylon (Sri Lanka) for four months. The rest of the troops arrived in Australia in March and by August the 7th Division was in action in New Guinea. If the troops had gone to Rangoon they would almost certainly have been captured by the Japanese.

## Uncle Sam to the Rescue

The fall of Singapore, followed by the air raid on Darwin and the landings at Ambon and Timor caused extreme concern to the Australian Government, whose military advisers now expected that Japan might soon attack Australia, probably from the north-east through New Guinea. The first Japanese air raids on Port Moresby (New Guinea's capital and main port on the south coast of Papua) began on 3 February and on 8 March Japanese forces landed at Lae and Salamaua on the north coast of New Guinea.

By the middle of March, an air of panic or desperation hung over some quarters of the Australian population. The federal and state governments began considering a 'scorched earth policy', by which civilians would be evacuated from certain areas where facilities and resources would be destroyed to deny them to the enemy. Some families living in seaside suburbs of Sydney despatched their women and children inland. Although the possibility of invasion didn't diminish during March, towards the end of the month several events caused a revival of confidence in the community:

- The 7th Division and one brigade of the 6th Division arrived back in Australia from the Middle East. The brigade hurried north to help defend Darwin.

- General Sir Thomas Blamey returned to Australia to become Commander-in-Chief of the Army, and his presence, along with the arrival of other officers with recent combat experience, helped raise the standard of the militia.

- General MacArthur arrived in Australia to command the combined Australian, American and Dutch forces of the newly formed South West Pacific Area. Already American forces had started to arrive in Australia, but MacArthur's presence showed that Australia wasn't alone in the coming struggle.

## MacArthur takes charge

In December 1941 Roosevelt and Churchill divided the world into theatres of war, each to be commanded by a single officer who would report to the Combined Chiefs of Staff (the American and British chiefs of staff sitting together as one committee). As the situation deteriorated in the South West Pacific the Combined Chiefs decided to form a new theatre of war and to appoint General Douglas MacArthur, commander of the American and Filipino forces in the Philippines, to command it.

MacArthur arrived in Australia on 17 March 1942 and formally assumed command of the South West Pacific Area on 18 April, with his headquarters in Melbourne. By that time some American forces, including two American divisions, were arriving in Australia. His forces consisted of:

- Allied Naval Forces, commanded by Vice-Admiral Herbert Leary (US Navy), and including Australian and American naval vessels.

- Allied Land Forces, commanded by General Sir Thomas Blamey and including all the Australian Army in the Australian area and assigned American divisions.

- Allied Air Forces, commanded by Lieutenant General George Brett (US Army Air Forces) and including all American, Australian and Dutch air squadrons in the Australian area.

The land forces formed the largest component and these, under Blamey's command, were deployed to defend Australia as follows:

- First Army, Lieutenant General Sir John Lavarack (defending eastern Australia).
  - 1st Corps: 3rd and 7th Divisions (southern Queensland)
  - 2nd Corps: 1st, 2nd and 10th Divisions (New South Wales)
  - 5th Division (North Queensland)
  - 1st Motor Division (in reserve)
- Second Army, Lieutenant General Sir Iven Mackay (southern Australia).
  - 2nd Motor Division
  - 32nd US Division
  - 41st US Division
- Third Corps, Lieutenant General Henry Gordon Bennett (Western Australia).
  - 4th Division
- Northern Territory Force, Major General Edmund Herring, one division.
- New Guinea Force, Major General Basil Morris, only a brigade.
- Land Force Reserve, 1st Armoured Division.

Most units were from the part-time Australian militia, mobilised for full-time duty at the beginning of the war with Japan, and still being trained and equipped. The 7th Division and a brigade in the Northern Territory had served in the AIF in the Middle East, and the 1st Armoured Division was also an AIF formation. The 32nd and 41st American Divisions were from the National Guard, similar to the Australian militia, and weren't fully trained.

## *The Yanks are here!*

The arrival of thousands of American servicemen had a huge influence on Australia. At the end of April 1942 they numbered 38,000 and increased to 200,000 by the end of June 1943. Under threat of Japanese invasion, Australians were delighted by the American invasion.

## Finding a messiah

General Douglas MacArthur had already had a long and distinguished military career when he arrived in Australia. By 1930 he was Chief of Staff of the US Army, serving under President Roosevelt. Later he became military adviser to the Philippines Government, eventually retiring from the American Army, but he was recalled in July 1941 to command the US forces in the Philippines. His command hadn't been successful. His air force had been destroyed on the ground by Japanese air attacks and his troops on the Bataan peninsula suffered a disaster exceeded only by that of the British at Singapore. MacArthur should have been relieved of his command, but Roosevelt needed a well-known general to boost America's reputation in Australia.

MacArthur's defeat rankled deeply and soon after arriving in Australia he declared: 'I shall return'. Henceforth his campaign to recover the Philippines would become a personal crusade. Aloof, intelligent, widely hated but also admired throughout the American Army, he believed that it was his destiny to lead an Allied force to victory in the Pacific. General Brett, his air commander, described him as 'a brilliant, temperamental egoist; a handsome man, who can be as charming as anyone who ever lived, or harshly indifferent to the needs and desires of those around him'. General Blamey said that the best and worst things you heard about MacArthur were both true.

MacArthur was a man of contradictions. As US Chief of Staff he had kept a Eurasian mistress, formerly a Shanghai chorus girl, while his mother, ignorant of this arrangement, helped him with official entertainment. He married, for the second time, in the Philippines and arrived in Australia with his wife, young son and Chinese housemaid. In January 1942, in the midst of his battle for the Philippines, Filipino President Quezon secretly awarded him $500,000 as 'recompense and reward' from the Philippines' people.

For all his faults, MacArthur gained the confidence of the Australian Government, which hoped that his appointment would ensure American support. He harassed Washington for more troops and slowly put together his new command. He quickly established a close relationship with the Prime Minister, John Curtin. As he said: 'Mr Prime Minister, we two, you and I, will see this thing through together .... You take care of the rear and I will handle the front'. It was a strange pairing of the anti-conscriptionist Labor leader and the imperious, conservative 62-year-old general.

American troops were based in most states, but the largest concentrations of camps were in Queensland. At the peak of the war, Brisbane's pre-war population of 325,000 increased by more than 80,000 American troops. In northern Australia, American bomber squadrons operated from air bases, often built by black American construction troops. Aspects of the American 'occupation' were noteworthy:

- Australians were exposed to American culture, including music (played on the radio to entertain the Americans), eating habits (cafes began selling coffee and hamburgers) and sports such as baseball and American football.

- The American troops were better paid than the Australians, and taxi-drivers and shopkeepers often gave them preference.

- Australian girls were attracted to the well-paid, neatly dressed, polite American servicemen. Between 12,000 and 15,000 Australian women married and followed their husbands or fiancées to the United States at the end of the war.

- In mid-1942 an American soldier, Eddie Leonski, was arrested in Melbourne for strangling three women. He pleaded guilty before an American court martial and was hanged at Pentridge Prison in November 1942.

- American and Australian troops brawled following disputes about rates of pay, women, food rations, race relations and alleged fighting skills. The most notorious incident was the Battle of Brisbane on 26–27 November 1942. Hundreds of servicemen fought each other in the streets of Brisbane. After the American Military Police produced weapons an Australian serviceman was killed, eight people suffered gunshot wounds and several hundred were injured. Censorship kept news of the incident out of the press.

# Thwarting Japan's Plans

Many Australians believe that Japan planned to invade Australia, but this was not the case. Japan's rapid success caught their planners unprepared. On 5 January 1942, when it looked as though they would achieve all their targets by the middle of March, the chief of staff of the Japanese Combined Fleet wrote in his diary: 'Where shall we go from there? Shall we advance into Australia, attack Hawaii; or shall we prepare for the possibility of a Soviet sortie and knock them out if an opportunity arises?' For two months Japan's Imperial General Headquarters debated this question. In the meantime, on 29 January the Commander-in-Chief of the Combined Fleet, Admiral Yamamoto Isoroku, was ordered to capture Lae and Salamaua in New Guinea and, at the proper time, Port Moresby in New Guinea and Tulagi in the Solomons Islands. Lae and Salamaua were seized on 8 March (refer to Figure 14-3).

The Japanese Navy General Staff were keen to invade Australia. On 14 February, one day before the fall of Singapore, a Navy Ministry official told Navy and Army staff in Tokyo that they had 'a good chance to make a clean sweep of Australia's forward bases'. Again, on 27 February, after the successful strike against Darwin and the landings in the East Indies, the Navy General Staff insisted on invading the north-east coast of Australia.

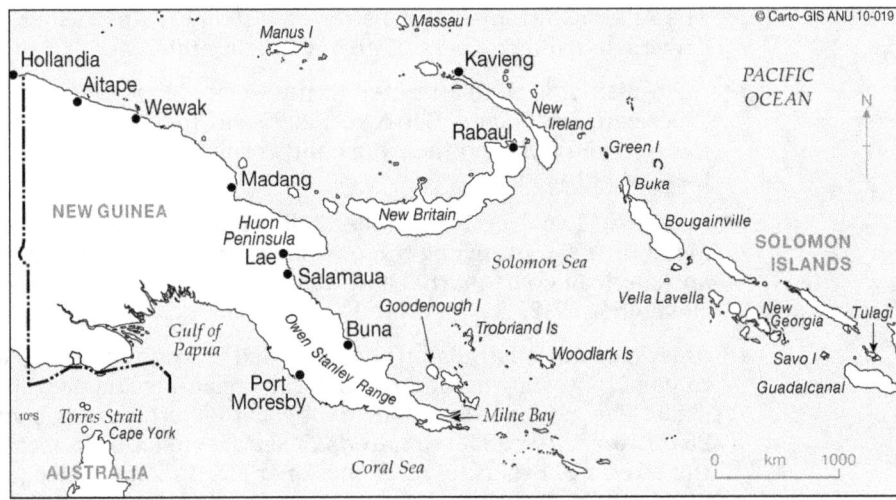

Figure 14-3: Eastern New Guinea and the Solomon Islands.

The Japanese Army resisted the Navy's plans because it couldn't spare the necessary 10 or perhaps 12 divisions from China or Manchuria. If the Red Army collapsed before the German blitzkrieg in the Soviet Union, Japan might launch an invasion of Siberia. Even more crucially, a major assault on Australia would require 1.5 to 2 million tonnes of shipping, most of which was needed to transport the newly gained raw materials back to Japan. Instead, the Army preferred an offensive in Burma and India.

The Navy wasn't unanimous about the need to invade Australia. Admiral Yamamoto wanted to attack Midway in the central Pacific, to draw the US Pacific Fleet into battle. A compromise was reached: The invasions of Australia and India were put aside and on 15 March General Headquarters agreed to capture Port Moresby and the southern Solomons, and 'to isolate Australia' by seizing Fiji, Samoa and New Caledonia. The Japanese planned to form a defensive ring around their Greater East-Asia Co-prosperity Sphere. If they could isolate Australia it would no longer be a base for an American counteroffensive. The security of Australia would therefore depend on the battle for Port Moresby, for if it were captured the Japanese could strike at will at the north coast of Queensland. Further, if the Japanese extended their air and naval bases to Fiji they could interdict the lines of communication between Australia and the United States.

## Assessing enemy intentions

Australian and American military chiefs struggled to assess Japan's intentions. Observing Japan's relentless onslaught, including the raid on Darwin, the capture of Timor and the landing on the north coast of New Guinea, it was reasonable to expect the next step would be an attempted invasion of Australia. The Australian Chiefs of Staff expected the main attack would come through New Guinea and recognised that Port Moresby was the critical point, because aircraft based there could dominate the Coral Sea. The Port Moresby garrison, however, consisted of only one militia brigade, and there were insufficient aircraft and naval ships to reinforce it. Instead, MacArthur and Blamey deployed most of their land forces along the east coast of Australia to repel an attack. The air forces concentrated their bombing squadrons in northern Queensland from which they could attack the Japanese base at Rabaul; it was too dangerous to locate them at Port Moresby.

Soon, however, the military chiefs began to receive intelligence that was to transform their ability to assess the enemy's intentions. Before the war, top-secret British and American intelligence teams had begun intercepting Japanese radio communications and had tried to break the Japanese codes and ciphers. Information gathered in this way was known as *signals intelligence*. During 1941 the Americans broke the Japanese diplomatic cipher traffic (known as *Magic intercepts*) and obtained early warning that the Japanese were planning an offensive in South-East Asia. By early April 1942 two important code-breaking units had been established in Melbourne:

- The US Navy's Fleet Radio Unit in Melbourne (FRUMEL) was staffed by American and Australian naval personnel, and was linked with other US Navy intelligence units in the Pacific.

- Central Bureau, set up by MacArthur, was staffed by American and Australian army and air force personnel, and was linked with British and American signals intelligence organisations around the world.

The existence of the code-breaking units was highly secret, as were their intelligence reports, because if the Japanese knew that the allies were reading their mail they would change their codes and tighten their security procedures. In late April 1942 signals intelligence began providing evidence that the Japanese would soon attempt an invasion of Port Moresby. This intelligence would have an important influence on the course of the war.

## Saving Port Moresby: The Battle of the Coral Sea

In early May 1942 the Japanese planned to send an invasion convoy, escorted by the small aircraft carrier *Shoho*, four cruisers and a destroyer squadron, from Rabaul to seize Port Moresby. Nearby would be a powerful carrier strike force with two large carriers, *Shokaku* and *Zuikaku*, three heavy cruisers and seven destroyers.

Warned by signals intelligence, Allied naval forces sailed to intercept the Japanese convoys. Rear Admiral Frank Jack Fletcher, US Navy, had a task force with the aircraft carriers *Lexington* and *Yorktown* and a separate cruiser force, which included two Australian cruisers, *Australia* and *Hobart*, and was commanded by Australian-born Rear Admiral John Crace, Royal Navy. After halting a Japanese landing at Tulagi in the Solomon Islands, Fletcher sent Crace's cruisers to block the invasion convoy as it turned the corner around eastern Papua, while his carrier force dealt with the Japanese carrier strike force farther east. The confusing battle took place on 7 and 8 May.

In the first sea battle in history in which neither side's ships set eyes on each other, Japanese aircraft sank an American destroyer and crippled an American oil tanker. Crace's cruiser squadron came under heavy air attack (including by American bombers based in Australia), but escaped without loss of ships. Then American aircraft located and sank the light Japanese carrier *Shoho*. The opposing carrier groups were so close to each other that on the first night several Japanese aircraft tried to land on *Yorktown*. Next morning *Yorktown*'s and *Lexington*'s aircraft attacked the heavy carrier *Shokaku*, forcing her to withdraw with damage. Then the experienced Japanese air squadrons struck *Yorktown* and *Lexington*. Lady Lex (as the aircraft carrier was known) was crippled so severely that she was later sunk by American destroyers. *Yorktown* was damaged.

The Americans had lost one large carrier and had another damaged, out of the four available in the Pacific, as well losing a destroyer and a tanker. The Japanese lost one small carrier, one destroyer and several smaller craft, and one of their six fleet carriers had been damaged. But the Japanese called off their sea-borne invasion of Port Moresby, which would now have to await the conclusion of their next offensive, the attack on Midway in early June. Had the invasion fleet not been halted, the Japanese would probably have taken Port Moresby and the war would have taken a different course.

## Threatening our shores: Submarines sneak into Sydney Harbour

Despite the Allied success in the Coral Sea, MacArthur still expected another Japanese attack on Australia and his expectations seemed to be confirmed during the following month. On 20 and 30 May 1942 Japanese aircraft were detected over Sydney and on the night of 31 May Japanese midget submarines entered Sydney Harbour. They tried to sink the US cruiser *Chicago*, missed, and sank an Australian barracks ship, HMAS *Kuttubul*, instead, killing 19 sailors. On the night of 7 June large Japanese submarines fired several shells into Sydney and Newcastle. Already, Japanese submarines were conducting an effective campaign off the Australian coast, sinking three merchantmen during a period of nine days. For the sake of public morale it was fortunate that this news was balanced by better news from the central Pacific.

## Breathing more easily: The Battle of Midway tips the balance

The outcome of the Battle of Midway, fought in the central Pacific on 4 and 5 May 1942, was determined partly by the Battle of the Coral Sea (see the section 'Saving Port Moresby: The Battle of the Coral Sea'). *Shokaku* had too much damage to be repaired in time for the Midway campaign, while *Zuikaku* was retained in home waters to train replacements for the pilots lost in the Coral Sea. Their absence was perhaps crucial. When American code-breakers discovered that the Japanese strike force of four carriers intended to attack Midway, Admiral Chester Nimitz, Commander-in-Chief of the Pacific Ocean Area based at Hawaii, deployed his limited forces. *Yorktown* limped back to Pearl Harbor from the Coral Sea, was quickly repaired in an outstanding feat of engineering, and joined the US carrier task force of *Enterprise* and *Hornet*, under the careful, clear-thinking Rear Admiral Raymond Spruance. Not expecting to encounter American carriers, on 4 June the Japanese were caught off guard. By the end of the battle on 7 June the Japanese had lost all four fleet carriers, while *Yorktown* was damaged and finally sunk by a Japanese submarine. It was the first decisive defeat inflicted on the Japanese and changed the naval balance in the Pacific.

Japan now postponed its plans to seize New Caledonia, Fiji and Samoa; instead, it was now even more urgent to capture Port Moresby. With the loss of the carriers, an amphibious operation was no longer possible and on 7 June Lieutenant General Hyakutake Harukichi, commanding the Japanese forces in the New Guinea–Solomons area from his headquarters in Rabaul, was ordered to plan a land approach over the forbidding Owen Stanley Range to Port Moresby. Six months after the attack on Pearl Harbor, the tide of war was beginning to turn, but the Japanese could still mount a deadly offensive and Australian troops would be in the forefront of halting it.

# Chapter 15

# New Guinea Battles — A Jungle Hell, 1942–44

### In This Chapter
▶ Winning fame on the Kokoda Trail
▶ Fighting bloody battles at the beachheads
▶ Mastering jungle warfare
▶ Coordinating the land, sea and air forces of two nations
▶ Reconquering New Guinea in a brilliant campaign

*B*etween July 1942 and May 1944 Allied forces fought several military campaigns in New Guinea and the Solomon Islands that halted Japan's South Pacific thrust and then drove the enemy back in a series of coordinated offensives, which became a major turning point in the Pacific War.

The first campaign was conducted by the South Pacific Command, with mainly American naval forces, but with some Australian and New Zealand ships. Based in New Caledonia and initially commanded by Vice-Admiral Robert Ghormley, this command halted the Japanese at Guadalcanal and then advanced north through the Solomon Islands to Bougainville.

The second campaign was conducted by the South West Pacific Area Command, under General Douglas MacArthur with his headquarters in Brisbane, Australia (MacArthur opened his headquarters in Brisbane on 20 July 1942, two days before the Japanese landed in Papua). The United States provided most of MacArthur's naval and air forces, while Australia supplied most of the land forces, all under Australian General Sir Thomas Blamey. MacArthur's command, with the Australians playing a major role, stopped the Japanese offensive in Papua and then mounted a counteroffensive along the north coast of New Guinea.

In this chapter I describe Australia's part in these campaigns, concentrating on the exploits of the Australian Army on the Kokoda Trail, at Milne Bay, on the north coast of Papua, in the advance to Salamaua, in the seizure of Lae, and in the fighting around Finschhafen and on Shaggy Ridge. The chapter also describes what it was like to fight and how our troops won against an unrelenting foe in New Guinea's jungles, swamps and mountain ranges.

## Halting Japan's South Pacific Offensive

Following the US Navy's success at the Battle of Midway in June 1942 (see Chapter 14), on 2 July the US Joint Chiefs of Staff ordered an offensive in New Guinea and the Solomon Islands to capture the major Japanese base at Rabaul.

- Ghormley's South Pacific Command was to seize Tulagi and Guadalcanal in the southern Solomons and then proceed north through the island chain towards Rabaul.
- MacArthur's South West Pacific Area was to occupy Buna on the north coast of Papua, construct airfields for his air forces, advance along the north coast of New Guinea and then, at the appropriate time, capture Rabaul.

MacArthur had already started preparing for this offensive and after the Battle of the Coral Sea in May (see Chapter 14) he belatedly began reinforcing New Guinea, sending the militia 14th Australian Brigade to Port Moresby (to join the militia 30th Brigade that had been there since December 1941), and the militia 7th Brigade to Milne Bay, at the eastern tip of New Guinea, to protect the airfields that he had ordered to be constructed there.

### Volunteers and chocos

The Defence Act of 1903 mandated that the Australian Army would consist primarily of part-time militiamen who weren't permitted to serve outside Australia (refer to Chapter 2). For that reason, the Australian Imperial Force (AIF) was raised from volunteers to serve in the First World War and similarly a Second AIF was formed in the Second World War. While the 2nd AIF fought in the Middle East in 1940–42, the militia divisions served in Australia. Some militia soldiers were volunteers, but most were conscripts. The AIF described the militiamen as *chocos*, because they would melt in the sun, or more sarcastically as *koalas*, because they lived only in Australia and were a protected species. At first the militia brigades were not as well trained as the experienced, battle-hardened AIF brigades. Because Papua was an Australian territory, the militia were deployed there before the AIF arrived back in Australia in 1942. Once the AIF divisions returned to Australia, the Army consisted of both militia and AIF divisions and brigades.

# Chapter 15: New Guinea Battles — A Jungle Hell, 1942–44

The Americans failed to realise that the Japanese were still on the offensive. Unlike the Allies, the Japanese fought a single integrated campaign. Lieutenant General Hyakutake Harukichi in Rabaul planned to establish a foothold at Guadalcanal, while other forces seized Buna and marched over the Owen Stanley Range to take Port Moresby (refer to Figure 15-1). Major General Horii Tomitaro, commander of the Japanese South Seas Force, was to conduct a reconnaissance to see if it was indeed feasible to advance overland. While the Allies prepared for their offensive the Japanese moved first. On 21 July their advance party landed at Buna.

Figure 15-1: Eastern New Guinea.

## The Japanese landing at Buna

By the beginning of July 1942 Major General Basil Morris, Commander of New Guinea Force in Port Moresby, had forces in three areas:

- Bulolo Valley (inland from Salamaua). Small elements of the New Guinea Volunteer Rifles and commandos kept watch over the Japanese at Salamaua.
- Port Moresby, 14th and 30th Brigades. Airfields were being prepared for the arrival of Allied fighter and bomber squadrons.
- Milne Bay, 7th Brigade and airfield construction troops.

In preparation for the offensive, General Blamey ordered Morris to send troops to occupy the Buna area, and the locally enlisted Papuan Infantry Battalion and the militia 39th Battalion started trekking over the Kokoda Trail, the narrow footpath that wound a tortuous way over the Owen Stanley Range from Port Moresby to the north coast. (The Kokoda Trail is also called the Kokoda Track and in general conversation was known as 'the track'.)

Only the leading troops had reached the north coast when the Japanese came ashore at Buna. In superior numbers the Japanese forced the Australian and Papuan troops to withdraw towards the village of Kokoda, where there was an airstrip. The Japanese captured Kokoda on 29 July, killing the commanding officer of the 39th. The depleted 39th recaptured Kokoda on 8 August. But the Japanese forces were gaining in strength; the 39th couldn't hold Kokoda and withdrew up the mountain to Isurava.

Realising the threat at last, MacArthur sent more reinforcements.

- Lieutenant General Sydney Rowell, commander of the 1st Australian Corps, went to Port Moresby to take over as Commander of New Guinea Force. Rowell was chief of staff of the Anzac Corps in Greece in 1941 (refer to Chapter 11).
- Major General Arthur (Tubby) Allen, commander of the 7th Division of the Australian Imperial Force (AIF), went to Port Moresby to command the forces there. Allen, a citizen soldier, had led a brigade in North Africa and Greece and the 7th Division in Syria (see chapters 10 and 11). He was accompanied by his division's 21st Brigade.
- Major General Cyril Clowes, a regular army gunner, went to Milne Bay to command the newly formed Milne Force. He was accompanied by the 7th Division's 18th Brigade.

## Guadalcanal and the sinking of HMAS Canberra at Savo Island

In the southern Solomon Islands it was the turn of the Japanese to be surprised. On 7 August US Marines landed on Tulagi and Guadalcanal and quickly overcame the small Japanese garrisons. The American operation was supported by a large naval force that included three aircraft carriers, a battleship and 14 cruisers. Rear Admiral Victor Crutchley, Royal Navy, commanded a squadron of eight cruisers, including the Australian cruisers *Canberra*, *Australia* and *Hobart*.

Not pleased to be pushed off their new airstrip on Guadalcanal, the Japanese attacked the Americans with aircraft based at Rabaul. Vice-Admiral Frank Jack Fletcher therefore withdrew his three carriers, exposing the remaining forces to the Japanese ships. On the night of 8–9 August Japanese cruisers, under Vice-Admiral Mikawa Gunichi, struck at the Allied naval forces protecting the American landing. In the battle of Savo Island, Japanese cruisers, displaying superior night-fighting ability, sank *Canberra* and three US cruisers in one of the US Navy's worst defeats. Captain Frank Getting and 83 others of *Canberra*'s company were killed.

Following this victory, the Japanese landed 1,000 men on Guadalcanal, but on 21 August they lost heavily in an ill-prepared attack on Henderson airfield. While the Americans held the airstrip, where US Marine aircraft were now based, they controlled the surrounding seas by day. But at night the Japanese dominated, bringing in reinforcements to seize the vital airstrip.

The fighting on land and at sea around Guadalcanal turned into a campaign of attrition and on 18 October Vice-Admiral William Halsey relieved Ghormley of command of the campaign. Both sides lost heavily at sea, but eventually the odds began to tilt towards the Americans. The campaign strongly influenced the fighting in New Guinea because the Japanese commander in Rabaul sent most of his forces to Guadalcanal.

## Breaking the Japanese spell at Milne Bay

In the early hours of 26 August Japanese Marines began to land in Milne Bay and advance along the coast towards the Australian positions. Major General Clowes, commander of Milne Force, was still organising his troops. The 18th Brigade had only recently arrived and he had only taken command on 22 August. In addition to the 18th Brigade his force included the 7th Brigade, some American engineers and two squadrons of RAAF Kittyhawk fighters.

On 27 August the Japanese attacked with tanks and drove back the Australians. Operating from rain-soaked jungle airstrips just behind the front, the Kittyhawks flew at tree-top level to support the Australian infantry. The Australians and American engineers eventually halted the Japanese on the edge of one of the airstrips. By 31 August the Australians had regained the initiative and the 18th Brigade advanced, in swamp and jungle, back along the north shore of the bay. Japanese ships withdrew their troops on the nights of 5 and 6 September. The Japanese had lost about 750 killed, while Australian battle casualties were 373. For the first time in the Second World War the Allies had defeated a Japanese offensive on land.

## *Retreating over the Kokoda Trail*

The Japanese began their offensive in the Owen Stanley Range in the morning of 26 August, and at Isurava the militiamen of the depleted 39th Battalion, now under Lieutenant Colonel Ralph Honner, were engaged in a bitter struggle. The 21st Brigade reached the battle area that evening to relieve the 39th. The Japanese South Seas Force had some 13,500 troops and a well-balanced fighting group of five infantry battalions, mountain and anti-aircraft artillery, engineers and pioneers. But not all of them could be deployed and at Isurava about 3,500 Japanese attacked a force of about 2,300 Australians.

A worse area to conduct military operations couldn't be imagined. The track wound its way through thick jungle and across raging mountain streams. All supplies had to be brought forward by native porters and casualties had to be carried back in the same manner. Troops arrived in the forward area after marching for days up and down lung-bursting mountains. The track was awash with mud and soldiers pulled themselves up the slopes by holding onto protruding roots. During the day it was hot and humid. At night the troops were lashed by chilling rain. Soon they were sick with tropical diseases. Supplies were inadequate. Attempts were made to drop supplies by parachute, but many of them disappeared into jungle-covered crevasses.

In these conditions the 21st Brigade under Brigadier Arnold Potts fought a crucial battle. Bravery was commonplace. Private Bruce Kingsbury of the 2/14th Battalion posthumously won the Victoria Cross when he attacked the Japanese with his Bren light machine gun (an excellent British-made long-barrel weapon). At the height of the battle, 30 walking wounded of the 39th, who had been evacuated, heard of their comrades' plight. All but three immediately, and at their own initiative, returned to the forward area; of the three who didn't, one had lost a foot, one a forearm and the third had been shot in the throat.

## Chapter 15: New Guinea Battles — A Jungle Hell, 1942–44

At Isurava the Australians delayed the enemy for four days and inflicted heavy casualties. For the next two weeks the 21st Brigade conducted a fighting withdrawal, always keeping itself between the Japanese and Port Moresby, delaying the Japanese long enough for it to be relieved by the 25th Brigade that had just arrived in New Guinea. By 14 September the 25th Brigade, commanded by Brigadier Ken Eather, had taken up positions on the Kokoda Trail at Ioribaiwa, but next day he withdrew to a firmer position at Imita Ridge, about 45 kilometres by air from Port Moresby. When Eather informed General Allen, the latter approved but made the situation quite clear: 'There won't be any withdrawal from the Imita position, Ken. You'll die there if necessary. You understand that?' Eather said that he did.

MacArthur, who hadn't been to New Guinea and had no idea of the conditions, was highly critical of the Australians, claiming that they were unable to match the Japanese in jungle fighting and that aggressive leadership was lacking. Convinced that the Australian commanders had failed, MacArthur persuaded Prime Minister Curtin to send General Blamey to Port Moresby to take command. When Blamey arrived on 23 September General Rowell saw Blamey's arrival as an indication that he had lost confidence in his ability. Blamey denied that this was the case, but they argued and in one of the most sensational episodes in Australian military history, on 28 September Blamey dismissed Rowell from his command.

Rowell's dismissal made no difference to the outcome, because he had put in place all the actions that eventually were to lead to victory. The tide of battle had already turned. The Guadalcanal campaign was demanding the Japanese main effort and on 18 September General Hyakutake ordered the Japanese South Seas Force in the Owen Stanleys to withdraw to the north coast of Papua.

---

### A harrowing ordeal

Shot in the ankle at Isurava on the Kokoda Trail, Corporal John Metson refused to be borne on a stretcher. 'It will take eight of you chaps to carry that thing', he said. 'I'll get along somehow.' He wrapped torn blankets around his hands and knees and began crawling through mud and rain toward Port Moresby 130 kilometres across the mountains. Two days later the war correspondent Osmar White found him, still crawling, and offered to find some stretcher-bearers. 'If you can get bearers,' Metson snarled, 'then get them for some other poor bastard! There are plenty worse off than me'. A party of wounded soldiers, cut off, set out on an unmapped route, living off sweet potato plants. The Japanese overtook a group of the weakest Australians and killed the helpless men, including Metson, who had crawled for nearly three weeks.

## MacArthur Orders a Counterattack

Once the Japanese offensive had been halted MacArthur ordered a counterattack. The 7th Division, with the 25th Brigade and the newly arrived 16th Brigade, was to advance back over the Kokoda Trail. The untried 32nd American Division flew to New Guinea and was ordered to send some troops via alternative routes to strike the Japanese base area at Buna. General Blamey remained in Port Moresby to supervise, although Lieutenant General Edmund Herring relieved Rowell as Commander of New Guinea Force. Herring was a lawyer who had commanded the 6th Division's artillery in the Middle East and then the force in the Northern Territory.

On 3 October MacArthur and the Army Minister, Frank Forde, visited New Guinea and farewelled the troops as they headed into the mountains. Forde naively told the Diggers of Brigadier John Lloyd's 16th Brigade, some of whom had fought in Libya, Greece, Crete and Syria, that they were about to have their baptism of fire! MacArthur was more eloquent. 'Lloyd' he said, 'by some act of God, your brigade has been chosen to do this job. The eyes of the world are upon you ... Good luck and don't stop'.

## Regaining Kokoda

The 7th Division's advance back over the Kokoda Trail was much harder than it seemed to generals like MacArthur sitting in Brisbane. Because of the narrowness of the track and the ruggedness of the mountains the Australians were restricted to a narrow front. As supplies needed to be carried by native porters the numbers that could be maintained in the forward areas were limited and when supplies were dropped by parachute they were often lost in the jungle. The 25th Brigade cleared Templeton's Crossing before the 16th Brigade took over and struck strong Japanese defences at Eora Creek.

MacArthur in Brisbane and Blamey in Port Moresby believed that the 7th Division wasn't moving fast enough and sent General Allen frequent messages, urging him to speed up the advance. Allen resented this criticism from officers who hadn't visited the front and had no understanding of his problems. Eventually Allen was relieved of his command and Major General George Vasey, who had arrived in Port Moresby to take over its local defences, flew into a newly opened airstrip in the mountains and took over the 7th Division on 28 October. Vasey was a colourful regular soldier who had led the 19th Brigade in Greece and Crete (refer to Chapter 11). Before Vasey could influence the fighting, the Australians overcame the Japanese defences. On 2 November the first troops of the 25th Brigade entered Kokoda, securing its airfield to allow the supply problems to be eased.

## Trapping the enemy at Oivi–Gorari

Moving out of the mountains Vasey set out in pursuit of the Japanese. Soon the 16th Brigade was halted by a strong Japanese position around the village of Oivi. While the 16th Brigade pressed the enemy, Vasey sent the 25th Brigade in a bold sweep through the jungle to swing around the enemy, capture the village of Gorari and cut the enemy's withdrawal route to the Kumusi River. The plan worked and the Japanese were trapped between the two Australian brigades. The battle raged for two days as the Japanese tried to escape. By nightfall on 11 November the Japanese regiment had been completely shattered. Possibly 600 Japanese were killed while others were lost in the rugged country or, like their commander, Major General Horii, drowned trying to cross the Kumusi River.

'"Buna or Bust" is our motto and we will not bust!' signalled Vasey to Herring as his troops reached the Kumusi River on 13 November. But first they had to cross the formidable river, because all the bridges had been destroyed.

## Stalemate at Buna, Gona and Sanananda

While the Japanese were withdrawing through the mountains, others were building strong defences at the beachheads around Buna, Gona and Sanananda on the north coast of Papua. More than 9,000 Japanese were deployed across an 18-kilometre front, mostly swamp and jungle.

On 16 November 1942 the Allies began their offensive to clear the coastal defences. MacArthur had arrived in Port Moresby to provide personal supervision. Vasey's 7th Division advanced on Sanananda and Gona from the east, while the 32nd American Division approached Buna from the south. The attack on the Japanese strongholds was some of the bitterest experienced by the Australians and Americans, as they tried for some two months to break the defences. The Americans were inexperienced and initially performed very poorly. Soon MacArthur called another American general, Robert Eichelberger, up from Australia. He told him to sack the American divisional commander and 'to take Buna or not come back alive'.

Over at Gona and Sanananda, Vasey's troops, after fighting in the mountains, were sick with malaria and his units were under strength. More troops, including the weakened 21st Brigade, flew in but could make little headway. Gona was captured early in December but the Japanese at Sanananda wouldn't give in. By this time General Herring had flown across the mountains with the headquarters of the 1st Australian Corps to coordinate operations of the 7th Australian and 32nd US Divisions. MacArthur urged the troops to move faster so that he could achieve a victory before the US Navy defeated the Japanese at Guadalcanal, but it cost many men their lives.

To break the impasse, General Blamey brought the 18th Brigade around from Milne Bay to support the Americans and a small number of Australian-manned light tanks were sent to Buna by barge. The confident, experienced 18th Brigade and the tanks did the trick at Buna, but not without heavy casualties. By this time, under Eichelberger's leadership, the Americans were learning about jungle warfare.

## A costly victory

After a six-month campaign, the last Japanese resistance in Papua ceased on 22 January. The Japanese committed about 20,000 troops and about 13,000 of these died. Over 2,000 Australians were killed, 3,500 were wounded and 15,500 came down with infectious diseases, mainly malaria. Combined with the victory at Guadalcanal, the Kokoda campaign marked the turning point of the war in the South West Pacific. The Japanese would never again be able to threaten Australia with direct attack. Port Moresby and the Buna area became major bases for the Allied advance during 1943.

# Figuring Out Jungle Warfare

Once the Japanese had been driven out of Papua, the US Joint Chiefs of Staff ordered MacArthur to close in on the Japanese base at Rabaul, giving him two more divisions of ground troops, 524 additional combat aircraft and 336 non-combat aircraft. MacArthur was ordered to:

- Establish airfields on the islands of Kiriwina and Woodlark (refer to Figure 15-1).
- Seize Lae, Salamaua, Finschhafen, Madang and western New Britain (Cape Gloucester).
- Seize the Solomon Islands to include the southern portion of Bougainville.

The third task was given to Halsey's South Pacific Command, operating under MacArthur's strategic direction. To implement this plan, MacArthur divided his troops into four task forces, not counting the South Pacific forces, as follows:

- New Guinea Force, commanded by General Blamey, was composed mainly of Australian Army units, but included some Americans. It had the task of seizing Lae, Salamaua and the Huon Peninsula up to Madang.

- ✔ New Britain Force, commanded by Lieutenant General Walter Krueger of the US Army, was an American force based on the newly formed Sixth US Army. Its task was to seize the islands of Kiriwina and Woodlark and the western end of New Britain.

- ✔ Allied Naval Forces, under Vice-Admiral Arthur Carpender of the US Navy, was composed mostly of US Navy ships with some Australian ships. Its task was to transport and protect the land forces for their amphibious landings. It included a newly formed amphibious force, but no aircraft carriers.

- ✔ Allied Air Forces, under Lieutenant General George Kenney of the US Army Air Forces, included large numbers of American fighter and bomber squadrons, but also an RAAF operational group. They were to destroy enemy aircraft and shipping and provide air transport for the land forces.

General Kenney appreciated that the most effective way to conduct the war wasn't to confront the main Japanese land forces, but to seize airfields, preferably in areas where the Japanese were weakest. Because MacArthur had only a relatively small navy, his air force, based on jungle airstrips rather than on aircraft carriers, became his main striking force. The role of the army was to seize and hold the areas needed for the airstrips and for the naval anchorages and bases. But until the forces had been trained and prepared for the big offensive, other troops had to keep the enemy at bay.

## Air power wins the battle at Wau

In the latter months of 1942 Australian commandos of the 2/5th and 2/7th Independent Companies, operating out of the gold-mining town of Wau in New Guinea, began harassing the Japanese at Salamaua. Wau is only 50 kilometres by air from Salamaua, but the country is extremely rugged with thick jungle, steep mountains, rushing streams and no roads — perfect territory for commandos, but a difficult place to keep troops supplied.

In January 1943 the Japanese decided to capture Wau and, advancing along the jungle trails, began pushing the commandos back to Wau. General Blamey tried to counter the move by flying in the 17th Brigade, under the command of Brigadier Murray Moten, to Wau's airstrip. However, New Guinea's high mountains and thick clouds made flying in the troops by the C-47 Dakota transport aircraft a very slow process.

## A new style of combat

The war in New Guinea forced the Australian Army to learn how to fight in jungle and mountains.

- Infantry divisions, brigades and battalions were restructured to operate with few vehicles and heavy equipment.

- Soldiers learned to live and navigate in the jungle, while carrying all their ammunition and food on their backs. They learned jungle tactics, such as how to counter ambushes and not to panic when cut off from withdrawal routes. Commanders had to use initiative when out of contact with their superiors.

- New resupply techniques were developed, including using native carriers and dropping supplies by parachute.

- Because the artillery often couldn't be dragged through the jungle, troops learned how to call for support from the Allied air forces. Troops were given a higher allocation of weapons such as submachine guns that were effective over short ranges. The Australian-designed Owen submachine gun became famous.

- With no roads in most areas of New Guinea, troops and supplies needed to be moved by aircraft or sea.

- The scourge of tropical illnesses, especially malaria, needed to be combated by the use of newly developed drugs and the disciplined application of rules such as wearing long trousers and sleeves, and sleeping under mosquito nets.

As the 2/6th Battalion's troops arrived progressively, Moten sent them forward, but they weren't in sufficient strength to stop the Japanese, who were cutting new jungle tracks and advancing on several approaches. Captain Bill Sherlock's company fought a heroic rearguard action that delayed the Japanese long enough for more troops to arrive, but he was killed as his company withdrew. By the time the Japanese reached Wau the 2/5th Battalion had arrived. The Japanese attacked on 29 January and while the Australians held them off, aircraft landed under fire and the 2/7th Battalion and two artillery guns unloaded and went straight into action. Some soldiers were shot as they disembarked and at least one went back on the same aircraft that had brought him. By 1 February the Australians had began pushing the Japanese back towards Salamaua.

## Destroying enemy shipping in the Bismarck Sea

Defeated in Papua and in their thrust toward Wau the Japanese began to build up their forces at Salamaua and Lae. At the end of February 1943 a Japanese convoy of eight transports and eight destroyers, escorted by fighter aircraft, left Rabaul carrying 6,000 to 7,000 troops and supplies, bound for Lae.

Alerted by signals intelligence, on 2 March American B-17 Flying Fortress bombers attacked the convoy off the north coast of New Britain and sunk three transports. Next day, 22 RAAF Boston bombers struck the airfield at Lae to keep the Japanese fighters on the ground. Meanwhile, 90 Allied aircraft, including 13 Bristol Beaufighters from No 30 Squadron RAAF, attacked the convoy. The Beaufighters strafed the ships at mast height, while American P-38 Lightning fighters held off the Japanese fighters, destroying 20 of them.

All eight of the Japanese transports and four of the destroyers were sunk. About 3,000 Japanese troops were killed and only about 800 made it to Lae. By any calculation it was an outstanding victory for the Allied air forces, which lost five American and one Australian aircraft. But this wasn't good enough for MacArthur. He released a communiqué stating that 12 transports, 3 cruisers and 7 destroyers had been sunk with a loss of exactly 12,762 men and he tried to take disciplinary action against anyone who disputed these fanciful figures.

## *Closing in on Salamaua*

Although the 17th Brigade had repulsed the Japanese attack on Wau and had started to push the enemy back towards Salamaua, it could only move very slowly because the size of the Australian force was determined by the amount of supplies that could be flown in and then carried forward by native porters. In April Major General Stan Savige, who had earlier commanded a brigade in Libya, Greece and Syria, and the headquarters of the 3rd Division arrived at Wau to take command of the advance on Salamaua.

In preparation for the wider Allied offensive, Savige was ordered to threaten but not capture Salamaua, although initially he wasn't told why. To assist his advance, on 30 June an American infantry regiment landed at Nassau Bay, south of Salamaua, and was placed under his command. Savige's division was built up so that in addition to Moten's 17th Brigade, several independent companies and the Americans, it included the militia 15th Brigade. His troops fought a difficult series of battles against stubborn Japanese defences along the jungle-covered ridges leading to Salamaua.

Savige's troops did their job well, drawing the Japanese forces away from Lae, where the Australians planned to strike next (see the next section). But Savige wasn't to see the final victory. On 29 August Major General Edward Milford and the headquarters of the 5th Division took over the battle. The 29th Brigade relieved the tired 17th Brigade. Once other Australian forces began their attack on Lae on 3 September there was no need to delay the assault on Salamaua and it fell on 11 September. More than 2,000 Japanese had been killed defending Salamaua.

## *Seizing the Enemy Base at Lae*

While the 3rd Division was advancing to Salamaua, MacArthur was putting the finishing touches on his broader campaign to capture the main enemy base at Lae.

Earlier MacArthur had been ordered to capture the Japanese stronghold at Rabaul. But he really was on a personal crusade to recover the Philippines and he wanted to advance along the north coast of New Guinea so that he could strike at the Philippines. Then in August 1943 the Joint Chiefs confirmed that MacArthur need not capture Rabaul, but instead could continue to the western end of New Guinea. MacArthur therefore needed to clear a passage through the Vitiaz Strait that separates the New Guinea mainland from New Britain (see Figure 15-2). To achieve this, his first objective was to capture Lae, after which he could:

- Develop Lae into a major base as it had a good harbour and airfield.
- Undertake an amphibious landing at Finschhafen, which could then become another port and forward operating base.
- Send troops into the Markham and Ramu valleys and build airstrips, from which Allied aircraft could strike Japanese positions farther along the New Guinea coast.

Opposing MacArthur was Lieutenant General Adachi Hatazo's Eighteenth Army, based at Madang, which included:

- The 20th Division, with a strength of about 20,000 troops, at Madang.
- The 51st Division, with about 15,000 troops, in the Lae–Salamaua–Finschhafen area.
- The 41st Division, with about 20,000 troops, at Wewak, 290 kilometres north-west of Madang.

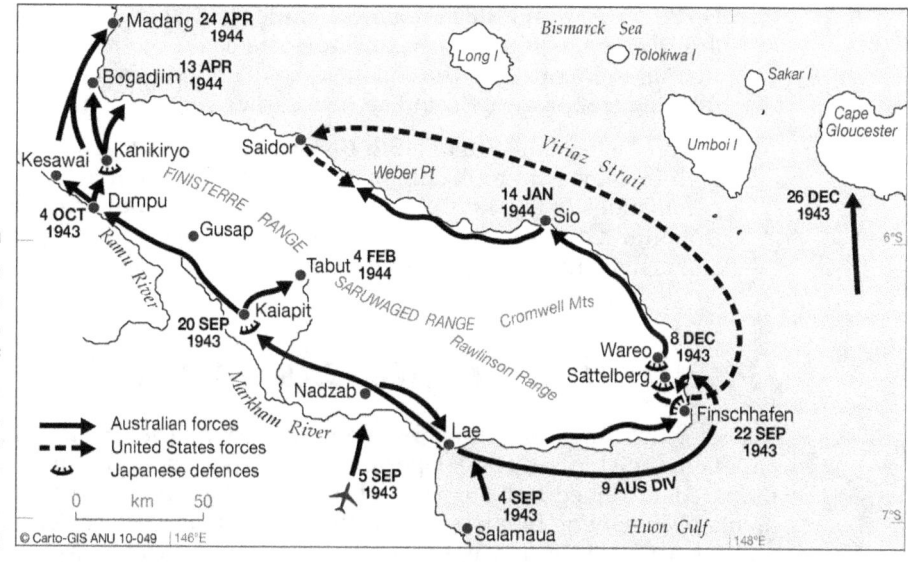

Figure 15-2: The envelopment of the Huon Peninsula, September 1943–April 1944.

## The preparation: Training and planning

General Blamey's Australian troops had the task of capturing Lae, and his plan involved the coordination of Australian and American land, sea and air forces. The main offensive was due to begin in early September, but before then months of careful training and planning were necessary.

- The Australian Army established a new training area on the Atherton Tableland behind Cairns in North Queensland to prepare the troops for jungle warfare.

- Major General George Vasey's 7th Division, worn out from the Papuan campaign, needed to recuperate and begin intensive training in jungle warfare to consolidate the lessons learned in Papua.

- The 9th Division had returned to Australia from the Middle East (where it had fought at El Alamein — refer to Chapter 12). It began training for jungle warfare and also for amphibious operations. Major General George Wootten, who had led the 18th Brigade at Tobruk, Milne Bay and Buna, took over the division.

- While Blamey supervised training and planning in Australia, Lieutenant Generals Sir Iven Mackay and Edmund Herring commanded New Guinea Force, and kept the pressure on the Japanese.

- On 30 June an American regiment landed at Nassau Bay to assist the 3rd Division as it advanced towards Salamaua. By threatening the town the Allies encouraged the Japanese to maintain a large garrison there, drawing troops away from Lae (see earlier section).

- In mid-August, the 7th and 9th Divisions moved to New Guinea, along with Blamey, who took command of New Guinea Force. Herring, commander of the 1st Corps, established his headquarters at Dobodura, on the north coast of Papua, and assumed responsibility for Salamaua and the amphibious landing at Lae.

## Devastating air attacks on Wewak

A key for the Allies was some pre-emptive work by the US Fifth Air Force and its associated 9th RAAF Operational Group. General Kenney secretly prepared advanced airfields west of Wau and even in the New Guinea highlands, enabling him to strike at the Japanese in greater depth. By mid-August 1943 the Japanese had amassed 200 aircraft at Wewak to mount a strong air offensive. Kenney was warned by signals intelligence and on 17 August his Liberators and Flying Fortresses attacked in strength. The Japanese were caught on the ground on four airfields and about 100 aircraft were destroyed. After the war the Japanese air commander described this as a 'decisive Allied victory'. It meant that the Allies would come under fewer enemy air attacks during the coming offensive.

## Landing our troops near Lae

On the night of 3 September 1943 Rear Admiral Daniel Barbey's 7th Amphibious Force, carrying the 9th Division, sailed west along the coast of New Guinea through the Bismarck Sea heading for beaches 25 kilometres east of Lae and Australia's first amphibious landing since Gallipoli in 1915. Before the landing five destroyers bombarded the beaches for ten minutes and when the troops of Brigadier Windeyer's 20th Brigade went ashore just after 6.30 am on 4 September they encountered no opposition. Later in the morning Japanese fighters and bombers attacked, damaging two landing craft and causing 120 casualties, but most were kept at bay by Allied fighters. By 10.30 am 7,800 troops were ashore along with vehicles and guns, and within 36 hours the whole division had landed.

The 9th Division advanced towards Lae, with the 24th Brigade near the coast, the 26th farther inland, and the 20th guarding the beachhead. They met only light resistance, but were held up by the rapidly flowing Busu River. The troops waded across under fire and secured the far bank. Wootten was given the militia 4th Brigade to secure the beachhead and the 20th Brigade joined him for the advance towards Lae.

## Paratroops secure Nadzab

Major General Vasey, commander of the 7th Division, had been ordered to secure the abandoned airstrip at Nadzab, some 30 kilometres north-west of Lae, and he persuaded MacArthur to give him an American parachute regiment. In the morning of 5 September, the day after the 9th Division's amphibious landing, the 503rd American Parachute Regiment, supported by a battery of Australian gunners who, unlike the Americans, were making their first parachute drop, boarded 87 Douglas transport aircraft in Port Moresby and, with a protective screen of fighter and bombers, headed towards Nadzab. The para drop was successful with no Japanese resistance and next day the first troops of Brigadier Ken Eather's 25th Brigade began landing.

In the midst of the operation tragedy struck in Port Moresby. Troops of the 2/33rd Battalion were waiting in trucks near the airfield when a Liberator bomber crashed on take-off, ploughing into five of the trucks. Fifty-nine soldiers died and 92 were injured. The operation continued. The first complete battalion, along with Vasey and his headquarters, arrived on 7 September, and when the remainder of the brigade joined them on 8 September Vasey ordered the brigade to advance towards Lae.

## Racing to take Lae

General Adachi now realised that he had been sucked into Salamaua and ordered his troops there to pull back to Lae. Wootten's 9th Division, closing in from the east, and Vasey's 7th Division, approaching from the north-west, were in a race to capture Lae. On 15 September two battalions of the 7th Division were engaged in a fierce battle in which 15 Australians and more than 100 Japanese were killed. Adachi saw that he could be trapped in Lae, so he ordered his troops to withdraw north through rugged mountain ranges. Alerted by signals intelligence, Vasey sent the 21st Brigade, which had just flown into Nadzab, on a jungle trek to cut them off. They were too late.

In the morning of 16 September Eather's patrols entered the abandoned town of Lae and they were joined by the first troops of the 9th Division that afternoon. Between them the two divisions had accounted for at least 2,200 Japanese, for a combined loss of about 550 Australians killed and wounded. More than 8,000 Japanese had escaped over the towering Saruwaged mountains, but they faced a nightmare journey and the 6,000 survivors reached the north coast in poor shape.

# Forcing the Enemy from the Huon Peninsula

The fall of Lae and Salamaua, coupled with defeat in the central Solomons and elsewhere, caused the Japanese to withdraw to western New Guinea, leaving the garrisons at Rabaul, Bougainville and in eastern New Guinea to fend for themselves. To hold the Vitiaz and Dampier Straits and to deny the Allies access to the Bismarck Sea, however, the Japanese sent reinforcements to Finschhafen. Warned of this move, MacArthur ordered Windeyer's 20th Brigade to take Finschhafen before the Japanese reinforcements arrived.

## A close shave at Finschhafen

On 22 September Admiral Barbey's Amphibious Force landed the 20th Brigade at a beach ten kilometres north of Finschhafen. The troops met some resistance from Japanese machine pieces, and later in the day more than 70 Japanese bombers and fighters appeared over the beachhead; some 90 American fighters beat off the attack and shot down half the Japanese planes. By 1 October the advancing Diggers had captured the village and harbour.

Things then started to go wrong. MacArthur's intelligence staff had estimated that there were between 350 and 2,100 enemy troops at Finschhafen. Blamey's intelligence staff had a much higher estimate (actually, there were 5,000, with more on the way), so Blamey directed the corps commander, Herring, to be prepared to move in the headquarters of the 9th Division and another brigade.

MacArthur and then Blamey headed back to Australia, believing that the campaign had been won. Admiral Barbey said that he had received no orders from MacArthur to transport another brigade to Finschhafen and refused Herring's request to do so. General Mackay, standing in for Blamey as Commander New Guinea Force, couldn't persuade Barbey. By this time the Japanese reinforcements were drawing closer. Mackay appealed to Blamey in Australia. Blamey spoke to MacArthur and on 29 September he directed Barbey to move the troops. The 24th Brigade arrived just in time to repel the Japanese attack.

# Chapter 15: New Guinea Battles — A Jungle Hell, 1942–44

## Scaling the heights of Sattelberg

Major General Wooten, commander of the 9th Division, moved forward to Finschhafen to take command. He was opposed by the Japanese 20th Division, which was hurrying to the area from Madang. The key position was Sattelberg Mountain, which dominated the plain and was held by the Japanese. Wootten directed the 20th Brigade to capture Sattelberg while the 24th Brigade defended the beachhead. But before this offensive began the Japanese mounted a sustained counterattack, which included a heavy air raid and a seaborne landing. The battle continued for several days and as the Australians gained the initiative the 26th Brigade disembarked with tanks.

### An extraordinary soldier

Tom ('Diver') Derrick was one of the Australian Army's most courageous and accomplished soldiers. Born in 1914 he had left school early and had struggled to find employment in the Great Depression. Serving in the 2/48th Battalion, he fought at Tobruk and at El Alamein, where he was awarded the Distinguished Conduct Medal. Those present thought he should have been awarded the Victoria Cross. Slightly wounded, he was promoted to sergeant.

A year later the battalion was in New Guinea. During the assault on Sattelberg, Derrick was commanding the leading platoon when the battalion commanding officer (CO) ordered a withdrawal. Derrick appealed to his company commander: 'Bugger the CO. Just give me twenty minutes and we'll have this place'. He set off up an almost vertical incline covered in jungle. In peacetime the climb is barely possible using both hands and feet. Covered by his platoon members, Derrick alone clambered up the cliff, holding on with one hand, throwing grenades with another, pausing to fire his rifle. He cleared ten machine-gun posts before, at dusk, he reached an open patch, just short of the crest. Fifteen Japanese dead remained on the spur. Derrick's platoon occupied the area. That night the remaining Japanese withdrew. Awarded the Victoria Cross, Derrick said that the achievement was due mainly to his mates.

By May 1945 the battalion was fighting on Tarakan, Borneo, when Derrick, now a lieutenant, led his platoon in a successful attack. As grenades burst among them, 'Diver was everywhere, encouraging, shouting orders, pressing us on', recalled one of his soldiers. They thought his actions were worthy of a bar to his Victoria Cross. That night a shot from an enemy machine gun struck him in the abdomen. 'I've been hit. I think it's curtains', he said, 'I've copped it in the fruit and nuts' (rhyming slang for 'the guts'). He insisted that the other wounded be evacuated first and died next day. Not overtly religious, he asked a friend to get the padre so that he could 'bring on the hocus pocus'. Cheerful to the end, he had done his duty as he saw it.

The 26th Brigade led the assault on Sattelberg, assisted by tanks, artillery and the 24th Brigade. But it took another month of fighting before Sergeant Tom Derrick's platoon from the 2/48th Battalion captured the crest on 24 November (see the sidebar 'An extraordinary soldier').

## Stepping up the pace of the advance

Once the Finschhafen area had been secured and the harbour developed, MacArthur was able to launch his attacks on the other side of the Vitiaz Strait. On 15 December troops of the American 1st Cavalry Division landed at Arawe, New Britain, and secured the area. Then on 26 December troops of the 1st Marine Division landed at Cape Gloucester.

Meanwhile, the 9th Division advanced along the north coast of New Guinea and in mid-January the militia 5th Division, under Major General Alan Ramsay, who had commanded the 9th Division artillery at El Alamein, took over. In the four months since landing at Finschhafen, the 9th Division had defeated the Japanese 20th Division. More than 3,000 Japanese had been killed, while 283 Australians were killed.

On 2 January troops from the American 32nd Division landed at Saidor and cut off the Japanese withdrawal route. The Japanese were able to strike inland and bypass Saidor, but they suffered extreme hardship and reached Madang in an exhausted condition. About 2,500 Japanese were killed or died of starvation and illness in this final phase.

## Into the Finisterre Range: The 7th Division's Offensive

While the Finschhafen campaign was being played out, the 7th Division was conducting a remarkable operation elsewhere. Between the mountains of the Huon Peninsula and the main mountain ranges of central New Guinea are the broad valleys of the Markham and Ramu Rivers, one flowing south-east and the other north-west. In this valley MacArthur planned to build airstrips, from which his air force could support his advance along the north coast of New Guinea by striking at Hollandia in Dutch New Guinea. The task went to Vasey's 7th Division, which had just captured Lae.

## Quick thinking captures Kaiapit

Soon after the capture of Lae, Vasey learned that the Japanese were planning to push down the Ramu valley towards the village of Kaiapit on the Markham side of the watershed between the two rivers. Moving quickly, he flew the 2/6th Independent Company to a pre-war airstrip near to Kaiapit. The approach to Kaiapit was through high kunai grass in stifling heat, but the commandos caught the Japanese by surprise and, attacking with grenades and bayonets, cleared them from the airstrip late on 19 September. Next day the Japanese counterattacked. The Australians held off the Japanese, who lost almost 200 killed. The independent company had begun the action 190 strong, but now numbered fewer than 140 and was low in ammunition.

In the morning on 21 September some of the weary commandos, assisted by local natives, cleared the airstrip, and late in the day Vasey landed in a Piper Cub aircraft to test the airstrip. That evening Brigadier Iven Dougherty, commander of the 21st Brigade and the first troops of his brigade started to land in transport aircraft, with more arriving the next day. Lieutenant General Nakai Masutaro, commander of the Japanese 20th Division, had planned to hold Kaiapit with a regiment.

## Chasing the Japanese through Death Valley

Vasey urged the 21st Brigade to advance into the steaming Ramu valley, known by the natives as Death Valley because of the high incidence of malaria, and after a few sharp actions the 21st captured Dumpu on 4 October. Vasey depended on supplies being flown into the forward airstrips, but as the 9th Division became embroiled at Finschhafen, the air support was withdrawn from Vasey. He flew in the 25th Brigade when aircraft could be spared, but that was the limit of his force. The Japanese were withdrawing, but Vasey lacked sufficient strength to press them strongly.

## A one-man front on Shaggy Ridge

By early October the Japanese had been chased out of the central and upper Ramu valley, while Australian commandos patrolled the swamps of the lower valley. Vasey now turned his attention to the towering, jungle-covered Finisterre Range that separates the Ramu valley from the north coast of New Guinea. The Japanese had tried to build a road across the mountains from Madang and now they constructed strong defences along the narrow ridges, manned by 12,000 men, to stop the Australians reaching Madang. The 21st Brigade pushed into the mountains and in determined battles gained a foothold on a long razor-edge spur known as Shaggy Ridge. Vasey rotated the 21st and the 25th Brigades, but with limited supplies and conscious that his main task was to defend the airfields, which were being rapidly developed, he couldn't mount a major offensive.

Early in January 1944 Vasey received fresh troops. His third brigade, the 18th, relieved the 21st, and the militia 15th Brigade, which had fought at Salamaua, took over from the 25th. Vasey decided to make a major effort to break through in the mountains using Brigadier Fred Chilton's 18th Brigade. The advance was supported by the RAAF's No 10 Operational Group that included fighters and dive bombers. The Diggers were forced to advance on a one-man front because of the narrow precipitous ridges, supported with heavy artillery concentrations and strafing attacks by Kittyhawks.

Vasey's instructions were reported to have included a typical order. 'The 7th Division will advance on a one-man front. Anyone disobeying this order will break his bloody neck.'

On 21 January the 18th Brigade attacked the main enemy position at Kankiryo Saddle, defended by determined Japanese in well-constructed and concealed log emplacements. Under heavy artillery, mortar and air attack the Japanese finally withdrew on 1 February. The 15th Brigade threatened the Japanese lines of communication, and on 8 April Major General Alan Boase and the headquarters of the 11th Division took over the offensive. The troops entered Madang on 24 April, just ahead of those of Ramsay's 5th Division. The advance through the mountains with limited supplies, native carriers and support troops had been a remarkable effort, especially when Vasey had been ordered merely to defend the airstrips in the Ramu valley.

## The final prize: Madang

For almost a year the Australians had strived to reach Madang, but the final prize proved to be an anticlimax. The exhausted Diggers withdrew to Australia for rest and retraining, leaving smaller forces to maintain pressure on the Japanese. Already, the Australian campaign had been completely overtaken by American operations elsewhere. On 29 February 1944 MacArthur's American troops carried out a daring 'raid' to seize Los Negros in the Admiralty Islands and complete the encirclement of Rabaul. The Joint Chiefs now told MacArthur to abandon any plans of capturing Rabaul.

Instead, MacArthur directed a series of landings by American troops along the northern New Guinea coast that isolated 40,000 Japanese in the Wewak area. His forces took Aitape and Hollandia on 23 April, Sarmi and Wakde on 17 May, Biak on 27 May, Noemfoor on 2 July and Sansapor on 30 July. In three months MacArthur's forces had advanced 1,400 kilometres.

The naval support for the American landings included Task Force 74, commanded by Rear Admiral Crutchley, and comprising the Australian cruisers *Australia* and *Shropshire*, the Australian destroyers *Arunta* and *Warramunga* and two American destroyers. Later Commodore John Collins took over from Crutchley, becoming the first graduate of the Royal Australian Naval College to command an Australian naval task force. Three former Australian passenger ships, *Manoora*, *Kanimbla* and *Westralia*, which had been converted to become naval landing ships, were among the 19 transports involved in the amphibious operations. The RAAF's No 10 Operational Group, commanded by Air Commodore Frederick Scheger and later Air Commodore Harry Cobby, provided Kittyhawk squadrons, which supported the landings by bombing and strafing enemy positions.

The story of the spectacular American advance shouldn't be allowed to overshadow the Australian Army's brilliant campaigns of 1943. Between March 1943 and April 1944 the Australians, under Blamey, had deployed five infantry divisions, losing about 1,200 killed. Japanese losses numbered about 35,000. In an impressive orchestration of the land, sea and air forces of two countries the campaign provided the firm base for the next phase of MacArthur's advance towards the Philippines.

# Chapter 16

# Fighting to the Finish, 1944–45

*In This Chapter*

▶ MacArthur sidelines our soldiers and airmen
▶ Blamey's army fights its own war
▶ Liberating British and Dutch territory in Borneo
▶ Winning our seat at the peace table

From April 1942, when General Douglas MacArthur took command of the South West Pacific Area, until April 1944, when Australian troops captured Madang in New Guinea, the Australian Army formed the largest component of MacArthur's land forces. Australian troops conducted most of the fighting during the New Guinea campaign, while Australian naval and air units supplemented MacArthur's forces. Australia also provided MacArthur with an indispensable mounting base and much of his logistic support came from Australia.

As increasing numbers of American troops, aircraft and ships arrived in the South West Pacific, however, MacArthur was determined to exclude Australian land and air forces from future offensive operations. In March 1944 he told the Prime Minister, John Curtin, that three Australian divisions and an American paratroop division would spearhead his advance, but this wasn't true; his plans didn't include the Australians in the next main offensive.

By that time the American Army was advancing rapidly along the north coast of New Guinea. Most of the naval and air forces were American, although Australian ships and an RAAF operational group assisted. MacArthur had his eyes firmly fixed on his next target, the Philippines. MacArthur's forces continued advancing towards the Philippines from New Guinea, while the US Navy attacked across the Pacific. On 15 September the US Joint Chiefs approved a landing by MacArthur's forces on Leyte (see Figure 16-1), beginning on 20 October. In the last year of the war MacArthur's forces secured the Philippines and then prepared for the invasion of Japan.

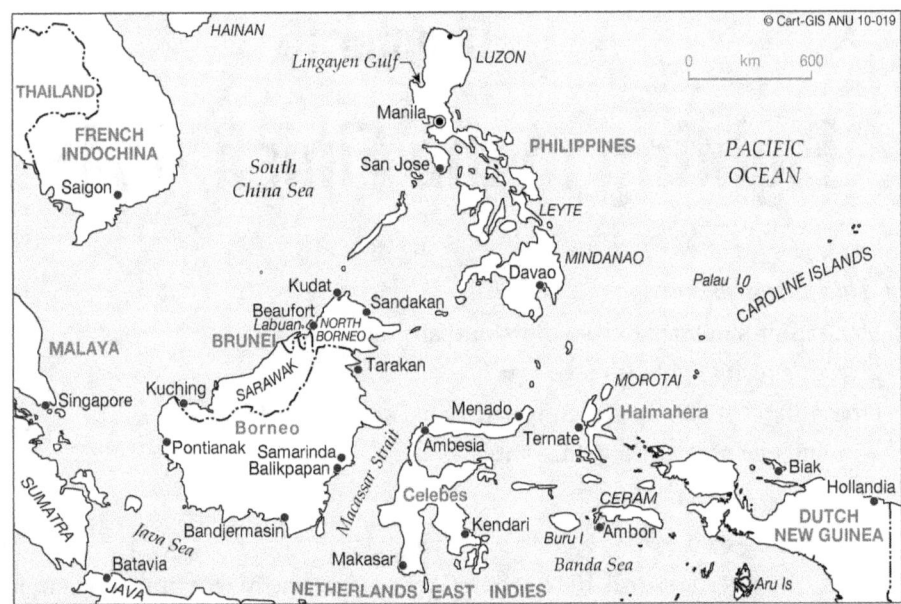

Figure 16-1: Borneo and the Philippines.

In this chapter I describe Australia's operations in the last year of the war. While the torch had passed from Australian troops to American forces in the most-publicised offensives, Australian forces still had important work to do. Our ships helped MacArthur in the invasion of the Philippines, and our troops continued fighting in New Guinea and fought in New Britain, Bougainville and Borneo. Though controversy still rages over whether our troops really needed to conduct their final campaigns, when the fighting stopped in August 1945 we had more troops in combat than at any other time in the war.

# With MacArthur to the Philippines

In preparation for his operations in the Philippines, MacArthur reorganised his command.

- He had been given control of the American forces in the Solomons (formerly under South Pacific Command) and he now had 18 American divisions.

- In addition to Lieutenant General Walter Krueger's Sixth Army, MacArthur formed a new army, the Eighth, under Lieutenant General Robert Eichelberger.

✓ General Blamey was still nominally Commander of the Allied Land Forces, but MacArthur effectively ignored Blamey's role and issued orders directly to the Sixth and Eighth Armies.

MacArthur ordered Blamey to relieve the six American divisions engaged in garrison or holding operations in the Solomons (primarily Bougainville) and New Guinea so that they would be available for the Philippines. Blamey produced plans to use seven Australian brigades. MacArthur insisted that Blamey use 12 brigades — or four Australian divisions — thus making fewer Australian divisions available for the Philippines. The 6th and the 9th Divisions, which had performed so well in New Guinea, could still be used in the Philippines, but in truth, MacArthur had no intention of using the Australians in what he intended to be a purely American operation. In effect, he was holding the Australians in reserve in case of an emergency.

The Royal Australian Air Force (RAAF) was similarly sidelined. In the New Guinea campaigns RAAF squadrons had operated effectively as part of the US Fifth Air Force. In October 1944 No 10 Operational Group, under Air Commodore Cobby, was retitled the First Tactical Air Force, and it included eight flying squadrons and four airfield construction squadrons, which already had made a significant contribution to MacArthur's strategy of seizing and developing airfields. Cobby moved his headquarters to Morotai and his squadrons assisted in the invasion of Leyte, but thereafter his squadrons were generally restricted to supporting the Australian Army's operations.

## Our ships at Leyte: The greatest sea battle

The Leyte landing on 20 October 1944 was one of the larger military operations of the war. The invasion force consisted of the US 7th Fleet under Vice-Admiral Thomas Kinkaid and four infantry divisions of Krueger's Sixth Army. Admiral Halsey's powerful US Third Fleet, with 16 carriers, provided support. Assembled at short notice, the total force numbered 700 ships and some 160,000 men and was mounted from multiple bases, some more than 1,000 kilometres distant. By the end of the first day at Leyte, 50,000 men were ashore, plus 4,500 vehicles and 107,000 tons of stores.

MacArthur waded ashore at Leyte on the afternoon of 20 October, the occasion well captured by waiting photographers. The Philippines President, Sergio Osmena, accompanied him and both delivered radio broadcasts. 'People of the Philippines, I have returned!' said MacArthur, 'By the grace of Almighty God, our forces stand again on Philippine soil . . . Rally to me!'

Ships of the Royal Australian Navy (RAN) were part of the invasion force. Commodore John Collins's Task Force 74 included the Australian cruisers *Australia* and *Shropshire* and the Australian destroyers *Arunta* and *Warramunga*. Three Australian landing ships, *Kanimbla*, *Manoora* and *Westralia*, were among the troop transports. In the Leyte Gulf for the first time the Japanese started using the *Kamikaze* (suicide) tactic of piloting aircraft directly into Allied ships and the Australian flagship *Australia* was the first ship to be struck. A Japanese dive bomber ploughed into its foremast, killing or mortally wounding 30 of the crew, including Captain Emile Deschaineux, and wounding 64 others, including Collins, who was seriously wounded.

Meanwhile, the Japanese Navy, under the tactical command of Vice-Admiral Ozawa Jizaburo, converged on the US fleet. Ozawa lured Halsey north away from the landing area while he sent two striking forces into the Leyte Gulf. The Battle of the Leyte Gulf, beginning on 24 October, was the largest and one of the most decisive naval battles in history. *Shropshire* and *Arunta* formed part of the southern blocking force and *Shropshire* engaged the Japanese battleship *Yamashiro* with eight inch shells, contributing to her destruction. By 26 October the Japanese had lost four carriers, three battleships, nine cruisers and ten destroyers. The Japanese Navy never recovered from this defeat.

## Combating Kamikaze attacks at Lingayen Gulf

After securing Leyte, MacArthur moved north and on 9 January 1945 the Sixth Army landed at Lingayen Gulf on the main Philippines island of Luzon. Commodore Harold Farncomb had taken over Task Force 74 from the wounded Collins and the Australian ships included *Australia* (repaired after the Leyte battle), *Shropshire*, *Arunta*, *Warramanga*, the frigates *Gascoyne* and *Warrego* and three transport ships.

By this time the Japanese had perfected their Kamikaze techniques and the naval force came under sustained attack, in which 25 American ships were sunk or damaged. *Australia* was struck five times, survived, but was forced to withdraw from operations having lost 44 of her crew killed and many others wounded. *Arunta* was also damaged, but *Shropshire*, which now became Farncomb's flagship, was one of the few ships to escape unharmed.

## The secret story of our code breakers

In 1942 MacArthur formed the Central Bureau, primarily from Australian army and air force and American army personnel, to provide signals intelligence for his command. Signals intelligence is gained by intercepting and decoding enemy wireless and cable communications. Central Bureau and the US Navy Fleet Radio Unit in Melbourne (FRUMEL) gave MacArthur access to priceless intelligence about Japanese strengths and intentions. In April 1943 signals intelligence warned that Admiral Yamamoto, Commander-in-Chief of the Japanese Combined Fleet, would be visiting his forces in the Solomon Islands. Eighteen American fighters from Guadalcanal intercepted Yamamoto's bomber and its escorts over Bougainville and shot it down in flames.

The most important break came in January 1944, when Australian infantry, pursuing the Japanese at Sio on the New Guinea coast, found a steel trunk near a river and recovered the entire cipher library of the Japanese 20th Division. MacArthur was able to plan his operations during 1944 with full confidence in his understanding of his adversary's capabilities. Australian army and air force personnel deployed into forward area with wireless intercept units to provide immediate intelligence to Australian and American commanders. Some of these worked with the Americans on Leyte and Luzon. By May 1945, when the Central Bureau began moving from Brisbane to Manila, it had a strength of 4,000 scattered across the theatre; about half of these were Australians. The men who served in the wireless intercept units and the men and women who worked in Central Bureau played a vital role in the Allied victory, but were sworn to secrecy. Their stories didn't begin to be told until the early 1990s.

# Mopping Up in New Guinea and the Islands

Between October 1944 and the end of the war in August 1945 Australian forces fought a series of mopping-up operations in the Australian territories of New Guinea, New Britain and Bougainville (refer to Figure 16-2). The operations were commanded by Lieutenant General Vernon Sturdee, commander of the First Australian Army, with his headquarters at Lae in New Guinea. Sturdee had been Chief of the General Staff in 1941 and the desperate days of early 1942. His forces were deployed as follows:

- Aitape-Wewak area of New Guinea, 6th Division, Major General Jack Stevens
- Madang, 8th Brigade, Brigadier Maurice Fergusson (garrison duties)
- New Britain, 5th Division, Major General Alan Ramsay
- Bougainville, 2nd Corps, Lieutenant General Stanley Savige

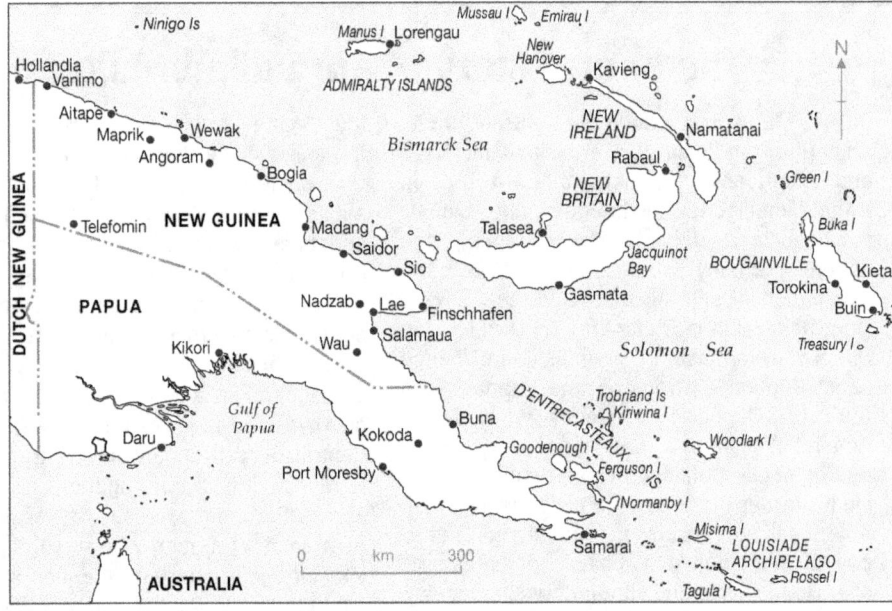

Figure 16-2: The Territories of Papua and New Guinea, including Bougainville.

The campaigns conducted by these forces have been the subject of much controversy, being seen as unnecessary and a waste of Australian lives. Blamey has been criticised for ordering them without consulting the Australian Government. However, MacArthur was ultimately responsible for all the operations conducted in his command, which included New Guinea, and his American forces were already undertaking similar operations in the southern Philippines islands. Yet when asked by Prime Minister Curtin whether the operations were necessary, MacArthur replied that 'if he was doing the job himself, he wouldn't jeopardise a single Australian life in an offensive in these back areas'.

Public disquiet about the operations was heightened by the lack of information about them. MacArthur insisted that no news of Allied operations could be released except in his own communiqués and these failed to mention the Australian operations in New Guinea. The Australian official historian Gavin Long wrote: 'Probably never in the history of modern war had so large a force, although in action, been hidden from public knowledge for so long'.

In May 1945 Blamey argued the case for the offensives to the War Cabinet.

- If the troops maintained a passive role their morale would suffer. This argument was difficult to sustain as the morale of the troops that merely patrolled their areas of responsibility was no lower than that of those engaged in offensives.

- Blamey was required to demobilise some troops and make others available for the invasion of the main island of Japan in March 1946. To withdraw his troops from New Guinea and Bougainville, where they were likely to suffer from tropical diseases, he needed to eliminate the Japanese forces there. He didn't know that the war would end abruptly in August 1945.

- Japanese forces were occupying Australian mandated territories. As Blamey argued, 'Were we to wait until Japan was finally crushed, it could be said that the Americans, who had previously liberated the Philippines, were responsible for the final liberation of the natives in Australian territories, with the inevitable result that our prestige both abroad and in the eyes of the natives would suffer much harm'.

The War Cabinet endorsed the operations retrospectively. We can now see that the offensives had no bearing on the outcome of the war and even at the time many soldiers resented the loss of lives in unnecessary battles. But the government considered it to be in the national interest to keep substantial forces in the field so that Australia could be seen to be a major partner in the war and hence entitled to a seat in future peace negotiations.

## *Resenting every death in Bougainville*

When the Americans invaded Bougainville in November 1943 they occupied an area around Torokina on the west coast, but made no effort to eliminate the Japanese army, thought to number 12,000, occupying the rest of the island. The Japanese, who actually numbered almost 40,000, were cut off from resupply but were growing food and still posed a powerful force. The 2nd Australian Corps, under Lieutenant General Savige, began relieving the Americans in October 1944. Savige's forces included Major General William Bridgeford's 3rd Division (7th, 15th and 29th Brigades), and the 11th and 23rd Brigades (from the 11th Division). All were initially based at Torokina except for the 23rd Brigade, which deployed battalions to each of Emirau, Green and Treasury islands, scattered to the north and south of Bougainville. Savige had led the militia 3rd Division in the advance to Salamaua in 1943 (see Chapter 15) and his brigades, all from the militia, had previously served in New Guinea.

As his forces built up, Savige began three offensives:

- In the north the 11th Brigade sought to destroy the enemy in a peninsula at the northern end of the island. The offensive struck heavy resistance, particularly during an abortive amphibious landing at Porton Plantation, and halted in May 1945 without reaching its objective.

- In the centre the 7th Brigade aimed to clear the island's central ridge line and threaten enemy communications. This objective was reached by January 1945, but other troops continued to patrol the area.

- In the south the 3rd Division began a more substantial offensive towards the main Japanese base at Buin at the southern end of the island. On 30 March the Japanese mounted a major counterattack at Slater's Knoll against the 25th Battalion (7th Brigade), which repelled the week-long attack with tanks and artillery. The 15th and the 29th Brigades continued the southern offensive in rain, swamp and jungle.

When hostilities ceased in August 1945 the Australians had lost 516 killed and 1,572 wounded, but had still not captured Buin. In the campaign, about 8,500 Japanese had been killed in combat, about 9,800 died of illness and 23,571 surrendered. The Australians had shown great fortitude in pressing an offensive that they knew wouldn't change the outcome of the war.

## *Keeping watch over Rabaul*

In October 1944 the militia 5th Division, under Major General Alan Ramsay, landed at Jacquinot Bay on the south coast of New Britain to take over from the Americans. The division had previously served at Salamaua and in the advance to Madang. The Australians believed that the Japanese army in New Britain was concentrated around Rabaul in the Gazelle Peninsula and was about 38,000 strong. In fact the Japanese army numbered about 93,000. The Australian troops quickly crossed the island and then advanced eastwards, driving the enemy's outposts back into the Gazelle Peninsula.

The Japanese commander at Rabaul, General Imamura Hitoshi, held his main forces closer to Rabaul, where they could be better supplied. He hoped that the Allies would launch a major attack on Rabaul as he expected that their casualties would reach at least 100,000. But the Australians were too wise for this. They refused to mount a major attack. Instead, the Australians and Japanese were involved mainly in patrol clashes at the southern end of the Gazelle peninsula. By the time hostilities ceased in August 1945, in a period of ten months of operations the 5th Division had suffered only 182 battle casualties, 48 of whom were killed. More than 100,000 Japanese surrendered in New Britain and New Ireland. The Allies were amazed at the numbers of Japanese troops in Rabaul, because their intelligence estimates had put the figure much lower.

## Slogging it out at Aitape and Wewak

In April 1944 American troops landed at Aitape on the northern New Guinea coast, bypassing and trapping Lieutenant General Adachi Hatazo's Eighteenth Japanese Army at Wewak, about 300 kilometres to the east. The Japanese tried to break through the Americans at the battle of Driniumor River east of Aitape in July, but lost heavily. By the time the 6th Division, commanded by Major General Jack Stevens, took over from the Americans at Aitape in October 1944 the Japanese army had been reduced in size, but still numbered 35,000. The AIF 6th Division had been the first division to serve in the Middle East in 1940–41. Its 16th Brigade had fought on the Kokoda Trail and the 17th at Wau, but the 19th had not seen action since Crete in May 1941.

Stevens began an offensive towards Wewak, with the 19th Brigade advancing along the coast. The 17th headed into the Torricelli Mountains to clear Japanese gardens and support the natives who, with Australian commandos, were conducting a guerrilla campaign against the Japanese. Then the 17th Brigade advanced east on an inland route. The 16th Brigade relieved the 19th and by April it was approaching Wewak. In early May the Australians attacked Wewak, with the 19th Brigade resuming the advance along the coast while the 2/6th Cavalry (Commando) Regiment landed by ship east of Wewak to cut off the Japanese escape route. The naval force, commanded by Commodore Farncomb, included the cruisers *Hobart* and *Newfoundland* (British), the destroyers *Arunta* and *Warramunga*, the sloop *Swan* and the corvettes *Colac* and *Dubbo*. Air support came from RAAF and American aircraft.

The Australians successfully captured Wewak, but the Japanese withdrew into the mountains and were still resisting when hostilities ceased in August. In the ten-month campaign the Japanese lost 9,000 killed, while 12,000 to 14,000 died of illness. Australian casualties were 442 killed and 1,141 wounded. The Australians showed that they could operate effectively in the jungle during the hard-fought campaign. Most of the air and naval support had been provided by Australian forces, rather than by the Americans, as had been the case in the past.

## Unnecessary Battles in Borneo

In the last months of the war MacArthur ordered the 1st Australian Corps, including the 7th and 9th Divisions, to conduct three major operations in Borneo to secure Tarakan, Brunei and Balikpapan (refer to Figure 16-1). In preparation, Blamey moved his advance headquarters forward to Morotai where Lieutenant General Sir Leslie Morshead, the corps commander, was also located. Morshead had commanded the 9th Division at Tobruk and El Alamein (see Chapter 12), and the 2nd Corps during the fighting around Finschhafen and Sattelberg in late 1943 (see Chapter 15).

For these final operations the RAAF's main operational command, known as RAAF Command, led by Air Vice-Marshal William Bostock, was given responsibility for all Allied air force operations south of the Philippines. Bostock moved his headquarters to Morotai so that he could coordinate his operations with those of the Australian Army. His command consisted of RAAF and New Zealand squadrons.

The necessity for these final operations is even more questionable than the mopping-up operations in Bougainville and New Guinea. On 1 April 1945 American forces from Pacific Ocean Command began a large-scale invasion of Okinawa, a Japanese island midway between the Japanese home islands and Taiwan. The battle lasted two and a half months, but it made all other operations further south strategically irrelevant because the Americans were now closing in on the Japanese home islands, cutting their lines of communication to South-East Asia.

Nonetheless, MacArthur wanted to capture the Borneo oilfields. He also wanted to demonstrate that he had regained the former British and Dutch territories in Borneo, and the Dutch colony in Java. Blamey reluctantly agreed to the operations in Borneo, but refused to allow MacArthur to use the 6th Division to invade Java. Curtin supported Blamey. MacArthur's biographer, D Clayton James, observed that it was 'most fortunate for the lives' of the Australian soldiers that MacArthur didn't get 'his way on the Java plan, for the two-division invasion could have produced the most tragic blood bath of the Pacific War'.

## Seizing Tarakan for oil and airfields

Tarakan is a small island off the north east coast of Borneo and MacArthur wished to capture it because it would

- Provide a naval and air base to support future operations in Borneo
- Re-establish the Netherlands Indies government
- Conserve the oil installations

The task went to Brigadier David Whitehead's 26th Brigade, which was strongly reinforced with two pioneer battalions, commandos and tanks and numbered nearly 12,000. The Japanese defenders numbered 2,100. The Allied naval force included six Australian warships and two Australian landing ships. The landing began on 1 May and the brigade was soon safely ashore, advancing against light opposition. The Japanese, however, occupied strong defensive positions in the centre of the island and while the Australians systematically destroyed the enemy defences not all of them had been dealt with by the end of hostilities in August.

Engineers laboured hard to repair the airfields, but they were hampered by a high watertable, rain and lack of materials, and the airfields couldn't be made operational in time to support the other Borneo landings. Similarly, the oilfields took a year to bring back to production. During the campaign the Australians lost 225 killed and 669 wounded. The Japanese lost 1,540 killed, 252 captured before the ceasefire, and more than 300 captured after it.

## Secret and special warriors

Australian military personnel served in several special units that fought their own secret wars across South-East Asia and the South West Pacific. One celebrated group was the Coastwatchers, generally long-time residents of New Guinea and the islands, who served as Navy reservists. During the last half of 1942 Coastwatchers in the Solomons observed Japanese ships sailing through the islands and radioed warnings to the Americans at Guadalcanal. Many of the Coastwatchers were tracked down by the Japanese and killed.

Later, Australian servicemen in the Special Reconnaissance Department, popularly known as Z Special Force, worked with the natives in New Guinea and Borneo, carrying out guerrilla campaigns against the Japanese.

The most famous operation (Operation Jaywick) was the raid on Singapore in September 1943 by 11 Australian and 3 British commandos, led by a British officer, Major Ivan Lyon. The raiders sailed from Australia in a captured Japanese fishing vessel, the *Krait*, disguised as a local fishing boat until they were close enough to approach Singapore in kayaks. Using limpet mines, they sank or seriously damaged seven Japanese ships in Singapore Harbour.

In October 1994 Lyon led a larger group of commandos on Operation Rimau. They travelled to the Singapore area by submarine, commandeered a Malay junk and planned to attack with semi-submersible canoes. A Japanese patrol intercepted them and the group was dispersed. A small party apparently made it into the harbour and sank three ships. Ten of the party were captured and executed at Singapore, some were killed during a fight with the Japanese and several escaped and tried to reach Australia by canoe. They were eventually caught and executed.

## Regaining British Borneo

The next landings were made on the small island of Labuan, off the coast of British North Borneo, and on the mainland in Brunei Bay, and were undertaken by Major General George Wootten's 9th Division. His division didn't include the brigade still fighting on Tarakan, but with support troops it numbered nearly 30,000 men. The substantial Allied naval force included five Australian warships and three landing ships. Air Vice-Marshal Bostock commanded the air operations, with aircraft from the RAAF's First Tactical Air Force, based at Morotai, other RAAF aircraft operating from the Northern Territory, and American aircraft from the Fifth and Thirteenth Air Forces.

The landings began on 10 June, when Brigadier Victor Windeyer's 20th Brigade went ashore on the mainland and Brigadier Selwyn Porter's 24th Brigade landed on Labuan. The 24th Brigade cleared stubborn pockets of Japanese with the help of naval gunfire and then, having already sent a battalion to the North Borneo mainland, began advancing towards Beaufort. The 20th Brigade landed another battalion on the Sarawak coast and advanced south. By the end of hostilities in August the 9th Division had begun re-establishing civilian government. The division had lost 114 killed or who died because of their wounds. More than 1,200 Japanese had been killed.

## Against our wishes — fighting the last battle at Balikpapan

By the time the third Borneo operation was approaching, Blamey had become more wary, and he, as well as his subordinate corps and divisional commanders and supporting naval and air force commanders, were opposed to the landing of the 7th Division at Balikpapan on the east coast of Borneo. Fearing that the division would become absorbed in garrison duties and wouldn't be available for the invasion of Japan, Blamey recommended to the government that it withdraw the division from the operation. MacArthur told the Australian government that to cancel the operation 'would disorganise completely not only the immediate campaign but also the strategic plan of the Joint Chiefs of Staff'. Sir Frederick Shedden, Secretary of the Department of Defence, drafted a reply, took it to Curtin and then cabled MacArthur that the Australian government agreed with him and the operation should go ahead.

The Australians didn't know that MacArthur had told the Joint Chiefs that the Balikpapan operation was necessary because not to carry it out would 'produce grave repercussions with the Australian government and people'. The truth was that MacArthur wanted to capture Balikpapan so that he could show the Dutch government that he had recovered part of its territory. The reason didn't appeal to either the Australian Government or the Joint Chiefs.

The landing by Major General Edward Milford's full-strength 7th Division was supported by a three-week aerial bombing campaign commanded by Air Vice-Marshal Bostock. Commodore Collins, recovered from the wounds he sustained when the Japanese attacked *Australia* (see the section 'Our ships at Leyte: The greatest sea battle'), commanded the Australian naval squadron, which included the cruisers *Hobart* and *Shropshire* and the destroyers *Arunta* and *Bataan*. The landing on 1 July was supported by gunfire from 5 cruisers and 14 destroyers. Brigadier Fred Chilton's 18th Brigade and Brigadier Iven Dougherty's 21st Brigade landed side by side and advanced inland supported by tanks and flame throwers. While the 21st Brigade moved along the coast to secure the airfield, Brigadier Ken Eather's 25th Brigade came ashore and thrust inland. By the end of hostilities in August the Japanese had been pushed into the jungle, leaving behind 1,783 killed. A total of 229 Australians were killed.

The amphibious assault was the last one conducted in the war and the largest by the Australians, demonstrating the high level of expertise which the Australian services had reached by this stage of the war; but the war didn't end one minute earlier because of the campaign. As with Australia's other operations in 1945, however, the government wished to keep substantial forces in the field to cement Australia's future postwar relationships.

# Dealing with a Defeated Japan

While the Australian Army, supported by the RAN and the RAAF, was conducting a series of demanding, but ultimately unnecessary campaigns in New Guinea, Bougainville and Borneo, the Allies were involved in six major military campaigns that crushed Japan:

- **Liberation of the Philippines.** After landing at Leyte in October 1944, the Americans moved on to Luzon in January 1945, liberated the shattered city of Manila and by the end of June had defeated the Japanese Army. The Philippines became the base for the invasion of Japan, planned to begin in November.

- **Blockade of Japan.** During 1944 American submarines destroyed Japan's merchant shipping. Then American aircraft attacked coastal shipping between China, Korea and Japan. Finally mines, dropped by aircraft, sealed the blockade. Short of food, Japan couldn't have continued beyond the spring of 1946.

- **Burma–China theatre.** During 1945 British–Indian forces successfully invaded Burma. The British then prepared to land in Malaya in September 1945.
- **Iwo Jima and Okinawa.** The landing by US Marines at Iwo Jima in February 1945 saw the only battle in which US casualties exceeded those of the Japanese. Central Pacific forces invaded Okinawa on 1 April. The fierce Japanese resistance on both islands caused the Americans to worry about possibly huge casualties if they invaded Japan.
- **Strategic bombing.** American B-59 Superfortresses started bombing Japan from China, but in October 1944 moved to the Marianas, from where they carried out devastating firebomb attacks. By July 1945, 60 per cent of the ground areas of Japan's 60 largest cities and towns had been burnt out, some 260,000 people had been killed and 2 million were homeless. In the atomic bomb attack on Hiroshima on 6 August, 50,000 to 80,000 inhabitants were killed — slightly less than in the first conventional firebomb attack on Tokyo (many others were to die from the effects of the bomb attack). Another atomic bomb was dropped on Nagasaki on 9 August.
- **Manchurian campaign.** On 9 August a massive Soviet Army invaded Manchuria. In this short, little-known campaign the Russians claimed to have killed more than 80,000 Japanese, and 600,000 Japanese were taken prisoner and transported to Siberia to be used as forced labour.

## *Joining the British Pacific Fleet in Japanese waters*

Australian ships took part in some of these final campaigns. Britain had undertaken to send a large fleet to support the Americans for the last stages of the war. Many of the ships came from the British fleet, which had been operating in the Indian Ocean, and the Australian destroyers, *Napier*, *Nepal* and *Norman,* had been working with this fleet along the Burmese coast. Later, as the new British Pacific Fleet headed towards Australia, the destroyers *Quiberon* and *Quickmatch* escorted British aircraft carriers in attacks on Japanese installations in Sumatra.

The British Pacific Fleet started to arrive in Australia in January 1945 and eventually numbered about 250 ships, including 21 aircraft carriers, 11 cruisers, 35 destroyers, 18 sloops, 14 frigates, 19 corvettes, 31 submarines and more than 90 support ships. In addition to the six Australian destroyers (including *Nizam*), which had accompanied the fleet from the Indian Ocean, Australia provided 18 corvettes that served in the mine clearance squadron.

The fleet, including *Quiberon* and *Quickmatch,* took part in the naval and air battles during the Okinawa campaign in March–April 1945, coming under attack from Japanese Kamikazes. They were joined later by *Napier*, *Nepal* and *Nizam.* After the battle many fleet units withdrew for rest and resupply. By July the fleet was off the coast of the Japanese home islands, carrying out air strikes and bombardment, but it was withdrawn from operations shortly before the end of the war.

## Taking the Japanese surrender

At noon on 15 August the Japanese Emperor broadcast his orders to cease hostilities. Not mentioning surrender, he said that the war had 'developed not necessarily to Japan's advantage' and that the enemy had employed 'a new and most cruel bomb'. Japan had 'resolved to pave the way for a grand peace for all the generations to come by enduring the unendurable and suffering what is insufferable'. Across the remnants of the Empire the members of the Japanese armed forces faithfully obeyed the order to cease hostilities.

The Australian forces needed to take the surrender of the local Japanese forces in their areas of operations, but they weren't permitted to do so until the Japanese Government formally surrendered. The surrender was signed on board the American battleship *Missouri* in Tokyo Bay on 2 September. Seven Australian ships were in the bay. General MacArthur signed on behalf of the Allied forces and Blamey signed on behalf of Australia. On 9 September Blamey accepted the surrender from Lieutenant General Teshima Futsataro of the Second Japanese Army at Morotai. Other Australian commanders conducted similar ceremonies, taking the surrender of almost 350,000 Japanese. By the time of the Japanese surrender, soldiers from six Australian divisions were serving on operations and Australia had more troops in combat than at any other time in the war.

## Punishing the war criminals

In 1946 the Allies set up the International Military Tribunal for the Far East in Tokyo to prosecute 28 top-level Japanese military and civilian leaders for alleged war crimes. Sir William Webb, a Justice of the High Court of Australia, was president of the tribunal. Six defendants were sentenced to death by hanging for war crimes, crimes against humanity and crimes against peace, one defendant was sentenced to death by hanging for war crimes and crimes against humanity, and 16 more were sentenced to life imprisonment.

> ## Tough words from Blamey
>
> General Blamey's comments in accepting the surrender on Morotai have become well known and reveal much about his approach to fighting the Japanese:
>
> 'In receiving your surrender I do not recognise you as an honourable and gallant foe, but you will be treated with due but severe courtesy in all matters. I recall the treacherous attack upon our ally, China ... upon the British Empire and upon the United States of America in December 1941, at a time when your authorities were making the pretence of ensuring peace. I recall the atrocities inflicted upon the persons of our nationals as prisoners of war and internees, designed to reduce them by punishment and starvation to slavery. In the light of these evils, I will enforce most rigorously all orders issued to you, so let there be no delay or hesitation in their fulfilment at your peril.'

The Allies conducted trials of other officers and soldiers in the liberated territories. Between 30 November 1945 and 9 April 1951 Australian military officers presided over 296 trials at Darwin, Hong Kong, Labuan, Manus Island, Morotai, Singapore, Rabaul and Wewak. Crimes included massacres of soldiers, ill-treatment of prisoners of war, execution of airmen and ill-treatment of civilians. A total of 924 enemy personnel were tried for war crimes in Australian military courts and of those found guilty, 148 were sentenced to death and executed, and 496 were given prison sentences.

# Chapter 17

# The Civilian Side of the War

*In This Chapter*

- Managing a wartime government
- Looking after our interests in the wartime coalition
- Living under a regime of austerity
- Finding ways to serve beyond the battlefield
- Building a foundation for the future

Australia's involvement in the Second World War was the biggest enterprise in its history and no-one living in Australia at the time was untouched by it. In most of Australia's wars the civilian population has been remote from the conflict. Even in the First World War, life in Australia had gone on much as in pre-war times, except of course for the many families of the men serving overseas, who lived in constant fear of the telegram advising of the death of a loved one. But in the Second World War Australia was engaged more fully as a nation, especially after Japan brought the conflict to Australia's doorstep.

Australian civilians were deeply involved in the war at all levels and for a range of reasons:

- For the first time, government ministers were concerned with directing where and how the armed forces would fight. In the First World War the Australian forces had been largely handed over to the British.
- Australia came under direct military attack from the Japanese, with the possibility of invasion. Ordinary people in locations such as Darwin, Broome, and even Sydney Harbour, found themselves under enemy fire. Civilian seamen manning ships around the Australian coast also came under enemy attack.
- Australia sought to expand its industrial capacity to build ships, aircraft and munitions, and workers in these industries knew that they were playing their part in the war.

- Australia became the main logistic and support base for Allied operations in the South West Pacific Area. Infrastructure needed to be built up, much of it constructed by civilian workers. Thousands of American servicemen also trained in Australia and civilians found themselves interacting with them.
- Improved communications, such as the wireless and cinema, meant that events around the world, including those involving Australians, could be reported to the civilian population more graphically than at any previous time.

In this chapter I describe how the government — particularly John Curtin's Labor Government, which came to power just two months before the outbreak of war with Japan — went about raising, equipping and supporting large numbers of troops. The government also needed to look after Australia's interests while cooperating with larger, more powerful allies. I relate how the government marshalled the nation's resources to support the war effort, imposing unprecedented restrictions on the general public. Finally, I tell how the effect of the war reshaped Australia during the next 50 years.

# Governing the Nation during War

In September 1939 the Menzies Government established a War Cabinet, consisting of the prime minister and five (later ten) senior ministers, to make the major decisions about the conduct of the war (refer to Chapter 10). The armed forces chiefs attended to advise the government on military matters. The War Cabinet was smaller than the Full Cabinet; it met more frequently and had access to information that wasn't available to the other ministers.

Under Menzies, the War Cabinet generally met in Victoria Barracks, Melbourne, where the Defence Department and the headquarters of the three services were located. This was convenient because Menzies and several other senior ministers were from Melbourne.

## Involving the Opposition

In May 1940 Winston Churchill became Prime Minister of Britain, heading an all-party government that continued until just before the end of the war. After the Australian federal election in October 1940, Prime Minister Menzies, who had been returned with a very slender majority, tried to form a similar national government, but the Opposition Leader, John Curtin, declined.

To involve the Opposition in the running of the war, Menzies established another body, the Advisory War Council, which included four government ministers and four members of the Opposition, including Curtin. This structure, with a War Cabinet and an Advisory War Council, remained in place for the duration of the war, even when the participants shuffled chairs.

## Curtin and his War Cabinet

In October 1941 two independents voted with the Opposition and Curtin and the Labor Party formed a new government. Curtin had a long union background and had been the editor of a union newspaper in Perth when he was first elected to parliament in 1928. He was an alcoholic but eventually stopped drinking in the late 1930s. He had been leader of the Opposition since 1935, but nonetheless very nearly lost his seat in the elections of 1940.

After becoming Prime Minister Curtin served as his own Minister for Defence and deserves credit for rallying the country — and for putting up with the egotistical American General Douglas MacArthur. The Labor Government generally put aside its more socialist agenda and was probably able to impose more restrictions on workers than would have been acceptable under a non-Labor government.

Leading the government, Curtin needed to work with some former foes, but the strain of dealing with them while doing the best for the nation took a toll on his health. His War Cabinet, which met mainly in Canberra, consisted of:

- Francis Forde, Deputy Prime Minister and Minister for the Army. A long-serving, loyal Labor politician from Queensland, he had served in the Scullin Labor Government in 1929–31 and had been deputy leader since 1932.

- Joseph Benedict (Ben) Chifley, Treasurer and Minister for Postwar Reconstruction. A former engine driver from Bathurst, he had served in the Scullin Government, but had lost his seat in 1931 and had returned to parliament in 1940.

- Herbert Vere (Bert) Evatt, Attorney General and Minister for External Affairs. A brilliant and ambitious lawyer, he had earlier been elected to the New South Wales Parliament, became a Justice of the High Court of Australia in 1930 (aged 36) and stepped down in 1940 to enter federal parliament.

- John Beasley, Minister for Supply and Shipping. A former Sydney unionist, he joined a faction headed by the radical New South Wales Premier Jack Lang, which helped bring down the Scullin Government and was thereafter known as Stabber Jack. When the faction dissolved, he returned to the main Labor Party.

- Norman Makin, Minister for the Navy and Minister for Munitions. A long-serving Labor politician (and Methodist lay preacher) from Adelaide.
- Arthur Drakeford, Minister for Air and Minister for Civil Aviation. A former engine driver from Melbourne.
- John Dedman, Minister for War Organisation of Industry. Born in Scotland, Dedman had served in the British Army in the First World War. He migrated to Australia in 1922, became a dairy farmer in Victoria and entered parliament in 1940. He was the only War Cabinet member with military experience.

## *Conscription for overseas service*

In many countries young men (and in some cases, women) are required by law to serve for a certain period in their nation's armed forces and this is known as *conscription* or *national service*. Conscription of young men for overseas military service has been one of the great contentious issues in Australian politics. Before the First World War both Labor and non-Labor politicians supported conscription for the part-time military forces, which were not permitted to serve outside Australia. In the First World War, Prime Minister Billy Hughes split the Labor Party when he tried unsuccessfully to introduce conscription for service overseas (refer to Chapter 7). John Curtin was gaoled briefly for refusing to attend a compulsory medical examination. The Labor Party subsequently opposed any form of conscription and abolished it when the party came to power in 1929.

### Prime ministerial wisdom

Since Federation Australia has had 27 prime ministers and 11 of them played major roles in Australia's conduct of the Second World War. Indeed, every prime minister from 1915 to 1968, except for Joseph Lyons (1932–39), was involved in policy making in the Second World War. The Advisory War Council (which Curtin maintained after coming to power) included eight men who served at some time as prime minister: Billy Hughes (1915–23), Sir Earle Page (1939), Menzies (1939–41, 1949–66), Arthur Fadden (1941), Curtin (1941–45), Forde (1945), Chifley (1945–49) and John McEwen (1967–68). Harold Holt (1966–67) was a minister (but not a War Cabinet member) in 1940–41. As prime minister, Curtin relied on James Scullin (prime minister 1929–32) for advice. Stanley Melbourne Bruce (prime minister 1923–29) was Australian High Commissioner in London throughout the Second World War and at times represented Australia in the British War Cabinet.

On the outbreak of the Second World War, the Menzies Government re-introduced conscription for the part-time militia, which was still restricted to service in Australia and its territories. When Japan entered the war, the Curtin Government brought the militia to full-time service and because Papua was an Australian territory, militia units served there, fighting at Milne Bay and on the Kokoda Trail.

Curtin was under pressure to change the law to allow conscripted militiamen to serve beyond Australia. In October 1942 General Douglas MacArthur, Commander-in-Chief of the South West Pacific Area, reminded Curtin that conscripted American troops were already fighting in the Pacific and suggested that he 'find a way' to allow Australian militiamen to serve beyond Australian territory. At Curtin's instigation, the Cabinet agreed to extend the boundary to enable the militia to serve up to the equator. After a bitter argument the Labor Party Federal Conference approved the change and it became law in February 1943. Curtin had shown considerable courage in pushing through a measure which, although relatively benign, aroused great opposition in some quarters of his party.

## Wartime politics

After the Labor Government came to power, party politics were stifled for a while by the existence of the Advisory War Council. The Opposition was in disarray. The Country Party's Arthur Fadden became Opposition Leader and the ageing Billy Hughes led the United Australia Party (UAP).

Politics heated up as the nation prepared for the federal election in September 1943. The left-wing Minister for Labour and National Service, Eddie Ward, claimed that the Menzies Government had planned to abandon the whole of northern Australia in the event of invasion. The controversy over the alleged plan to withdraw to the Brisbane Line (refer to Chapter 25) led to a Royal Commission to investigate Ward's claims of a missing document. Ward was suspended from his portfolio and refused to cooperate with the Royal Commission.

The Government won the election handsomely and Curtin reinstated Ward. Curtin apparently said: 'I've given Ward External Territories and Transport. The Japs have got external territories and the Army's got the transport'.

Menzies returned to the political fray as Leader of the Opposition and of the UAP. He promptly pulled his party out of the Advisory War Council and, as the UAP disintegrated, in 1944 he formed the Liberal Party. It took him another five years to regain government.

Worn out by the cares of office Curtin died on 5 July 1945. His deputy, Forde, succeeded him for a week until a party ballot elected Ben Chifley as prime minister.

## Cooperating with Allies

From the outbreak of the war, Australian ships, army units and air force squadrons were deployed as part of a British Empire war effort and they served under British commanders on the oceans, in Britain and in the Middle East. Once the United States entered the war in December 1941, Australians became part of the Allied forces under the general strategic direction of the Combined Chiefs of Staff (chiefs of staff of the United States and Britain). Australian forces then came under the command of Allied theatre commanders, such as General Wavell and later Admiral Mountbatten in South-East Asia, and General MacArthur in the South West Pacific Area.

The challenge for Australian leaders was to find ways to influence the strategic direction of the war. Early in 1941 Prime Minister Menzies visited London and briefly joined the British War Cabinet as it discussed matters such as the deployment of troops to Greece in March 1941 (refer to Chapter 11). Menzies hoped to return to Britain as Australia's permanent representative, but he lacked support from his colleagues and instead Sir Earle Page, a former Country Party prime minister, went to London; he never achieved the influence and access that the Australian Government wished.

Once the United States joined the war, Australia hoped to influence Allied strategy through Pacific War Councils established in London and Washington (where Australia's representative was the former politician Richard Casey and then Justice Owen Dixon). But the British and Americans rarely consulted the Pacific War Council.

## Handing control to MacArthur

In April 1942 General Douglas MacArthur, who had previously commanded the American forces in the Philippines, took over as Commander-in-Chief of the South West Pacific Area, which covered Australia, New Guinea, the Netherlands East Indies (Indonesia) and the Philippines. He therefore commanded all of Australia's armed forces except those serving under British command in Europe and the Middle East. (For the military aspects of his command refer to chapters 14 to 16.) MacArthur — a foreign general — became the government's principal military adviser, in effect supplanting the Australian chiefs of staff. In granting this power to MacArthur, the government had abrogated a considerable degree of sovereignty, although in the emergency of early 1942, perhaps there was no alternative.

To formalise this arrangement, Curtin established a body called the Prime Minister's War Conference, which consisted of himself, MacArthur, Frederick Shedden (Secretary of the Defence Department and of the War Cabinet), and anyone else he chose to invite. Shedden became the crucial link between Curtin and MacArthur: As Curtin wrote to MacArthur, 'if I should not be readily available, Mr Shedden has my full confidence in regard to all questions of War Policy'. Australia's top army officer, General Sir Thomas Blamey, was not included in Curtin's inner circle.

Fortunately for Australia, at least initially MacArthur and Curtin's aims were almost the same. The Combined Chiefs of Staff had given priority to the war with Germany, but MacArthur and Curtin worked together to try to persuade President Roosevelt and the American Joint Chiefs of Staff to send more resources to Australia. They were generally successful and additional American ships, troops and aircraft continued to arrive in the theatre.

By October 1943, however, Blamey believed that MacArthur's strategic policy, by which Australia provided support services for American troops and reduced the numbers of its combat troops, was not appropriate for Australia. Nevertheless, Curtin was still under MacArthur's spell and continued to look to him for advice. He commented that if MacArthur 'had been born in Australia and gone to [the Royal Military College] Duntroon he could not have shown higher concern for Australia's interests'. In a broadcast, Curtin said that he 'was indebted to General MacArthur for the high statesmanship and breadth of world vision he has contributed to the discussion. The complete integration of our concepts, which has been a source of such strength, will continue to the end'. Astonishingly, these two sentences had been written by MacArthur himself; he had requested Curtin add them to his statement.

## *Balancing the war effort*

By mid-1943 it was becoming clear that Australia didn't have sufficient manpower to undertake all the tasks to which it was committed. At that time the Army had a strength of more than 12 divisions; some were needed to defend Australia and others for the offensive in New Guinea. The Royal Australian Air Force had 48 squadrons, with 17 serving in Europe. Australia was providing food and supplies to MacArthur's American troops and was also sending food to Britain. MacArthur preferred Australia to continue to supply his troops and also wanted Australia to provide three divisions for future offensive operations.

Mindful of MacArthur's demands, the War Cabinet struggled to decide how to balance the war effort. After a discussion lasting five and a half hours, on 1 October 1943 the War Cabinet agreed that by June 1944 the Services should release 20,000 men, the munitions and aircraft industries should release 10,000 men, and the monthly intake into the Services should be fixed at 5,000 men and women. But the War Cabinet didn't wish to reduce its fighting forces in the Pacific substantially because it was vitally important 'to the future of Australia and her status at the peace table in regard to the settlement in the Pacific that her military effort should be concentrated as far as possible in the Pacific and that it should be on a scale to guarantee her an effective voice in the peace settlement'. Nonetheless, as it became clear that Australia was no longer under direct threat of attack, the Army could be reduced.

Eventually MacArthur accepted, as inevitably he had to, 'that it was for the Australian Government to decide the nature and extent of its war effort'. It was not until Curtin, Blamey and Shedden visited Washington and London in April and May 1944 that the American and British governments agreed to the new shape of Australia's war effort. The episode showed how Australia believed that it needed to cooperate with its Allies in determining its wartime priorities.

The decisions of 1 October 1943 were fundamental to setting the direction of Australia's war effort for the remainder of the war. Against strong resistance from Blamey, in August 1944 Curtin directed the Army to release 30,000 men and the RAAF 15,000 men over the next nine months. By 1945 the Army had shrunk to six divisions, all of which were in action in the Pacific. If Australian troops had stopped fighting it would have made little difference to the outcome of the war, but Australian forces needed to remain on operations to strengthen the alliance with the United States and Britain in the post-war world. While the War Cabinet hadn't displayed a complete grasp of the problem and hadn't performed particularly well, it was nevertheless frustrated by the arrangement established the previous year whereby strategic matters were in the hands of General MacArthur.

# *Marshalling the Nation's Resources*

The Menzies Government started the process of gearing the nation for total war and laid a strong foundation. The Curtin Government came to power only two months before the war with Japan began. Faced by a possible invasion, it needed to apply more drastic measures.

## Building wartime industries

The Second World War became a catalyst for the development of Australia's modern industrial economy. From soon after Federation successive governments had tried to develop munitions industries and these expanded to a moderate degree during the First World War. After the war the Munitions Supply Board struggled to keep the munitions factories alive. In 1933 the government began to order more munitions and the factories were revived. In 1935 a consortium led by Essington Lewis, chief general manager of BHP Co Ltd, established the Commonwealth Aircraft Cooperation, which began constructing the American-designed Wirraway trainer.

With the outbreak of the Second World War the Menzies Government set up the Department of Munitions, with Essington Lewis as director general. A year later the Department of Aircraft Production was formed, also under Essington Lewis. Before the end of the war, Australian factories were producing all manner of guns, ammunition, vehicles and aircraft, including British-designed Beaufighters, Beauforts and Mosquitoes and the Australian-designed fighter the Boomerang, used for air–ground cooperation, marking targets in the jungle of New Guinea. During the war, Australian factories manufactured about 3,500 aircraft of all types.

Australia also began a substantial ship-building program at Cockatoo Island in Sydney and in new centres in Adelaide, Whyalla, Newcastle, Brisbane and Maryborough (Queensland). These shipyards built 60 corvettes (36 for the Royal Australian Navy), as well as 14 frigates and three 2,000-tonne *Tribal*-class destroyers. Merchant ships were converted to become armed merchant cruisers or landing ships and thousands of small craft were constructed.

One notable weapon success was the Owen submachine gun, invented by Evelyn Owen. Originally manufactured by John Lysaght's factory at Port Kembla near Wollongong, about 50,000 Owens were produced during the war. It was a popular and effective weapon for jungle fighting in New Guinea and Borneo, and was also used in the Korean and Vietnam Wars.

## Regulating all aspects of life

Soon after the outbreak of war with Japan, Curtin gave notice that the government was planning 'a complete revision of the whole Australian economic, domestic and industrial life', and a little later he added that to achieve defence requirements the government would act ruthlessly. During February 1942 the government instituted a series of National Security Regulations. One regulation gave the Minister for the Army power to declare an emergency in any part of Australia should that be required for defence purposes. Another regulation required any person resident in Australia to perform any services for the nation. On 16 February Curtin said: 'It is now work or fight as we have never worked or fought before'.

The details of the government's economic plan were coordinated by the Production Executive, which was a committee of nine ministers chaired by the Minister for War Organisation of Industry, John Dedman. On 18 February 1942 he announced the first of a series of measures prohibiting the manufacture of a wide range of non-essential products.

## Conscripting the workers

In January 1942 the government established a Manpower Directorate, to control all manpower (human resources) in Australia. It had exceptional powers and could decide where every person should work. The Directorate published lists of essential and non-essential industries and advised that men and women could be directed ('manpowered') to work in essential industries. This publication encouraged many men and women to move voluntarily to war industries, food production or to join the forces, rather than to risk being 'directed' to work in whatever job the Directorate thought fit. Between December 1941 and June 1942 the numbers of workers engaged in civil production (excluding rural and domestic work) fell by about 140,000, while those in war production went up by 70,000 men and nearly 40,000 women. At the same time, 228,000 men and 12,000 women enlisted in the services.

Pansey Hickey, a textile worker in Sydney, recalled her experiences with the manpower. 'They used to get around in a car like police officers and we were very afraid of them — they used to carry a lot of power. If you were to have a day off from work, you had to have a very good reason to do that, and people were really too scared to have time off from work without reason.'

## Rationing and restricting

The Menzies Government introduced rationing of petrol and tyres for civilian vehicles because these products needed to be imported, using valuable merchant shipping. As the war progressed, however, the Curtin Government introduced rationing for food and clothing. For example, in 1944 the weekly ration scale for each adult was 2 ounces (60 grams) of tea, 1 pound (500 grams) of sugar, 6 ounces of butter and 2.5 pounds of meat. Everyone was issued with a ration booklet containing coupons to be surrendered when purchasing goods.

In September 1942, Curtin asked the Australian people 'to reconcile yourself to a season of austerity to make your habits of life conform to those of the fighting services'. His austerity campaign was designed to support the raising of a loan of £100 million on the home market; to announce a series of decisions such as restrictions on horse and dog races; but also to strengthen moral standards in the community. He called for 'clean and honest thinking ... By doing so we will be a nation which is morally and spiritually rearmed'. The public was soon confronted by the reality of the austerity campaign. Regulations required tailors to make only single-breasted suits, dresses had fewer pleats, and icing of cakes was prohibited, except for wedding cakes when only white icing was permitted.

Life was regulated in other ways. For example, railways were vital for transporting troops and war supplies, and soon regulations prohibited civilians from moving from one state to another without a permit.

While there was much sacrifice of personal comfort, it was not always shared equally. Food and other goods could be obtained on the black market. Workers in munition industries received high wages; others found their work conditions frozen at pre-war levels. Workers in key industries such as coal mining and on the docks went on strike even at times when Australia was in great peril.

## The man who killed Santa Claus

As Minister for War Organisation of Industry, John Dedman, a dour Scot, was responsible for the austerity campaign. In mid-1942 his department introduced the Victory Suit, which consisted of a single-breasted two-button coat, without waistcoat, and trousers without cuffs. It was thought that the Victory Suit would save cloth and manpower, and a glum Dedman modelled one to show how sensible and good-looking it was. When he reduced the permitted size of the tails on men's shirts he earned the nickname 'Lumbago Jack'.

As Christmas 1942 approached, the government feared that the public would spend heavily and take time off from work. Dedman banned the use of words such as 'Christmas', 'festive season' and 'Yuletide' in advertisements. In the eyes of retailers and many in the public, he became 'the man who killed Santa Claus'. A *Bulletin* cartoon showed 'Mr Dedman Scrooge' speaking to young children waiting anxiously at their fireplace for their Christmas presents. 'It's nae use waitin' for Father-r-r Chr-r-istmas, ye ken. Ah've r-r-rationalised him', he said in his Scots accent.

Dedman later became Minister for Postwar Reconstruction in the Chifley Government. He helped establish the Snowy Mountains Scheme and the Australian National University.

## Serving in Other Ways

Australians could contribute to the war effort in many ways beyond serving in the armed forces. In February 1942 the government established the Allied Works Council under former Queensland Premier and Federal Treasurer Edward Theodore, with wide powers to carry out the big construction tasks necessary to support the Americans once they started to arrive in large numbers. Camps, airstrips, roads and ports needed to be constructed, often in remote areas of Australia. Much of the labour was provided by the Civil Construction Corps. Men who were over military age (between 45 and 60) and not working in a protected industry, could be required to serve in the Corps. By June 1943 the Corps had a strength of 53,500, of whom 16,600 had been conscripted. Some of these men had a conscientious objection to serving in the armed forces.

The Civil Aliens Corps was formed from 4,400 men who weren't eligible to serve in the armed forces because they were born in an enemy country. It included Italian-Australians who had earlier been interned in Australia, and men who had escaped from Germany before the war, had been interned in Britain and then sent to Australia.

The Volunteer Defence Corps was the equivalent of Britain's Home Guard, made famous by the British television comedy *Dad's Army* in the 1960s and 1970s. Formed by the Returned Servicemen's League, it was later taken over by the Australian Army. The VDC included older men, many of whom had served in the First World War, and younger men who were working in essential industries. Its peak strength was 100,000 and the men served at nights or on weekends. At first they were involved in defending static positions (bridges and power stations), but later operated anti-aircraft batteries and searchlights.

## Lost at sea — our merchant navy's war

As an island nation, Australia relies on the sea for commerce and trade, and during the Second World War it had a substantial merchant navy. The merchant navy consisted of commercial shipping and crews. The crewmen were civilians but faced as much danger as servicepeople. According to some sources, more than 14,000 Australians served on merchant ships during the war, about 12,500 of them in Australian-registered ships.

The men of the merchant navy served on convoys around the world and endured attacks by enemy submarines and aircraft, some being lost in the notorious Arctic Ocean convoys bringing supplies to Murmansk in northern Russia. Convoys and individual vessels also sailed around the Australian coast, where 76 merchant ships were lost to mines laid by German raiders, and torpedoes from Japanese submarines. Of these ships, 29 were Australian and 349 Australian seamen were killed. A further 37 died while prisoners of war. The numbers killed while serving in foreign vessels isn't known. Many of the seamen were either too young or too old to serve in the armed forces.

The greatest loss of life on an Australian merchant vessel occurred when the Australian hospital ship *Centaur* was illegally torpedoed by a Japanese submarine off North Stradbroke Island, Queensland, in the early hours of 14 May 1943, while sailing to New Guinea to deliver medical personnel and to return with sick and wounded troops. The ship was well lit, was painted white and was displaying the Red Cross. Under the Hague Convention it should have been protected from attack. The survivors were in the sea for 36 hours before they were discovered and an American ship began their rescue. Sister Nell Savage of the Australian Army Nursing Corps was awarded the George Medal for her attempts to rescue some of the injured survivors in the water. Of the 332 personnel on board, only 64 were rescued. The dead comprised 45 civilian crewmen and 223 medical personnel.

## *Allowing women to do men's work*

The Second World War gave women opportunities to work in areas not normally available to them, both in the civil community and in the services. At first, women simply applied for jobs that became vacant because men had gone off to war, or because new industries were established. In 1943, however, the Manpower Directorate was given power to direct women without children and between the ages of 18 and 45 to work in specific industries, including munitions factories.

Building on voluntary organisations, in 1942 the government established the Australian Women's Land Army to provide women to work on farms and in rural industries. Most women came from the cities: as one commented, 'The country girls were too wise, they knew how hard the work was, they all went and joined [the services]'. At its peak in December 1943 the Land Army included 2,300 permanent members and 1,000 auxiliary members who worked for periods of not less than four weeks at nominated times in the year.

At the beginning of the war the only women in the services were those in the Australian Army Nursing Corps, but as the war continued, in 1941 the service chiefs began pressing the government to allow the recruitment of women to serve in certain occupations within the armed forces to release men for combatant duties. Women served in the following services:

- Australian Army Nursing Corps (AANC). Australian nurses had first served overseas in the Boer War and they continued that tradition in the First World War. Almost 3,500 women served in the AANC during the Second World War. They served overseas in most theatres of war and some became prisoners of war of the Japanese.

- Royal Australian Air Force Nursing Service (RAAFNS). Established in July 1940, by the end of the war it numbered more than 600 women, some of whom served in New Guinea.

- Women's Australian Auxiliary Air Force (WAAAF). Formed in March 1941 it was the largest of the women's services, reaching a strength of 18,664 at its peak in October 1944. More than 27,000 women served in the WAAAF, but none served overseas.

- Women's Royal Australian Naval Service (WRANS). Formed in April 1941 it was relatively small: A total of 2,000 women served during the war.

- Australian Women's Army Service (AWAS). Formed in August 1941, it had an establishment of 6,000 and a total of 24,000 women served during the war. At the end of the war small numbers were serving at Lae in New Guinea.

- Australian Army Medical Women's Service (AAMWS). Members of the Red Cross's Voluntary Aid Detachments served in the Middle East. In March 1942 members working full-time in the Army were accepted as being a separate service and in December 1942 the name was changed to the AAMWS. More than 8,500 women served in the AAMWS, including in New Guinea and Borneo.

The women in the WAAAF, the WRANS and the AWAS generally worked as administrators, clerical assistants, drivers, catering staff, telephone and telegraph operators, code-breakers and stores people. They didn't work in combat jobs, except for a few who operated searchlights and radars, and assisted in operations rooms of coast defence units.

## Working for no pay: The volunteers

A vast number of Australians, mainly women, devoted countless hours to volunteer work in support of the war effort. One way was through membership of patriotic organisations that provided recreational activities, food, accommodation and comforts for soldiers and their dependents. The largest patriotic fund was the Australian Comforts Fund, which raised almost £7 million across Australia. Other prominent organisations included the National Emergency Services, the Volunteer Air Observation Corps, the Young Women's Christian Association and the Australian Red Cross.

# Reshaping the Nation

Australia as we know it today was shaped largely by the experiences of the Second World War. Australia's independence was strengthened. The government realised that it would need to establish the capability to make its own assessments of international affairs. Australia could no longer rely solely on Britain but would seek security within a wider framework of alliances, including the British Commonwealth and the United States. At the same time, the nation would need to look more to its own defences by establishing a Regular Army and expanding the peacetime Navy and Air Force.

As rationing, quotas and other restrictions were lifted, the energy displayed during the war was transferred to national development. Thousands of young men were demobilised and they sought to pick up careers, marry, start families and carve out for themselves lives that they could only have dreamt about for six years. In the 1930s few Australians ever travelled outside their own state, let alone overseas. During the war about 550,000 servicemen and women served outside Australia. The effect of overseas service is hard to quantify, but it probably made this generation of Australians more aware of the outside world, while service around Australia broke down state-centred attitudes and encouraged a feeling of belonging to one nation.

## Calculating the cost

Fewer Australians were killed in the Second World War than in the first — almost 40,000 compared to more than 60,000 in the earlier war. But many more Australians took an active part in the war. From a population of a mere seven million, about one million served in uniform at some stage. At its peak, over 500,000 Australians were serving in the Australian Army and throughout the war 735,781 Australians spent some time in the Army. More than 200,000 Australians served in the RAAF.

The First World War had cost Australia about £364 million. Australia's total Second World War expenditure was almost £2.5 billion. In the year 1942–43, war-related expenditure amounted to about 40 per cent of the national income. Many funds were raised from loans. Australia received a large amount of goods from the United States under lend-lease arrangements, but because it also provided many goods and services to American forces, on balance the nation didn't end up with a large overseas debt.

## Opening our doors to migrants

The threat of Japanese invasion in 1942 came as a great shock. With a small population and a limited industrial base Australians knew that they couldn't withstand a powerful enemy without help from their allies, Britain and the United States. They also understood that Britain hadn't been able to come to their aid and that there was no guarantee that assistance would be available in the future. Australia needed a larger population both to provide for larger armed forces and to build up a more substantial industrial base. Immediately after the war the Chifley Government launched a massive immigration program and the first Minister for Immigration, Arthur Calwell, promoted it with the slogan 'populate or perish'.

Up to 1951, more than 180,000 refugees from Europe were settled in Australia. Meanwhile, migrants were sought from Britain and later from other European countries. The immigration policy was maintained by successive government over the next 50 years. By 2008 about 6.5 million people had migrated to Australia, comprising a significant proportion of the expansion of Australia's population from 7 million to more than 21 million.

Migrants contributed substantially to national development. For example, more than 100,000 migrants worked on the Snowy Mountains Hydro Electricity Scheme and they provided workers for new industries. Large-scale production of the Holden motor car began in 1949, using some of the factories that had been established in the war. Ironically, many of the migrants came from countries such as Italy and Germany, which had been enemies in the Second World War. The immigration program enriched the nation's cultural and social life, and helped transform Australia in the second half of the twentieth century.

# Part VI
# The Aussies Do Their Bit in the Cold War

*How the Cold War heated up*

## In this part ...

For 45 years after the Second World War the international system was dominated by the Cold War between the American-led Western Alliance and the Soviet bloc. The Cold War was marked by continuing ideological, political, economic and military confrontation. Although no actual military conflict occurred between the Soviet Union and the United States, there were numerous so-called proxy wars, in which the warring parties were supported by the opposite sides of the ideological divide. The greatest danger was that one of these limited conflicts would develop into a major international war, in which the exchange of nuclear weapons would lead to unimaginable destruction.

In this part I explain that as a member of the Western Alliance, Australia fought in two of the biggest conflicts of the Cold War — the Korean War (1950–53) and the Vietnam War (1962–72). Australian forces also supported Britain against communist insurgents in Malaya in the 1950s, and against Indonesia's efforts to disrupt the new nation of Malaysia in the 1960s. Australia's defence policy of maintaining forces in South-East Asia to deal with the communist threat was known as 'Forward Defence'. The Cold War was a distinct phase in Australian military history, but conscious of the heavy casualties in the world wars, successive Australian governments sought to limit Australia's involvement, trying to reap the maximum benefit from the contribution, while paying as small an insurance premium as possible.

# Chapter 18

# Taking up Arms for the United Nations in Korea, 1950–53

## In This Chapter

- Adjusting to the Japanese occupation and the Cold War
- Fighting up and down the Korean peninsula
- Winning respect in a forgotten war
- Bombarding North Korea from the sea and the air
- Reaping benefit from our military commitment

*I*n July 1950, not quite five years after the end of the Second World War, Australian forces were again committed to war, this time in support of the United Nations (UN) in Korea. The five years had been a turbulent and challenging period for Australia's political and military leaders. The Pacific War had come as a great shock to Australia which, for the first time since white settlement, had faced the prospect of invasion, and the government was determined that Australia would never again face such a threat.

In shaping its defence policies for the future, the government had to deal with a range of issues. Australia needed to contribute to the occupation of Japan to ensure that it abided by the peace arrangements and would never again pose a threat in the Pacific, but Australia had never previously maintained a permanent Army in peacetime, and needed to work out how to raise and maintain the force in Japan. The government also needed to determine the future size and shape of its armed forces.

With the formation of the United Nations in 1945, Australia optimistically hoped that the UN would play the major role in promoting world peace. But the outbreak of the Cold War posed a major threat to world peace and Australia needed to determine what part it should play. Conflicts in China, Indochina, Malaya, Indonesia, the Philippines and finally Korea emphasised that Australia needed to take its defences seriously.

In this chapter I explain how the Australian Government responded to these issues, and why, when North Korea invaded South Korea in 1950 and the United Nations authorised the United States to assist South Korea, Australia sent forces to help. I describe how our newly raised regular army went to war and made its name in Korea, and also outline the part played by our naval and air forces. Finally, I reveal how our contribution, made under UN auspices, cemented our relationship with the United States.

# The Occupation of Japan

After Japan ceased hostilities in August 1945 the British Government suggested that Australia join a British Commonwealth Occupation Force (BCOF) in Japan that would include army and air force units from Australia, Britain, India and New Zealand. BCOF would join the larger occupation force, to be provided by the Americans, all under the Supreme Commander for the Allied Powers, General Douglas MacArthur. The government of Prime Minister Ben Chifley believed that Australia had played a major role in fighting Japan and insisted on a separate commitment to the occupation to increase Australia's influence over the future of Japan and in particular the form of the peace treaty.

When Britain offered Australia the command of BCOF, Australia dropped its plans for a separate force and Lieutenant General John Northcott was appointed Commander-in-Chief of BCOF. The force was to include infantry brigades from Australia, New Zealand, Britain and India, as well as two air force wings and shore-based naval personnel, although naval ships from the respective countries didn't serve as part of BCOF.

## Signing on for more military service

Providing an infantry brigade for BCOF posed a problem as Australia had never previously possessed permanent infantry battalions in peacetime and indeed they were not permitted under the Defence Act. Most of the troops serving overseas were anxious to return home, so it wasn't a simple matter of sending an existing wartime brigade to Japan. The government therefore extended the wartime regulations to form a special BCOF brigade. The 34th Brigade, as it was known, was formed on the island of Morotai (northeastern Indonesia) and consisted of three newly raised battalions, the 65th, 66th and 67th. Volunteers were sought from the six Australian divisions serving across the South West Pacific and they began arriving at Morotai in October. Troops were required to serve for 12 months in Japan.

The battalions completed their training on Morotai and embarked in January 1946, arriving at Kure, Japan, the following month. BCOF was responsible for southern Honshu and nearby Shikoku island, and the Australian brigade was allocated to the Hiroshima Prefecture, which included the city of Hiroshima that had been destroyed by the atomic bomb in August 1945 and the former Japanese naval base at Kure. The Royal Australian Air Force (RAAF) provided three squadrons, flying Mustang fighters, while 10 Australian warships operated in Japanese waters.

## Living with the former enemy

The Australian troops in Japan were required to maintain military control, supervise the demilitarisation and disposal of the remnants of the Japanese war machine, and deal with the large numbers of Japanese troops that were returning home from their wartime service overseas. Initially the occupation troops were not permitted to fraternise with the local population, but as time passed restrictions were eased and some soldiers married Japanese women.

In April 1946 Lieutenant General Horace Robertson succeeded Northcott (who had become Governor of NSW) as Commander-in-Chief. By the end of 1948 the other nations' forces had withdrawn and Australia's commitment had been reduced to one infantry battalion, one RAAF squadron, and a naval support unit of one ship and shore personnel. The government of Prime Minister Robert Menzies, elected in December 1949, decided to withdraw the remaining forces, but they were still there when the Korean War began in June 1950.

## Seeking Future Security

The Pacific War had a deep effect on the Chifley Government as it sought to ensure Australia's future security. At home, the government concentrated on national development and initiated a massive immigration program to increase the country's population.

In addition to ensuring that Japan's military potential was totally eliminated, the government had several objectives in terms of defence and foreign policy:

- Support the United Nations Organisation in its peacekeeping role
- Establish regional defence arrangements with powerful allies
- Build up Australia's own defences

## Pinning our hopes on the United Nations

The Australian Labor Party has a long history of seeking to promote international peace by encouraging countries to work together (political scientists call this collective security). Dr H V (Bert) Evatt, Australian Minister for External Affairs from 1941 to 1949, followed this tradition and took an active part in drafting the charter of the United Nations, which was signed by 50 countries in San Francisco in June 1945. Evatt was President of the UN General Assembly in 1948–49.

Evatt hoped that the United Nations could be used to help prevent future wars and to resolve some of the conflicts then breaking out around the war. The Defence Department preferred to seek security by establishing cooperative arrangements within the British Commonwealth and by strengthening the alliance with the United States. The Prime Minister, Ben Chifley, supported the Defence view, but Evatt still advocated relying on the United Nations. Australia sent military observers under UN auspices to Indonesia in 1947 to help maintain the ceasefire between the Dutch and Indonesian nationalists.

## Restructuring our defences

Post-war assessments concluded that Australia's security depended primarily on its geographic isolation, but because of its limited industrial and economic capacity Australia needed to seek allied support. Australia therefore had to structure its forces so that they could cooperate with British Commonwealth forces in the Pacific.

In June 1947 the Defence Minister, John Dedman, announced the post-war defence policy and outlined the structure of the new Australian services:

- The Royal Australian Navy (RAN) would consist of 2 light cruisers, 2 cruisers, 6 destroyers and 13 support ships. The ships were left over from the war, but Australia would acquire two aircraft carriers. The RAN's permanent strength would be 10,450 rising to 14,753 in 1951–52.

- A Regular Army would be formed, to include three infantry battalions. It would have a strength of 19,000. The Citizen Military Forces (CMF) would be revived, and would include two infantry divisions and a strength of 50,000.

- Relying on aircraft left over from the war, the RAAF would consist of 12 permanent and 3 Citizen Air Force squadrons. The permanent strength would be 13,922.

 For the first time Australia would have a Regular Army. The three battalions raised for service in BCOF became part of the Regular Army and by 1949 they were known as the 1st, 2nd and 3rd Battalions of the Royal Australian Regiment.

## Responding to the Cold War

Despite the high ideals of men such as Bert Evatt, Australia couldn't stand aloof from the Cold War. When the British Government provided evidence that officials in the Australian Department of External Affairs had been passing information to the Soviet Union, in March 1949 Chifley established the Australian Security Intelligence Organisation (ASIO) to improve Australia's counter-espionage capacity. Also in 1949 Chifley ordered troops from the newly formed Regular Army to take over the mining of coal in New South Wales to break a strike by communist-led unions.

## Breaking the Berlin Blockade

After the Second World War the wartime allies — Britain, France, the Soviet Union and the United States — divided Germany into occupied zones. Berlin, in the Soviet zone in East Germany, was similarly divided into Soviet and Western sectors. In June 1948, the Soviet Union imposed a land blockade on Berlin's Western sector to gain control of the city, and American and British air forces began a massive airlift of food and supplies to the people of Berlin.

Britain sought assistance and in August 1948 the Chifley Government offered ten RAAF Dakota transport aircraft with crews as a demonstration of Australia's opposition to Soviet polices. The aircraft weren't needed but the aircrews took part in the airlift between September 1948 and August 1949. The flying was often dangerous, involving poor weather and congested skies. Realising that their tactic had failed the Soviet Union lifted the blockade in April 1949, but the airlift continued until September 1949.

# The Korean War — The Cold War gets Hot

At the end of the Pacific War, Soviet forces occupied the northern half of Korea and Americans occupied the south, with the border at the 38th Parallel. North Korea had a communist government while the south was nominally democratic. On 25 June 1950 North Korea, encouraged by the Soviet Union, invaded South Korea, seeking to reunify the country under communist rule. The South Korean Army, supported by a weak American division, was driven south in disarray.

When two Australian officers, in South Korea as part of a UN monitoring team, reported to UN headquarters that the North Koreans were the aggressors, the UN Security Council authorised the United States to lead a UN force to eject the North Korean Army from South Korea. The Soviet Union was boycotting the Security Council at that time, so was unable to exercise its power of veto over the Security Council's decision.

General Douglas MacArthur, commanding the occupation force in Japan, was appointed commander of the UN force in Korea and began transferring US Eighth Army units from Japan to Korea. Meanwhile, American aircraft based in Japan attacked the North Korean Army. Nonetheless, by September 1950 the North Koreans had occupied all of South Korea except for an enclave around the southern port of Pusan (refer to Figure 18-1). The Americans were, however, building up their forces for a major counteroffensive.

At MacArthur's request, the Australian Government approved the use of the RAAF's No 77 Squadron, based in Japan, and by 2 July its Mustang fighters were in action over South Korea. The Australian Government also offered the destroyer *Bataan* and the frigate *Shoalhaven*, then serving in Japanese waters.

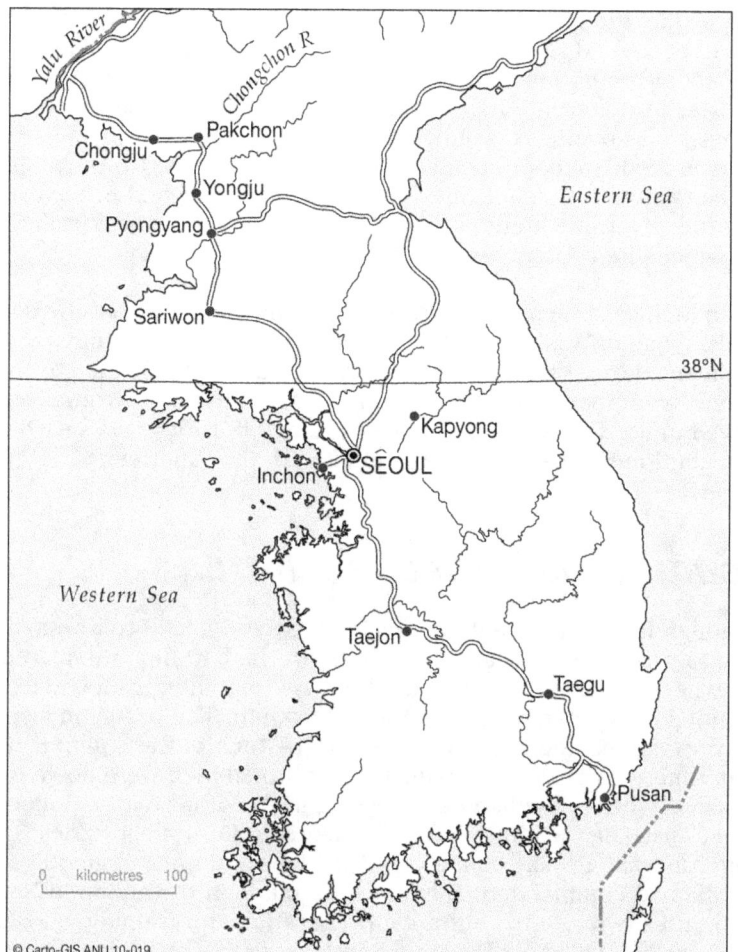

Figure 18-1: Korea, 1950–53.

## Winning friends in Washington

At first Prime Minister Robert Menzies and his government saw little purpose in sending Australian ground troops to Korea. With only a small Regular Army, Australia could send only a few soldiers, which couldn't affect the outcome. But before long General Macarthur asked General Robertson, Commander-in Chief of BCOF, for the use of the 3rd Battalion, the Royal Australian Regiment (3 RAR) located in Japan. Australia's military chiefs agreed, even though 3 RAR was understrength and poorly equipped.

Meanwhile, the Department of External Affairs learned that Britain, which hadn't consulted Australia and had previously declined to send troops, was about to announce its commitment of ground forces. Percy Spender, Minister for External Affairs, believed that Australia needed to act quickly. Menzies was overseas, sailing from Britain to the United States, and couldn't be consulted. Spender spoke by phone to the Acting Prime Minister, Arthur Fadden, and the Defence Minister, Phillip McBride, and in the evening of 26 July the government announced the commitment of the battalion. Britain announced its commitment an hour later.

When Menzies reached New York on 27 July he learned of the decision and arriving in Washington the following day he was warmly received by President Harry Truman who 'attached great political value to the provision of even a comparatively small force'. Eventually forces from 21 countries served under UN Command in South Korea, but Australia's early contribution carried particular weight with the Americans.

## Sending our forces to Korea

Although the government had decided to send 3 RAR to Korea, it took some time to prepare it for war. At full strength the battalion numbered 1,000 men, but when war broke out the battalion was just above half its strength and included many men who were too old or unfit. The battalion also needed heavy weapons and additional transport. Much of the equipment came from American stores in Japan. The additional men were flown in from Australia where they had been serving in the other two battalions of the Royal Australian Regiment. Finally, Lieutenant Colonel Charles Green arrived from Australia to take command of the battalion. Although only 30 years of age, he had commanded an infantry battalion in the action in New Guinea in 1945. After two months of frantic preparation and training, on 27 September the battalion sailed for Pusan in South Korea.

## The Royal Australian Regiment's First War

By the time 3 RAR arrived at Pusan on 28 September 1950 the war had been transformed. On 15 September, under MacArthur's command, American troops conducted a daring amphibious landing at Inchon, on the west coast, near the South Korean capital of Seoul. The Americans recaptured Seoul and the North Korean Army, faced with being cut off, withdrew quickly from the Pusan perimeter. The 3rd Battalion joined the British 27th Brigade, which had two relatively weak British battalions and was renamed the 27th Commonwealth Brigade. The brigade moved north to join MacArthur's army near Seoul. Many of the Diggers had served previously in the Second World War and were experienced and confident, but the coming battles would be the first for any battalion of the Royal Australian Regiment.

## Mustangs and Meteors take on the MiGs — air combat over Korea

When the Korean War began the RAAF's No 77 Squadron, equipped with Mustang fighters, was serving in Japan as part of the Occupation Force and on 2 July its aircraft began operations over South Korea, escorting American bombers and attacking enemy ground positions with rockets. Wing Commander Lou Spence, the squadron's commander, was shot down and killed by enemy ground fire in September and he was succeeded by Squadron Leader Dick Cresswell, who had earlier raised and commanded No 77 Squadron in 1942. The Mustangs provided excellent close support to 3 RAR during a major attack at Pakchon in the far north of Korea in November. Australia's commitment increased with the arrival of a transport squadron flying Dakotas and a communications flight, and all the units were brought together as No 91 Composite Wing.

In November 1950 the Chinese Air Force entered the war, flying the Soviet-built MiG-15 jet fighter. Because the MiG-15 was far superior to the Australian Mustangs, No 77 Squadron was then restricted to ground attack roles. The RAAF hoped to replace the Mustang with the American Sabre fighter, but the US Air Force needed all the Sabres then being built.

Britain offered the Gloster Meteor 8 jet, even though it was likely to be inferior to the MiG-15. No 77 Squadron flew its first operational mission with Meteors in July 1951, but it was soon obvious that they were no match for the MiGs. In their first clash in August 1951, in which eight Meteors took on six MiGs, one Meteor was lost and another badly damaged for no enemy losses. After a few more engagements No 77 Squadron returned to attacking ground targets, such as bridges, railways and ground positions, often in the face of intense anti-aircraft fire.

By the end of the war No 77 Squadron had lost 37 men killed while flying and 7 taken prisoner. The squadron had lost 13 Mustangs and 46 Meteors. Australian aircraft had shot down five MiGs, but only four Meteors had been lost to MiGs — most had been lost to ground fire.

## Advancing to the Yalu River

MacArthur's forces crossed the 38th Parallel and pushed into North Korea. The 27th Brigade took over the advance on 16 October and moved rapidly northward against light opposition. The first major action took place in an apple orchard at Yongju, where American paratroopers were fighting a North Korean regiment. The Australians came to the aid of the Americans, caught the North Koreans by surprise, killed between 150 and 200 of them, and captured more than 200 prisoners.

Shortly before this action, Major Bruce Ferguson, second-in-command of 3 RAR, was waiting in the dark with a small party of guides for the arrival of ration trucks when a large column of North Korean troops approached, thinking Ferguson was a Russian. Shots were fired and a battle began. Ferguson mounted a tank, drove into the centre of the North Korean column and through an interpreter told them they were surrounded and had two minutes to surrender. 'They were the longest two minutes of my life', recalled Ferguson. 'A deadly hush fell over the area and you could hear your own heart beats.' The bluff worked and 1,982 North Koreans surrendered.

By the end of October the brigade had crossed the Chongchon River, deep in North Korea, but was encountering strong resistance. In the battle of Chongju on 29 October they endured a fierce attack from the North Koreans, which was halted by American artillery and the battalion's mortars. The following night six enemy shells landed near battalion headquarters. Five exploded harmlessly, but shrapnel from the sixth shell struck Lieutenant Colonel Green and he died two days later. The American divisional commander's message congratulating 3 RAR on its 'splendid and sensational drive into enemy territory' was cold comfort for Diggers, who had quickly recognised the quality of their young commander.

## Retreating to Seoul

As the North Korean Army retreated north, more than 180,000 troops from the Chinese Army started crossing the Yalu River that separates the two countries. Outnumbered, the UN forces began to pull back. The 27th Brigade conducted a fighting withdrawal while elsewhere American and South Korean troops were cut off and fought desperate battles.

By the beginning of January 1951 the UN forces had withdrawn south beyond the 38th Parallel and for the second time Seoul was abandoned to the enemy. General Walton Walker, commander of the US Eighth Army, was killed in a motor accident, and Lieutenant General Matthew Ridgeway took over. Having reached Seoul the Chinese halted their offensive and Ridgeway was able to stabilise the line. The Australians, under newly promoted Lieutenant Colonel Ferguson, occupied defensive positions in the bitterly cold winter.

Towards the end of January Ridgeway mounted a limited offensive that gradually pushed the Chinese back. By mid-March the UN forces had recovered Seoul. Since the previous September the Australians had lost 46 dead, 220 wounded and 2 missing. The 27th Brigade had been in constant action, but fortunately it was strengthened by the arrival of a Canadian infantry battalion and a New Zealand artillery regiment.

Earlier, General MacArthur had dismissed evidence that the Chinese were going to enter the war and he now proposed bombing bases inside China, thus risking a full-scale war with China. When MacArthur publicly disagreed with President Truman's policy of limiting the conflict to Korea to avoid a larger war with China, Truman relieved him of command. General Ridgeway took command of the UN forces.

## *Kapyong — a remarkable achievement against great odds*

By April 1951 the 27th Commonwealth Brigade and the newly arrived 29th British Brigade were consolidating along a line just south of the Imjin River. The 3rd Battalion held a hill overlooking the Kapyong River valley and the brigade commander ordered Lieutenant Colonel Ferguson to place his headquarters some distance to the rear of his company localities.

### Hoping to celebrate Anzac Day

The Turkish brigade, which arrived late in 1950, proved to be one of the toughest fighting units in Korea. When the Turks met the Australians they realised their shared bond of fighting, although on opposite sides, at Gallipoli in 1915. The Turks planned a special party to celebrate Anzac Day in 1951 and invited the Australians. The party never eventuated. By Anzac Day 3 RAR was in the midst of the Kapyong battle.

In the evening of 23 April a massive Chinese offensive began against the Commonwealth positions. Advancing in waves, the Chinese overran the forward Australian defences. Meanwhile, other Chinese troops bypassed the main Australian position and attacked Ferguson's headquarters. Major Bernard O'Dowd, commander of A Company, took control of the other companies and ordered local counterattacks to regain the forward positions. The Diggers fought with great determination, causing numerous Chinese casualties, but the enemy had a seemingly limitless supply of men. Late in the afternoon of 24 April the Australians began a fighting withdrawal, eventually reaching a defensive location held by a British battalion.

In a brilliant defensive battle, 3 RAR lost 32 killed, 53 wounded and 3 men captured, while holding off a far superior force. The battalion was awarded the US Presidential Citation. The Canadian battalion also fought a successful defensive battle. These actions, along with those of the other Commonwealth battalions, supported by American tanks, halted the Chinese offensive. Kapyong is one of the iconic battles of Australian military history.

## An embarrassing Australian

Captain Reg Saunders, who commanded a company of 3 RAR during the battle of Kapyong, was the first Aboriginal Australian to be commissioned in the Australian Army. He had previously served in North Africa, Greece, Crete and New Guinea, and after being commissioned in 1944 commanded an infantry platoon in the Wewak campaign. He volunteered to serve in the Occupation Force, but Aborigines weren't accepted. After working in low-paid jobs he rejoined the Army in 1950 and was soon in Korea. He observed that after Kapyong: 'At last I felt like an Anzac and I imagine there were 600 others like me'. Looking at the rugged Maryan San feature before 3 RAR's attack on it, one officer commented that it was 'no country for white men'. 'It is no country for black men, either', added Saunders. The Australian journalist Harry Gordon, who worked in Korea and published a biography of Saunders entitled *The Embarrassing Australian*, wrote of him: 'He was accepted unreservedly by the men who served with him because false values do not flourish among front-line soldiers'.

## Showing great skill and determination at Maryan San

In mid-1951 the 28th Commonwealth (previously the 27th), 25th Canadian and 29th British Brigades joined together to form the Commonwealth Division. Along with two British battalions, 3 RAR remained part of the 28th Brigade. Lieutenant Colonel Frank Hassett took over 3 RAR, most members of which had been replaced by reinforcements from Australia.

As part of a general UN advance to a new position, known as the Jamestown Line, the Commonwealth brigades were ordered to capture a series of well-defended Chinese strongholds in an operation dubbed Operation Commando. The 3rd Battalion's objective was a hilltop position known as Maryan San. The attack began on 3 October 1951 and in a brilliantly executed battle successive companies attacked along the ridgeline. Hassett controlled the battle, deploying his reserve companies to relieve the attacking companies and to keep up the pressure. By 5 October the Australians had reached the summit and next morning Hassett joined his troops to direct the defences successfully against a heavy Chinese counterattack that left 120 enemy dead.

In an outstanding action 3 RAR had defeated two Chinese battalions, but had lost 20 dead and 89 wounded. Hassett received an immediate award of the Distinguished Service Order, while 37 other battalion members received decorations. It was the last full-scale battalion attack against a strongly defended position by the Australian Army, with none on this scale being carried out in the Vietnam War or later campaigns.

## Raiding, patrolling and probing on the Jamestown Line

The Commonwealth Division's battles of October 1951, of which 3 RAR's triumph at Maryan San was a significant part, marked the end of the 16-month war of manoeuvre. The opposing forces then faced each other for another 21 months along a defensive line that stretched across the peninsula. Each side dug trenches, constructed bunkers, erected barbed wire and laid minefields for a new phase that was similar to the trench warfare of the Western Front in the First World War. In April 1952, 1 RAR arrived to join 3 RAR on the Jamestown Line, north of Seoul. An Australian officer, Brigadier Tom Daly, took command of the 28th Commonwealth Brigade, which now had two Australian and two British battalions.

## Brainwashing our prisoners

A relatively small number of Australian servicemen, 29 in all, became prisoners of war in Korea. By comparison with the dreadful privations endured by Australian prisoners of the Japanese in the Second World War, those in Korea suffered no worse treatment. They were beaten, starved and exposed to artillery fire. But there was a new aspect to the prisoner of war experience, namely the attempts by the North Koreans and Chinese to extract false confessions, to force prisoners to issue propaganda statements and to re-educate the prisoners about the superior values of communism. The re-education campaigns became known as 'brainwashing' and while the captors were unsuccessful with the Australians they had some limited successes among the larger numbers of Americans. Captain Philip Greville, the most senior Australian soldier to be captured, recalled that lectures would continue for eight hours, followed by written tests. Private 'Slim' Madden refused to cooperate, was beaten, deprived of food and eventually died; he was awarded the posthumous George Cross.

An Australian-born journalist, Wilfred Burchett, covered the war from the Communist side and helped spread false stories of American germ warfare. Australian prisoners testified that he visited them dressed in the uniform of a Chinese army officer. In a later court case, one former prisoner claimed that Burchett said that if he collaborated and swore allegiance to the Chinese he would get better treatment. Greville and others were adamant that Burchett was a traitor. Burchett reported the Vietnam War from the North Vietnam side and died in Bulgaria in 1983.

The static war was still dangerous and arduous. The Australians, along with the other Commonwealth battalions, sought to dominate no-man's land — the area between the opposing trenches — to prevent the Chinese getting into position for a surprise attack. The Diggers patrolled at night, sometimes in an attempt to capture a prisoner to obtain information, or just to observe the enemy. At times they raided the Chinese to inflict casualties and to keep them off balance. Often they clashed with opposing Chinese patrols. During these patrols the Australians faced the danger of stumbling into Chinese minefields.

Life in the trenches and dugouts was trying, as the soldiers tried to sleep during the day, before embarking on their night-time patrols. In summer it was hot. In winter it was bitterly cold and the patrols often found themselves negotiating frozen paddy fields. Those occupying the defensive positions needed to remain alert to repel a sudden Chinese attack, or to take cover during a bombardment by Chinese artillery.

## Blockade and bombardment — the Navy in the Korean War

Soon after the outbreak of the Korean War the Australian destroyer *Bataan* and the frigate *Shoalhaven*, then serving in Japanese waters, joined a British naval task group operating off the coast of Korea. Along with the much larger American naval force, the British and Australian ships ensured that North Korea was unable to mount operations or send supplies along the Korean coast. They also bombarded North Korean shore positions. Australia attempted to maintain two ships on station for the remainder of the war and a total of nine RAN vessels served there, some returning for a second tour. One of the most notable incidents took place in July 1951 when the frigate *Murchison* was patrolling the Han River estuary just south of the 38th Parallel.

In constricted waters with shoals and narrow channels, *Murchison* came under heavy enemy fire which she returned at the shore batteries.

In October 1951 the aircraft carrier *Sydney* relieved a British aircraft carrier. Hawker Sea Fury and Fairy Firefly fighter-bombers from *Sydney* attacked enemy bridges, railways and defensive positions. During a typhoon *Sydney* lost four aircraft overboard and in all lost nine aircraft in operations. In one incident an American helicopter, flown from *Sydney* rescued a downed Navy pilot, while Sea Furies and Meteors kept the approaching North Korean troops at bay. *Sydney* ended its tour in February 1952 having conducted 2,366 sorties.

# *Holding on at the Hook*

While the troops occupied the defences, the politicians and generals tried to negotiate a ceasefire. The Commonwealth Division withdrew from the line in February and March 1952. When it returned in April, 2 RAR had arrived to take over from 1 RAR and Brigadier John Wilton had succeeded Daly as commander of the 28th Brigade. The Australians resumed the aggressive patrol programs that had characterised their earlier periods in the front-line.

In mid-July, South Korea accepted the terms of the armistice and a final truce seemed near. As a ceasefire became more likely the Chinese became more aggressive, hoping to capture vital positions before the ceasefire came into effect. In July the brigade was holding a key ridge, known as the Hook, overlooking the Samichon River. Earlier, US Marines had repulsed a heavy Chinese attack there and a British battalion had a similar experience.

On the night of 24 July the Chinese attacked in huge numbers, reaching the forward Australian positions. During the next two nights 2 RAR lost 5 killed and 24 wounded, while the division's artillery fired almost 23,000 rounds. Nineteen-year-old Sergeant Brian Cooper of 2 RAR, commanding an isolated section, called down the artillery on his own position to repel the attackers who were almost upon him. Wilton wrote later that after the battle, 'The floor of the valley between the Hook and the Chinese position was almost covered with dead Chinese who had been caught in our deadly defensive fire artillery concentrations ... It was a terrible and gruesome sight. We estimated that the Chinese lost about 2,000 men in that useless unnecessary attack'. The armistice came into effect on 27 July 1953.

## Remembering the forgotten war

The widespread description of the Korean War as the 'forgotten war' is a cliché, but many soldiers who fought there believed that they weren't given adequate recognition. By comparison with the world wars, Australia's contribution was relatively small. Nonetheless, the soldiers had fought in a major war in which about half a million South Koreans and more than 33,000 Americans were killed, along with about 1.5 million Chinese and North Koreans. Of the 339 Australians killed in the war, 293 were from the Army, which also had 1,210 wounded and 23 taken prisoner. While the battalions included many men who enlisted specifically to fight in Korea (they were known as K Force) they served in regular army battalions, which didn't have the same link to the Australian community as had been the case with the units that had fought in the world wars. Officers and soldiers gained valuable combat experience that would prove its worth in the Vietnam War.

## Cementing our Alliance with the United States

Australia's commitment to the Korean War helped build and strengthen its alliance with the United States. The United States was anxious to conclude a peace treaty with Japan to end the Second World War formally, but Australia and New Zealand were reluctant to agree to a treaty that would allow for Japanese rearmament. Australia and New Zealand relented only when the United States agreed to a separate three-way security treaty with them. In the negotiations between Percy Spender, Australia's Minister for External Affairs, and Dean Acheson, the US Secretary of State, the Americans indicated that they appreciated Australia's assistance in Korea.

## Chapter 18: Taking up Arms for the United Nations in Korea, 1950–53

The ANZUS treaty, as it was known, was signed at San Francisco on 1 September 1951 and came into force on 29 April 1952. The three countries merely agreed to consult in the event of an armed attack on any of them in the Pacific, but the treaty provided the basis for further military cooperation and is still seen as a fundamental pillar of Australian defence and foreign policy.

One example of defence cooperation is the Radford–Collins agreement, signed by the US Commander-in-Chief in the Pacific, Admiral Arthur Radford, and the Australian Chief of Naval Staff, Vice-Admiral John Collins, in Hawaii in September 1951. The agreement provided for peacetime naval liaison, naval planning and cooperative arrangements for protecting the sea lines of communication in the Pacific in time of war.

# Chapter 19

# Backing the Brits in Malaya and Borneo, 1950–66

## In This Chapter

▶ Defending Australia through a policy of 'Forward Defence'
▶ Learning about counterinsurgency in Malaya
▶ Developing skills in jungle patrolling and ambushing
▶ Fighting a secret war in Borneo

Australia's involvement in South-East Asia grew out of the experience of the Pacific War when Japanese forces occupied the region and threatened Australia. Australian leaders were determined to prevent the region again falling under the control of hostile governments, so Australian military forces were deployed under a defence policy known as 'Forward Defence'. Some forces served with the Americans in South Vietnam between 1962 and 1972 (refer to Chapter 20). Others supported Britain by fighting communist insurgents in Malaya and Indonesians in Borneo. In the context of the Cold War, a communist government was seen as hostile. But with only a small population, a weak industrial base and a tiny regular defence force, Australia had only a limited capacity to influence events in the region.

As in the past, Australia sought to strengthen its security by cooperating with Britain, but cooperation was a two-way street. Britain looked to Australia to help meet the broader threat from the Soviet Union. At first, Britain sought assistance in the Middle East, but then changed its focus to South-East Asia, which was of more immediate concern to Australia. Britain, Australia and New Zealand then worked together to help defend the region in a variety of ways, including through treaties, deployment plans, combat troops, basing forces in the region and assisting regional countries to improve their defences.

In this chapter I describe how Australia joined with its allies in cooperative arrangements to defend the region and sent troops to fight the Communist Terrorists in Malaya. I also explain why Australian combat troops fought in an undeclared, low-level war against Indonesia in Borneo, while amazingly Australia still kept up diplomatic relations with its populous neighbour.

# The British Empire's Last Gasp

At the end of the Second World War Britain was exhausted economically and militarily, yet still saw itself as a great power. The British Empire was intact, but it was already showing signs of disintegration and Britain faced a myriad of military demands. India and Pakistan became independent in 1947, followed by Burma in 1948. British troops fought terrorists in Palestine before Israel came into existence in 1948. An insurgency began in Malaya in 1948. Britain maintained occupation forces in Germany and Japan, and felt compelled to join the Korean War in 1950 (refer to Chapter 18).

Under pressure to meet its commitments around the world, Britain tried to persuade Australia to prepare to send forces to the Middle East if war broke out with the Soviet Union, just as it had done in the two world wars. For its part, after relying on the United States in the Pacific War, Australia wanted to strengthen its connection with Britain. When the British Commonwealth Occupation force (BCOF) went to Japan early in 1946 (refer to Chapter 18) the countries involved in it set up the Joint Chiefs of Staff in Australia (JCOSA) to exercise higher direction over BCOF. JCOSA consisted of Australia's military chiefs plus senior officers from Britain, India and New Zealand. Through JCOSA, Australia, Britain and New Zealand made the first steps towards joint planning for the defence of the Malaya region, which they dubbed the ANZAM (Australia, New Zealand and Malaya) arrangement. But Britain continued to urge Australia to plan on sending troops to the Middle East.

# Defending the Middle East from Malta

With the outbreak of the Korean War in June 1950 and the intensification of the insurgency in Malaya, the Australian Government was reluctant to agree to Britain's request for support in the Middle East. Nonetheless, the Liberal–Country Party Government, which had come to power in December 1949 under Prime Minister Robert Menzies, feared that these Cold War conflicts would expand into a major war with the Soviet Union. The government therefore introduced a national service scheme to bolster the Citizen Military Forces so that it could send large numbers of troops to the Middle East in a general war.

Eventually, in December 1951 the Australian Government gave in to British pressure and agreed to commit Army and Air Force units to the Middle East in time of war and to maintain two fighter squadrons there in peacetime. In July 1952 the RAAF's No 78 Wing, consisting of two half-strength fighter squadrons and base units, deployed to the British-ruled Mediterranean island of Malta. Flying mainly Vampire fighters on lease from Britain, the squadrons conducted training and exercises throughout the Middle East and the Mediterranean. No 78 Wing returned to Australia in January 1955.

## *Protecting the countries to our north — ANZAM and SEATO*

In the early 1950s Australia began promoting a series of alliances and arrangements with allied countries to help defend South-East Asia against encroachment by the communists and to strengthen Australia's security. The first of these was the ANZAM arrangement between Australia, Britain and New Zealand. The second was the ANZUS Pact between Australia, New Zealand and the United States in which the parties agreed to consult if one of them was attacked in the Pacific (refer to Chapter 18).

The third attempt to promote security resulted from the war in Vietnam between France and communist-led guerrillas. The communists defeated the French at the battle of Dien Bien Phu in 1954 and the subsequent Geneva agreement divided Vietnam into the communist north and non-communist south. Following on from the communist victory in China in 1949 and the Korean War (1950–53), Australia, Britain and the United States were deeply concerned at the prospect of communism spreading in South-East Asia.

In April 1954 US President Dwight Eisenhower claimed that if Indochina fell to communism, Burma, Thailand, Malaya and Indonesia might follow. The 'domino' theory, as it was known, was widely believed by Western leaders.

Responding to this threat, in September 1954 Australia, Britain, France, New Zealand, Pakistan, the Philippines, Thailand and the United States formed the South East Asia Treaty Organization (SEATO). Member countries were supposed to come together to respond to a communist attack against a fellow member, as well as against one of the so-called protocol states of South Vietnam, Laos and Cambodia.

# Countering the 'CTs' in Malaya

After the Japanese occupied Malaya in 1941–42 the British organised a guerrilla war against the Japanese, fought mainly by an underground army based strongly on the Malayan Communist Party (MCP). After the war the party started a campaign to overthrow the British colonial government. The MCP was formed mainly from Malaya's Chinese community, which had fewer rights than the majority Malays. Initially the MCP organised strikes, seeking better conditions for workers, but then moved on to guerrilla warfare, using weapons left over from the war. The guerrillas started sabotaging industries and attacking rubber plantations, culminating in the murder of three estate managers on 18 June 1948. The British colonial government declared an 'Emergency', and British, Gurkha and Malay battalions began to take action against the guerrillas, which the British called 'Communist Terrorists' or 'CTs'.

## The Malayan Emergency

Early British efforts to deal with the insurgents were weak and poorly coordinated, but the communists also took a while to organise an effective guerrilla war. By early 1950, however, the insurgents were attacking isolated police posts and plantations and the numbers of incidents were rising rapidly.

In April 1950 Lieutenant General Sir Harold Briggs became Director of Operations. He produced a plan of action which required the authorities to:

- Coordinate all aspects of government policy.
- Deal with the Chinese communities' political, social and economic grievances.
- Move the Chinese living in settlements near the jungle into 'New Villages', where they could receive better services and where they could be physically separated from the insurgents in the jungle, who relied on their support.
- Dominate the populated areas so that the people there could feel secure.
- Eliminate the guerrilla bases in the jungle and force the guerrillas to attack the security forces on their own ground.

The Briggs Plan proved to be highly successful, but it took some time to put into action and to show results. In the meantime, on 6 October 1951 the guerrillas ambushed and killed the British High Commissioner, Sir Henry Gurney. In March 1952 General Sir Gerald Templer took over as both High Commissioner and Director of Operations. With unprecedented power, Templer could now coordinate all government and military agencies. Within a few years the British campaign was proving effective in crushing the CTs.

## Bombing the jungle

Britain asked Australia for assistance in Malaya in June 1950 just as the Korean War was beginning and the Australian Government saw Korea as a higher priority for its ground troops. Nonetheless, the government sent a flight of Dakota transport aircraft from No 38 (Transport) Squadron and No 1 (Bomber) Squadron, flying Lincoln bombers. The Dakotas served in Malaya until December 1952 and were useful for transporting supplies and troops (including parachute drops) and dropping propaganda leaflets.

Based in Singapore and Kuala Lumpur, the Lincolns conducted most of the British bombing operations until they were withdrawn in 1958. Initially the bombers conducted pinpoint strikes on targets identified by ground patrols, aerial reconnaissance or other intelligence, but later they undertook night-time harassing raids over wide areas. The Lincoln was a most suitable bomber for the conditions in Malaya as it carried 14, 450-kilogram bombs, machine guns and cannon, and it could travel at slow speeds and at low altitudes. The effectiveness of the bombing campaign has been subject to much criticism, as the bombers killed only 23 CTs in 4,000 sorties. But many years later Chin Peng, the leader of the Malayan Communist Party, testified that the bombing raids severely disrupted life in the guerrilla camps deep in the jungle.

## Contributing to Malaya's Defences

It might seem somewhat fanciful now, but following the communist victory in Vietnam over the French, Western leaders were concerned that Chinese or North Vietnamese forces might advance through Laos into Thailand and then continue towards Malaya. In response, at the Commonwealth Prime Ministers' Conference in London in January 1955 the Australian, British and New Zealand leaders agreed to establish the British Commonwealth Far East Strategic (BCFESR) to be located in Malaya. The main role of the BCFESR was to deter an attack and to be available at short notice to move forward to Thailand under SEATO command to counter an enemy attack should this occur. Australia undertook to contribute two destroyers or frigates, an aircraft carrier on an annual visit, additional ships in an emergency, an infantry battalion with supporting arms, a fighter wing of two squadrons, a bomber squadron and an airfield construction squadron. The land component of the BCFESR was to consist of the 28th Commonwealth Infantry Brigade Group, with battalions and supporting troops from Australia, Britain and New Zealand.

## Sending our soldiers to Malaya

As part of its contribution to the BCFESR, Australia deployed the 2nd Battalion of the Royal Australian Regiment (2 RAR) to Malaya in October 1955. Although it had been sent to help defend Malaya and Singapore from external attack, 2 RAR was permitted to participate in operations against the CTs. Under the command of Lieutenant Colonel James Ochiltree, 2 RAR joined the 28th Brigade on Penang Island, north-west Malaya (refer to Figure 19-1). For the first time, Australian soldiers served overseas accompanied by their families.

The battalion began its first counterinsurgency operations early in 1956. By this time the CTs had been cleared from much of the populated area of Malaya and the operations were designed to ensure that the CTs weren't able to interfere with the population and eventually to eliminate them in their jungle bases. The battalion's operations, and those of the later Australian battalions, took place in the north-west of the Malayan peninsula in the states of Perak and Kedah. The battalions conducted two sorts of operations:

- ✔ Framework operations. A battalion was allocated to a district where it established company bases. Platoons patrolled throughout the district, laid ambushes, checked security passes and ensured that the CTs couldn't contact the local villagers.

- ✔ Federal Priority Operations. After months of preliminary work a brigade-size force would move into a district, cordon the villages and undertake operations into the jungle to locate and destroy CT bases.

The Diggers conducted jungle patrols for long periods but with only limited success. In June 1956 a group of CTs ambushed Lieutenant Wally Campbell's platoon and three Australians were killed. Two enemy bodies were recovered. Another 2 RAR patrol found an enemy camp in June 1957.

### Chapter 19: Backing the Brits in Malaya and Borneo, 1950–66

Two Diggers were killed, two were wounded and the enemy escaped. By the end of its tour in October 1957, two months after Malaya was granted its independence, 2 RAR had lost seven soldiers killed in action for only a moderate return.

Under the command of Lieutenant Colonel John White, 3 RAR took over from 2 RAR in October 1957. The new battalion conducted similar operations to its predecessor, but with a little more success, killing ten CTs for the loss of two soldiers wounded in action. By the time 1 RAR arrived in October 1959 to take over from 3 RAR, the CTs had generally withdrawn into Thailand and the battalion conducted operations along the Thai–Malayan border to prevent the CTs returning to Malaya. On 31 July 1960 the Prime Minister of Malaya formally declared the end to the Emergency.

**Figure 19-1:** Malaya, showing states, 1950.

## Tracking and ambushing in the jungle

The Australian Army's operations in the Malayan Emergency introduced it to the techniques of counterinsurgency warfare and refined its skills in jungle patrolling. Platoons patrolled deeply into the jungle for periods of up to two weeks, sometimes assisted by local trackers or tracker dogs. Soldiers learned to move silently, communicating with field signals or by whisper. They needed to lie quietly in ambush for days, waiting to spring into instant action. But actual contacts were rare. In 1954, an infantryman would spend, on average, 1,000 hours on patrol and 300 hours in ambush for every contact, but this period became greater as the CTs became less active and 1 RAR, which served in 1959–61, had no contacts.

The Australians did, however, have a few notable successes. In July 1957 three soldiers from 3 RAR ambushed a group of CTs approaching a shed in a rubber plantation where food appeared to have been left. They killed three CTs and wounded another. Next day the wounded CT surrendered. He later led the security forces to his comrades' camps, resulting in the elimination of several large CT groups.

During five years of operations the three Australian battalions were involved in 45 contacts and killed 17 CTs for the loss of 7 soldiers killed in action. Twice as many Diggers had been killed in accidents. Success, however, shouldn't be measured by statistics. Although they had arrived late in Malaya, the Australians had played their part in the security operations that contributed substantially to the success of the counterinsurgency war.

## Maintaining our presence in Malaya

When the Lincoln bombers departed in 1958 they were replaced by Canberra bombers from No 2 Squadron RAAF, based at Butterworth air base in north-west Malaya, where they were joined by the Sabre fighters of Nos 3 and 77 Squadrons. The squadrons were part of the Strategic Reserve, although the Canberras conducted a few bombing sorties against the CTs.

During 1961 the 28th Commonwealth Brigade moved from Penang to Terendak near Malacca in southern Malaya. The new Australian battalion, 2 RAR, trained for its role as part of the Strategic Reserve and its headquarters and a rifle company took part in a SEATO exercise in Thailand. The battalion also conducted operations against the remnants of the CTs near the Thai border, killing one in a successful contact in August 1962.

> ## The British Raj with the Beatles
>
> Living in a large military complex near Malacca in a country which had recently been a British colony, the soldiers and their families enjoyed a life similar to that in India during the British Raj; although as one officer observed, it was 'less stuffy, and more congenial than in India — it was the British Raj with the Beatles'. For the soldiers there was good, hard training, ceremonial parades, plenty of sport, the limited fleshpots of Malacca, and occasional excursions to Kuala Lumpur and Singapore. The families lived in a manner that they couldn't attain in Australia. Young Australian mothers had *amahs* (Chinese maids) to run their homes and to look after their children.

## *Avoiding Conflict with Our Indonesian Neighbours*

In 1961 the British Government agreed to a plan, proposed by Malaya, to form a new nation, the Federation of Malaysia, by joining Malaya, Singapore, the British colonies of North Borneo (Sabah) and Sarawak and the protectorate of Brunei (refer to Figure 19-2). President Sukarno of Indonesia strenuously objected to this plan, claiming that it was a form of 'neo-colonialism' that would threaten his country. He eventually declared that Indonesia would pursue a policy of *Konfrontasi* or Confrontation with Malaysia and that he was going to 'crush Malaysia'.

At the last minute Brunei declined to join the Federation and in December 1962 a revolt broke out in Brunei that was put down by British troops flown in from Singapore. The rebels had been trained and supported by Indonesian forces in Kalimantan (Indonesian Borneo). In the first half of 1963 so-called volunteers (mainly Indonesian soldiers not in uniform) conducted raids into Sarawak and Sabah trying to foment opposition to the formation of Malaysia.

At the time of Malaya's independence in 1957 Britain had agreed to help defend the nation and by extension this applied to Malaysia. By September 1963, when Malaysia came into existence, Britain had deployed seven infantry battalions to Sarawak and Sabah to deal with the Indonesian regular troops that were now making more substantial incursions into Malaysian territory. The British operations were commanded by Major General Walter Walker, who had his headquarters on Labuan Island, near Brunei.

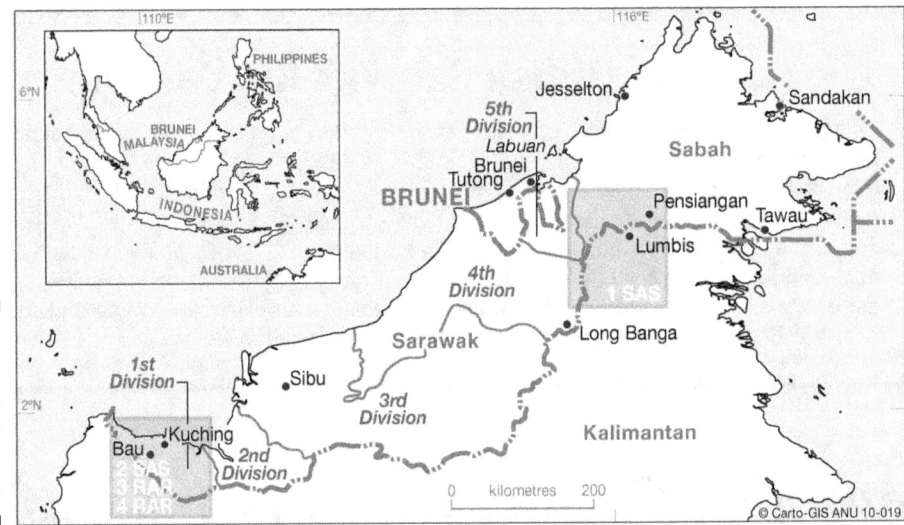

Figure 19-2: Sarawak, Sabah, Brunei and northern Kalimantan.

## Reluctantly edging into war

Sharing a border with Indonesia in New Guinea, Australia had no desire to become involved in a military conflict with its large neighbour. Australia was more concerned about the conflicts in Laos and South Vietnam (to which Australia had already sent Army trainers — refer to Chapter 20). Unlike Britain, Australia was not obliged to defend Malaysia from attack by Indonesia, but in September 1963 Prime Minister Menzies agreed to do so, although at this stage he offered no actual troops.

Australia already had forces based in the Malay Peninsula, including 3 RAR at Terendak and RAAF squadrons at Butterworth. Early in 1964, Australia agreed that 3 RAR could conduct counterinsurgency operations near the Thai border (where the CTs were still eking out an existence) to release Malaysian troops to fight in Borneo. In April 1964 the Malaysian Government formally asked Australia for assistance against Indonesia. Australia agreed to:

- Allow 3 RAR to be used if Indonesians landed on the Malay Peninsula.
- Deploy a squadron of Army engineers to build a road and an airfield in Sabah.
- Send Army signallers to work in the British headquarters at Labuan.
- Provide two minesweepers and four helicopters to assist the Malaysians.

In August 1964 Indonesian guerrillas landed on the coast of the Malayan peninsula in the southern state of Johore and in September Indonesian paratroops dropped into Johore. When late in October more guerrillas came ashore near Malacca, Lieutenant Colonel Bruce McDonald, commanding officer of 3 RAR, commanded a force, including elements of 3 RAR, which rounded up 29 infiltrators. The operation had been extremely minor, but for the first time Australians had been in action against the Indonesians.

## *Patrolling the borders of Borneo*

The pressure on the Australian Government to send combat forces to Borneo was becoming irresistible and in January 1965, at the request of Malaysia, Australia agreed that 3 RAR could be deployed to Borneo. The 3rd Battalion arrived in Borneo in March 1963 to join four British, four Gurkha and three Malaysian battalions that were serving there. The Australians operated along the border of western Sarawak, where most infiltrations were occurring. With its headquarters at Bau, 3 RAR deployed companies to separate bases near to the border and the troops began patrols in thick jungle and along steep ridges.

By the time 3 RAR arrived in Borneo, Major General George Lea had succeeded Walker as Director of Operations. The 3rd Battalion was not permitted to conduct Claret patrols (refer to sidebar 'Claret and the secret cross-border war') across the border until it had spent a mandatory period of one month patrolling the Malaysian side of the border. It then completed some outstanding ambush patrols in Indonesian territory. Lieutenant Pat Beale's platoon killed 15 Indonesians, Lieutenant Robert Guest's platoon killed 8 Indonesians, and Second Lieutenant Douglas Byers' platoon killed at least 17 and perhaps 25 enemy. The battalion completed its four-month tour in July having lost three men killed to mines on the Malaysian side of the border, but none to direct enemy action.

In April 1966 4 RAR, which had relieved 3 RAR at Terendak, arrived in Sarawak and occupied similar bases to 3 RAR. Under Lieutenant Colonel David Thomson, the battalion sent Claret patrols into Indonesian territory. The battalion also dealt with several Indonesian thrusts into Sarawak. In one action four enemy and one Australian were killed.

By this time the conflict was winding down. In September 1965 Indonesian generals took over the government, while Sukarno remained as a figurehead. The generals then negotiated a peace treaty between Malaysia and Indonesia, which was ratified on 11 August 1966. The 4th Battalion completed its tour in Sarawak at the end of August 1966. Australian artillery and field engineers also served in Sarawak, while an engineer construction squadron continued building roads in Sabah until December 1966.

### Claret and the secret cross-border war

Britain's success in Borneo can be attributed primarily to the so-called Claret operations. During 1964 the British Government permitted General Walker to send patrols secretly into Indonesian territory to gather information and to ambush Indonesians as they prepared to cross into Malaysia. By December 1964 the patrols were operating up to 10,000 yards (9,140 metres) across the border. The patrols were planned in meticulous detail, troops were sworn to secrecy, they weren't to carry anything that could identify them, and they weren't to 'be captured by the enemy — alive or dead'. The Claret operations kept the Indonesians on the defensive, but their existence was kept secret and they were never mentioned in official reports. Obviously the Indonesians knew about the patrols, especially when they were on the receiving end of ambushes, but they were too embarrassed to admit publicly that the British could operate at will in their territory. When high-level visitors came to the 3 RAR headquarters they were shown false maps, which disguised the fact that the Australians were operating in Indonesia.

In a remarkable diplomatic balancing act the Australian Government maintained cordial relations with Indonesia while its troops were killing Indonesians in Kalimantan. An Australian Army officer even attended the Indonesian Staff College during this period.

## *The Special Air Service's secret missions*

Borneo was the scene of the first operations by the elite troops of Australia's Special Air Service (SAS). The SAS had been formed at Swanbourne, near Perth, Western Australia, in 1957 to conduct long-range reconnaissance patrols behind enemy lines. British SAS squadrons served in Borneo before the Australian SAS arrived in February 1965 and they helped the Australians to refine their techniques. Commanded by Major Alf Garland, the 1st SAS Squadron (100 soldiers) initially conducted 'hearts and minds' operations among the tribes people in southern Sabah and north-west Sarawak.

In May the SAS began reconnaissance patrols, going up to 18 kilometres into Indonesian territory. Patrols were extremely arduous as they lasted from 10 to 14 days and the four-man teams needed to carry all their provisions with no prospect of resupply. In June the SAS began offensive patrols, guiding Gurkhas for an attack on an Indonesian camp at Lumbis and ambushing Indonesian river craft. By the end of their tour in August 1965 the squadron had killed 17 Indonesians for one fatal casualty, killed by a rogue elephant (see the sidebar 'A horrendous death').

## A horrendous death

On 24 May 1965 Sergeant Roy Weir led a four-man SAS team on a reconnaissance patrol from Sabah into Indonesia. Dropped by helicopter at a Landing Zone (LZ) 35 kilometres south of Pengsiangan, they moved through deep jungle with steep ridges, but saw no sign of Indonesian troops. On 2 June they were advancing along a ridge when they spotted an elephant about 200 metres away. Suddenly the elephant charged. Weir and Lance Corporal Stephen Bloomfield fired at least nine shots directly at the elephant as it ploughed into the Australians. Apparently unaffected it headed off into the jungle, but the patrol's radio operator, Lance Corporal Paul Denehey, had been seriously injured. He had been gored below the ribcage by the elephant's broken tusk.

The patrol applied first aid and carried Denehey to an area that they could defend if the rogue elephant attacked. Their radio had been damaged, but they managed to send a message. Headquarters received it, although the patrol heard no reply on their damaged radio. Next day, concerned that Denehey's condition was deteriorating and knowing that the three others couldn't carry him, Weir and Corporal Bryan Littler went for help, leaving Bloomfield to look after Denehey. Avoiding the elephant, which they saw patrolling the ridge, they reached the LZ. Next morning, accompanied by other SAS soldiers and Gurkhas, they headed back into Indonesia. Late on 6 June they recovered Denehey's body. Bloomfield had remained with Denehey until midday on 5 June, but running out of medication and unaware that help was coming he had gone to seek help himself. He reached the LZ about the time the others found Denehey. Ten Gurkhas were needed to carry the body out through the jungle. Denehey, the Australian SAS's first fatality on active service, had died an agonising and lonely death.

---

The 2nd SAS squadron, commanded by Major James Hughes, served in western Sarawak from January to July 1966. The 2nd SAS conducted reconnaissance patrols in Indonesian territory and in one patrol two Australians were drowned and lost while crossing a flooded river at night. Their bodies, which had been recovered and buried by the Indonesians, were eventually located by an Australian Army team in 2009.

## *Watching the waterways*

At the beginning of Indonesia's Confrontation two Australian destroyers or frigates were operating in Malaysian waters as part of the Far East Strategic Reserve and these vessels joined in patrols to prevent Indonesians infiltrating into Malaysia. In May 1964 the six ships of the RAN's 16th Minesweeping Squadron arrived to contribute to naval operations. On one occasion the minesweeper *Teal* fired upon and stopped a vessel approaching Singapore, killing three of the seven Indonesians aboard. Australian ships also served along the coast of Borneo.

## Securing the peace

After Confrontation, Australian ships, army units and aircraft remained in Malaysia. Successive Australian battalions, along with artillery and engineers, served in the 28th Commonwealth Brigade, which moved from Terendak to Singapore in 1970. The British Labour Government had already announced that it was going to withdrew its forces 'from east of Suez', but Malaysia and Singapore wanted Australia, Britain and New Zealand to remain in the area. The incoming British Conservative Government reversed its predecessor's decision and in November 1971 Australia, Britain, Malaysia, New Zealand and Singapore signed the Five Power Defence Arrangements, by which the countries agreed to consult in the event of attack or threat against Malaysia or Singapore. The 28th Commonwealth Brigade became the 28th ANZUK Brigade, under Australian command. When the Whitlam Government was elected in December 1972 it decided to withdraw Australia's ground forces. The last Australian battalion left Singapore in 1973.

Two RAAF fighter squadrons flying Sabres and later Mirages remained at Butterworth in north-west Malaya until the last squadron withdrew to Australia in 1988. But RAAF P3-C Orion maritime patrol aircraft still deploy forward to Butterworth to conduct patrols in the Indian Ocean and South China Sea, and an Australian rifle company serves at Butterworth on a rotational basis. A senior RAAF officer commands the Integrated Air Defence System covering Singapore and Malaysia. And 30 years later the Five Power Defence Arrangements remain one of Australia's key defence treaties.

# Chapter 20
# Fighting Alongside the Yanks in Vietnam, 1962–72

*In This Chapter*
- Earning a reputation for courage and professionalism while advising the South Vietnamese
- Gaining control of a previously Viet Cong–dominated province
- Employing the full range of the Army's weapons against an elusive enemy
- Taking on Viet Cong and North Vietnamese Main Force battalions
- Finding useful roles for the Navy and the Air Force
- Coming to grips with an unpopular and unwinnable war

The Vietnam War (1959–75) was a major conflict within the broader context of the Cold War. Sometimes the Vietnam War is called the Second Indochina War to differentiate it from the 1946–54 war that led to the end of French control in Indochina and the separation of the country at the 17th Parallel to form communist North Vietnam and anticommunist South Vietnam. The later Vietnam War ended in 1975 when North Vietnamese forces captured the southern capital of Saigon. Vietnam was then reunited as the Socialist Republic of Vietnam. The Vietnamese tend to call the Vietnam War the American War, asserting that it was fought against American imperialism.

The 1954 Geneva Agreement, which negotiated the end of French involvement in Vietnam, stipulated elections in both North and South Vietnam, but the South refused, claiming that elections in the North wouldn't be free. The United States provided military training assistance to South Vietnam, while North Vietnam encouraged communist guerrillas in the South, known as the Viet Cong (Vietnamese Communists), to go to war against the South Vietnamese Government. As the war intensified the United States sent more advisers until in 1965 it deployed combat troops. North Vietnam also sent regular soldiers to the South. The ensuing war included large conventional battles, a savage guerrilla war and extended bombing campaigns over North Vietnam. The United States withdrew in 1973 and North Vietnam triumphed in 1975.

By contrast with the United States, which deployed more than half a million troops and lost almost 60,000 killed, Australia played only a relatively small part. Nonetheless, the war became Australia's third largest in terms of numbers of servicemen involved, the longest in duration (1962–72) and was more controversial and divisive than any previous war.

In this chapter I describe how the first Australians in Vietnam were the advisers of the Training Team. I then tell the story of how our infantry battalions fought in Phuoc Tuy and nearby provinces, engaging in fleeting clashes against local Viet Cong (VC) guerrillas and major battles with Main Force North Vietnamese units. I also explain how Australia's commitment expanded to include Navy and Air Force units. Finally I touch on how the war was viewed at home.

# Advising and Training the South Vietnamese Army

By early 1962 the numbers of US military advisers in South Vietnam were growing and the South Vietnamese army, known as the Army of the Republic of Vietnam (ARVN), was having some success against the Viet Cong. But the United States sought allies to share the burden. The Australian Government was concerned about the spread of communism in the region and on 24 May 1962 announced that it was sending up to 30 military advisers to instruct the ARVN in jungle warfare and in other military skills.

The 30 specially selected officers, warrant officers and sergeants of what became known as the Australian Army Training Team Vietnam (AATTV) arrived in Vietnam in August 1962 and were deployed in various training camps, working alongside American Army advisers. The Australians were not permitted to accompany the ARVN on operations.

The commander of the AATTV was Colonel Francis (Ted) Serong. He set the standards for the AATTV, which soon gained a high reputation for its dedication and expertise. At the end of his tour with the AATTV in 1965 Serong remained in Vietnam as senior adviser to South Vietnam's Police

Field Force. In 1968 he left the army with the rank of brigadier and became an adviser to the South Vietnamese Government. As the war deteriorated and the Australians and Americans departed he remained in Saigon almost to the end, flying out on the last helicopter from the American embassy in Saigon on 29 April 1975.

## The advisers take to the field

In June 1964 the Australian Government increased the numbers of advisers in the AATTV to 83 (later 100) and permitted them to deploy in the field with the Vietnamese units they were advising. Some served with the US Army's Special Forces, which raised and led battalions formed by the Montagnard hill tribes. A small number of Australians worked with the American Central Intelligence Agency, running a controversial program, Operation Phoenix, which assassinated key Viet Cong officials. The advisers served in all ARVN corps zones (refer to Figure 20-1), but mostly in the I and II Corps areas.

The Australians soon found themselves engaged in combat. The Team became the most decorated unit in the Australian Army and four members were awarded the Victoria Cross:

- Warrant Officer Kevin Wheatley was advising a South Vietnamese company during a contact in November 1965. Another Australian warrant officer was badly wounded and the company began to scatter. Wheatley dragged his dying mate to comparative safety, but the South Vietnamese withdrew leaving Wheatley and the wounded Australian to meet the enemy. Facing certain death, Wheatley refused to abandon his comrade. Both their bodies were found next day.

- Warrant Officer Ray Simpson had three tours of duty with the AATTV. On his second tour in 1964 he was awarded the Distinguished Conduct Medal. In May 1966, while commanding a Montagnard company, he moved forward under intense fire to cover the evacuation of casualties.

- Major Peter Badcoe's VC was awarded for three actions between February and April 1967 while advising Regional Force and ARVN companies. When the ARVN company faltered under fire he rallied it and led it in an assault in which he was killed.

- Warrant Officer Keith Payne was commanding a Montagnard company that was attacked and almost surrounded in May 1969. Wounded, he organised a withdrawal to a defensive position, but found that many of his soldiers had been wounded and left behind. He returned to the battle scene and under fire organised the evacuation of 40 wounded soldiers.

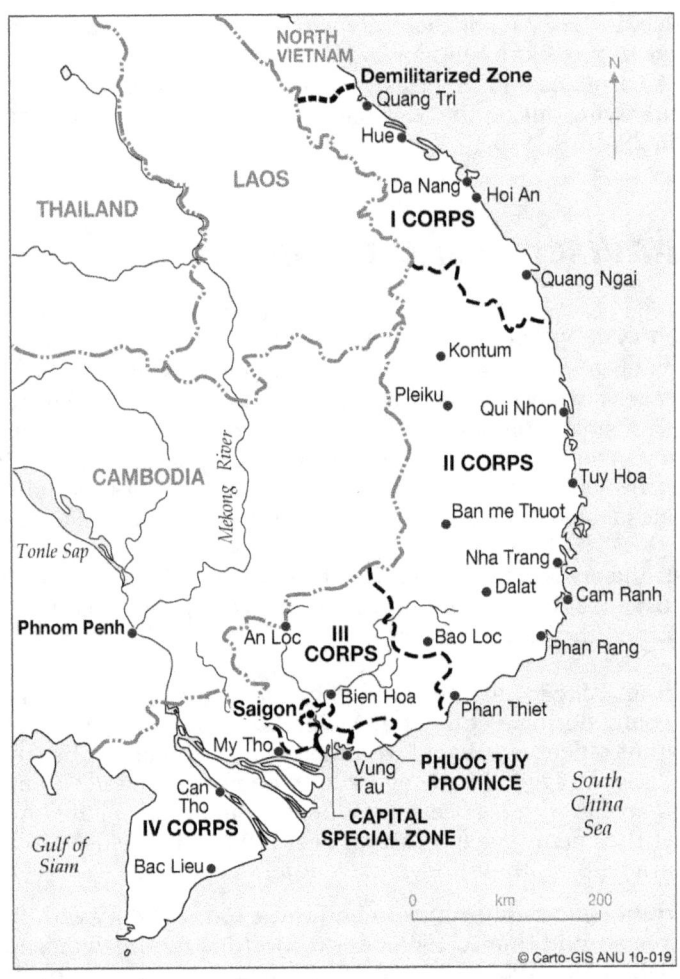

Figure 20-1: South Vietnam, showing ARVN corps zones.

The Team's advisers experienced some of the most intense fighting of the Vietnam War. Serving in ARVN units they needed to display tact when advising ARVN commanders. The advisers could never be confident that their troops would prove reliable in combat, and the success of ARVN operations was often decided by their determination and leadership. A total of 990 advisers served in the Team and 33 died on service.

## Commanding a Montagnard battalion

Australian officers and warrant officers helped raise and command Montagnard battalions, known as *Mike Force* battalions, often filling positions that would normally be held by more senior officers in the Australian Army. In 1970 Major Pat Beale, aged 30, was commanding the 300-strong 1st Mike Force Battalion. His three companies were commanded by an Australian captain, an Australian warrant officer and an American Special Forces captain, while six other warrant officers commanded platoons.

Early in April 1970 a Montagnard battalion camp at Dak Seang in Kontum Province, opposite the Cambodian–Laos border, was surrounded by three North Vietnamese Army (NVA) Regiments. Beale was ordered to relieve the Dak Seang battalion. Inserted by helicopter only 2,800 metres from Dak Seang, Beale's force fought its way through successive NVA defences, against almost overwhelming odds, until after ten days it relieved the beleaguered camp. His battalion suffered more than 100 casualties, dead and evacuated wounded; nearly as many had been wounded and had kept fighting. Of the ten Australians, one was dead and three wounded. Beale was awarded the Distinguished Service Order, the only Australian major to receive the award in the Vietnam War, all others going to more senior officers.

## Sending Combat Troops

In mid-1964 the Australian Army had little capacity to send combat troops to Vietnam as it had only four infantry battalions. One was serving in Malaysia and another was preparing to relieve it. The other two battalions had a large unwieldy structure and were known as Pentropic battalions. In November 1964 the Government announced that it was doubling the numbers of infantry battalion from four to eight. The Pentropic battalions were split in two and two more battalions were to be raised.

The additional soldiers would come from a selective National Service scheme. If a young man was aged 20, medically fit and his birth date was drawn from a barrel, he was required to serve in the Army for two years. Married men, tertiary students, apprentices, those who had joined the part-time Citizen Forces and certain other categories could have their service deferred or they could be exempted.

Contrary to popular perceptions, the government didn't introduce conscription to provide troops for service in Vietnam. Rather, the government was concerned about a possible war with Indonesia and in January 1965 it sent a battalion to combat operations in Borneo (refer to Chapter 19). But undoubtedly the decision to increase the numbers of battalions made it possible to send one of them to Vietnam.

## A contentious decision

In December 1964 the United States advised that it was considering sending combat troops to Vietnam and suggested that Australia send 200 advisers. The Menzies Government was anxious to support the Americans, and as the Army couldn't find enough qualified officers and soldiers to expand the Training Team it proposed sending a battalion. No decision was made, but early in April 1965 the Chairman of the Chiefs of Staff Committee, Air Chief Marshal Sir Frederick Scherger, attended discussions in Hawaii with senior American officers and, exceeding his authority, he offered a battalion even before the Americans asked for it. Scherger had, however, astutely assessed the mood of the Cabinet, because on his return it approved the deployment. On 29 April Menzies announced that the 1st Battalion of the Royal Australian Regiment (1 RAR) and support troops would be deployed to Vietnam.

Much controversy has surrounded Menzies's announcement in which he stated that the government 'was in receipt of a request' for assistance from South Vietnam. In fact, after deciding to send the battalion the government had then asked the South Vietnamese to request it and the message from Saigon arrived a few hours before Menzies' announcement. Menzies described the commitment as a major contribution to the Australian–American alliance, but also noted that the 'takeover of South Vietnam would be a direct military threat to Australia and all the countries of South and South-East Asia'.

The Leader of the Opposition, Arthur Calwell, criticised the decision, claiming that South Vietnam was engaged in a civil war, 'aided and abetted by the North Vietnamese Government'. Instead of sending troops, he argued that the United States and Australia should have sent economic assistance to South Vietnam. But he failed to acknowledge that without military help the Saigon Government would soon fall.

## The first battalion

The first American combat troops arrived in South Vietnam in March 1965. Australia's first troops, 1 RAR, arrived in June 1965 and were deployed to defend the approaches to the Bien Hoa air base on the outskirts of Saigon. Under the command of Lieutenant Colonel Lou Brumfield, 1 RAR became part of the American 173rd Airborne Brigade (Separate).

The American brigade conducted major operations to locate and destroy Viet Cong units in an area north of Bien Hoa to a distance of about 30 kilometres, but at times moved further afield, almost to the Cambodian border. At first, 1 RAR wasn't permitted to operate much beyond 30 kilometres, because the Australian Government and the Chief of the General Staff, Lieutenant General Sir John Wilton, were determined to limit casualties and didn't want to expose Australian troops to capricious American operations. The limitation was extended in September 1965.

The Australians found that they had a different approach to the Americans, who blustered into an area with much noise and firepower, challenging the Viet Cong to engage in a major battle. By contrast, mindful of their experience in Malaya, the Australians moved stealthily through the jungle, hoping to catch the enemy offguard. The Australians had fewer contacts than the Americans, killed fewer enemy and had fewer casualties. The Australians had much to learn about large-scale operations, especially with helicopters, but they also showed the value of their more careful tactics. They successfully cleared the enemy from around Bien Hoa and then took part in major operations with the American brigade. At the end of its tour in June 1965 the battalion had lost 18 Diggers killed. Numbers of enemy dead aren't known. In a major operation in January 1966 the battalion lost 8 killed and accounted for 27 VC killed.

## Dominating Phuoc Tuy Province

As the Americans increased their forces in South Vietnam, they pressured the Australian Government to do likewise. In March 1965 the Australian Prime Minister, Harold Holt, who had succeeded Menzies, announced that 1 RAR would be replaced by the 1st Australian Task Force (1 ATF), which would include two infantry battalions (5 RAR and 6 RAR), a Special Air Service squadron, additional combat and logistic support units and eight RAAF Iroquois helicopters. With a larger force the Australians could be given their own area of responsibility and would be able to conduct their operations as they saw fit, rather than as part of an American force. General Wilton agreed that 1 ATF would be located in Phuoc Tuy Province, which was dominated by the Viet Cong. Located south-east of Saigon, the province bordered the South China Sea. If the war turned into a disaster, the Australians could be evacuated through the port of Vung Tau, which was on a nearby and isolated peninsula (see Figure 20-2).

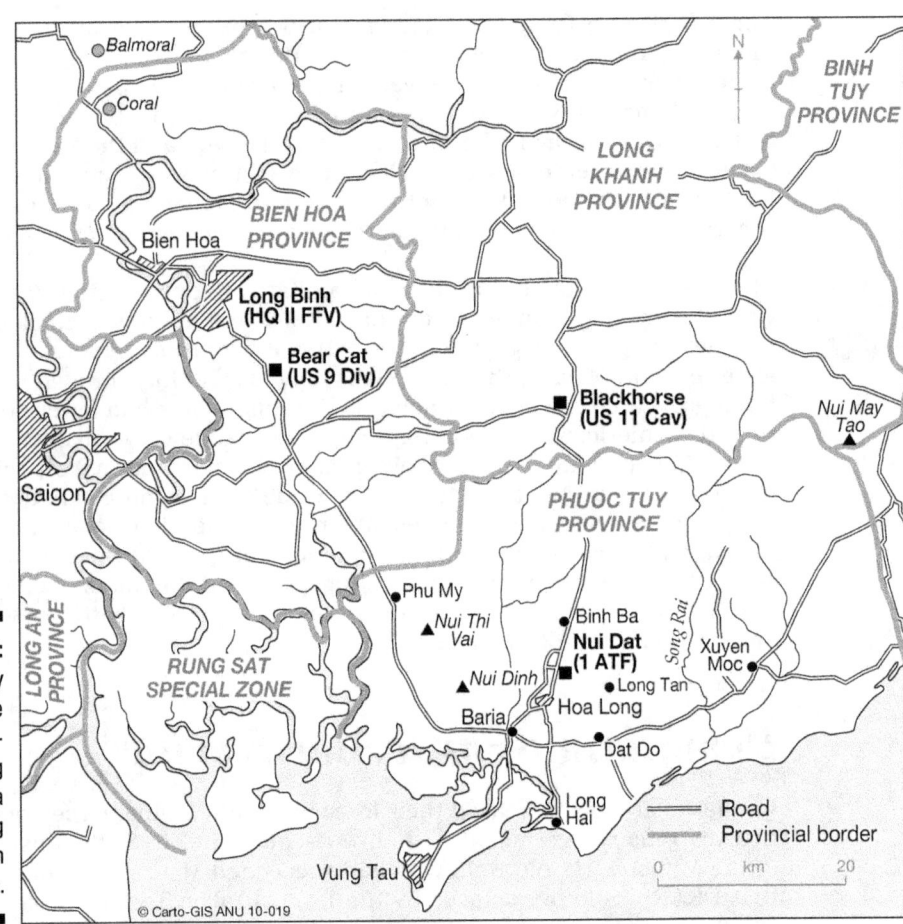

Figure 20-2: Phuoc Tuy Province and neighbouring Bien Hoa and Long Khanh provinces.

Brigadier David Jackson, the commander of 1 ATF, worked under the direction of an American general (commander of the 2nd Field Force), who controlled operations in the ARVN III Corps tactical zone. Jackson didn't 'own' Phuoc Tuy Province, which was still the responsibility of the South Vietnamese Government, but the Task Force was given four tasks:

- Secure the province against enemy Main Forces.
- Open the highway from Saigon to Vung Tau.
- Help the South Vietnamese authorities to pacify Phuoc Tuy so that normal civilian movement could be restored.
- Be prepared to operate anywhere else in the III Corps area and even in the neighbouring province in the II Corps area if necessary.

## Building the Task Force base at Nui Dat

Brigadier Jackson located 1 ATF at Nui Dat (which means small hill) in the centre of the province, just north of the province capital of Baria, while the Australian supply and support base was established at Vung Tau. The two Australian battalions, which included National Servicemen, arrived in Vietnam in May 1966 and, after clearing the Nui Dat area, they began establishing the base. Eventually, as well as the infantry battalions, the base would include an airfield, several helicopter landing areas, artillery, engineers, armoured personnel carriers and support units.

Within Phuoc Tuy Province the Viet Cong (VC) Main Force and Regional Force units occupied bases in the jungle-covered hills and mountains in the north-east of the province, and in hill areas to the west and south. The VC intimidated the villagers, taxing them and seeking food that was then transported to the jungle bases.

To ensure his base's security, Jackson arranged for two nearby villages to be destroyed and their inhabitants relocated, which hardly endeared the Australians to the people of these villages. His battalions then started patrolling out from Nui Dat to locate and destroy the VC. The troops also conducted cordon and search operations, in which at night they inserted a cordon of troops around a village. At first light other Australian troops, with South Vietnamese police, searched the village for VC and hidden weapons. With only two battalions, initially Jackson needed to retain one battalion to defend the base, while the other battalion was used for operations further away. During July the Australians engaged groups of VC in several intense fire fights, indicating that they were disrupting the VC's activities. The big question was how long it would take before the VC tried to challenge the Australian presence in the province.

## Identifying the enemy

The common picture of a Viet Cong soldier — known by the Australians and Americans as Victor Charlie, or just Charlie — is of a man or woman dressed in black pyjamas with a straw conical hat and wearing sandals made from old tyres, called Ho Chi Minh sandals. These VC lived in the villages, tended their paddy fields during the day, but quickly turned into a deadly enemy when the occasion presented itself. This picture is only partially correct.

The Viet Cong were the soldiers of the National Liberation Front. The communists tried to pretend that the Front was a popular home-grown organisation formed in South Vietnam to overthrow the allegedly tyrannical South Vietnam Government. In truth, the Front was controlled from Hanoi. The Viet Cong included regular Main Force regiments that wore uniforms and could be deployed in large-scale offensives wherever they were ordered. Main Force 274 and 275 VC Regiments fought in Phuoc Tuy Province. Each had three battalions, but in practice they were considerably smaller than an Australian infantry battalion.

VC Regional Force units were also full-time, but served within their own province. The largest VC Regional Force unit in Phuoc Tuy Province was D445 Battalion, which fought the Australians on many occasions. The local part-time village guerrillas were the black pyjama brigade. They were equipped with fewer heavy weapons and conducted minor operations such as ambushes and the laying of mines. The basic weapon in all the units was the Russian-designed AK-47 assault rifle.

Large numbers of North Vietnamese Army (NVA) regular soldiers fought in South Vietnam. They wore uniforms (often with pith helmets) and were equipped with heavier weapons such as mortars and heavy rocket launchers. The Australians fought the NVA and soldiers from the 33rd NVA Regiment often deployed into Phuoc Tuy Province.

## *Desperate defence at Long Tan*

On the night of 17 August 1966 VC mortars and rockets landed in the Nui Dat base, wounding 22 Australians. Next morning Brigadier Jackson deployed company-sized patrols to locate the enemy. In the afternoon of 18 August D Company 6 RAR, commanded by Major Harry Smith, entered the Long Tan rubber plantation about five kilometres east of Nui Dat. The company's 11 Platoon contacted a small group of VC, but was soon fighting for its life against a larger enemy force. The platoon commander was killed, more than a third of the platoon became casualties and Sergeant Bob Buick took command. Smith deployed 10 Platoon to assist but it too came under heavy fire. Buick conducted a fighting withdrawal to join the rest of the company.

Smith gathered his troops in all-round defence as, in torrential monsoonal rain, well-trained and disciplined VC attacked in waves. Australian and New Zealand artillery, located at Nui Dat, brought down heavy fire on the attacking VC, wiping out complete rows of the enemy. Outnumbered, running short of ammunition, the Australians faced annihilation. In fading light, Australian helicopters dropped ammunition. Then as the VC launched another assault, armoured personnel carriers (APC) carrying A Company 6 RAR appeared through the gloom, raking the attacking VC with their machine guns. The VC broke off the attack and D Company had been saved.

Next day D Company's troops swept through the battle area to recover their dead comrades and some of their mates who had been wounded and had lain alone on the battlefield. The Australians lost 18 killed and 24 wounded, but found the bodies of 245 VC. Many others had been carried away. The VC had deployed the three battalions of the 275 VC Regiment and the D445 Battalion. About 100 Diggers, supported by artillery, had withstood concerted attacks by a force at least ten times their size. D Company was awarded the US Presidential Unit Citation. The date the battle began, 18 August, is commemorated in Australia as Long Tan Day, also known as Vietnam Veterans' Remembrance Day.

## *The two-edged sword — the disastrous barrier minefield*

Because 1 ATF had only two combat battalions and two companies needed to be assigned permanently to defend Nui Dat, it didn't have enough troops to prevent the VC moving between the villages and their jungle camps. Brigadier Stuart Graham, who had succeeded Jackson as Task Force commander, came up with the imaginative idea of laying an 11-kilometre minefield and fence from the coast to a small old volcano crater called the Horseshoe (just north of Dat Do), where the Australians located some artillery and infantry. The minefield would prevent the VC moving between the villages and the jungle and thus deprive them of vital food and supplies. South Vietnamese forces, based in each village, were supposed to guard the minefield.

The barrier minefield, in which 20,000 M-16 anti-personnel mines were laid by Australian Army engineers between March and June 1967, has sometimes been called Graham's Folly and it proved to be disastrous for the Australians.

- Because of the need for haste, five Australian engineers were killed and eight wounded in accidents during the laying of the minefield.
- The South Vietnamese troops failed to guard the minefield adequately and the VC crept in at night and stole many mines. In effect the minefield became the VC mine supply depot.

- The VC laid the captured mines in areas where the Diggers were likely to patrol, causing heavy Australian casualties, especially in 1969–70. Those who weren't killed often lost limbs. While exact figures are not available, one historian claims that 55 Australian soldiers were killed by Australian M-16 mines. About 11 per cent of all Australian deaths in Vietnam and 8 per cent of all those wounded were caused by Australian mines.
- The Task Force needed to devote considerable resources to removing the mines in 1969 and 1970.

# Our Contest with Victor Charlie

The popular picture of Australian operations in Vietnam is of Diggers patrolling silently through the jungle, occasionally meeting small bands of VC, or of helicopters dropping soldiers in the field before they set out on patrol. In fact, 1 ATF troops took part in a wide range of activities. At its largest, 1 ATF had a strength of about 8,000 troops, including three infantry battalions, a Special Air Service squadron, a squadron of tanks, a squadron of APCs, a regiment of artillery, a squadron of field engineers, a flight of army helicopters and fixed wing aircraft, and numerous support troops.

## The grunts carry the load

The main work was carried out by the infantry. In 1965–66, 1 RAR served in Bien Hoa and then in mid-1966 1 ATF began operations in Phuoc Tuy Province with two battalions (see preceding section). In December 1967 the Task Force expanded to a force of three battalions. Each battalion generally served in Vietnam for a year. Some battalions included a company or two of New Zealanders and were known as Anzac battalions. In November 1970 the government withdrew one of the battalions and the Task Force operated with two battalions until August 1971, when the government decided to withdraw the force. Over a period of six and half years all nine battalions of the Royal Australian Regiment served in Vietnam and eight of them served there twice.

The battalions generally numbered about 750 troops and had the following structure:

- Battalion headquarters
- Support Company, with mortar, signals, assault pioneer and anti-tank platoons, although the latter often became a tracker platoon with dogs

- Administrative Company, with medical, supply and transport platoons
- Four rifle companies, each with a support section and three rifle platoons

A rifle platoon, commanded by a lieutenant, consisted of three ten-man sections each led by a corporal. The section included one and sometimes two M-60 machine guns and the soldiers carried either M-16 Armalite carbines or the heavier SLR rifles, as well as grenade launchers, lightweight anti-tank rocket launchers and Claymore mines (fixed direction mines that were laid around defensive positions and were initiated with an electric charge).

As in the world wars, Korea and Malaya, the main burden of the fighting was borne by the infantry soldiers, who called themselves grunts. The grunts patrolled in the jungle, lay in ambush, assaulted enemy bunker systems, manned machine guns in defensive positions, stayed awake on sentry duty, dug shallow trenches (shell scrapes) each night, slept on the ground, ate combat rations and took the most casualties. Apart from 1 RAR, all the battalions included National Servicemen (Nashos), but in the field there was no distinction between the Nashos and the Regular soldiers (Regs).

The work of the cavalry squadron, equipped with M113 A1 armoured personnel carriers (APCs), shouldn't be discounted. The 'Tracks', as the APCs were called, patrolled and ambushed on their own, but also transported the infantry when they deployed through the province and at times carried them directly into battle.

## *Patrolling and ambushing*

Much of the infantry's time was spent patrolling through the jungle, searching for signs of the enemy. Platoons carried sufficient rations to operate for about six days, but this time could be extended for up to 30 days, during which the troops were resupplied by helicopter. Patrolling wasn't just a leisurely stroll through the jungle. Soldiers needed to remain alert for any indication of an enemy. Forward scouts knew that if they didn't spot the enemy first they were likely to be the first casualty. If an infantry patrol came across a recently used track it might lay an ambush. Ambushes were also laid on the approaches to villages to prevent the VC moving in or out of the villages at night to collect taxes and food.

An example of such an ambush took place in August 1970 when a platoon of C Company 8 RAR commanded by Sergeant Chad Sherrin took up an ambush position on the approaches to Hao Long village. At 9.00 pm Sherrin's rear protection group reported that 50 to 60 VC had moved into Hoa Long along a separate path about 100 metres away across a paddy field. Sherrin redeployed his platoon in four groups, each with five men and a machine gun, to cover the other track. About 3.15 am the VC returned heavily laden. When the enemy were ten metres away one of the ambush groups fired its Claymore mines and the other groups engaged the enemy with machine guns. The VC tried to counterattack, but were driven off. Sherrin's platoon recovered 19 enemy bodies, with large quantities of weapons, supplies and food.

## Search and destroy

At times the Australians took part in large-scale operations, often with American units, to locate and destroy the VC. One standard tactic was to deploy one battalion in a blocking position while another battalion swept through an area where VC were thought to be based. The VC often deployed small forces to delay the sweeping battalion while the rest escaped. In that case the sweeping battalion was engaged in some battles, while the blocking battalion might conduct successful ambushes. But often the VC were able to melt away and avoid the Australians.

In a search and destroy operation in August 1967 A Company 7 RAR, under Major Jake O'Donnell, struck a VC rearguard of similar size and a fierce two-hour battle ensued. The company's artillery observer, Lieutenant Neville Clark, called down artillery fire on the VC positions. When the VC moved closer to the Australians, Clark brought the exploding artillery to within 50 metres of the Diggers. The weight of artillery induced the VC to withdraw. Six Australians died and 20 were wounded. Only five enemy bodies were recovered but the tally would have been much higher. O'Donnell, Clark and several other members of the company received awards for bravery.

The fiercest fighting occurred when the Australians struck VC camps that were protected by bunkers, often connected by tunnels. If the situation allowed the Australians would withdraw from close proximity to the bunker system and pound it with artillery and air strikes, before they assaulted the enemy position. If the enemy remained to fight the Australians would find themselves advancing against machine guns that had been sited to cover the obvious approaches.

The Australian infantry preferred to attack bunker systems with the assistance of Centurion tanks, which were heavy enough to crash their way through the jungle. The tanks would fire high explosive rounds from their 20-pounder main guns directly at the enemy bunkers and would also be used to crush enemy bunkers. An example of such a battle took place in July 1971 when C and D Companies of 4 RAR and tanks of C Squadron 1st Armoured Regiment fought their way into a bunker system occupied by the 1st Battalion of 274 VC Regiment.

## Phantoms of the jungle

The most effective Australian combat unit was the Special Air Service (SAS), which maintained a squadron on operations from June 1966 to October 1971. With a strength of about 100 soldiers, the SAS squadron generally deployed patrols of four to six soldiers commanded by a junior officer or sergeant. At first the SAS conducted reconnaissance patrols to locate enemy camps, but gradually they were permitted to mount ambushes and eventually the SAS patrols dominated the VC rear areas.

The SAS and the RAAF helicopters cooperated closely and often SAS patrols were lifted out of the jungle, dangling on the end of ropes, while other helicopters firing machine guns kept the enemy at bay. The SAS soldiers were highly trained and moved stealthily through the jungle. They were experts at camouflage and during one ambush an SAS soldier had to lean backwards so that the muzzle of his rifle didn't actually touch the VC he was about to shoot. For good reason, the VC referred to the SAS as *Ma Rung* — phantoms of the jungle.

An Australian Army study in late 1968 found that the three infantry battalions (two until December 1967) had been involved in 74 per cent of all Australian contacts, compared with 24 per cent for the SAS squadron, which was one-seventh the size of an infantry battalion. Of the 410 enemy killed to that time, the infantry had accounted for 188, the SAS 173 and minor units, the remainder.

The statistics of the SAS's operations are remarkable. As far as can be determined, the SAS had 298 contacts in Vietnam, inflicted 492 kills, 106 possible kills, 47 wounded, 10 possibly wounded and they captured 11 prisoners. A total of 5,366 enemy had been sighted (counted) in 801 sightings. Australian and New Zealand SAS casualties (some New Zealanders served with the Australians) were six deaths, only two of whom were the result of enemy action.

## *Hitting the enemy hard — the guns in the jungle*

Standard army practice was to deploy a battery of field artillery to support a battalion of infantry on operations and by the time the two infantry battalions of 1 ATF arrived at Nui Dat in mid-1966 they were supported by a regiment of artillery consisting of two Australian field batteries (each with six guns) and a New Zealand battery. The guns were 105 mm howitzers with a range of about 10 or 11 kilometres depending on the model being used. The infantry conducted their patrols within range of the guns so that if they struck the enemy they could call for artillery support by radio. In the three-hour battle of Long Tan in August 1966 Australian and New Zealand gunners fired 3,198 rounds of 105 mm ammunition. The artillery caused tremendous casualties to the attacking VC, saving D Company 6 RAR from annihilation.

When the infantry moved further away from Nui Dat the artillery deployed to temporary positions known as Fire Support Patrol Bases (FSPB). Artillery officers patrolled with the infantry to direct artillery fire in support of the infantry, and they often found themselves under enemy fire. They were assisted by junior artillery and mortar observers who deployed with the infantry platoons, but all infantry platoon commanders were proficient in giving simplified fire orders and often did so in an emergency.

## *Bushrangers and dust-offs — helicopters prove their worth*

Helicopters became an iconic image of the Vietnam War. The Australian Task Force was supported by No 9 Squadron of the Royal Australian Air Force (RAAF) flying 8, later 16, UH 1 Iroquois helicopters, which became an integral part of the army's operations. Popularly known as the Huey, the Iroquois helicopter carried out a wide range of tasks:

- Inserting and withdrawing infantry at the beginning and end of an operation.
- Evacuating battle casualties, often from a temporary landing zone near a battle. A medical evacuation was known as a 'dust-off'.
- Resupplying the infantry with ammunition during a contact. In the battle of Long Tan the helicopters dropped vital ammunition under fire and in appalling weather.
- Resupplying the infantry with food and other stores while on patrol.
- Spraying chemicals to kill mosquitoes or to defoliate the jungle (so that the enemy would have fewer places to hide).
- Providing fire support to the infantry from helicopters armed with machine guns and rockets. These helicopter gunships were known as 'bushrangers'.
- Inserting and withdrawing Special Air Service patrols (see sidebar 'Phantoms of the jungle').

The helicopters enabled 1 ATF to redeploy its troops quickly throughout Phuoc Tuy Province. By the use of helicopters, wounded soldiers could be evacuated to the Australian field hospital at Vung Tau within an hour of being wounded and the speed of evacuation saved many Australian lives.

# Challenging the Enemy's Main Force — the Tet Offensives

At the end of 1967 the Australian Government increased the size of the Task Force by deploying a third battalion (3 RAR) and a squadron of 12 Centurion tanks. With the arrival of a third battalion the Task Force could now send two battalions on operations outside the province, while the third battalion protected Nui Dat and patrolled in Phuoc Tuy Province.

In January 1968 the American high command received intelligence that the VC were planning a major offensive for the Tet (Chinese Lunar New Year) holiday period at the end of the month, when traditionally both sides had observed a truce. On 23 January the headquarters of 1 ATF, now commanded by Brigadier Ron Hughes, and with 2 and 7 RAR (which had replaced 5 and 6 RAR) moved out of Phuoc Tuy Province to the border of Bien Hoa and Long Khanh Provinces, just east of Saigon, on Operation Coburg.

In the early hours of 31 January the Viet Cong violated the Tet truce and launched major attacks all over South Vietnam. The ferocity of the VC offensive and their ability to seize key points in many cities caused considerable dismay among the American public. Actually the South Vietnamese and the Americans fought well and inflicted a stunning military defeat on the Viet Cong and NVA. While the ARVN lost 4,000 troops and the Americans 2,000, they claimed to have killed 50,000 VC. The two Australian battalions on Operation Coburg were astride the line of communication of the VC 5th Division and they had almost daily contacts, often against company sized Main Force VC groups moving in and out of Saigon.

## Street fighting in Baria and Long Dien

While most of 1 ATF operated in Bien Hoa Province on Operation Coburg, the VC attacked the main towns in Phuoc Tuy Province. The provincial capital, Baria, was occupied by heavily armed and reinforced D445 Battalion. Colonel Donald Dunstan, deputy Task Force Commander, despatched A Company 3 RAR, commanded by Major Brian (Horrie) Howard, in APCs to assist the government forces in the town. The Diggers cleared the VC in a series of savage contacts. For 3 RAR's soldiers who had recently arrived in Vietnam prepared for jungle warfare, it was a new and challenging experience to find themselves engaged in street fighting through a major town.

The VC also moved into the village of Long Dien, five kilometres east of Baria. D Company 3 RAR, commanded by Major Peter Phillips, with APCs helped ARVN Rangers clear the village. Major Bert Irwin's B Company 3 RAR operated in the village of Hoa Long, three kilometres south-west of Nui Dat, then moved on to Long Dien to help the Rangers.

Having blunted the VC offensive in Phuoc Tuy, 3 RAR replaced 7 RAR in Operation Coburg and established Fire Support Patrol Base (FSPB) Andersen astride the enemy's line of communication. Over a ten-day period at the end of February 1968 the VC attacked Andersen in force on three occasions, being driven off by machine-gun, mortar and artillery fire. In a month of action all three Australian battalions had helped crush the VC Tet offensive.

## *Coral and Balmoral — the biggest battles*

In May the VC and NVA began another attempt to take over Saigon and again the Australians were deployed to intercept the VC battalions moving in and out of the city. On 12 May, 1 ATF including 1 RAR (which had recently arrived to take over from 7 RAR) and 3 RAR moved by helicopter into an area north of Bien Hoa. By last light the headquarters of 1 RAR, commanded by Lieutenant Colonel Phillip Bennett, was establishing FSPB Coral, while its companies began patrolling. Coral was occupied by the battalion's mortars and assault pioneers and six guns of the 102nd Field Battery.

In the early hours of 13 May rockets and mortars rained down on the Coral defenders before soldiers from the 141st NVA Regiment attacked in force. The NVA overran 1 RAR's mortars, captured one of the Australian 105-mm howitzers and damaged another. While three Australian guns fired in support of the 1 RAR companies that were also in contact in the jungle, the remaining gun lowered its barrel to the horizontal position and fired splintex rounds (rounds filled with thousands of small darts) over the Australian mortar position. The Australian mortar men lay flat in shallow trenches, while the splintex rounds passed overhead, striking the attacking NVA. By dawn the Australians had lost 9 killed and 28 wounded. At least 52 NVA bodies were found. The NVA tried again, without success, on 16 May.

Australian tanks arrived from Nui Dat and some of these joined 3 RAR in FSPB Balmoral. Soldiers from the 7th NVA Division attacked Balmoral early on 26 May. The infantry of 3 RAR were supported by artillery, mortars and tanks, which fired directly at the attacking enemy, halting their assault. The NVA resumed the attack two nights later and paid a heavy price. Between 12 May and 6 June, 1 RAR and 3 RAR engaged in some of the fiercest fighting the Australians experienced in Vietnam, and 21 Diggers were killed. The Australians identified 267 enemy bodies, but many more were killed.

## Denying food to the enemy

Captain John Bullen was on duty in the 1 ATF Command Post one evening, shortly before the battle of Coral, when an RAAF aircraft sought permission by radio to shoot six cattle. Bullen recorded the conversation with the RAAF pilot:

'Did you say cattle, i.e. cows?' said Bullen.

'That is affirmative.' (RAAF people aren't capable of a simple yes or no.)

'Why do you want to shoot them?'

'Because they're Viet Cong cattle, that's why.'

'How can you divine the political beliefs of a cow when you're in an aircraft and the cow's on the ground?'

'If we don't kill the cattle, the Viet Cong will eat them, so let's get in first.'

'What, and kill the poor beasts in case someone else does? Fair go, mate.'

'May I engage them with machine-gun fire?'

'No. Leave them alone.'

'What! Are you Viet Cong or the bloody RSPCA?'

Eventually a senior officer approved the attack and the RAAF pilot replied that he was 'engaging the enemy'. Next morning the RAAF reported the 'successful slaying' of two cattle — killed in action — but that four others had escaped. (From Paul Ham (ed.), *Captain Bullen's War*, HarperCollins, Sydney, 2009, p. 110.)

## *The enemy confronts our tanks at Binh Ba*

During 1968 and the first half of 1969 the Australian battalions continued their battles with VC Main Force units both within and beyond the border of Phuoc Tuy Province. The VC tried another Tet offensive in February 1969, but it wasn't as dangerous as the offensive in 1968. One of the last enemy Main Force battles with the Australians took place in early June 1969, when a company of NVA regulars, along with local guerrillas, occupied the village of Binh Ba just five kilometres north of Nui Dat. On 6 June, D Company 5 RAR, under the command of Major Murray Blake, along with four Centurion Tanks of B Squadron, 1st Armoured Regiment and APCs, hurried to the village.

As the Australians entered the village they struck fierce resistance from the NVA and VC who had occupied the houses. When more NVA and VC headed towards the village several of the tanks manoeuvred to meet them and Blake had to withdraw from Binh Ba. Another company of 5 RAR, along with four more tanks, arrived and Lieutenant Colonel Colin Khan took command. D Company, assisted by tanks, then cleared the village street by street. Much of the village was destroyed as the tanks fired high explosive rounds into each house that was occupied by the enemy. By the time the battle ended on 8 June the Australians had killed 91 enemy and had taken 11 prisoners.

# Striking the Enemy from Sea and Air

Although the Army carried the heaviest burden in Vietnam, deploying the largest numbers and suffering the most casualties, the Royal Australian Navy (RAN) and the RAAF were also involved in a variety of ways.

## The Air Force's war

The RAAF's first commitment to Vietnam began in August 1964 when the first of eventually six Caribou twin-engine transport aircraft arrived at Vung Tau. The unit was later renamed No 35 (Transport) Squadron, but was known in Vietnam as 'Wallaby Airlines'. The aircraft carried out resupply regular flights, known as milk runs, up and down the country, often landing on short, rough airstrips at American Special Forces bases in remote localities, where they were vulnerable to enemy fire.

In April 1967 the RAAF's No 2 Squadron, equipped with eight Canberra bombers, deployed to Phan Rang air base (refer to Figure 20-1). The base was protected by RAAF airfield defence guards, who patrolled around the base and sometimes were in contact with the VC. Operating by day and at night the Canberra bombers attacked concentrations of VC and North Vietnamese troops, winning recognition for accuracy. By the time the squadron withdrew in June 1971 five members had died, two on operations.

Flying Officer Michael Herbert and Pilot Officer Robert Carver were lost in November 1970 when their aircraft failed to return from a mission south-east of Da Nang. The mystery of their disappearance continued for almost 40 years, until in April 2009 a joint Army–Air Force team remarkably located their crashed aircraft near the Laotian border and recovered their remains for burial in Australia.

## The Navy's war

Between March 1967 and October 1971 the RAN maintained a destroyer on operations off the Vietnamese coast, working as part of the US Navy's 7th Fleet to deliver naval gunfire support to ground forces and to help prevent the VC using small craft to move supplies along the coast. The destroyers *Hobart* and *Perth* had three six-month tours, *Brisbane* two and *Vendetta* one. They rarely came under enemy fire, but in June 1967 American aircraft attacked *Hobart* in error, killing two Australians and wounding several others.

Most of the Australian soldiers who served in Vietnam were transported there and home again by HMAS *Sydney*, an aircraft carrier that had been converted to a troop carrier. It was known as the 'Vung Tau Ferry'. Other navy personnel to serve in Vietnam included clearance divers, who helped clear mines from ports, and an RAN helicopter unit that served with great distinction alongside American army helicopters at Bear Cat air base, southeast of Bien Hoa. Five RAN aircrew were killed on operations.

# Protest and Dissent

Australia's involvement in the Vietnam War is replete with myths and misconceptions. One popular image is that the war was extremely unpopular among the Australian population. However, after Australia sent combat troops the Liberal–Country Party Government was re-elected twice, with a large majority in November 1966 and with a reduced majority in October 1969.

## Opposing conscription

The government announced the introduction of conscription or National Service in November 1964. The first intake began training in mid-1965 and the first national servicemen to serve overseas arrived in Vietnam in mid-1966. Conscription was opposed by some Australians for a variety of reasons:

- Some people were philosophically opposed to conscription in any circumstances.
- Because national servicemen were selected according to whether their birth date was drawn by a lottery, national service could be seen as unfair because the burden wasn't shared equally. The ballot was called the 'lottery of death'.
- Many people increasingly saw the war as immoral, illegal or at best unwise and objected that men could be compelled to take part in it.

Most young conscripts obeyed the law and served in the Army to the best of their ability. Of 50,000 Australian servicemen who went to Vietnam, 17,424 were conscripts. Some young men publicly flouted the law hoping to increase opposition to conscription by the subsequent publicity. At times the police's efforts to chase the dissenters looked like episodes involving the Keystone Cops. Opposition groups included the Draft Resisters Union and Save our Sons, which was made up of middle-aged women who organised petitions, lobbied Members of Parliament, engaged in protests and conducted silent vigils in public places. During demonstrations some militant groups deliberately sought to turn peaceful protests into a violent confrontation with the police.

## The moratorium marches

As the war continued and especially after the 1968 Tet offensive, opposition to Australia's involvement gathered strength. Opposition groups included members of the Australian Labor Party, trade unions and academics. Following the example of protests in the United States, various groups in Australia organised days of mass protest known as the Vietnam Moratorium. The first of these took place in early May 1970. The largest crowd, estimated to be between 50,000 and 100,000, gathered in Melbourne. The second Moratorium march was held in September 1970 and the third in June 1971.

The Moratorium marches emphasised the extent to which the Vietnam War had bitterly divided the community and families. Among the protesters were a small number who actively supported the Viet Cong and carried North Vietnamese flags and pictures of Ho Chi Minh. While in the main the demonstrators directed their protests at the government, some took aim at the soldiers serving in Vietnam. Nonetheless, when battalions returned from Vietnam the troops marched through the city where the unit was based and were generally welcomed by the public.

## Our troops go home

Despite the demonstrations by protesters the main reason why Australia withdrew from Vietnam was that the United States had decide to withdraw. At the end of 1968 the United States introduced a policy of Vietnamisation, in which the conduct of the war would be taken over by the South Vietnamese Army, and the Americans began gradually to withdraw their forces. Australia followed suit and when 8 RAR ended its tour in November 1970 it wasn't replaced. The Australian Task Force continued operations in Phuoc Tuy Province with two battalions, while the Army increased its training effort for the South Vietnamese Army in the province. The following March the Prime Minister, William McMahon, withdrew the RAN helicopters and clearance divers, the Canberra bombers and some Caribous. Finally in August 1971 the government announced the withdrawal of the remainder of the combat forces.

Hoping for a last victory, towards the end of September the 33rd NVA Regiment moved back into Phuoc Tuy Province and clashed with 4 RAR. Five Australians were killed and 30 were wounded in the Task Force's last major action of the war. All the combat units withdrew before the end of the year and most of the Training Team withdrew during 1972. By the time the Whitlam Labor Government was elected in December 1972 just 128 members of the Training Team were in Vietnam and they were winding down their activities. Whitlam recalled these last few soldiers immediately. Of the 50,000 Australian servicepeople who served in Vietnam between 1962 and 1972, 519 were killed and about 2,400 were wounded.

# Part VII
# On Overseas Service

'Who'd have thought you'd need so many weapons to be a peacekeeper?'

## In this part ...

After the withdrawal from Vietnam in 1972 it seemed that Australia would never again send troops to fight overseas. Suddenly, however, peacekeeping, which for almost three decades had appeared to be a less dangerous and demanding activity, took on more prominence. When the Cold War ended in the late 1980s, peacekeeping commitments increased in number and complexity, and soon members of the Australian Defence Force were serving around the world. The difference between peacekeeping and war became blurred. Finally, Australian forces went to war in Iraq in 1991 and 2003 and in Afghanistan in 2001.

By the new millennium, members of the Australian Defence Force were accepting overseas service as a normal part of their professional duties. These more recent operations need to be accorded their place in Australian military history.

In this part, I describe how Australia became involved in international peacekeeping in 1947. I follow the story through more than a dozen major and many other minor peacekeeping missions over the subsequent 60 or more years. I show how, after the hesitancy that followed the Vietnam experience, Australia again sent forces overseas on combat missions. These commitments were finely calibrated to limit Australia's involvement and to minimise casualties, but to show that the nation was pulling its weight as part of the American alliance and more broadly as a contributor to international security.

# Chapter 21

# Peacekeeping Near and Far, 1947–2010

## In This Chapter

- Standing on ceasefire lines around the world to prevent further fighting
- Bringing peace to war-torn nations after the fighting stops
- Deploying Australian troops to deal with the bandits, thugs and illegal militias

Until at least the 1990s, Australia's involvement in international peacekeeping didn't figure in books on Australian military history. But that view has now changed. Australia's military forces exist not just to defend the nation by fighting or deterring enemies, they also contribute to Australia's defence by helping to maintain international peace and security.

Between 1972 and 2000 peacekeeping was the largest and most significant form of Australian overseas military activity. Although Australian peacekeepers have suffered few deaths, many missions have been arduous and dangerous. In this chapter I describe some of the many peacekeeping activities carried out by almost 40,000 Australian military personnel and police who have taken part in peacekeeping missions since 1947.

## Observing and Reporting when the Fighting Stops

When the United Nations (UN) was formed in 1945 one of its aims was to stop wars and to maintain international peace. But there was no actual provision for international peacekeeping, which only developed as the need arose. The easiest form of peacekeeping was to deploy observers to monitor the implementation of a peace agreement once one had been agreed by the warring parties. Most peacekeeping missions between 1947 and 1987 were of this nature. Successive Australian governments have supported UN peacekeeping efforts. Between 1947 and 2000 Australia sent military and police on almost 20 observer-type missions. Some of the larger missions are described in the following sections. As we will see, Australia sent people around the globe. Some of the locations are shown in Figure 21-1.

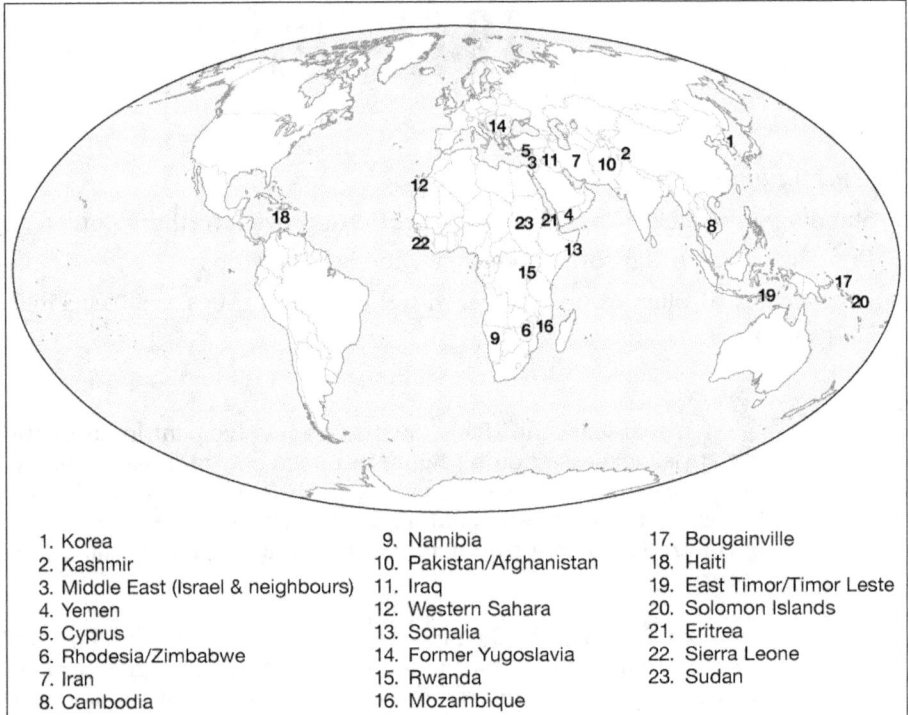

**Figure 21-1:** Australia's contribution to peacekeeping missions, 1947–2007.

1. Korea
2. Kashmir
3. Middle East (Israel & neighbours)
4. Yemen
5. Cyprus
6. Rhodesia/Zimbabwe
7. Iran
8. Cambodia
9. Namibia
10. Pakistan/Afghanistan
11. Iraq
12. Western Sahara
13. Somalia
14. Former Yugoslavia
15. Rwanda
16. Mozambique
17. Bougainville
18. Haiti
19. East Timor/Timor Leste
20. Solomon Islands
21. Eritrea
22. Sierra Leone
23. Sudan

## *The first peacekeepers — the mission in Indonesia*

At the end of the Second World War Indonesian nationalists proclaimed the formation of the new Republic of Indonesia, but when the Dutch colonial authorities tried to reassert their rule fighting broke out. The United Nations organised a ceasefire. A special commission, set up to report on the observance of the ceasefire, recommended the deployment of 24 military observers. Australia sent four officers and because Australia was closer geographically to Indonesia than the other countries involved, they arrived first. The four officers — two Army officers, one navy and one air force — stepped off the plane in Batavia (Jakarta) on 13 September 1947 and began work the next day. Australia therefore became the first country to deploy military peacekeepers as part of a UN operation. The military observers' task was to ensure that the Dutch and Indonesian forces abided by the ceasefire arrangements. By 1949, when Indonesia formally became an independent nation, Australia's contribution had grown to 15 officers. The commitment ceased in April 1951.

## In the mountains of Kashmir

After India and Pakistan became independent in 1947, fighting broke out over the status of the northerly state of Kashmir, which was claimed by both sides. The United Nations tried to negotiate a ceasefire and eventually formed the United Nations Military Observer Group in India and Pakistan (UNMOGIP). At the same time an Australian High Court Judge, Sir Owen Dixon, was appointed to try to mediate between the two sides. He was unsuccessful and the observers were left to try to keep the peace.

In October 1950 an Australian officer, Major General Robert Nimmo, was appointed Chief Military Observer, a position he held until 1966. In 1951 Australia sent eight military observers to UNMOGIP. The observers were drawn from the part-time Citizen Military Forces (CMF) or the Retired List. Australian observers served in Kashmir until the end of 1985, by which time about 150 officers had served there. The Australian Government thought that because the conflict wasn't being resolved, Australia 'had done its bit'. Observing in the mountainous country was arduous because the terrain was steep and the observers had to climb up and down very high mountains to fulfil their task. Some Australians were affected by altitude sickness. When short wars broke out between India and Pakistan in 1965 and 1971, the observers came under artillery fire. Between 1975 and 1979 the RAAF deployed a Caribou transport aircraft to Kashmir to move the observers and their supplies.

## Keeping the Arabs and the Israelis apart

In 1948 the newly formed state of Israel was attacked by its Arab neighbours. Later that year the UN Truce Supervision Organisation (UNTSO) was set up to supervise the various armistices and truces that had been arranged. Australia wasn't involved at first, but in 1956 after the Suez Crisis (when Britain, France and Israel attacked Egypt), and in response to a UN request, Australia sent four CMF officers. This number gradually increased and finally stabilised at its present level of 12 officers, all now regular officers. For more than five and half decades Australian observers have served in UNTSO, during which time they have witnessed the 1967, 1973 and 1982 Arab–Israeli wars, the Israeli invasion of Lebanon in 2006 and the Israeli attack on the Gaza Strip in 2008–09. Australia has twice provided commanders for UNTSO. The officers were Major Generals Tim Ford and Ian Gordon.

During time of conflict work as an observer could be dangerous. Major Keith Howard was lightly wounded during the 1967 Six Days War. In January 1988 Captain Peter McCarthy was killed when his jeep was blown up by a landmine during a patrol in Lebanon.

After the 1967 War Major Roy Skinner, an Australian observer from UNTSO, arrived at the Suez Canal to find that Egyptian aircraft and artillery were attacking an Israeli-held town. The Israelis were returning fire from a building that was to become the UNTSO local headquarters. Dressed in his Australian uniform and wearing a blue UN beret, Skinner stood on the canal bank, in full view, shouting at the Israelis until they stopped firing.

After the 1973 War the United Nations established a separate force to monitor the ceasefire between Israel and Egypt, and between 1976 and 1979 Australia provided four RAAF UH1H Iroquois helicopters with crews to transport observers and carry out aerial patrols along the Suez Canal and in the Sinai Desert. The helicopter unit was the first actual Australian unit, as distinct from individual observers, to take part in a peacekeeping mission.

Eventually a peace treaty was signed between Egypt and Israel, but because of Cold War politics the peacekeeping force, known as the Multinational Force and Observers (MFO), was formed by the United States, not the United Nations. The MFO was located in the Sinai Desert. Between 1986 and 1989 Australia provided eight UH1H helicopters with crews, as well as officers to work in the MFO headquarters. In 1993 Australia renewed its commitment to the MFO, providing headquarters staff. The officers are still serving in the Sinai Desert.

## *Policing in Cyprus*

The island of Cyprus in the Eastern Mediterranean became an independent country in 1960 within the British Commonwealth, but by 1964 violence had broken out between the majority Greek and minority Turkish citizens. The United Nations therefore formed the UN Force in Cyprus (UNFICYP) to help maintain peace between the two communities. Australia sent 40 civilian police, drawn from all states and territories. The police contingent arrived in May 1964 as part of the 173 police from various countries who were part of UNFYCYP. Their role was to observe and 'apply moral pressure' to persuade the local police to act fairly in their dealings with the warring communities.

 The Australian police had no authority and didn't carry their pistols, because to do so would only have provoked trouble in a country where automatic weapons were prevalent. The police later joked that they only had the power to call out 'Stop, or I'll say stop again'. They could take no other action.

Three Australian police have died while serving with UNFICYP, two from road accidents and one from a landmine. Chief Inspector Jack Thurgar, who had been wounded while serving with the Special Air Service in Vietnam, was awarded the Star of Courage when he rescued a wounded civilian from a minefield.

Australian police continued to serve on a rotating basis, including during the Turkish invasion of 1974 and the later partition of the country. After 1976 the Australian contingent was provided by the Commonwealth (later Australian Federal) Police. By 2007 more than 1,000 Australian police had served in Cyprus and the commitment is still continuing.

## *Monitoring the ceasefire in Zimbabwe*

In 1965 the white minority government of the British colony of Rhodesia declared unilateral independence. Black nationalists, the Patriotic Front, conducted a guerrilla war against the Rhodesian Government. By 1979 the Rhodesians were losing the war and at a meeting at Lancaster House, London, in December that year both sides agreed to allow free elections. Britain undertook to set up a Commonwealth Monitoring Force to supervise the arrangement by which the Rhodesian forces would be confined to their bases and the guerillas would gather at assembly places throughout the country.

In a force that grew to 1,300 personnel, including troops from Britain, Fiji, Kenya and New Zealand, Australia provided 151 officers and non-commissioned officers, under the command of Colonel Kevin Cole. The troops arrived on Christmas Day 1979 and deployed around the country to observe and monitor compliance with the Lancaster House Agreement. At times the Australians were involved in tense situations as both sides sometimes broke the agreement, seeking to provoke the other side into action. The election was held towards the end of February and most of the Australians headed home early in March 1980. Rhodesia (now Zimbabwe) became independent on 17 April 1980 with Robert Mugabe as prime minister.

## Overseeing the end of the Iran–Iraq war

In 1980 Iraq, under President Saddam Hussein, invaded Iran, setting off the Iran–Iraq War. The United Nations tried to broker a ceasefire and eventually in August 1988 both sides agreed to halt hostilities along the existing frontline. The United Nations set up the UN Iran–Iraq Military Observer Group (UNIIMOG) to ensure that both sides abided by the ceasefire.

Australia sent 15 officers as part of the 180 observers on the Iranian side. Iraq refused to allow Australian observers on their side because Australia had criticised Iraq over the use of chemical weapons during the war.

Led by Lieutenant Colonel Kerry Gallagher, the Australian observers arrived in Tehran on 16 August 1988 and were deployed in multinational observer teams along the front-line by the time the ceasefire came into effect on 20 August. The mission proved to the most arduous undertaken by Australian observers to that time. Some teams lived in Iranian bunkers, where they were kept under tight control by the Iranian Army, allegedly for their own protection. At times the observers were threatened by members of the Iranian Revolutionary Guard, the more fanatical element of the Iranian armed forces. Some team members found themselves in the middle of artillery duels between the opposing sides. Mines were a constant threat and several Australians were involved in incidents in which Iranian soldiers were killed or maimed by mines, although fortunately there were no Australian casualties. Australian observers also helped prevent the outbreak of fighting (see the sidebar 'Preventing an outbreak of hostilities').

After Iraq invaded Kuwait in August 1990 Saddam Hussein decided formally to end the war with Iran and Iraq began to withdraw all its troops from Iranian territory. UNIIMOG supervised the withdrawal and the last Australians departed in December 1990. Five contingents, each of 15 Australian observers, served in Iran, each for about six months.

## Preventing an outbreak of hostilities

In March 1989 Captain Craig Orme, a 30-year-old Armoured Corps officer, was serving at a teamsite on the southern Iran–Iraq border when he heard that the Iranians were threatening to fire on the Iraqis over an alleged violation. Orme and a Ghanaian officer went to investigate, arriving at 1.00 pm. The Iranians brought a T-54 tank into a firing position on the embankment where Orme and his Ghanaian colleague were standing. Then, as Orme wrote in his diary, when a platoon of Iranian soldiers with RPG-7 rocket launchers took up their firing positions, the Ghanaian 'shot through to about 400 metres away with our vehicle leaving me with the tank and the Iranians, a real mate in a crisis!' At one stage the tank's barrel rested between the legs of Orme and the senior Iranian Revolutionary Guard officer as he tried to calm the situation.

As Orme wrote: 'Eventually we were able to have [the tank] removed to calm things. I might add that I was walking around slowly as we were having our discussions in order to hide the fact that my legs were shaking!' The argument was over a bunker that the Iraqis had built, a mere 100 metres away, and the Iranians were demanding that it be removed by 2.00 pm. Communicating with UNIIMOG sector headquarters, Orme had the ceasefire extended until the next day, but that information didn't reach the local Iranian commander until 4.30 pm. Orme remained until then. Twenty years later Orme was still serving in the Australian Army, as a major general. (Extract from Captain Craig Orme's diary and interview with the author, 8 December 2004.)

## *Hopes dashed in Western Sahara*

Perhaps the most remote location where Australians served was in Western Sahara. In 1975 Spain withdrew from its Western Sahara territory and the local Sahrawi people then fought a 15-year guerrilla war to resist annexation by neighbouring Morocco. The Moroccans constructed a remarkable earth wall, called a *berm*, for 2,700 kilometres through the eastern part of the territory. Guarded by Moroccan troops and protected by thousands of landmines, the berm divided the territory into the larger Moroccan and smaller Sahrawi-ruled areas.

The United Nations planned a referendum to allow the Sahrawi people to vote either for independence or integration into Morocco. Australia agreed to send a 45-person contingent to provide radio operators and drivers. Before the force could be deployed Morocco decided to permit only a force to monitor the ceasefire. Australia's initial deployment in early September 1991, led by Lieutenant Colonel Ian Gordon, comprised only eight personnel. Obviously this group was too small and the UN Force Commander obtained permission for the remainder of the Australian unit to be deployed by the end of the month.

Australian radio operators served at all the observation sites, on both sides of the berm, to maintain communications. They lived in extremely trying conditions, at times operating in the desert without break for a month, working up to 15 hours per day. English was the official language of the mission, but because many of the military observers from a variety of countries had poor English language skills the Australian radio operators performed a key function in maintaining communications. Five contingents were deployed, each for six months, before the force was withdrawn in May 1994, with no decision concerning the referendum in sight. The UN force is still operating in Western Sahara.

On 21 June 1993 Major Susan Felsche, the fourth contingent's medical officer, was killed in a plane crash while on a medical mission. She was the first Australian female to die on overseas military service since the Second World War.

## *Unarmed in Bougainville*

Bougainville, the most easterly island of Papua New Guinea, has long been seeking independence. In 1989 Bougainvillean rebels began a campaign of sabotage and guerrilla warfare, forcing the giant Panguna copper mine to cease operations. The Papua New Guinea Defence Force deployed to the island and low-level conflict ensued for several years until in September 1994 the Papua New Guinean Prime Minister and Bougainvillean leaders agreed to a ceasefire with the purpose of conducting a peace conference. Australia organised and led a South Pacific Peacekeeping Force, which was deployed the following month to the Arawa area of Bougainville where the talks were to take place, but the talks failed.

Conflict continued until October 1997 when the parties met in New Zealand and agreed to a truce. A Truce Monitoring Group (TMG) was established on Bougainville in December 1997 to monitor the terms of the agreement. The TMG was led by New Zealand and included 100 Australians and personnel from Fiji and Vanuatu. The monitors included military personnel, police and civilians, and in a courageous move, they went unarmed, thereby placing their safety in the hands of the Bougainvillean people. Following the signing of the ceasefire agreement at Arawa on 30 April 1998 the TMG became the Peace Monitoring Group (PMG) and Australia took over leadership of it.

 Commanded by an Australian brigadier (initially Brigadier Bruce Osborn), the PMG included five monitoring teams, support troops, a field hospital, four orange-painted Iroquois helicopters, two small army landing craft and one heavy navy landing craft. The PMG's tasks included:

- Monitoring and reporting compliance with the terms of the ceasefire.
- Promoting and instilling confidence in the peace process.
- Informing Bougainvilleans about the ceasefire and peace process.

To achieve these tasks, teams undertook patrols, awareness tours, attendance at reconciliations or other peace-related meetings, ceasefire violation investigations, provision of transport to facilitate local nationals attending meetings, and attendance at churches and markets to distribute the newspaper known as *Nius Blong Peace*.

The parties to the conflict signed a peace agreement in 2001 and the military operation concluded in June 2003. Operation Bel Isi, as it was known, had lasted for more than five years and about 2,000 Australian military personnel, over 200 Australian Federal Police and more than 2,500 peace monitors from the Australian Public Service had served on Bougainville.

# Rebuilding Shattered Nations

At the end of the Cold War in 1988–90 the United Nations moved beyond the previous, and longstanding, idea that peacekeepers should be used to help end conflicts, to the notion that they could also be used to help rebuild nations that had been shattered by conflict. These missions included the operations in Namibia and Cambodia to monitor and conduct elections, and in Pakistan to train local Afghans to clear land mines.

## Supervising elections in Namibia

Between 1966 and 1988 South Africa fought a guerrilla war against a black nationalist body movement known as the South West Africa People's Organisation (SWAPO), both within South West Africa (later called Namibia) and also across the border in Angola. South Africa ruled the territory even though its United Nations mandate was revoked in 1966. In 1979 the United Nations developed a plan for elections in Namibia, which would then became independent, and the Australian Government, led by Malcolm

Fraser, agreed to contribute to the UN force. All the interested parties didn't sign off on the plan until late in 1988, when the end of the Cold War caused the Soviet Union and the United States to withdraw support for Angola and South Africa respectively. Australia then sent a 300-person contingent including an engineer construction squadron and a headquarters with engineer staff officers, all commanded by Colonel Richard Warren.

The Australians arrived in Namibia on 11 March 1989, but most of the other members of the UN force hadn't arrived by 1 April, when the South African troops were supposed to withdraw to their bases. On that day, contrary to the peace agreement, SWAPO forces crossed the border from Angola and fighting erupted. As one of the few UN units in the country the Australians played a key role in defusing this dangerous development by setting up and staffing assembly points in northern Namibia, where the Australians were based. The peace process could then proceed, and the Australian engineers cleared mines and prepared camps for SWAPO members who were returning to the country.

In September 1989 a new contingent arrived in Namibia, commanded by Colonel John Crocker, to relieve the first contingent, and it played a vital role in supporting the elections in northern Namibia in early November. Members of the Australian Electoral Commission were part of the UN group that monitored the elections. Namibia formally became independent on 21 March 1990, and the last Australians departed on 9 April 1990.

## *Resolving the conflict in Cambodia*

During 1991 the Australian Foreign Minister, Gareth Evans, was instrumental in setting up the peace process in Cambodia where four armies had been at war for many years. The aim was to produce a neutral environment in which the four armies would disarm and demobilise, and so allow free and fair elections. In October 1991 Australia contributed a 65-strong communications unit to the UN Advance Mission in Cambodia.

A much larger organisation, the UN Transitional Authority in Cambodia (UNTAC), was established in March 1992, and an Australian officer, Lieutenant General John Sanderson, was appointed to command the UNTAC military force, which numbered 16,000 personnel from 32 different countries. The force's 12 infantry battalions came from 11 different countries. Australia provided the Force Communications Unit with 488 personnel drawn mainly from the Army, but with a few Navy and Air Force communicators, as well as an extra 40 New Zealanders. Australia also provided 14 staff for the Force Headquarters. The dispersal of the Australian signallers attached to units in 56 locations across Cambodia enabled Sanderson to maintain a strong grip on the force. These deployments imposed a heavy responsibility on relatively junior personnel, who often found themselves in delicate and at times dangerous situations. From May to July 1993, in the period covering the election, Australia contributed a further 115 soldiers and six Black Hawk helicopters.

With Sanderson as the Force commander, Australia gained credit for the successful outcome of the mission. An Irish lieutenant colonel said that Sanderson 'was the most competent force commander' he had seen in seven UN missions. Australia also gained respect for the quality of its personnel. Perhaps more importantly, the UN mission brought a measure of peace to Cambodia and the wider South-East Asia region.

## *Clearing landmines in Afghanistan*

After Soviet forces withdrew from Afghanistan, in February 1989 the United Nations initiated a program to clear huge numbers of unmarked landmines left behind in the contested areas. In July 1989 Australia deployed nine Army engineers on a four-month tour to Pakistan as part of the UN Mine Clearance Training Team (UNMCTT). At first the team trained Pakistan-based Afghan refugees in basic mine clearance techniques, but later teams helped plan and supervise mine clearance operations within Afghanistan. The Australian teams varied in strength from 6 to 12 members and by the time the last team was withdrawn late in 1993, ten Australian teams had been deployed. A total of 92 Australian Army personnel served with the UNMCTT.

At the height of the program nine countries provided teams, but Australia was one of only two countries to maintain soldiers there after 1991. The Australian engineers gained great satisfaction from helping to clear mines around villages, thereby allowing the people to start farming their land again. Many of the Australians went on to work in mine clearance programs elsewhere, either as part of an Australian army commitment to places such as Cambodia and Mozambique, or as civilian contractors. The Australian military personnel who served in Pakistan and Afghanistan became leaders in humanitarian mine clearing around the world.

## *Enforcing Peace*

Until the early 1990s the United Nations generally refrained from interfering in the internal affairs of countries, but then the United Nations changed its view and authorised the deployment of troops to enforce peace, rather than merely to observe a previously agreed peace arrangement.

After the 1991 Gulf War the Kurdish people in Iraq revolted against the government, which reacted with savage reprisals. The subsequent humanitarian crisis induced the United Nations to authorise action against Iraq. Australia's part in the war and the humanitarian operation is described in Chapter 22.

The end of the Cold War led to the breakup of Yugoslavia, followed by savage ethnic conflict. The United Nations initially sent observers, but belatedly the UN authorised the use of armed force to stop the conflict. About 260 Australian military personnel served in the former Yugoslavia between 1994 and 2004 in small groups, mainly attached to British forces.

## *Guarding aid workers in Somalia*

During 1992 Somalia was wracked by civil war with no effective government. Non-government aid organisations, trying to bring humanitarian assistance to the starving population, were attacked by marauding bandits and armed groups loyal to local warlords. In October 1992 the United Nations sent in peacekeepers and Australia contributed 30 members of a movement control unit. The situation deteriorated and early in 1993 the United Nations authorised the deployment of a larger force, to be led by the United States.

Between January and May 1993 Australia sent a force of almost 1,000 military personnel, consisting mainly of an infantry battalion group based on the 1st Battalion of the Royal Australian Regiment (1 RAR), commanded by Lieutenant Colonel David Hurley. The battalion group was required to establish its authority in the town of Baidoa and the surrounding countryside, restore law and order, and protect the humanitarian relief efforts. These tasks placed a heavy responsibility on junior leaders and soldiers who had to observe strict rules of engagement, only firing when in direct danger or when they were being fired upon. Patrols had several contacts with bandits. For example, on 17 February 1993 a patrol led by Corporal Adrian Hodges came across a group of bandits dismantling a water pump. In the ensuing firefight three Somalis were shot, a fourth was detained and several escaped.

During their four-month tour the Australians had few casualties (none fatal) as a result of action with the bandits. On 2 April 1993, however, Lance Corporal Shannon McAliney was accidentally shot dead on patrol. Conditions were extremely trying with high temperatures, few facilities and limited opportunities for rest and recreation. The operation was highly frustrating because corruption and local customs often nullified the Australians' efforts.

When the force returned to Australia in May 1993 the movement control unit remained and was joined by Australian air traffic controllers. The Australians experienced tense periods, especially during the battle in October 1993 made famous by the book and movie *Black Hawk Down*, when US Rangers were surrounded and lost 18 killed in a 14-hour battle. After that incident the Australians were joined by a patrol of the Special Air Service to provide protection. The final Australian contingent withdrew in November 1994. Despite the success of Australia's operations, overall the UN operations in Somalia failed to bring peace to the country, and when the UN forces withdrew they left the country in the hands of the most prominent warlord.

## *Genocide in Rwanda*

During 1993 the United Nations sent a small force to Rwanda in central Africa to monitor a peace agreement between the government forces (from the Hutu people) and a rebel force (mainly Tutsis). The inadequacies of the UN force, which was much too small to stop the genocide attempted by the Hutus against the Tutsis, were described graphically in the memoirs of its commander, General Roméo Dallaire, called *Shake Hands with the Devil*, and in the movie *Hotel Rwanda*. After ethnic violence in which between 200,000 and 800,000 people were reported missing or dead, the Tutsi force, known as the Rwanda Patriotic Army (RPA) took control of the country and in mid-1994 invited UN assistance to stabilise the situation. The second UN mission numbered 5,500 personnel and Australia contributed a medical team.

The Australian force of 308 members was commanded by Colonel Wayne Ramsey, a medical officer, and included a medical company, with a strong infantry company for protection, and support troops. The Australians arrived in Rwanda in August 1994 and began operating from the Kigali central hospital, which had been badly damaged and looted during the fighting. In very difficult circumstances, the Australians treated refugees who were often in a poor state, and sometimes under threat from RPA soldiers. As one young surgeon put it: 'This place is like a surgical textbook written in a mad house. If you thought too much about it you would go stark raving mad'.

In February 1995 a second Australian contingent, commanded by Colonel Peter Warfe, replaced the first. During April RPA forces carried out a massacre of Hutus at the Kibeho refugee camp, killing perhaps 4,000 and injuring about 600. A seven-person Australian medical team under Army Captain Carol Vaughan-Evans struggled to give medical aid to the injured refugees while protected by about 20 Australian infantrymen. The episode was extremely distressing for the young Diggers who, under the UN rules of engagement, weren't permitted to open fire to protect the refugees. They could only return fire if they or the medical teams were attacked. The second contingent returned to Australia in August 1995.

Vaughan-Evans and four others were awarded the Medal for Gallantry as a result of their actions during the Kibeho massacre. They were Australia's first decorations for gallantry awarded since the Vietnam War and the first under the Australian rather than the British honours system (see Chapter 2).

## Safeguarding the new nation of East Timor

In 1975 Indonesia forcibly took over the former Portuguese colony of East Timor and made it an Indonesian province. Under international pressure, particularly from Australia, in January 1999 Indonesia announced that it was willing to let East Timor have independence if it rejected an offer of autonomy within the republic. During 1999 Indonesian-backed militia groups in East Timor stepped up violence against those favouring independence. A UN mission, including Australians, went to East Timor to monitor the referendum on the question of independence. The ballot took place on 30 August and in early September the United Nations announced that 78.5 per cent favoured independence.

The militia bands went on a wild rampage of killing and looting, and Indonesia accepted a UN request to permit an international coalition force to restore peace and security in East Timor. Meanwhile, Australian C-130 Hercules transport aircraft were busy evacuating threatened UN staff and other refugees from East Timor, flying them to the nearby northern Australian port of Darwin. In a highly charged atmosphere some senior Indonesian military officers said that they wouldn't accept Australians as peacekeepers and militia leaders vowed to kill any Australians in East Timor.

Australia was the only country capable of deploying large forces rapidly to East Timor, and it quickly put together the International Force East Timor (INTERFET). Eventually the force included elements from 22 nations, but at first it was mainly an Australian force with a few New Zealand and British troops. Major General Peter Cosgrove was appointed commander of INTERFET and he displayed a great deal of tact and diplomacy, working with his Indonesian counterpart in East Timor to ensure that there was no clash between INTERFET and Indonesian soldiers.

The Australian-led force began to land from ships and aircraft at the East Timor capital of Dili on 20 September 1999. The land force component included the headquarters of the 3rd Brigade and three infantry battalions, with Special Air Service troopers, engineers, armoured personnel carriers, helicopters and support troops. The naval force included nine Australian warships and one each from Britain and New Zealand. Australian transport aircraft brought in troops and supplies from Darwin. Faced by this show of strength the militia generally avoided confrontation and stability was restored, although the territory's infrastructure had been largely destroyed by the militia. A few militia groups initiated contacts with the Australians, but although some Australians were wounded none were killed by enemy action. The Indonesians withdrew from the territory. By mid-November Australia's commitment had grown to 5,700 in a force strength approaching 11,500.

In February 2000 INTERFET handed over the task of peacekeeping in and governing of East Timor to the UN Transitional Administration. Some of the Australian troops, now wearing blue UN helmets, remained in the new peacekeeping force, which helped to protect East Timor from occasional forays by militia groups from across the border in Indonesia. East Timor, renamed Timor-Leste, became an independent nation on 20 May 2002, but a UN force remained in the country until June 2004. Nine Australian infantry battalions served in six-month tours in East Timor from February 2000 (when INTERFET departed) until June 2004. Gradually the militia incidents declined. During the 6th Battalion's tour in 2000 it killed or wounded seven infiltrators. When the battalion returned to East Timor between October 2003 and June 2004, it had no contacts.

## Wearing the right hat

Australian soldiers serving overseas on peacekeeping mission almost always wear Australian uniforms, but when part of UN missions they wear either blue berets or blue helmets, indicating that they're working on behalf of the United Nations rather than Australia. Wearing their Australian uniforms, with blue berets, they're still identifiable as Australians. Troops serving with the Multinational Force and Observers (MFO) in the Sinai wore orange caps and an MFO badge on their sleeves. Members of the Peace Monitoring Group in Bougainville wore yellow T-shirts and yellow caps, along with their national uniforms. The International Force in East Timor (INTERFET) was authorised by the United Nations but wasn't a UN force. Its members wore their national uniforms, but with an INTERFET badge on their sleeves. The only troops not to wear Australian uniforms were the members in the UN Mine Clearance Training Team in Pakistan. They wore khaki safari suits with both Australian and UN shoulder flashes, without military insignia, but on more formal occasions they wore these 'uniforms' with their Australian slouch hats. Whatever uniform or headdress that the Australians wore, they were identifiable as Australians, representing Australia abroad.

In April 2006 riots broke out in Dili, followed in May by fighting between government troops and former guerrilla fighters. At the request of the Timor-Leste Government, Australian troops returned to the island under the command of Brigadier Mick Slater, who had commanded the 2nd Battalion when INTERFET landed in Dili in 1999. The Australians restored some stability to the island. An Australian infantry battalion, along with troops from Malaysia and New Zealand, remained in Timor-Leste, although their numbers gradually reduced over the years.

## *Quelling unrest in the Solomon Islands*

During 2000 law and order began to break down in the Solomon Islands, and in July the Solomon Islands Prime Minister sought regional military and police intervention. A peace agreement was signed at a meeting in Townsville, and Australia sponsored an International Peace Monitoring Team, but it wasn't permitted to use force. Troops from the 3rd Battalion merely sat in navy ships offshore from the main Solomons island of Guadalcanal for about three weeks before the mission lapsed.

In 2003 the law and order situation had again deteriorated with fighting between people from Guadalcanal and those from Malaita Island, who had moved to Guadalcanal. At the request of the Solomon Islands Prime Minister, Australia helped set up the Regional Assistance Mission to Solomon Islands (RAMSI). The mission was headed by Nick Warner, an official from the Australian Department of Foreign Affairs and Trade. He was supported by a multinational police contingent headed by an Australian, Ben McDevitt, and including police from Australia, New Zealand and 13 other Pacific Island countries. The police were backed by a military force, commanded by Lieutenant Colonel John Frewen, based on an Australian infantry battalion (2nd Battalion), and including infantry companies from Australia, New Zealand and Fiji and platoons from Tonga and Papua New Guinea.

Working together the police and the military managed to withdraw weapons from the warring groups and they gradually restored law and order. By late 2004 the military force had been reduced to just a platoon of infantry. But when in December 2004 Australian Federal Police Officer Adam Dunning was shot and killed while on a RAMSI patrol, the military force was quickly reinforced with an infantry company from Australia. After riots in the Solomons capital, Honiara, in April 2006 additional infantry companies arrived from Australia until the situation became calmer. RAMSI is still operating with civilian administrators and advisers, a multinational police contingent and an Australian infantry company provided by the Army Reserve.

# Chapter 22

# Flying the Flag in Iraq and Afghanistan, 1990–2010

*In This Chapter*

▶ Sending our ships to the Persian Gulf
▶ Keeping the pressure on Saddam Hussein
▶ Fighting alongside the Yanks and other buddies in Iraq and Afghanistan

After the last Australian troops withdrew from Vietnam in 1972 the possibility that Australia might again deploy combat forces overseas was dismissed by politicians and military leaders. The war had been controversial at home and abroad, and in the end, Australia's participation didn't prevent the North Vietnamese from winning once US and Australian troops were withdrawn. Australia's new Defence policy, announced in 1976 by the Liberal–National Party Coalition Government under Malcolm Fraser, meant that in future the Australian Defence Force (ADF) would concentrate on preventing an enemy approaching the Australian coast, rather than sending forces overseas.

When in 1978 the Fraser Government announced that it was sending helicopters on a peacekeeping mission in the Sinai Desert (refer to Chapter 21) the Leader of the Opposition, Bill Hayden, criticised it as a potential 'Vietnam'. For a while the Labor Party was lukewarm about peacekeeping, but eventually Hayden, as Foreign Minister in the Hawke Labor Government in the 1980s, saw the merit of contributing to peacekeeping. His successor, Gareth Evans, who took over as the Cold War was ending, became a strong advocate of peacekeeping, promoting Australia as an 'international good citizen'. This led to some peacekeeping missions (described in Chapter 21) and eventually to a decision to send naval ships to the Persian Gulf region after Iraq's invasion of Kuwait in August 1990.

In this chapter I tell how Australia's commitment to the Gulf in 1990 developed into a 20-year involvement in the region. More particularly, I describe how in recent years the ADF has fought in four wars: The 1991 Gulf War, the 2003 invasion of Iraq, the subsequent security operations in Iraq and the fight against the Taliban in Afghanistan, in which for the first time since the Vietnam War Australian soldiers were killed in combat.

## *Iraq Invades Kuwait — We Defend our Vital Interests*

Between 1980 and 1988 Iraq, under its ruthless president, Saddam Hussein, fought a costly and exhausting war with Iran. Neighbouring Kuwait loaned Iraq billions of dollars, but after the war Kuwait asked for it to be repaid. Iraq was unable to pay and had several long-standing grievances with Kuwait. Saddam therefore sought to resolve the problem. On 2 August 1990 Iraq invaded Kuwait and quickly took over the country.

In deciding to invade Kuwait, Saddam made several miscalculations:

- Saddam misinterpreted comments by the American ambassador to imply that the United States would take no action if he moved against Kuwait.

- He didn't understand that because the Cold War had ended there was a new mood of cooperation between the United States and the Soviet Union.

- He didn't contemplate that Saudi Arabia, which feared it was next on the list to be attacked by Iraq, would allow American forces to be based in its country.

- Saddam didn't expect other Arab countries to join together to oppose him.

Immediately the UN Security Council passed a resolution condemning Iraq and demanding its withdrawal from Kuwait. After the end of the Cold War many countries thought that the United Nations could now play a major role in dealing with threats to international peace. The Soviet President, Mikhail Gorbachev, talked of a 'new world order', an idea that was soon embraced by America's President, George H W Bush. Along with other countries, Australia applied economic sanctions against Iraq.

Apart from espousing high ideals about respecting the sovereignty of a UN member such as Kuwait, the United States didn't wish to see Saddam gain control of the region's vast oil reserves. The United States immediately began sending military forces to defend Saudi Arabia and also began planning a multinational naval force to enforce the sanctions against Iraq.

## *Reaffirming our friendship with the United States*

When Australia's Prime Minister, Bob Hawke, heard about the proposed multinational naval force he immediately concluded that Australia should take part because, as he said, 'Australia had vital interests at stake'.

- Australia relied heavily on oil from the Persian Gulf and even in the best case Saddam's actions would drive up the price of oil.

- A nation such as Iraq shouldn't be permitted to 'gobble up Kuwait' in what Hawke described as a 'blatant act of aggression'.

- The United Nations was likely to authorise action against Kuwait and Australia needed to boost its efforts to deal with problems of international security.

- Australia had a long-standing alliance with the United States and needed to demonstrate that it was a reliable alliance partner, or a 'good ally'.

By joining the American-led multinational naval force early, even though it hadn't yet been authorised by the United Nations, Australia would win much approval from the United States. On Friday 10 August, Hawke announced that Australia would send two guided missile frigates, *Adelaide* and *Darwin*, and the supply ship *Success* to the Gulf region, and that the ships would depart on Monday 13 August.

Across Australia there was widespread public support for the decision, but there was considerable criticism in some quarters and some demonstrations. Hawke argued his case in parliament on 21 August, and on 25 August, 15 days after he had announced Australia's commitment, the UN Security Council authorised maritime forces to apply the sanctions against Iraq.

## Boarding and searching — our ships in the Gulf of Oman

The Australian naval task group, commanded by Commodore Don Chalmers, didn't reach the operational area of the Gulf of Oman until 3 September. The Gulf of Oman was a key area because ships heading for Iraq need to sail through it to enter the Persian Gulf (refer to Figure 22-1). The frigates *Darwin* and *Adelaide* worked closely with American and British ships to intercept, board and search suspicious vessels. On 14 September, in its first difficult interception, *Darwin*, commanded by Captain Russell Shalders, fired its machine guns across the bows of an Iraqi oil tanker, *Al Fao*, to compel it to stop.

By the time the Australian ships headed for home in early December the multinational force in the Gulf of Oman had diverted 19 ships to other ports and of these 11 had initially refused to stop. Ten incidents involved the firing of warning shots, with the Australian ships involved in five of these incidents.

The destroyer *Brisbane* and the frigate *Sydney* took over from *Darwin* and *Adelaide*, with Commodore Chris Oxenbould now in command of the task group. On 16 December the ships sailed into the Persian Gulf to work with the American aircraft carriers in preparation for war with Iraq. In the midst of these preparations *Sydney*, commanded by Commander Lee Cordner, returned to the Gulf of Oman to assist with the apprehension of an Iraqi ship, *Ibn Khaldoon*, which was attempting to break the blockade with peace activists aboard. In tense operations US Marines, who boarded the ship first before being joined by Australian sailors, were violently attacked by the peace activists and had to fire shots to restore control.

**Figure 22-1:** Persian Gulf and the Gulf of Oman.

## A small part in the Gulf War

After it became clear that Saddam Hussein was thumbing his nose at the United Nations and would remain in Kuwait, on 29 November the UN Security Council passed a resolution which, in effect, authorised the United States to lead a coalition of forces to drive Iraq out of Kuwait. The United Nations gave Iraq an ultimatum to withdraw from Kuwait by 15 January 1991. On 4 December Prime Minister Hawke announced that the Australian ships could sail into the Persian Gulf and operate with the coalition forces in the event of war. The decision was generally supported by the Australian public, but as the deadline approached various groups, including some in the Labor Party, increased their criticism. Demonstrations, with crowds numbering in the thousands, took place in several Australian cities.

The war began on 17 January, when American and British aircraft began bombing Iraq, while American ships launched cruise missiles at Iraqi cities. *Brisbane* and *Sydney* helped provide the protective screen around the American aircraft carriers *Midway* and *Ranger*. As the bombing campaign continued, the coalition ships sailed north up the Persian Gulf, where they became more vulnerable to Iraqi air attack and to the sea mines that the Iraqis had released into the Gulf. While no Iraqi aircraft actually attacked the coalition ships it was a tense time, made worse when on 18 February two large American warships were damaged by Iraqi sea mines.

The coalition ground forces, mainly American and British troops, but with units from France, Kuwait, Saudi Arabia and Syria, launched the ground attack on 24 February. The war was swift and ruthless, as American and British tanks thrust through the desert, liberated Kuwait and surrounded many Iraqi units. Iraq surrendered and the ceasefire came into effect on 28 February. After the surrender an Australian naval clearance diving team moved into Kuwait, where it worked hard in murky waters and in the smoke of burning oil wells to clear mines from Kuwaiti ports and harbours.

Australia had played only a small part in the 1991 Gulf War and had no casualties, but having joined the US-led coalition in August 1990 Australia would be committed to operations in the region for decades to come.

## Twisting Saddam Hussein's Arm

After the Gulf War the United Nations wanted to ensure that Iraq would no longer pose a threat to its neighbours and was particularly concerned about Iraq's weapons of mass destruction (WMD). WMD are weapons with the capacity to kill indiscriminately large numbers of people, animals and plants and they include nuclear, biological, chemical and radiological weapons. Saddam Hussein had already used chemical weapons against dissidents in his own country.

On 3 April 1991 the UN Security Council passed a resolution setting out the terms which Iraq needed to meet before sanctions could be lifted. Broadly, the United Nations would prevent Iraq from exporting oil (except for a small amount to pay for essential civilian needs) and restrict imports (except for medicine, health supplies and food) until all Iraq's WMD had been located and destroyed.

The problem was that Saddam Hussein believed that he needed to retain his WMD both as a defence against attack from his neighbours and also to retain face as a powerful leader in the Arab world. For the next decade a defiant Saddam would resist UN efforts to destroy his WMD and Australia would play a major role in the UN efforts.

## Humanitarian relief in Kurdistan

After the Gulf War the Kurdish people in north-east Iraq rebelled against the government. Attacked by the Iraqi army, hundreds of thousands of Kurds fled across the border into the mountains of Turkey where they were cold, wet and starving. Faced with this humanitarian disaster, in early April 1991 the United Nations authorised the United States to lead a rescue mission. Troops from the United States and allied countries provided humanitarian assistance, while other troops moved into northern Iraq to establish a secure area so that the Kurds could return safely to Iraq (refer to Figure 22-2).

Australia sent a small force of 75 troops, including 23 Army medical personnel, a field hygiene section and engineers to provide clean water. Commanded by Lieutenant Colonel David Ross, the force arrived in northern Iraq on 26 May 1991. Working with a British Royal Marine brigade, the Australians deployed medical teams, each with a doctor and a nurse, to provide medical assistance to the Kurds, who were returning to their country now that American, British and other troops were keeping the Iraqi soldiers away. The Australian team withdrew in mid-June.

**Figure 22-2:** Iraq, showing areas of operations.

 For a young Australian Army doctor, Captain Tam Tran, it was a poignant experience. Born in South Vietnam, she had come to Australia as one of the refugee 'boat people' and had joined the Army to pay her way through medical school. Now she was helping refugees. She recalled: 'Life for me in Vietnam was traumatic and when I was in Iraq I was always getting flashbacks'.

## *Disarming Iraq — sanctions and weapons inspection*

In April 1991 the UN Special Commission on Iraq (UNSCOM) was formed to look for Iraq's weapons of mass destruction (WMD). During the 1980s Australia had been a vocal critic of Iraq's use of chemical weapons and the government felt obliged to support UNSCOM's work. Between 1991 and 1999 about 135 ADF personnel and other Australian Government officials took part in the weapons inspection program. Their duties included:

- Engineer inspections of weapons sites
- Destruction of Iraqi chemical weapons and ballistic missiles
- Medical assistance to inspection teams

- Aerial surveys and inspections of Iraqi weapons sites
- Inspections of factories to determine if they were being used to make biological weapons
- Impromptu inspections (raids) to catch the Iraqis as they tried to hide their WMD
- Negotiations with Iraqi leaders and scientists
- Command, security and communications tasks within the UNSCOM teams

The Iraqis never completely cooperated with the UNSCOM inspectors. The inspectors faced threatening and dangerous situations, including dealing with leaking chemical weapons, extremes of temperature while wearing protective suits and physical threats from Iraqi military personnel.

In September 1991 an UNSCOM team, including two Australians, Major Colin Chidgey and Captain Brad Hampton, seized Iraqi documents about its nuclear weapons program. The Iraqis detained the inspectors at gun point as they tried to leave the inspection site in their UN vehicles. The inspectors refused to relinquish the documents and lived in their vehicles for four days, until a compromise was reached whereby the Iraqis and the inspectors would make an inventory of the documents. Chidgey managed to smuggle some of the documents out to a waiting UN aircraft at the airport. The German pilot dodged his aircraft around an Iraq truck that was blocking his path and took off for Bahrain. An Australian intelligence analyst assessed that the Iraqis were much closer to developing nuclear weapons than previously thought.

UNSCOM made considerable progress in eliminating Saddam's WMD, but periodically Iraq forced UNSCOM to halt its inspections. Sometimes the Americans and British carried out air strikes against Iraq to force Saddam to allow the inspections to continue. In 1997 an Australian diplomat, Richard Butler, was appointed Chairman of UNSCOM and he pressed Iraq strongly, but at the end of 1998 Saddam permanently banished the inspectors from Iraq.

Australian naval vessels took part in the multinational naval force that continued to apply sanctions against Iraq, seeking to force Saddam Hussein to abide by the UN Security Council resolution concerning Iraq's WMD. Australian frigates served on three-month tours in the Persian Gulf in 1991, 1996 and 1999, and in the Red Sea in 1991, 1992 and 1993.

Chapter 22: Flying the Flag in Iraq and Afghanistan, 1990–2010   **385**

Early in 1998 the Americans and British planned to carry out airstrikes against Iraq to force Saddam Hussein to allow UNSCOM inspections to resume. In February 1998 the Australian Government under Prime Minister John Howard sent an Australian Special Air Service (SAS) squadron and two RAAF tanker aircraft to Kuwait to support the expected strikes. With typical brinkmanship, at the last minute Saddam agreed to allow in the UNSCOM inspectors and the air strikes were called off. The Australian commitment was significant because it showed that the Howard Government was willing to agree to a request from the United States. The decision set the pattern for Howard's support for the Americans during the invasion of Iraq in 2003.

# Terror Attacks in the United States: the Start of a New War

On 11 September 2001 members of the Al Qaeda terrorist group hijacked four commercial jet airliners flying over the United States. Two of the airliners intentionally crashed into the twin towers of the World Trade Center in New York, destroying the buildings and killing more than 2,000 people. About the same time another airliner struck the Pentagon Building in Washington (headquarters of the US Department of Defense) causing more casualties. The fourth airliner crashed into a field in the Pennsylvania countryside. None of the hijackers, passengers or crew on the four airliners survived the attacks.

The origins of Al Qaeda can be traced to the Soviet invasion of Afghanistan in December 1979 and the subsequent war, in which Islamic guerrillas fought against the Soviet forces. After the war ended in 1989 Al Qaeda, led by Osama bin Laden, continued the *jihad* (holy war) against what he perceived to be anti-Islam nations around the world. Al Qaeda conducted many terrorist attacks over the following years. Meanwhile, an extreme Islamic political organisation known as the Taliban had come to power in Afghanistan and the country provided a safe haven and training area for Al Qaeda.

After 11 September, US President George W Bush — the son of George H W Bush of the Persian Gulf War — declared a War on Terrorism and he demanded that the Taliban government in Afghanistan hand over the Al Qaeda leaders and close the terrorist training camps. When the Taliban refused, on 7 October the Americans began airstrikes against terrorist targets in Afghanistan. American Special Forces soldiers entered Afghanistan and assisted anti-Taliban forces, known as the Northern Alliance, to wage war against the Taliban. The Northern Alliance captured the Afghan capital, Kabul, on 12 November. The Taliban were pushed back into the mountains along the border with Pakistan, where fighting continued.

## Joining the Americans in Afghanistan

At the time of the 11 September terrorist attacks the Australian Prime Minister, John Howard, was in Washington and within days Australia invoked the ANZUS alliance, by which the United States and Australia agreed to provide support if either were attacked. The Australian Government believed that the terrorist threat applied not just to the United States but to Western countries around the world and that the countries needed to stand together against the threat. Australia wasn't the only country to come to America's assistance. The North Atlantic Treaty Organization (NATO) declared that the attacks against the United States amounted to an attack on all NATO countries.

Australia provided military assistance to the United States in its war against terrorism, directed particularly at the terrorist base in Afghanistan. This support (known in Australia as Operation Slipper) consisted of about 1,300 ADF personnel, including the following forces:

- A Special Forces Task Group was deployed to Afghanistan.
- Two RAAF Boeing 707 air-to-air refuelling aircraft were based in Kyrgyzstan to support coalition air operations in Afghanistan.
- Australia already had one frigate in the Persian Gulf maintaining sanctions against Iraq. An additional frigate and an amphibious ship went to the Persian Gulf to support the war against terrorism.
- RAAF C-130 Hercules transport aircraft supported the movement of personnel and equipment to the area of operations.
- Two RAAF AP-3C Orion maritime patrol aircraft were deployed to the Persian Gulf regional to conduct surveillance operations.
- Four F/A-18 Hornet strike aircraft were based at Diego Garcia in the Indian Ocean to provide backup for the Americans.
- An Australian military headquarters was established in Kuwait, under Brigadier Ken Gillespie, to command the ADF units in the Persian Gulf–Afghanistan area.

The most noteworthy operations were carried out by the Special Air Service (SAS) in Afghanistan, serving mainly in Kandahar Province and east of Kabul (refer to Figure 22-3). The SAS group was commanded by Lieutenant Colonel Gus Gilmore and included an SAS squadron led by Major Dan McDaniel. Operating in rugged mountains and in the desert in extreme weather conditions, the SAS patrols carried out surveillance of Taliban positions and later took part in offensive operations.

Figure 22-3: Afghanistan, showing areas of operations.

In February 2002 Sergeant Andrew Russell was killed when his vehicle struck a mine; he was the first Australian soldier to die as a result of enemy action since the Vietnam War. The Special Forces Task Group was relieved by another group in March–April 2002 and a third group took over in August 2002. By the time the SAS soldiers withdrew at the end of 2002 they had cemented their reputation for professionalism and ability among the other coalition partners. The SAS troopers had engaged in the largest battles conducted by Australians since the Vietnam War and many soldiers received awards for courage under fire.

## Invading Iraq

President George W Bush was concerned that Saddam Hussein had refused to allow UN inspectors to complete their task of ridding Iraq of WMD. There was no evidence that Saddam was cooperating with Al Qaeda or even supporting it, but Bush and his advisers saw the Al Qaeda terrorist threat and Iraq's apparent possession of WMD as part of one general menace to America and more generally to world security. During 2002 the United States threatened to invade Iraq if Saddam did not relinquish his WMD. In

January 2003 the Australian Government decided to deploy forces to the Middle East so that they would be available if the invasion eventuated. The deployed forces, numbering about 2,000 personnel, included:

- The Royal Australian Navy (RAN) frigates *Anzac* and *Darwin* already operating in the Persian Gulf as part of Operation Slipper.
- The RAAF AP-3C Orion maritime patrol aircraft already operating in the Persian Gulf region as part of Operation Slipper.
- The amphibious ship HMAS *Kanimbla* with an RAN clearance diving team.
- A Special Forces Task Group with an SAS squadron, commandos, engineers and three Chinook helicopters.
- An RAAF air wing with 14 F/A-18 Hornet strike aircraft and 3 C-130 Hercules transport aircraft.
- An Australian national headquarters commanded by Brigadier Maurie McNarn.

All the forces arrived in the Middle East by early March 2003. The United States decided to go ahead with the invasion of Iraq, and Australia and Britain agreed to join in. The Australian Government claimed that because Iraq had failed to abide by the UN Security Council resolutions concerning its WMD, the United States and its allies had the necessary authorisation to undertake the invasion. Critics claimed that the United States should have waited for the outcome of inspections that Iraq had belatedly agreed to late in 2002 and that the invasion was not justified. Britain supported the United States with substantial forces, Australia sent 2,000 ADF personnel and Poland sent a miniscule token force.

## What's so special?

The military love to use jargon words that are confusing to the general public. One common term used in this chapter is Special Forces. These highly trained troops conduct unconventional warfare, often behind enemy lines. In the late 1990s the ADF formed a Special Forces Group, which included the Special Air Service (SAS) Regiment, Regular and Reserve commandos, and chemical, biological and radiological warfare specialists. The Special Forces Group was supported by specially trained helicopters crews. In 2002 the Special Forces Group became Special Operations Command, headed by Major General Duncan Lewis. The Special Forces Task Groups, which served in Afghanistan in 2001 and in Iraq in 2003, included SAS troopers, commandos and other Special Operations Command soldiers. The Special Forces Task Groups are sometimes called Special Operations Task Groups.

The Howard Government's decision to join the 'coalition of the willing' was highly controversial and was criticised by the Labor Opposition. The government claimed that it was intent on removing the threat of Iraq's WMD, but the most important factor was its desire to support the United States. Australia's commitment was finely managed to keep casualties to a minimum.

The invasion of Iraq began in the evening of 19 March 2003, when SAS troops and other coalition forces crossed into Iraq. American and British aircraft bombed Iraqi army positions. British troops seized the southern city of Basra, while American divisions with tanks advanced north towards Baghdad. Meanwhile American, Australian and British Special Forces took control of Iraq's western desert. Baghdad was captured on 9 April and President Bush declared the combat operations over on 1 May. Australian forces were involved in three main areas.

- HMAS *Anzac* provided naval gunfire support for British amphibious operations on the coast of Iraq and Naval clearance divers helped open some of the ports. Boarding parties from HMAS *Kanimbla* seized an Iraqi ship carrying sea mines.

- The Special Forces Task Group's mission was to prevent Iraq from using its ballistic missiles in western Iraq. The SAS squadron deployed deep into Iraq by vehicles and helicopters (refer to Figure 22-2). The SAS troopers carried out some outstanding operations, attacking Iraqi positions and quickly putting them out of action. When SAS patrols were attacked by superior numbers of Iraqis they held them off and defeated them using a variety of weapons. On 11 April the SAS patrols were brought together to capture the Al Asad air base.

- On 23 March the F/A-18 Hornets began flying strike missions against Iraqi positions. Once Baghdad was captured, C-130 Hercules transport aircraft flew in supplies to provide food for Iraqi civilians.

After Bush declared the war over, most combat forces returned to Australia, leaving smaller forces in the Middle East. Australia had no combat deaths during the 2003 Iraq War.

And what of the weapons of mass destruction that Iraq was supposed to have, which were one of the main justifications for the war? After the war the Americans found that Iraq had no WMD. We now know that UNSCOM, which had worked hard during the 1990s to eliminate Iraq's WMD, actually had been very effective before Saddam stopped the inspectors from interfering in 1998. Saddam had pretended that he possessed such WMD to maintain his prestige — and saw his country invaded as a result. The decision proved to be a fatal mistake for him and his regime.

## Dealing with the insurgency in Iraq

After the 2003 Iraq War the ADF maintained forces in the Persian Gulf–Iraq region including:

- A Navy frigate in the northern Persian Gulf to help protect Iraq's off-shore oil terminals
- C-130 Hercules transport aircraft based in Qatar
- AP3-C Orion maritime surveillance aircraft
- A logistic and support base in Kuwait
- A security detachment in Baghdad to protect Australian diplomats
- RAAF air traffic controllers at Baghdad airport

The US-led coalition in Bagdad soon found itself fighting a savage insurgency throughout the country in which the United States sent ever-increasing numbers of troops, supported by troops from other countries. As the situation deteriorated Prime Minister John Howard agreed to send troops to Iraq. In mid-2005 an Australian Army task force went to Al Muthanna Province to maintain security (refer to Figure 22-2). The task force (between 450 and 500 troops) was rotated every six months. It was based on a cavalry regiment or an infantry battalion and included light armoured vehicles, Bushmaster infantry patrol vehicles and infantry soldiers. Later the task force moved to Dhi Qar Province and took responsibility for security in southern Iraq. The task force had several contacts with insurgents but suffered no deaths. The Labor Government, led by Prime Minister Kevin Rudd, and elected in November 2007, had vowed to withdraw Australian combat and training units from Iraq and the withdrawal began in June 2008. By the time the last combat and training soldiers departed in July 2009, about 20,000 ADF personnel had served in and around Iraq over a six-year period.

The other units listed at the beginning of this section remained in the Iraq-Persian Gulf–Iraq region. Senior Australian naval officers periodically commanded the naval combined task force, which included Australian, British and United States vessels. This commitment was still continuing in 2010.

## Returning to the enduring war in Afghanistan

After Australia's initial commitment to Afghanistan in 2001–02 a new government was elected in Afghanistan, but the Taliban was still causing death and mayhem. In September 2005 an Australian Special Forces Task

Group returned to Afghanistan. Australia's commitment was supported by both major political parties, who believed that the Taliban were supporting terrorism and that the Kabul government shouldn't be allowed to fall to the Taliban. International support for the Kabul government was authorised by the United Nations and was provided by the International Security Assistance Force, under the control of the North Atlantic Treaty Organization (NATO).

The Australian Special Forces troops served in Oruzgan Province (see Figure 22-3) and worked with a US-led coalition task force, including the Dutch, as well as the Afghan National Army and police. Three Australian Special Operations Task Groups served in Afghanistan in 2005–06. In July 2006, fighting alongside Dutch troops, the Diggers killed 150 Taliban and Al Qaeda guerrillas in a fierce nine-day battle, which saw the heaviest fighting experienced by Australian forces since the Vietnam War.

In September 2006 an Australian Reconstruction Task Force, based on the 1st Combat Engineer Regiment, went to Afghanistan to undertake construction work and to train local tradesmen. The task force included a strong protection group with infantry and light armoured vehicles, and was supported by Australian helicopters.

The Australian Special Forces returned to Afghanistan in May 2007 to take the fight to the Taliban in Oruzgan province. The soldiers soon found themselves in intense battles. The Australian force in Afghanistan continued to grow and in mid-2009 the Reconstruction Task Force became the Mentoring and Reconstruction Task Force with a strong combat element, an engineering group, and a mentoring and liaison team to work with an Afghan infantry battalion. By this time more than 1,500 troops were serving in Afghanistan. Between October 2007 and July 2009, ten Australian soldiers were killed on operations in Afghanistan, either by improvised explosive devices (bombs), gun fire or, in one case, by a rocket.

In September 2008 an Australian Special Forces explosives detection dog called Sabi went missing during the battle which led to Trooper Donaldson being awarded the Victoria Cross (see the sidebar 'Acting naturally while engaging the enemy') and to nine Australians, including Sabi's handler, being wounded. Fourteen months later, in November 2009 an American soldier saw Sabi in a remote area of Oruzgan Province and realised that the dog had received military training. He sent the dog to the Australian base where Sabi's trainer recognised her. Sabi was soon taking orders again and playing her old games with her Army mates.

## Acting naturally while engaging the enemy

On 2 September 2008 SAS Trooper Mark Donaldson was part of a combined Afghan, US and Australian vehicle convoy that was ambushed by a numerically superior Taliban force. The combined patrol suffered numerous casualties and fought for two hours before it could break clear of the ambush site. During the battle Donaldson, while engaging the enemy, deliberately exposed himself to enemy fire to draw attention away from the wounded soldiers, allowing the wounded to be moved to safety.

The vehicles withdrew over a distance of about four kilometres and because the wounded were on the vehicles, Donaldson and others had to run beside the vehicles throughout. During the withdrawal a severely wounded Afghan interpreter was left behind. Disregarding his own safety, and on his own initiative, Donaldson ran alone across about 80 metres of exposed ground through intense enemy machine-gun fire to recover the interpreter. Carrying the interpreter on his back, he brought him to the vehicles where he provided first aid treatment. He then returned to the fight, engaging the enemy and administering first aid to other wounded soldiers.

On 16 January 2009 Donaldson was invested with the medal of the Victoria Cross of Australia. He commented that he didn't see himself as a hero. 'I'm a soldier, I'm trained to fight ... it's instinct and it's natural. I just saw him there. I went over and got him, that was it.'

By mid-2010 Australians had been serving on operations in Afghanistan for almost five years since the Special Operations Task Group returned there in 2005. Many of the soldiers serving in Afghanistan have been awarded medals for gallantry. Unfortunately, the full story of the exploits of the Australians in Afghanistan has yet to be recorded. When the story is told, it is sure to prove to be one of the more remarkable and praiseworthy chapters in Australian military history.

# Part VIII
# The Part of Tens

'We were only outnumbered fifty to one, so naturally the enemy didn't stand a chance.'

## In this part ...

This part provides an opportunity for a bit of fun as I make a perhaps contentious list of different aspects of Australian military history. The part also allows me to look back over 200 years of Australian military history and to highlight some of the important people and incidents. You may want to begin by reading these chapters first as a starting point so you can dip into other chapters and follow up some of the people and incidents mentioned here.

# Chapter 23
# Ten Top Australian Military Leaders

*In This Chapter*
- Leading our troops in combat
- Protecting Australia's interests at home and in the field
- Recognising the strategists and planners

Military commanders have one of the hardest jobs because they give orders that risk the lives of the many men and women under their care. Australians don't expect their military leaders to fail, especially with the safety of the nation at stake. Their task is particularly difficult because while military commanders are trying to do their job successfully, the enemy is doing its utmost to prevent them from doing it at all.

Military commanders must:

- Know their job
- Be physically and morally courageous
- Have the ability to lead and inspire their troops
- Be robust enough to bounce back from disasters
- Be lucky

Hundreds of Australian military leaders have commanded at battalion and brigade level, but relatively few have commanded at the top level in war. Australian forces have usually served as part of larger Allied organisations and not many Australian commanders have been responsible for large independent military operations. Fewer than 40 Australian Army generals have led forces in battle overseas. No Australian admiral has ever commanded Australian ships at sea in war. Only a handful of admirals, generals and air marshals have been required to advise the government on military strategy during a war.

I have selected some top military leaders who have commanded Australians in battle, as well as a few who have also commanded the Navy, the Army or the Air Force in war. To avoid making an impossible judgement as to who was the best, I have listed the military leaders alphabetically.

# Field Marshal Sir Thomas Blamey (1884–1951)

No Australian commander has been the subject of as much criticism and, in some quarters, contempt, as Blamey. Some, but by no means all, of it was deserved. He resigned as Chief Commissioner of the Victoria Police when he lied to protect the force's reputation. He ruthlessly sidelined anyone who was a contender for his position. He saved his own son during the withdrawal from Greece, when thousands of Diggers went into captivity. He criticised the troops who fought valiantly on the Kokoda Trail, almost causing a mutiny. Blamey had a tough hide; he didn't care much what others thought.

Yet no Australian commander held and retained such important positions as Blamey. In the First World War he was the respected chief of staff of the Australian Corps, under Monash. In the Second World War he commanded the AIF in the Middle East as well as the 1st Australian Corps during the ill-fated Greek campaign. He demanded that the British withdraw the Diggers from Tobruk when he believed the Diggers were becoming worn out.

As Commander-in-Chief of the Australian Army from 1942 to 1945, Blamey made it into the formidable force that defeated the Japanese. Commanding the troops in New Guinea, he orchestrated the brilliant offensives of 1943. Serving under the egocentric American General Douglas MacArthur, who held overall command and retained the confidence of the Australian government, Blamey tried to protect Australian interests.

The Australian Prime Minister John Curtin dismissed gossip about Blamey's private life with the comment: 'I want a commander of the Australian Army, not a Sunday school superintendant'. No other Australian commander had the toughness and political savvy to balance all the demands of the Army's top command in the war. In 1950 he became Australia's only field marshal. At his funeral 300,000 Australians lined the streets of Melbourne.

## General Sir Harry Chauvel (1865–1945)

Australia's famous Australian Light Horse will forever be linked with its equally illustrious commander, Harry Chauvel. In the Boer War he commanded mounted units and learned much about the use of light horsemen in battle. He continued serving after the war as a regular army officer, and at the beginning of the First World War he took command of the 1st Light Horse Brigade. When reinforcements were needed at Gallipoli he led his light horsemen at Anzac Cove and was noted for his coolness and courage.

After Gallipoli Chauvel took command of the Anzac Mounted Division and at the battle of Romani, in the Sinai Peninsula, helped defeat a major Turkish offensive. By June 1917 Chauvel was commanding the Desert Mounted Corps. He was the first Australian to be promoted to lieutenant general and the first to command a corps. Under his command the light horsemen carried out the famous charge at Beersheba.

In the last year of the war Chauvel's corps became the main British Army striking force in Palestine and Syria. In the offensive beginning in September 1918, Australian, British and Indian horsemen conducted one of the world's great cavalry operations. The Turks surrendered and Chauvel was present for the capture of Damascus. He was a careful planner, loyal, courageous and unpretentious. He never had to endure the horrendous casualties such as occurred on the Western Front, but in the desert and hills of the Middle East he was an outstanding commander. After the war Chauvel became Chief of the General Staff and Inspector General. He was promoted to general in 1929, the first Australian to attain this rank.

## Vice-Admiral Sir John Collins (1899–1989)

Although no Australian admiral has ever commanded Australian ships in battle, Collins was one of the few officers to command an Australian squadron on active service. As a young midshipman he served in a British battleship in the First World War. In 1940 in the Second World War he was in command of the Australian light cruiser HMAS *Sydney* in the Mediterranean when it sank an Italian cruiser in a famous Australian naval battle.

During the Japanese campaign to take Singapore in January 1942 Collins took command of British and Australian cruisers and destroyers, and evacuated civilians and military personnel. In May 1944 he was appointed commander of the Australian Squadron, with the rank of commodore. The squadron, with cruisers and destroyers, supported American landings along the coast of New Guinea and at Leyte in the Philippines. During the famous battle of Leyte Gulf in October 1944, in which large Japanese and American fleets clashed, a Japanese kamikaze aircraft struck the flagship *Australia* and Collins was severely wounded. He recovered in time to resume command of the squadron shortly before the end of the war.

Collins became Chief of Naval Staff in 1947, with the rank of rear admiral, and was promoted to vice-admiral in 1950. His tenure as Navy chief, which included the period of the Korean War, finished in 1955. He was clever, ambitious, cool and courageous in battle, and professional in his conduct. A member of the first intake to the RAN College in 1913, he became the first graduate to lead the Navy.

# General Peter Cosgrove (1947–)

In the first decade of the 21st Century, Cosgrove became the most widely recognised military leader in Australia. Traditionally, Australian generals hadn't sought publicity, but Cosgrove turned that on its head.

In 1999, as a major general, Cosgrove was commanding the 1st Division in Brisbane when Australia was invited to lead the International Force in East Timor. By that time Cosgrove had had years of command experience. In Vietnam in 1969 he was awarded a Military Cross for bravery. He subsequently commanded a rifle company, a battalion, a brigade, the ADF Warfare Centre, the Royal Military College and the division.

In East Timor he exercised great tact to prevent an outbreak of fighting with the Indonesians who were preparing to leave the territory, while his troops, including an Australian brigade, showed firmness and resolve while dealing with the local militia. Realising the importance of public relations, Cosgrove gave nightly news conferences, beamed by satellite back to the 'mums and dads' in Australia. In East Timor he commanded troops from all three services as well as from 22 countries. The force was about the size of a division — the first time an Australian had commanded a force of that size on operations since the Second World War.

By 2003 Cosgrove was Chief of the Defence Force, when the Howard Government directed the ADF to join with the United States and Britain in the invasion of Iraq. Howard had great confidence in Cosgrove's conduct of the operations. Although a brigadier commanded the Australian forces in the Middle East, with modern communications Cosgrove was able to keep a close watch on the operations.

An effective communicator with a common touch, Cosgrove continued to address the public at every opportunity. He was the epitome of the new, modern commander. Cosgrove was well trained and had years of military experience, but he never faced some of the trials endured by earlier commanders, such as defeats in battle or heavy casualties. No Australian troops were killed in action in East Timor or in Iraq.

# Lieutenant General Sir Talbot Hobbs (1864–1938)

Ten Australian officers commanded divisions in the First World War. Two were killed by enemy action, two were dismissed for poor performance, two were promoted to corps command, and four were still serving at the end of the war. One of the last group was J J Talbot Hobbs, who commanded his division, the 5th, longer than any other Australian officer.

A successful architect from Perth, Hobbs was a dedicated militia soldier who trained with the British Army in England at his own expense. He commanded the artillery of the 1st Division at Gallipoli where he performed with energy and courage. He continued in the same role during the division's costly battles at Pozières and Mouquet Farm in the Somme offensive in July and August 1916.

In January 1917 Hobbs, with the rank of major general, took command of the 5th Division and led it during the Ypres battles in 1917. He was largely responsible for one of the Australian Army's most famous victories, the recapture of Villers-Bretonneux in April 1918. In the remarkable offensive, which began in August 1918, his troops captured Pèronne and helped break the Hindenburg Line.

At the end of the war Lieutenant General Sir John Monash took over responsibility for repatriating the AIF to Australia, and Hobbs assumed command of the corps as a lieutenant general. After the war he played a major role in erecting memorials on the Australian battlefields. Hobbs's command was marked by his concern for his soldiers and his willingness to challenge his superiors to protect his men.

# General Sir John Monash (1865–1931)

Australia's most famous general, Monash commanded the Australian Corps in France from the beginning of June 1918 to the end of the war. At the outbreak of the war he was a successful Melbourne engineer and militia officer, but had already borne his share of trials. As a Prussian-born Jew he had struggled for acceptance in his hometown of Melbourne and he had rebuilt his business after it had collapsed, leaving him heavily in debt. Monash commanded the 4th Brigade at Gallipoli where his performance was patchy, but he learned his trade, cared for his men, and remained in command when others fell by the wayside. It has been said of Monash that he was a better divisional commander than a brigade commander, and a better corps commander than a divisional commander.

In mid-1916 Monash was promoted to major general to lead the newly formed 3rd Division, and he trained his brigades well. He showed his powers of planning and organisation in the battles at Messines and Ypres in 1917, and his flexibility in helping to stop the German offensive early in 1918.

The Australian Corps, with five divisions, had the strength of an army. Innovative, as corps commander Monash tried new, successful tactics at Hamel on 4 July 1918 and then planned his corps' remarkable offensive, which began on 8 August. Highly intelligent, he was the master of every detail, and in well-conducted conferences ensured that everyone understood their part. Monash's forceful personality gave confidence to subordinate commanders and their troops. Perhaps reflecting his background, he was eager for status, sought publicity and honour, and tended to exaggerate the achievements of his men and his own part.

At the end of the war, in another great feat of organisation, Monash managed the repatriation of the Australian troops back to Australia. In the 1920s he became chairman of the State Electricity Commission of Victoria, which developed the use of brown coal from the Gippsland region and built power stations to provide electricity for Melbourne. One of his friends wrote: 'He was a great leader and a genius in getting to the heart of any problem and finding its solution ... the ablest, biggest-minded and biggest-hearted man I have ever known'.

## Lieutenant General Sir Leslie Morshead (1889–1959)

All of Australia's higher level commanders in the Second World War had distinguished service in the First World War. Generals such as Morshead were militia soldiers and were at times derided by British professionals as amateurs, but they had a deep understanding of war and of how to command men in battle. Morshead went ashore at Gallipoli on 25 April 1915 as a captain, was major in the bitter fighting at Lone Pine, and commanded an infantry battalion on the Western Front, including in famous battles such as Messines, Villers-Bretonneux and Amiens. Between the wars, while building a business career, Morshead successively commanded four militia infantry brigades.

Morshead joined the AIF in the Second World War. In 1941, as a major general, Morshead led the 9th Division during the siege of Tobruk. A strict disciplinarian, he was known as 'Ming the Merciless'. At Tobruk he insisted on an aggressive defence, and counterattacked if any territory was lost. Morshead's troops were the first to halt and defeat a German blitzkrieg attack in the war. By holding Tobruk, he prevented German General Erwin Rommel from advancing into Egypt. The following year Morhead's division was heavily engaged in Egypt, culminating in the battle of El Alamein in October–November.

Morshead's division laid the foundations for the British victory by drawing onto itself the might of the German Panzers. He stood up to senior British officers when he believed his troops' best interests were at risk and, working alongside British professionals, he proved to be a skilful commander.

In the Pacific War, Morshead successfully commanded a corps, fighting in New Guinea and Borneo. He was Australia's most successful battlefield commander in the Second World War.

## Air Chief Marshal Sir Frederick Scherger (1904–84)

Officers of the RAAF have had fewer opportunities to demonstrate their capacity to command large formations on operations than their Army counterparts. As part of the Empire Air Training Scheme in the Second World War, Australian bomber squadrons served in England under British higher commanders (see Chapter 13). In the Pacific War, Australian air squadrons generally operated as part of an Allied air force led by an American general. The RAAF deployed an operational group in New Guinea, commanded by a succession of capable air commodores, of whom Scherger was the best known.

Scherger was in charge in Darwin when it was bombed by the Japanese in February 1942. Between November 1943 and August 1943 he led the 10th Operational Group in New Guinea, supporting Australian and American troops, and returned to operations in May 1945 as commander of the 1st Tactical Air Force. After the war Scherger was promoted to Air Vice-Marshal and in 1953 commanded all British Commonwealth air forces in Malaya during the Emergency (see Chapter 19).

Scherger was Chief of the Air Staff from 1957 to 1961 and then became Chairman of the Chiefs of Staff Committee, a relatively new position which was supposed to coordinate the work of the three services. He built up his position as the government's principal adviser on military matters, especially as the strategic situation grew more dangerous in the mid-1960s. Scherger played a major role in having Australian troops sent to Vietnam. In 1965, a year before the end of his appointment, he was promoted to Air Chief Marshal, the first RAAF officer to reach this 'four-star' rank. He strengthened the position of Chairman Chiefs of Staff Committee, which eventually became the Chief of the Defence Force, with command authority over all three Services.

## Major General George Vasey (1895–1945)

A great anomaly in Australian military command at the beginning of the Second World War was the belief, reinforced by Prime Minister Menzies, that senior leadership positions should be held by militia (part-time) officers rather than regulars. The senior militia officers had all commanded troops in the First World War and many believed that the role of regular officers was to act as their staff officers. Vasey was determined to overthrow this stereotype.

As a young Duntroon graduate Vasey saw plenty of front-line service in the First World War, gained solid training and experience in India between the wars, and believed that he was well-equipped for command. When he received his opportunity to lead the 19th Brigade in Greece and Crete he seized it with both hands (see Chapter 11). Cool in a crisis, colourful in language, 'Bloody George', as Vasey was known, quickly gained the respect and affection of his troops.

Promoted to major general, he commanded the 7th Division on the Kokoda Trail, and at Gona and Sanananda in Papua between October 1942 and January 1943. During the 1943 New Guinea campaigns, which included the landing at Nadzab, the capture of Lae, the seizure of Kaiapit and the gruelling Shaggy Ridge battles, Vasey demonstrated military expertise and personal leadership (see Chapter 15). One officer recalled providing a platoon to escort Vasey to Shaggy Ridge. 'They cleaned and tried to polish their sodden boots and equipment as though it was a ceremonial parade. Whenever General Vasey appeared, either on foot or in jeep, it was all the troops could do to avoid calling out "How are you George?" such a sense of comradeship prevailed between the general and his men.' He died in a plane crash near Cairns in March 1945, flying north to take command of the 6th Division. After Vasey demonstrated his capacity for command no-one said that regular officers should be restricted to staff appointments.

# General Sir John Wilton (1910–81)

Leadership of troops in combat is often seen as the high point in the exercise of command, demanding all the qualities of knowledge, character, courage and resilience. But if the government deploys its military forces to the wrong places for the wrong reasons, the brilliant work of the commander on the ground may still count for nothing. The work of top level commanders in advising the government on strategy is crucial.

Wilton was the government's principal adviser on the conduct of Australian operations in Vietnam for most of the ten-year commitment. Australian Army advisers went to Vietnam in 1962 and the following year Wilton became Chief of the General Staff, presiding over the deployment of an infantry battalion in 1965. In 1966 the battalion was expanded to a task force, and RAAF and RAN elements were also sent. Because the three services were involved, responsibility for the conduct of the war transferred to the Chairman Chief of Staff Committee, but at the same time Wilton took on this appointment. He remained in the job until the end of 1970, by which time the Australian forces were beginning to withdraw. He became the first Australian Army officer to be promoted to full general since Blamey in 1941.

Wilton didn't reach this top-level position by chance. By the time he became head of the army in 1963 he had accumulated many years of operational experience. A Duntroon graduate, Wilton had served in India and Burma between the wars. He had seen combat in Syria in 1941 and was chief of staff of the 3rd Division in New Guinea in 1943. In the last year of the war he worked on General Blamey's staff in the Philippines and Morotai. He commanded an infantry brigade in the Korean War.

Wilton believed that Australia should be involved in the Vietnam War, but he was careful to ensure that Australian troops weren't placed in positions where they were likely to suffer heavy casualties. 'Smiling Jack', as he was known, because of his lack of small talk or any hint of flamboyance, also set the Services on the course that led to the formation of the Australian Defence Force in 1976, a few years after he retired. Wilton was the most important and influential Australian Army officer in the second half of the 20th century.

# Chapter 24

# Ten Famous Australian Battles

## In This Chapter

▶ Establishing Australia's reputation in the First World War
▶ Changing the course of Allied campaigns in the Second World War
▶ Winning new battle honours in Korea and Vietnam

Throughout this book you can read about many battles in Australian military history. This chapter lists some battles, not all large, that mark particular turning points or triumphs. Some were defensive battles, some were victories. Many changed the course of the campaign in their particular theatre of war. They all give us a glimpse of the character of Australian fighting men.

## The Landing at Gallipoli

The landing of the 1st Australian Division on the Gallipoli Peninsula on 25 April 1915 (see Chapter 6) is the iconic battle of Australian military history. For the first time, Australian troops fought on the world stage. The troops unexpectedly found themselves scrambling up steep slopes under enemy fire, and they pushed inland with enthusiasm and daring against Turkish fire.

More dispassionately, the landing should be considered as a major military battle. A complete division was landed on a foreign shore in the face of enemy opposition. While many troops advanced inland on their own initiative, the Australian commanders tried to impose some order. Critics have suggested that the deep thrusts could have been exploited further and that Colonel Sinclair McLagan erred in persuading Colonel McCay to deploy his 2nd Brigade to the right flank, thereby allowing the Turks to mount a strong attack on the left. By failing to take the dominating heights on the left the Australians were contained in their beachhead.

On the positive side, the Australians managed to hold off a concerted Turkish counterattack late in the day. The Australian and New Zealand divisional commanders certainly took counsel of their fears and wanted to withdraw. But General Hamilton ordered them to dig in and hold on. The perimeter seized on the first day remained the limit of the Australian advance until the August offensive and in some areas, until the withdrawal in December that year.

## Beersheba

The charge of the 4th Australian Light Horse Brigade against Turkish defences at Beersheba on 31 October 1917 is one of the most exciting episodes in Australian military history (see Chapter 8). But its importance relates to how it transformed the strategic situation.

In March and April 1917 the British army had tried unsuccessfully to capture Gaza, which was preventing it from advancing into Palestine. After these failures the British commander planned a major new offensive. This time he would pretend to attack Gaza while sending his main forces against Beersheba, in the desert about 43 kilometres south-east of Gaza.

The infantry began the attack in the morning of 31 October, but by mid-afternoon they hadn't captured the town. Lieutenant General Harry Chauvel, commander of the Desert Mounted Corps, knew that if the town and its vital wells weren't captured soon he would need to withdraw his light horsemen as they would have no water for their horses. Chauvel ordered Brigadier General Grant's 4th Light Horse Brigade, which hadn't yet been in action, to seize the town. 'Put Grant straight at it', he ordered. In one of the great cavalry charges in history the light horsemen, using their bayonets as swords, galloped straight at the Turkish defences. Shocked by the audacious action the Turks were overwhelmed and surrendered. The town fell and the British Army advanced into Palestine.

## Villers-Bretonneux

The second battle of Villers-Bretonneux, fought on 24 and 25 April 1918, came at the end of the month-long German offensive in northern France (see Chapter 9). On 17 and 18 April the Germans mounted a strong attack on the town, which was beaten off by the 9th Australian Brigade. British troops then took over from the Australians. On 24 April the Germans tried again, supported by tanks and mustard gas, and captured the town.

A British divisional commander was given the task of recapturing the town using Brigadier General Glasgow's 13th Australian Brigade and Brigadier General Harold Elliott's 15th Australian Brigade. In a famous incident, Glasgow refused to attack at the time suggested by the British commander, instead attacking later at night, when conditions were better. Major General Hobbs, commander of the 5th Australian Division, played a major role in planning the operation. The attack was a resounding success, although not without heavy casualties. By 25 April the Australians were clearing the Germans out of the town street by street.

After three years of the war the Australian commanders had the ability to prepare plans quickly, and they had the confidence and courage to maintain their views when dealing with British commanders. The attack also showed that the Australian infantry battalions were now well trained and capable of executing an attack with the minimum of preparation and warning. The capture of the town marked the end of the German offensive. The battle added greatly to the already high reputation of the Australian infantry.

# Mont St Quentin

Three weeks after the great Allied offensive began on 8 August 1918, the Australian troops were tiring and the battalions were shrinking as casualties mounted, but the Corps Commander, General Monash, knew that it was important to keep the Germans off balance. However, the Somme River blocked his advance. Across the river lay Mont St Quentin, which dominated the nearby town of Péronne, 3 kilometres to the south, and was held by one of the German Army's best divisions.

The 3rd Division crossed the river on the left flank and secured a foothold. In the early hours of 31 August two battalions of the 5th Brigade, 2nd Division, began their assault up the mountain, without assistance from tanks or a creeping artillery barrage. The Australian battalions were desperately understrength, but yelling to make up for their small numbers, the Diggers charged up the mountain. After a seesaw battle they were held just below the crest, but next day another Australian brigade drove the Germans off the mountain. Other troops from the 3rd and 5th Divisions captured Péronne.

The capture of Mont St Quentin was one of the Australian troops' finest achievements of the war (see Chapter 9). As the Australian Official Historian described it, 'the Australians at a cost of 3,000 casualties dealt a stunning blow to five German divisions'.

## Sinking the Bartolomeo Colleoni

In mid-July 1940 Captain John Collins, with his light cruiser HMAS *Sydney* and a British destroyer, HMS *Havock*, was ordered to intercept Italian ships north of Crete. Collins also had to protect four other destroyers on antisubmarine patrol off the western end of Crete. Collins believed that he couldn't undertake both tasks properly and at his own initiative steamed south so that he was closer to the destroyers, maintaining radio silence so as not to warn the enemy of his presence.

Soon after dawn on 19 July the destroyers encountered two fast Italian light cruisers and, outgunned, the destroyers steamed north towards *Sydney* and *Havock*, which were approaching at full speed. As the ships drew closer, *Sydney* opened fire on the pursuing Italian cruisers. Receiving accurate fire, the Italian commander thought he had encountered two heavier British cruisers and turned away. *Sydney* put the *Bartolomeo Colleoni* out of action with gunfire and then chased the other Italian cruiser, which was badly damaged but eventually managed to escape. The British destroyers torpedoed and sank the *Bartolomeo Colleoni*.

The victory can be attributed to Collins's enterprise and the good training of *Sydney's* gun crews. Coming early in the war it boosted morale and helped establish the British Navy's superiority over the Italians. No other Australian cruiser achieved quite the same success against enemy cruisers; later the Australian cruisers *Sydney*, *Perth* and *Canberra* were to be sunk in engagements with enemy warships.

## Kokoda

As an iconic name in Australian military history, Kokoda now almost matches that of Gallipoli. Yet Kokoda wasn't a battle but an entire military campaign. It began with the Japanese landing at Buna on the night of 21 July 1942 and ended when Australian troops recaptured the Papuan village of Kokoda on 2 November 1942 (see Chapter 15). The campaign was fought along the Kokoda Trail, a narrow footpath that wound its way from Kokoda over the forbidding Owen Stanley Range towards Port Moresby.

The most important battle took place at Isurava between 26 and 29 August, when three Australian battalions fought a bitter defensive battle against the Japanese South Seas Force. The Australians were forced to conduct a fighting withdrawal in appalling conditions along the trail until the Japanese halted their offensive, on orders from their higher command, at Ioribaiwa. On 1 October two Australian brigades began a counteroffensive that regained Kokoda on 2 November.

The legendary status of the campaign relates to the belief that the defensive battles on the track prevented the Japanese from seizing Port Moresby, which would have increased the pressure on Australia (see Chapter 25). The troops were poorly supplied and casualties needed to be carried by native porters. The troops fought heroically against a battle-hardened Japanese force that appeared to be in superior numbers.

## El Alamein

Between 23 October and 3 November 1942, near El Alamien in northern Egypt, one of the great battles of the war was fought. The British Eighth Army, under General Sir Bernard Montgomery, defeated a German–Italian (Axis) Army under General Erwin Rommel (see Chapter 12).

The 9th Australian Division, commanded by Lieutenant General Sir Leslie Morshead, was just one of nine British Commonwealth divisions in the battle. The 9th Division held the most northerly position, near the coast and, along with other divisions, it was supposed to open a passage through the Axis defences for the British armoured divisions. When the British infantry failed to achieve their task, Montgomery ordered the Australians to mount a series of attacks which drew in most of the German panzers. At a critical point, with one of his brigades being destroyed before his eyes, Morshead relieved it with another brigade during the night. The next morning the brigade held off a fierce German attack. Once the German reserves were committed against the Australians, Montgomery ordered his armoured divisions to attack. After hard fighting the Axis defences collapsed and were forced to withdraw.

Montgomery knew that without the efforts of the Australians he wouldn't have won the battle. Forming just one-tenth of the attacking force, the Australians suffered more than one-fifth of the casualties.

## Bismarck Sea

Aircraft from the RAAF were engaged in hundreds of operations during the Pacific War. The battle of the Bismarck Sea stands out as distinct action that had a major effect on the conduct of the war in New Guinea (see Chapter 15).

On 28 February 1942 a Japanese convoy departed Rabaul bound for Lae in New Guinea, carrying 6,000 troops. Informed by intercepted radio messages, American and Australian aircraft located the convoy off the north coast of New Britain and attacked it on 2 and 3 March as it entered the Huon Gulf. The Australian aircraft included Boston bombers and Beaufighters from No 9 Operational Group under the command of Air Commodore Joseph Hewitt.

Complementing the work of the American bombers, the Beaufighters strafed the Japanese ships at mast height, while American fighters held off Japanese fighters. All eight of the Japanese transports and four destroyers were sunk. About half of the Japanese troops perished. The battle confirmed Allied domination over the seas, and after that the Japanese sent supplies and reinforcements on barges that hugged the coast at night.

# Kapyong

Australia's most famous battle in the Korean War was fought on a hill overlooking the Kapyong River on 23 and 24 April 1951 (see Chapter 18). By that time the 3rd Battalion of the Royal Australian Regiment (3 RAR), had been in action in Korea for more than six months, and although some troops had been replaced the officers and soldiers were experienced in battle. In the earlier battles 3 RAR (a component of the 27th Commonwealth Brigade) had advanced deep into North Korea, before the Chinese Army had entered the war, causing the United Nation forces to withdraw. By April the UN force occupied a line north of the South Korean capital, Seoul.

The Chinese began a massive offensive with more than 480,000 troops and in the evening of 23 April the companies of 3 RAR came under heavy attack. The Chinese attacked in waves, and despite being cut down in huge numbers by Australian fire, they continued their charges. The Australians repelled the Chinese with local counterattacks for almost 24 hours, but late on 24 April they were compelled to conduct a fighting withdrawal.

Along with a similar defensive battle by a Canadian battalion, the Australians managed to blunt the Korean offensive and prevented the Koreans breaking through the United Nations line. Both battalions were awarded the United States Presidential Citation. The infantry of Australia's new Regular Army had a worthy battle honour.

## Long Tan

The battle of Long Tan was not the largest battle conducted by the Australians in the Vietnam War, but has become emblematic of the Australian Army's involvement in the war (see Chapter 20). On the night of 17 August 1966 Viet Cong rockets landed in the Australian task force base at Nui Dat in the centre of Phuoc Tuy Province. The next day Australian patrols attempted to locate the enemy who had fired the rockets.

D Company 6 RAR struck a large enemy force in the Long Tan rubber plantation in the afternoon of 18 August and soon found itself surrounded and fighting for its existence against overwhelming numbers. The young soldiers, including national servicemen, showed the benefits of their training and discipline, but the company would have been wiped out except for the heavy and accurate artillery fire that decimated the ranks of the attacking Viet Cong. When ammunition ran low, Australian helicopters, in pouring monsoonal rain, dropped resupplies directly to the defenders. Just on dark, as the Viet Cong renewed their assault, another company of infantry arrived in Armoured Personnel Carriers (APCs). The machine guns on the APCs cut down the rows of VC attackers. D Company had been saved.

The Australians had lost 18 killed and 24 wounded. Next morning 6 RAR recovered 245 VC bodies. Many more would've been killed. About 100 Diggers had withstood an attack by a force ten times their size. The battle established the Australian Army's dominance in the province.

# Chapter 25

# Ten Myths of Australian Military History

*In This Chapter*
- Debunking strongly held perceptions about Australian military history
- Marvelling at the way certain stories survive despite evidence to the contrary

A veteran once told me that Prime Minister Curtin had implored the 8th Division to delay the Japanese in Malaya for eight weeks to prevent them from invading Australia. I asked him to give me some documentary proof of Curtin's request. Some weeks later a letter arrived enclosing a cutting of an article he had written, published in his local newspaper, in which, with no further evidence, he reiterated his statement. This, he said, was the proof.

Military history raises strong emotions, and those who have lived through a war often have firm ideas about what happened. Sometimes their perceptions are not matched by the evidence. People want to believe in dramatic explanations of past events, and when facts are lacking they sometimes accuse the government of a cover-up. Not all the myths of Australian military history (many more than the ten listed here) are caused by conspiracy theories. Nonetheless, once perceptions become widespread they are hard to shift.

## *The Aborigines Didn't Resist White Invasion*

Until the 1970s the accepted view among historians and the general public was that the Aborigines didn't effectively resist the arrival of the British in Australia; that is, the British had settled rather than invaded Australia.

Gradually that view changed. Henry Reynolds's 1982 book *The Other Side of the Frontier* described how the Aborigines reacted to the arrival of the British. Other authors showed that while the Aborigines didn't organise for war in the Western way, they adapted their own way of war and conducted guerrilla campaigns against the settlers across the nation (see Chapter 3).

Critics such as Keith Windschuttle have claimed that the authors fabricated the evidence, and that the numbers of deaths were highly exaggerated. While much evidence is still contested, there seems little doubt that the Aborigines did try to resist the invasion of the Whites. A question remains as to how the frontier wars should be integrated into the larger story of Australian military history, with its focus on the experiences of Australians fighting overseas.

# *Breaker Morant Wasn't a War Criminal*

In February 1902 two Australians, Harry (Breaker) Morant and Peter Handcock, then serving as officers in an irregular unit in South Africa, were executed by the British Army for murdering Boer prisoners (see Chapter 4). The Australian Government only found out about the court martial and execution after the event. Before the war Morant was a well-known figure and many Australians believed that he was innocent. Over the following century several histories and novels appeared about the case, which also received widespread publicity though the successful 1980 movie *Breaker Morant*.

Some authors claim that Morant and Handcock acted in accordance with secret orders from the British commander-in-chief, Lord Kitchener, to kill every Boer in sight. In their view, the British executed them to cover up the criminal order.

Recent scholarship by Craig Wilcox, however, has found no evidence of Kitchener's secret order and he has debunked many of the other claims. Yet in February 2010 the Commonwealth Attorney General sent a petition to the Queen seeking to have Morant and Handcock pardoned because their court martial was unfair and the lawyers involved had made mistakes.

## Incompetent British Generals Recklessly Sacrificed First World War Diggers

The notion that incompetent British generals recklessly sacrificed Australian soldiers in the First World War is based on two ideas.

- British generals were generally incompetent and insensitive, as illustrated by the well-known comment that the British soldiers were 'lions led by donkeys'.

- Because the Australian troops were 'colonials' the British generals used them as they saw fit. For example, an incompetent British general caused the slaughter of the 5th Division at Fromelles in July 1916 (see Chapter 7).

The truth is more complex. The Australian Government handed its troops over to Britain and Australian generals had no say over where and how their troops were used. In the first two years of the war all generals struggled to come to grips with the industrial scale of the fighting on the Western Front. All Empire troops, including Tommies (British troops) and Diggers, were affected equally by the decisions of the high command.

At brigade and division level, on the whole Australian generals proved no more competent than their British counterparts. Major General Harold Walker, a British officer who led the 1st Division for almost three years, was an excellent commander and argued with his British Army superiors to protect his Australians troops. By the last year of the war the Australian Corps had very good commanders, but there were many good British commanders also.

## Monash Could've Commanded the British Army on the Western Front

After the First World War the British military historian, Sir Basil Liddell Hart, declared: 'If that war had lasted another year [Monash] would almost certainly have risen from commander of the Australian corps to command of an army; he might even have risen to be Commander-in-Chief'. Liddell Hart's comments grew out of a dispute with the British military establishment. But a recent Monash biography has restated the view with approval.

There is no doubting Monash's ability. In commanding the Australian Corps with its five divisions he was already heading a force the size of an army. But he was just one of many corps commanders on the Western Front. As Monash was a part-time Jewish soldier from a dominion it is unlikely that the British military establishment would have agreed to his commanding a British Army on the Western Front. The Canadian Corps commander, General Currie, had held his command longer than Monash and was thought to be equally capable.

Glib and unsustainable comments that Monash would have risen to become Commander-in-Chief detract from the more reasoned conclusion that he was an outstanding and innovative commander.

## Curtin Demanded that Churchill Return Our Troops from the Middle East

Admirers of the Second World War Prime Minister John Curtin love to paint the image of the man who stood up to Winston Churchill, demanding that the Australian troops return from the Middle East to defend Australia. Curtin's performance is praiseworthy, but the facts are slightly different.

When Japan entered the war three Australian divisions were in the Middle East, but the Australian Government didn't request that they be sent home. By the end of December 1941 Japanese troops had advanced through Malaya, but the 8th Australian Division there hadn't yet been in action. The British Government wanted to send reinforcements and on 3 January 1942 it asked the Australian Government if it would permit two of its divisions in the Middle East to be transferred to the Far East. The Australian Government agreed.

By mid-February the troops were aboard a convoy heading towards the Far East when Singapore surrendered and the Japanese landed in Sumatra. Churchill suggested that the convoy be diverted to Burma, which the Japanese had invaded. Against strong demands from Churchill and US President Roosevelt, Curtin insisted that the convoy proceed to Australia. Churchill had no option but to accede to the demand, but Curtin allowed most of one of the divisions to help defend Ceylon (Sri Lanka) for four months.

## HMAS Sydney was Sunk by a Submarine

The story that the Australian cruiser *Sydney* was sunk by a Japanese submarine three weeks before the outbreak of the Pacific War is one of the quirkiest myths in Australian military history.

In November 1941 *Sydney* engaged the German merchant raider *Kormoran* off the Western Australian coast and was lost with all hands. *Kormoran* was also sunk, but most of her crew were rescued and became prisoners of war. Because no trace of *Sydney* was found numerous rumours developed to try to explain how an armed merchant ship could have sunk a cruiser. In his 1981 book *Who Sank The Sydney?* Michael Montgomery claimed that the cruiser was torpedoed by a Japanese submarine and the Australian sailors were killed to cover up Japan's involvement. Other history books have included this story.

In the face of the various theories and agitation by special interest groups, a parliamentary committee conducted an inquiry, which reported in 1999 that there was no evidence of a Japanese submarine in the vicinity. In March 2008 a multimillion dollar search project, partly funded by the government, located *Sydney*'s wreck. A further inquiry, assisted by photographic analysis of the wreck, was held in 2009. The two inquiries and the expensive search confirmed that the 1957 Official History's account was largely correct; namely, that inexplicably *Sydney*'s captain ventured too close to *Kormoran,* which crippled *Sydney* with its opening salvo.

## The Battle of the Coral Sea Stopped the Japanese from Invading Australia

Each year since 1946 the Battle of the Coral Sea, fought by aircraft from American and Japanese aircraft carriers in early May 1942, has been celebrated in Australia, usually accompanied by the statement that the battle saved Australia from invasion. Many people who lived through the war believed this statement to be true, bolstered by Prime Minister John Curtin's claim, during the battle, that the security of Australia was at stake.

In fact the Japanese invasion fleet, which turned back as a result of the battle, was not heading for Australia but for Port Moresby (see Chapter 14). In February and March 1942 Japanese Imperial Headquarters in Tokyo debated whether to invade Australia. Eventually the Japanese decided to put aside plans to invade Australia. Instead, they would isolate Australia by seizing Port Moresby in New Guinea, the southern Solomon Islands, Fiji, Samoa and New Caledonia.

If the Japanese had captured Port Moresby the strategic situation would have been transformed. Just possibly, the Japanese might have reconsidered their plans about the invasion. But that is a far cry from saying the Battle of the Coral Sea saved Australia from invasion.

## The Kokoda Battles Saved Australia

In 1992 the Australian Prime Minister, Paul Keating, claimed that at Kokoda 'young Australian men fought for the first time against the prospect of the invasion of their county'. The Diggers certainly thought they were fighting to protect Australia. Recent books, as well as the 2006 movie *Kokoda*, have continued the theme. In the previous section I explain that the Japanese didn't intend invading Australia, but rather wanted to capture Port Moresby. But what if the Australians hadn't stopped the Japanese on the Kokoda Trail?

When the Japanese South Seas Force under General Horii began the advance over the Kokoda Trail on 26 August 1942 he hoped to reach Port Moresby. But within days the Japanese high command ordered Horii to stop on the crest of the mountains. Stretching his orders, Horii continued on, looking for a suitable place to stop. Perhaps he secretly hoped that he could still reach Port Moresby, but he lacked supplies for the task. Eventually, after he reached Ioribaiwa, on 18 September Horii was ordered to withdraw to the north coast.

If the Australians hadn't delayed Horii's force, just possibly it might have crossed the mountains, but short of supplies it would have been defeated by the superior, well-supplied Australians in the Port Moresby area. Whichever way you interpret the campaign, the Kokoda battles didn't save Australia from invasion. But they were important battles because a different outcome would have put great pressure on Australia.

## The Menzies Government Planned to Defend Australia from the Brisbane Line

Some myths are generated for political purposes. Before the August 1943 federal election, a Labor Government minister, Eddie Ward, claimed that in 1941 Australian generals had planned to defend Australia by withdrawing behind a 'Brisbane Line'. He criticised the previous Menzies Government for endorsing such a defeatist defence plan, and cited a missing document as evidence.

There were elements of truth in the allegation. A senior Army general had proposed such a plan late in 1941, but it had never been endorsed by the Menzies Government. Military commanders in all states sensibly prepared local defences. Troops based in Brisbane prepared defences, in the same way as those in Sydney, Townsville and elsewhere. Those soldiers who dug and manned the Brisbane defences still believe that the Brisbane Line was real.

At the Royal Commission to investigate Ward's claims about the missing document, Ward refused to cooperate. The Royal Commission found that no document was missing. The Labor Government won the 1943 election.

In 1978 I asked Fred Daly, the only surviving member of the Curtin Government (and who had been elected unexpectedly in 1943), whether the Brisbane Line existed. 'It must have,' he replied as quick as a flash. 'We won the election didn't we?' Perhaps Daly was joking, but I'm not so sure.

## The Whitlam Government Withdrew the Troops from Vietnam

The Labor Party Opposition opposed the deployment of Australian troops to South Vietnam in 1966, and Gough Whitlam, who succeeded Arthur Calwell as party leader, continued to advocate the abolition of conscription and Australia's withdrawal from Vietnam. Dr Jim Cairns, a leading leftwing member of the Labor Opposition, led mass movements against the war.

But the Vietnam War didn't figure as prominently in the lead-up to the December 1972 federal election as might have been expected after Labor's record of opposition to it. Australia's withdrawal from Vietnam actually began in November 1970, and in August 1971 Prime Minister McMahon announced the complete withdrawal of all remaining combat troops. The last Australian operation took place in September 1971 and the last combat troops left Vietnam in February 1972. Army advisers wound down their training tasks and by December 1972 only 128 of them remained. After the election, the Whitlam Government immediately halted conscription and ordered the remaining soldiers home.

In later years many Australians forgot about the sequence of events. They remembered that the Labor Party had advocated the withdrawal from Vietnam and the end of conscription, and that it had been elected on those policies. They remembered the Whitlam Government's decision to end conscription. In a technical sense Whitlam withdrew the last troops from Vietnam, but the decision to withdraw was actually made more than two years before he was elected.

# Index

*Note:* Page number in bold type indicate maps

1939–45 Star, 34

## • A •

Aboriginal servicemen, 314
Aborigines
  frontier wars, 44–49, 413–414
  resistance to white invasion, 413–414
  traditional warfare, 45–46
aces, 148, 199, 212
Acheson, Dean, 318
Adachi Hatazao, 258, 261, 277
ADF Joint Logistics Command, 28
Admiralty Islands, Australian occupation, 82
Advisory War Council, 286–287, 288, 289
Afghan National Army, 391
Afghanistan
  American Special Forces soldiers wage war against Taliban, 385
  areas of operations involving Australians, **387**
  Australian involvement in ongoing war against Taliban, 390–392
  US attacks on terrorist targets, 385
Africa Star, 34
aircraft. *See also* types of aircraft, e.g. AP3-C Orion aircraft
  use in First World War, 120, 131–132, 134, 204
aircraft carriers, 25
aircraft production, 293
Airey, Captain Henry, 51, 66
*Al Fao* (Iraqi oil tanker), 380
Al Qaeda, 385, 387
Alexander, Field Marshal Sir Harold, 199
*All Quiet on the Western Front* (novel), 106
Allen, Major General Arthur ('Tubby'), 169, 174, 184, 248, 251, 252
Allenby, Field Marshal Sir Edmund ('Bull'), 129, 130, 131, 134, 135, 136
Allied Air Forces, 255
Allied Naval Forces, 255
American War. *See* Vietnam War
Amiens, 145

Anderson, Lieutenant Colonel Charles, 226
Angola, 370
Antill, Major General John, 99, 124
Anzac Day
  celebration in the midst of the Korean War, 313
  marches and memorial services, 18, 104, 153
Anzac legend
  and Australian identity, 15
  honouring, 18–19
  Man with the donkey, 97
Anzac spirit
  demonstration at Gallipoli, 103
  demonstration in later wars, 15
Anzacs. *See* Australian and New Zealand Army Corps (Anzac corps)
ANZAM (Australia, New Zealand and Malaya) arrangement, 322, 323
ANZUK Brigade, 334
ANZUS Alliance, 319, 323, 386
AP3-C Orion aircraft, 27, 386, 388, 390
Arab–Israeli wars, 364
armed forces
  at Federation, 74
  basic structure, 21
  structure following Second World War, 36
Armentières, 108
armoured personnel carriers (APCs), 26, 347
army organisations, 26
Army of the Republic of Vietnam (ARVN), 336–338, 351
Army Reserve, 31
Army Reservists, 31
artillery techniques, 109–110, 114–115, 116, 118–119
artillery units, 27, 44, 52
Ashmead-Bartlett, Ellis, 101
Asquith, Herbert, 101
Auchinleck, Field Marshal Sir Claude, 195, 196, 197, 198
austerity campaign, 295
'Australia Remembers' year, 19
Australia–US alliance, 318–319, 379, 385
Australian Active Service Medal, 34

Australian Army. *See also* Citizen Military Forces (CMF); Regular Army
  artillery units, 27
  depletion following First World War, 159, 160
  during Second World War, 246
  early disagreement over role, 75, 76–77
  establishment and organisation along British lines, 76
  fighting units, 25, 26
  front-line personnel, 31–32
  infantry battalions, 25, 26
  jungle warfare training, 259
  naming and numbering of units, 26
  operation prior to 1976, 28
  ranks, 33–34
  restrictions on size and role under Defence Act, 75, 76, 83, 161
  structure, 25
  structure following Second World War, 306
Australian Army Medical Women's Service (AAMWS), 298
Australian Army Nursing Corps (AANC), 297, 298
Australian Army Training Team Vietnam (AATTV), 336–338
Australian Central Flying School, 131, 149
Australian Comforts Fund, 299
Australian Commonwealth Horse, 70
Australian Defence Force. *See also* Special Forces Task Groups
  control of, 23–24
  enforcement of sanctions in Iraq, 383–385
  forces in Persian Gulf–Iraq region following 2003 Iraq War, 390
  formation, 28–29
  purpose, 377
  Special Forces Group, 388
  Special Operations Command, 388
Australian Defence Force Academy, 28
Australian Electoral Commission, 370
Australian Federal Police, 369, 376
Australian Flying Corps, 131, 147–149, 204, 205
Australian Government, role in military alliances, 22–23
Australian Horse (NSW), 61, 63
Australian identity, and the Anzac legend, 15
Australian Imperial Force (AIF) (1st AIF)
  deployment to France in 1916, 108
  deployment to France in, 108
  enlarging after Gallipoli, 106–108
  formation, 73
  raising of, 83–84
  volunteers, 30–31

Australian Imperial Force (AIF) units and formations
  1st Anzac Corps, 108
  2nd Anzac Corps, 108, 115
  Anzac Mounted Division, 107, 124–125, 125, 126, 128, 129, 130, 131, 134, 135, 136
  1st Division, 84, 88, 91, 107, 140
  1st Division Artillery, 84
  2nd Division, 107
  3rd Division, 107, 139, 140
  4th Division, 107, 139, 140
  5th Division, 107, 110
  1st Light Horse Brigade, 84, 88, 123, 124, 125, 127, 129
  2nd Light Horse Brigade, 87, 88, 123, 124, 125, 127, 129
  3rd Light Horse Brigade, 123, 124, 126, 128, 133, 135
  4th Light Horse Brigade, 123, 127, 128, 130, 133, 135
  5th Light Horse Brigade, 133, 134, 135
  8th Light Horse Regiment, 99
  10th Light Horse Regiment, 99, 131, 135
  1st Infantry Brigade, 84, 88
  2nd Infantry Brigade, 84, 88, 107
  3nd Infantry Brigade, 84, 88, 144
  4th Infantry Brigade, 87, 88, 107, 139, 140, 142, 144
  5th Infantry Brigade, 107, 113, 146
  6th Infantry Brigade, 114, 144, 146
  7th Infantry Brigade, 142
  8th Infantry Brigade, 107
  9th Infantry Brigade, 140, 143
  11th Infantry Brigade, 144
  12th Infantry Brigade, 107, 139, 144
  13th Infantry Brigade, 107, 139, 141, 142, 143
  15th Infantry Brigade, 110, 141, 142, 144
  4th Infantry Battalion, 98
  9th Infantry Battalion, 107
  10th Infantry Battalion, 107
  11th Infantry Battalion, 107
  23rd Infantry Battalion, 111
  36th Infantry Battalion, 140
  45th Infantry Battalion, 139
  59th Infantry Battalion, 142
  1st Australian Tunnelling Company, 115
Australian Imperial Force (2nd AIF)
  First Army, 237
  Second Army, 237
  1st Australian Corps, 164, 174, 234, 237, 248, 253, 260, 277
  2nd Australian Corps, 237, 273, 275, 278

6th Division, 163, 164, 165, 171, 174, 190, 234, 235, 236, 252, 273, 277, 278, 271, 277, 278
7th Division, 164, 165, 170, 182, 184, 190, 234, 235, 236, 237, 248, 252–253, 259, 260, 261, 264, 266, 277, 280, 281
8th Division, 222, 224, 227, 229
9th Division, 165, 190–191, 196, 197–198, 202, 259, 260, 264, 271, 277, 278, 280
11th Division, 266, 275
16th Brigade, 169, 170, 174, 176, 177, 178, 184, 252, 253, 277
17th Brigade, 169, 170, 174, 176, 185, 255, 257, 258, 277
18th Brigade, 164, 171, 190, 191, 192, 248, 249, 250, 254, 259, 266, 281
19th Brigade, 170, 174, 175, 176, 177, 252, 277
20th Brigade, 190, 191, 192, 200, 201, 260, 262, 263, 280
21st Brigade, 183, 184, 185, 248, 250, 251, 253, 261, 265, 266, 281
22nd Brigade, 187, 227
24th Brigade, 190, 191, 198, 202, 260, 262, 263, 264, 280
25th Brigade, 182, 183, 184, 185, 190, 251, 252, 253, 261, 265, 266, 281
26th Brigade, 190, 191, 197, 198, 201, 202, 263, 264, 278
27th Brigade, 224, 225
2/1st Battalion, 180
2/2nd Battalion, 176
2/3rd Battalion, 177, 184, 185
2/7th Battalion, 180, 181, 256
2/8th Battalion, 180
2/11th Battalion, 180, 181
2/14th Battalion, 250
2/28th Battalion, 198
A Company, 184, 226
B Company, 226
raising of, 163
training in Palestine, 164
Australian Labor Party, 288, 306, 356, 377
Australian Mounted Division, 129, 130, 133, 135
Australian Naval and Military Expeditionary Force, 80–82
Australian and New Zealand Army Corps (Anzac corps)
  in Egypt, 87, 87–88
  formation, 87
  initial composition, 88
  New Zealand and Australian Division, 88, 91
Australian police, in peacekeeping missions, 364–365, 369, 376
Australian Regiment, 60, 61, 63
Australian Security Intelligence Organisation (ASIO), 307
Australian War Cabinet, 174, 274–275, 292
  under Curtin Government, 287–288
  under Menzies Government, 286
Australian War Memorial (Canberra), 153
Australian Women's Army Service (AWAS), 298
Australian Women's Land Army, 297
Australianists' view on defence of Australia, 14, 76
Australia's involvement in wars
  compared to other countries, 11
  fighting style, 22
  global conflicts, 15
  impact on shaping the nation, 1, 15
  in South-East Asian region, 321–322
  wars in which Australians have fought, 13
  why Australians have fought, 13–14

• B •

Badcoe, Major Peter, 337
Baker, General John, 29
Barbey, Rear Admiral Daniel, 260, 262
Bardia, 168–170
Barrie, Admiral Chris, 29
Barrow, Major General Guy, 129
*Bartolomeo Colleoni* (Italian cruiser), 166, 408
Barton, Edmund, 74
'Battle of Australia', myth of, 19
Battle of Bismarck Sea, 256–257, 409–410
Battle of Britain pilots, 211
Battle of Bullecourt, 114
Battle of Colenso, 57
Battle of the Coral Sea, 242, 417–418
Battle of Diamond Hill, 64
Battle of Fromelles, 110–111
Battle of Leyte Gulf, 271–272
Battle of Long Tan, 344–345, 349, 411
Battle of Magersfontein, 57
Battle of Midway, 243–244
Battle of Passchendaele, 115–117
Battle of Romani, 125–126
Battle of the Somme, 109–112
Battle of Vinegar Hill, 40–41
battleships, 24
BE2c aircraft, 131
Beale, Brigadier Pat, 331, 339
Bean, Charles, 18, 85, 101, 110, 111
Beasley, John, 287
'Beat Hitler First' strategy, 186
Beatson, Stuart, 68–69

Beaumont, Admiral Alan, 29
Beersheba, 129–130, 406
Bennet, Donald, 215
Bennett, Major General Henry Gordon, 187, 222, 224, 225, 227, 237
Bennett, General Phillip, 29, 352
Bennett, Corporal Alfred, 51
Berbera, 167
Bergonzoli, General Annibale, 169, 171
Berlin Blockade, 307
*Berrima* (liner), 81
Berryman, Lieutenant General Sir Frank, 184
Bethune, Captain Frank, 141
biological weapons, 384
Birdwood, Field Marshal Sir William, 87, 90, 91, 92, 93, 97, 101, 106, 108, 114, 117, 142
'bite and hold' tactic, 114–115, 116
*Black Hawk Down* (film), 373
Black Hawk helicopters, 371
Black Line, 47
Blackburn, Brigadier Arthur, 185, 234
Blackforce, 234
Blake, Major General Murray, 353
Blamey, General Sir Thomas
  reputation as a military leader, 178, 195, 291, 396
  service in First World War, 83, 85, 111, 142
  service in Second World War, Middle East theatre, 23, 163, 164, 165, 171, 195, 202
  service in Second World War, Pacific theatre, 236, 248, 251, 252, 254, 259, 260, 262, 267, 271, 274–275, 280, 283, 284
Bligh, Captain William (Governor), 41
blitzkrieg (lightning war), 22
Bloomfield, Lance Corporal Stephen, 333
Boase, Major General Alan, 266
Boer War
  advance to Pretoria, 61–62
  arrival of Australians, 60
  Australian Hill, 62
  Australian Regiment, 60, 61, 63
  background, 55
  beginnings of conflict, 56
  the Black Week, 56–58
  Bushveldt Carbineers, 69–70
  Citizen Bushmen, 65
  Colesberg battles, 62
  commando raids and counterattacks, 57
  cost of Australian involvement, 70
  countering the Boer raids, 65–67
  defending Eland's River, 66–67
  departure of contingents from Australian colonies, 58–59
  guerilla warfare, 67–70
  Harry 'Breaker' Morant, 18, 69–70, 414
  humiliation at Wilmansrust, 69
  Imperial Bushmen, 65, 68
  Koster River ambush, 65–66
  march to Bloemfontein, 63
  opposition and support for Australian involvement, 59
  patrolling the veldt, 67–70
  Southern Africa 1895–1902, **57**
  Sunnyside Hill skirmish, 62
  tradition of the Light Horse, 122
bomber crews, front-line role, 32
bombers, described, 27
Borneo Battles
  battle at Balikpapan, 280–281
  overview, 277–278
  regaining British Borneo, 280
  seizing Tarakan for oil and airfields, 278–279
Botha, General Louis, 64
Bougainville
  Australian occupation, 82
  peacekeeping mission, 368–369
Boxer Rebellion, 52–53
Bragg, 2nd Lieutenant Lawrence, 119
brainwashing, of prisoners in Korean War, 316
Brazier, Lieutenant Colonel Noel, 99
*Breaker Morant* (film), 18, 69, 414
Brett, Lieutenant General George, 236
Bridges, Major General Sir William, 77, 83, 85, 91, 93, 95, 106
Briggs, Lieutenant General Harold, 324
Brisbane Line, 289, 419
Brisbane, Thomas (Governor), 47
Bristol Beaufighters, 208
Bristol Fighter (aircraft), 131
British Commonwealth Far East Strategic Reserve (BCFESR), 325, 326
British Commonwealth Occupation Force (BCOF), 304–305, 322
British Empire
  Australian support at outbreak of First World War, 79
  Australia's status as a dominion, 73, 83
  importance of trade with dominions, 165
  military demands following Second World War, 322
  status at end of Second World War, 322
British Expeditionary Force (BEF), on Western Front, 106
British Fifth Army, 114
British infantry units, in Australian colonies, 41, 42, 43–44
British Pacific Fleet, 282–283

British War Cabinet, 174, 288, 290
British–Indian Army, 187
Broome, Richard, 49
Bruce, Stanley, 159, 288
Brumfield, Brigadier Lou, 341
Brunei, 329, **330**
Buick, Sergeant Bob, 344
Bull, Gunner Joe, 225
Bullen, Lieutenant Colonel John, 353
Buller, Lieutenant General Sir Redvers, 57, 58
Burchett, Wilfred, 316
*Buresk* (German collier), 86
Burma, 235
Burma–China theatre, 282
Burnett, Captain John, 188
Bush, George H W, 378
Bush, George W, 385, 387
Butler, Richard, 384
Butterworth air base, 328, 330, 334
Byers, 2nd Lieutenant Douglas, 331

• **C** •

C-130 Hercules transport aircraft, 27, 386, 388, 390
cadets military training, 76
Cairns, Jim, 419
Callaghan, Major General Cecil, 227
Calwell, Arthur, 300, 340, 419
Calwell, Wing Commander Clive, 199
Cambodia, 370–371
Cameron, Major General Duncan, 50
campaign medals, 34
Campbell, Brigadier Ian, 180–181
Campbell, Brigadier Wally, 326
Canberra bombers, 328
Cape Helles, 88, 90, 93, 95
Caribou transport aircraft, 354
Carpender, Vice Admiral Arthur, 255
Carrington, Major General Frederick, 65
Carson, Sergeant Arthur, 177
Carver, Flying Officer Robert, 354
Casey, Richard, 290
casualties
  in Australian Flying Corp, 149
  in First World War, 151–152
  at Gallipoli, 92, 94, 95, 96, 97, 99, 101, 103
  Korean War, 318
  Malayan Emergency, 328
  in Palestine Campaign, 126, 128, 129
  Vietnam War, 338, 339, 341, 345, 348, 351, 352, 357
  on Western Front, 109, 110, 111, 112, 116, 141, 142, 147

cavalry, 26
Central Bureau, 273
Central Intelligence Agency (CIA), in Vietnam, 337
Ceylon, 235
Chalmers, Vice Admiral Don, 380
Chamberlain, Joseph, 56
Charrington, Brigadier Harold, 174
Chauvel, General Sir Harry
  reputation as a military leader, 397
  service in the Boer War, 397
  service in First World War, 84, 97, 100, 107, 123, 124, 125, 126, 127, 128, 129, 130, 133, 134, 135, 406
Chaytor, Major General Edward, 129, 133, 135
chemical weapons, 383
Chetwode, Lieutenant General Sir Philip, 126, 128, 129
Chidgey, Major Colin, 384
Chief of the Defence Force (CDF), role, 24, 28, 29
Chief of the Defence Force Staff, 28, 29
Chief of Joint Operations, 29
Chifley Government
  concentration on national development, 305
  defence and foreign policy, 305
  and occupation of Japan, 304–305
Chifley, Joseph Benedict (Ben), 287, 290
Chilton, Brigadier Sir Fred, 176, 266, 281
Chinese Air Force, in Korean War, 311
Chinese Army, in Korean War, 312–318
chlorine gas, 119
chocos, 246
Churchill, Sir Winston, 88
  failure to consult with Australian Government, 167
  and return of Australian troops from Middle East, 202, 235, 416
  support for Greece, 173–174
Citizen Military Forces (CMF), 31, 306, 363
Civil Alien Corps, 296
Civil Construction Corps, 296
Claret patrols, 331, 332
Clark, 2nd Lieutenant Neville, 348
Clemenceau, Georges, 152
Clisby, Flying Officer Leslie, 211
Clowes, Lieutenant General Cyril, 248, 249
'coalition of the willing', 389
coalition warfare, 22–23
Coastwatchers, 279
Cobby, Air Commodore Harry, 148, 267, 271
code-breaking units, 241, 273
Cold War. *See also* Korean War; Malayan Emergency; Vietnam War
  overview, 302
  responding to, 307

Cole, Brigadier Kevin, 365
collective security, 306
Collins, Vice Admiral Sir John, 166, 267, 272, 281, 319
   reputation as a military leader, 397–398
   service in First World War, 397
   service in Second World War, 397–398, 408
colonial era conflicts
   Battle of Vinegar Hill, 40–41
   Boxer Rebellion, 52–53
   defensive fortifications, 44
   Eureka Stockade, 42–43
   frontier wars with Aborigines, 44–49, 413–414
   loyalty to the British Empire, 49–53
   Maori Wars, 43, 50
   the Rum Rebellion, 41
   Sudan, 51
   troops as strike-breakers, 52
colonisation of Australia
   establishment of new settlements, 42
   first infantry battalion, NSW Corps, 40
   first Marines, 40
   impact of discovery of gold, 43
   raising of volunteer and militia units, 43–44
   reasons for, 39
   role of British infantry units, 41, 42, 43–44
Combined Chiefs of Staff, 290
Commander-in-Chief of the ADF, 24
commissioned officers, 33
Commonwealth Aircraft Corporation, 206, 293
Commonwealth Military Forces, 74, 75
Commonwealth Naval Forces, 77, 78
Commonwealth War Graves Commission, 153
communism, concern over spread, 323
Companion of the Order of Australia (AC), 35
compulsory military service
   in the 1960s, 31
   following First World War, 158, 160
   in part-time militia, 76–77
   reintroduction following outbreak of Second World War, 162
conscription
   1916 and 1917 referendums, 112–113, 288
   for militia, 76–77, 162, 289
   opposition to, 288, 355–356, 419
Conspicuous Service Medal (CSM), 35
constitutional monarchy, 24
Cook, Sir Joseph, 79, 153
Cordner, Commodore Lee, 380
Cosgrove, General Peter
   awards, 35
   command of INTERFET, 374
   reputation as a military leader, 398–399
   role as Chief of Defence Force, 24, 29

counterinsurgency warfare, 328
Country Party, 289
Courtney, Able Seaman John, 82
Cox, Brigadier General 'Fighting Charlie', 126, 127
Cox, Major General Herbert, 107, 113
Coxen, Major General Walter, 119
Crace, Rear Admiral John, 242
creeping barrage tactic, 109–110
Cresswell, Squadron Leader Dick, 311
Creswell, Rear Admiral Sir William, 78
Crete Campaign
   Allied dispositions 19 May 1941, **179**
   casualties, 182
   evacuation, 181, 182
   naval battles, 181–182
   purpose, 179
   Retimo, 180–181
Crimean War, 43
Crocker, Colonel John, 370
Cronje, General Piet, 63
cruisers, 24, 78
Crutchley, Rear Admiral Victor, 249, 267
Cunningham, Phillip, 40
Cunningham, Admiral of the Fleet Sir Andrew, 166, 176, 181–182
Curtin Government
   Allied Works Council, 26, 296
   austerity campaign, 295
   and Brisbane Line, 419
   election, 187
   handing control to MacArthur, 290–291
   Manpower Directorate, 294, 297
   National Security Regulations, 293–294
   Prime Minister's War Conference, 291
   rationing and restrictions, 294–295
   War Cabinet, 287–288
Curtin, John
   death, 290
   as opposition leader, 286
   as prime minister, 187, 287, 288
   relationship with MacArthur, 291
   and return of troops from Middle East, 202, 234–235, 416
   and threat of Japanese invasion, 417–418
Cyprus, UN peacekeeping mission, 364–365

•  •

Dakar, 167
Dakota DC3 transport aircraft, 27, 311, 325
Dallaire, Lieutenant General Romeo, 373
Dallas, Stan, 149

Dalley, William (Premier), 51
Daly, Fred, 419
Daly, Lieutenant General Sir Thomas, 315
Dardanelles Commission, 101
Darling, Herbert, 68
Darwin, Japanese attack, 232
Davies, Walter Karri, 56, 60
Dawes, Lieutenant William, 41
Day, Captain Edward, 48
De Haviland Mosquitos, 208
Deakin, Alfred, 78, 79
Dedman, John, 288, 295
*Defence Act 1903* (Cwlth), 75, 76, 83, 161, 163, 246, 304
defence of Australia
   Australianists' view, 14, 76
   following Federation, 74–78
   Imperialists' view, 14, 77
   impetus for Federation, 52
   lack of preparation for Second World War, 158–161
   threat of Japanese invasion, 15
defence fortifications, 44
defence policy. *See also* Australia–US alliance; Western Alliance
   ANZAM, 322, 323
   ANZUS Treaty, 323
   of Chifley Government, 305, 306–307
   cooperation with Britain, 321, 322
   Five Power Defence Arrangements, 334
   following Second World War, 303
   'Forward Defence', 321
   Howard Liberal–National Party Government, 14–15, 385, 386, 389, 390
   new focus on preventing enemy approaching Australian coast, 377
   relations with Indonesia, 330, 332
   Rudd Government, 15, 390
   SEATO, 232
   support of US in Afghanistan, 386
Denehey, Lance Corporal Paul, 333
Department of Aircraft Production, 293
Department of Defence, formation, 28
Department of Munitions, 293
Dernancourt, 139–140
Derrick, Lieutenant Tom ('Diver'), 263
Deschaineux, Captain Emile, 272
Desert Mounted Corps, 129, 133, 134
destroyers, 24–25, 78
DHC-4 Caribou transport aircraft, 27
'diggers', origins, meaning and use of term, 30, 93, 105
disarmament, following First World War, 158, 160
Distinguished Service Cross (DSC), 35

Distinguished Service Order (DSO), 35, 315
Dixon, Owen, 290, 363
Dobell, Lieutenant General Sir Charles, 126, 128, 129, 281
dogfights, 120
'domino' theory, 323
Donaldson, Trooper Mark, 35, 391, 392
Draft Resisters Union, 356
Drakeford, Arthur, 288
*Dumont d'Urville* (French sloop), 167–168
Dunkirk evacuation, 164
Dunning, Adam, 376
Dunstan, Lieutenant General Sir Donald, 351

## • E •

East Timor, 374–376
Eastern Front, First World War, 106, 137
Eather, Major General Ken, 251, 261, 281
Eddy, Major George, 62
Egypt, 364
Egyptian Expeditionary Force, 124, 126, 129
Eichelberger, Lieutenant General Robert, 253, 270
Eisenhower, President Dwight, 323
El Alamein, 196–202, **197**, 409
election supervision, in Namibia, 369–370
Elliott, Major General Harold ('Pompey'), 110, 111, 141, 407
*Emden* (German cruiser), 74, 80, 85–86
Empire Air Training Scheme (EATS), 163, 206–211
*Espero* (Italian destroyer), 166
ethnic violence, 373
Eureka Stockade, 42–43
Evans, Gareth, 370, 377
Evatt, Herbert Vere (Bert), 287, 306
Evetts, Major General John, 184
expeditionary forces, 51
explosives detection dogs, 391

## • F •

F-111 strike aircraft, 27
F/A-18 Hornets, 27
Fadden, Arthur, 187, 288, 289, 310
Federation, 52
Federation of Malaysia. *See* Malaysia
Felsche, Major Susan, 368
Ferguson, Major Bruce, 312, 313, 313–314
Fergusson, Brigadier Maurice, 273
fighter aircraft, described, 27
fighter pilots, front-line role, 32
fighting styles, national differences, 22

Finucane, Wing Commander Paddy, 212
First Boer War, 56
First World War. *See also* names of specific battles, campaigns or theatres of war, e.g. Gallipoli Campaign
    Australia's contribution, 72
    Australia's support for Britain, 79
    casualties, 151–152
    commemoration of the fallen, 153
    dominance of artillery, 118–119
    end of the war, 147, 151
    first Australian overseas military expedition to seize German colonies in New Guinea, 80–82
    first RAN operation, 80
    first shot by British armies, 81
    gas attacks, 119–120
    impact of new technology, 117
    myth of incompetent British Generals sacrificing diggers' lives, 415
    Paris peace conference, 152–153
    repatriation of Australian servicepeople, 151
    use of aircraft, 120
Fisher, Andrew, 79, 113
Five Power Defence Arrangements, 334
the Fleet, 25
Fletcher, Vice Admiral Jack, 242
Ford, Major General Tim, 364
Forde, Francis (Frank), 252, 287, 288, 290
foreign policy
    of Chifley Government, 305, 306
    as a dominion of the British Empire, 73, 159
Forrest, Sir John, 75
Fort Nepean Battery, 81
forts, 44
*Forty Thousand Horsemen* (film), 18
Frankland, Noble, 218
Fraser (Liberal–National Party Coalition) Government, defence policy, 377
Fraser, Malcolm, 369–370
Free French Forces, 167
French Army, on Western Front, 106
French, General Sir John, 60, 62, 63
Frewen, Colonel John, 376
Freyberg, Lieutenant General Sir Bernard, 174, 178, 179–181
frigates, 25
Frontier Wars with Aborigines
    Aboriginal warfare, 45–46
    denial of magnitude of conflict, 49
    early conflict, 44–45
    extent of, 47–48
    settler, military and police methods of warfare, 46–47

## • G •

Gallagher, Colonel Kerry, 366
Galleghan, Brigadier Frederick, 225
Gallipoli Campaign
    AE2 in the Sea of Marmara, 93–94
    August offensives, 97–101
    and Australian identity, 15
    casualties, 92, 94, 95, 96, 97, 99, 101, 103
    charging the Turkish line at Helles, 95
    Chunuk Bair, 100–101
    conditions, 96–97, 102
    contribution of Light Horse brigades, 123–124
    decision to land troops on Gallipoli Peninsula, 88
    decision to withdraw, 101–102
    digging in at Anzac Cove, 92–93
    evacuation, 101–103
    holding on, 94–97
    landing at Anzac Cove, 90–94, 405–406
    Lone Pine, 98–99
    the Nek, 99–100
    overview, 89–90
    reassessing and remembering, 103–104
    repelling Turkish attack at Anzac Cove, 95–96
    Sari Bair ridge, 91, 92, 100
    Suvla Bay, 99, 101
    'The Silent Stunt', 102
    thrusting inland, 92
*Gallipoli* (film), 18, 99
Gallipoli Peninsula, **90**
Garland, Brigadier Alf, 332
gas attacks, at the Western Front, 119–120
gas masks, 119–120
Gatacre, Major General William, 57
Gaulle, President Charles de, 167, 168
Gellibrand, Major General Sir John, 83, 114, 139, 144
Geneva Agreement 1954, 335
George Cross, 316
George, David Lloyd, 152
George Medal, 297
German Africa Corps, 189
German Army, offensive against French at Verdun, 108
Germany, fighting style, 22
Getting, Captain Frank, 249
Giarabub, 171
Gillespie, Lieutenant General Ken, 386
Gilmore, Brigadier Gus, 386
Gipps, George (Governor), 48
Gladiator biplanes, 199

Glasgow, Major General Sir William, 124, 139, 141, 143
Glossop, Captain John, 86
Goble, Air Vice-Marshal Stanley, 205
Godfrey, Brigadier Arthur, 191, 202
Godley, Lieutenant General Sir Alexander, 91, 93, 106, 108, 115
gold
  discovery in Australia, 43
  discovery in Transvaal, 56
Gorbachev, Mikhail, 378
Gordon, Major General Charles, 51
Gordon, Harry, 314
Gordon, Major General Ian, 364, 367
Gordon, Brigadier General John, 63
Gose, Major Francis, 40
Gough, Lieutenant General Sir Hubert, 111, 114
Governor General, role as Commander-in-Chief of the ADF, 24
Graham, Major General Stuart, 345
Grant, Brigadier General William, 130, 133, 406
Gration, General Peter, 29
'Great Australian Silence', 49
Greater East-Asia Co-prosperity Sphere, 240
Greek Campaign. *See also* Crete Campaign
  Allied withdrawal from Greece, **175**, 176–177
  Brallos Pass, 177
  decision to send troops, 173–174
  evacuation, 178
  German invasion, 174, 175–176
  Olympus-Aliakmon Line, 174
  Pinios Gorge, 176
  Thermopylae line, 177
Greville, Brigadier Philip, 316
Grogan, Brigadier General George, 142
Guadalcanal, 249
Guest, 2nd Lieutenant Robert, 331
Gulf of Oman, 380, **380**
Gulf War (1991), 381
Gull Force, 231
Gun Ridge, 91, 92
Gurkhas, at Gallipoli, 100
Gurney, Sir Henry, 325

### • H •

Hague Convention, 297
Haig, Field Marshal Viscount Douglas, 106, 109, 113, 114, 117, 140
Haking, Lieutenant General Sir Richard, 110, 111
Halsey, Admiral William, 249, 254, 272
Ham, Captain David, 68

Hamel, 144
Hamilton, General Sir Ian, 63, 64, 90, 93, 95, 97, 98, 101, 103, 406
Hampton, Captain Brad, 384
Handcock, Lieutenant Peter, 69–70, 414
Handley-Page Halifax bombers, 131, 208
Harris, Air Chief Marshal Sir Arthur, 214
Harrison, Sergeant Kenneth, 225
Hart, Sir Basil Liddell, 415
Hassett, General Sir Francis, 28, 315
Hawke, R J L (Bob), 379
Hawke (Labor) Government
  commitment to join US-led coalition forces to drive Iraq out of Kuwait, 381
  commitment to join US-led multinational naval force to enforce sanctions against Iraq, 379
  peacekeeping missions, 377
Hawker Hurricane fighters, 208
Hayden, Bill, 377
Hazebrouck, 140
helicopters, 350
Herbert, Flying Officer Michael, 354
Herring, Lieutenant General Sir Edmund, 237, 252, 253, 259, 262
Hewitt, Air Vice-Marshal Joseph, 410
Hickey, Pansy, 294
Hindenburg Line, 113–114, 138, 146–147
Hiroshima, 305
HMAS *Adelaide*, 161, 168, 379, 380
HMAS *AE1* (submarine), 82
HMAS *AE2* (submarine), 93–94
HMAS *Anzac*, 388, 389
HMAS *Armidale*, 233
HMAS *Arunta*, 267, 272, 277, 281
HMAS *Australia*, 78, 81, 150, 158, 161, 167, 242, 249, 267, 272
HMAS *Bataan*, 281, 308, 317
HMAS *Brisbane*, 150, 355, 380, 381
HMAS *Canberra*, 161, 249, 408
HMAS *Centaur*, 297
HMAS *Cerebus*, 74
HMAS *Colac*, 277
HMAS *Darwin*, 379, 380, 388
HMAS *Dubbo*, 277
HMAS *Hobart*, 161, 167, 242, 249, 277, 281, 355
HMAS *Huon*, 150
HMAS *Kanimbla*, 165, 185, 267, 272, 388, 389
HMAS *Kuttabal*, 243
HMAS *Manoora*, 165, 267, 272
HMAS *Melbourne*, 78, 81, 86, 150
HMAS *Napier*, 194, 282, 283
HMAS *Nepal*, 282, 283
HMAS *Nestor*, 194

HMAS *Nizam*, 194, 282, 283
HMAS *Norman*, 282
HMAS *Paramatta*, 150, 194
HMAS *Perth*, 161, 182, 234, 355, 408
HMAS *Pioneer*, 78, 150
HMAS *Protector*, 53, 74
HMAS *Quiberon*, 282, 283
HMAS *Quickmatch*, 282, 283
HMAS *Shoalhaven*, 308, 317
HMAS *Shropshire*, 267, 272, 281
HMAS *Stuart*, 161, 166, 194
HMAS *Success*, 379
HMAS *Swan*, 150, 161, 277
HMAS *Sydney*, 24, 78, 80, 81, 86, 150, 161, 166, 188, 317, 355, 380, 381, 408, 417
HMAS *Teal*, 333
HMAS *Torrens*, 150
HMAS *Vampire*, 161, 166
HMAS *Vendetta*, 161, 166, 194, 195
HMAS *Voyager*, 161, 166, 194
HMAS *Warramunga*, 267, 272, 277
HMAS *Warrego*, 80, 150
HMAS *Waterhen*, 161, 166, 194
HMAS *Westralia*, 165, 267, 272
HMAS *Yarra*, 150, 161, 185, 194
HMS *Defender*, 194
HMS *Encounter*, 78, 81, 82, 150
HMS *Exeter*, 234
HMS *Havock*, 408
HMS *Newfoundland*, 277
HMS *Prince of Wales*, 187, 223
HMS *Queen Elizabeth*, 93
HMS *Repulse*, 187, 223
HMS *Vita*, 194
HMS *Wallaroo*, 53
Hoad, Major General John, 60, 63, 76
Hobbs, Lieutenant General Sir J J Talbot
　reputation as a military leader, 399–400
　service in First World War, 59, 84, 113, 141, 144, 407
Hodges, Corporal Adrian, 372
Hodgeson, Major General Sir Henry, 129, 133
Holmes, Major General William, 80, 82, 113, 116
Holt, Harold, 288
Honner, Lieutenant Colonel Ralph, 250
Hore, Lieutenant Colonel Charles, 66
Horii, Major General Tomitaro, 247, 253, 418
Hornet strike aircraft, 386, 388, 389
*Hotel Rwanda* (film), 373
Howard, Major General Brian (Horrie), 351
Howard, Colonel Keith, 364
Howard Liberal–National Party Government, defence policy, 14–15, 385, 386, 389, 390

Howden, Captain Harry, 167
Howse, Major General Sir Neville, 64, 83
Hughes, Brigadier General Frederick, 97, 99, 123, 124
Hughes, Major General James, 333
Hughes, Pat, 211
Hughes, Major General Ron, 351
Hughes, W M (Billy), 59, 79, 113, 151, 152–153, 288, 289
Hurley, Lieutenant General David, 372
Hutton, Major General Sir Edward ('Curly'), 63, 74–75, 77, 122
Hyakutake, Lieutenant General Harukichi, 244

# • I •

*Ibn Khaldoon* (Iraqi ship), 380
icons used in this book, 6–7
Idriess, Trooper Ion, 96, 128
Imamura, General Hitoshi, 276
immigration policy, post-war immigration program, 300, 305
Imperial Camel Corps Brigade, 126, 127, 129, 133
Imperial conference 1911, 77
Imperial Light Horse, 60
Imperial Mounted Division, 127–128, 129
Imperialists' view on defence of Australia, 14, 77
Indian Army, 133
Indonesia
　confrontation with Malaysia, 329–334
　and East Timorese independence, 374–376
　UN peacekeeping mission 1947–51, 362–363
infantry battalions, front-line role, 25, 31
International Force East Timor (INTERFET), 374–376
International Military Tribunal for the Far East, 283–284
International Peace Monitoring Team (Solomon Islands), 376
Israel, 363–364
Iran–Iraq war, 366–367
Iranian Revolutionary Guard, 366
Iraq
　1991 Gulf War, 381
　areas of operations involving Australians, **383**
　fighting style, 22
　humanitarian relief to Kurdistan, 382–383
　insurgency following US-led invasion, 390
　invasion of Iran, 366
　invasion of Kuwait, 378–379
　sanctions and weapons of mass destruction, 382

UNIIMOG supervision of withdrawal from Iran, 366
US-led invasion, 387–389
weapons inspection, 383–385
Iraq Medal, 34
Iraq War 2003, 389
Iroquois helicopters, 350
Irwin, Major Bert, 352
Israel, use of pre-emptive strikes, 22
Iwo Jima, 282

## • J •

Jacka, Captain Albert, 96, 112
Jackson, Brigadier David, 343, 344, 345
Japan, League of Nations mandate over former German islands, 152, 158
Japanese Occupation, 304–305
Japanese possible invasion of Australia
  and Battle of the Coral Sea, 417–418
  Japanese plans, 239–240
  and Kokoda Campaign, 418
Japanese threat
  assessing enemy intentions, 241
  recognising, 186
  responses to, 158, 235–236
*jihad*, 385
Joffre, Marshal Joseph, 109
Johnston, Major George, 40–41
Joint Chiefs of Staff (JCOSA), 322
jungle patrolling, 328
jungle warfare, 256, 259

## • K •

Kalimantan, 329, 330
*kamikaze* (suicide) tactic, 272, 283
*Kanowna* (liner), 80, 81
Kapyong, 410
Kashmir, UN peacekeeping mission 1950–85, 363
Keating, Paul, 418
Kemal, Mustafa, 91–92, 100
Kennedy Regiment, 80, 81
Kenney, General George, 255, 260
Khan, Brigadier Colin, 353
Kingsbury, Private Bruce, 250
Kinkaid, Vice-Admiral Thomas, 271
Kirkpatrick, Private John Simpson, 97
Kitchener, Field Marshal Lord, 67, 68, 76, 87, 102, 414
Kittyhawk fighters, 199, 208

Knight, Lieutenant Colonel Guy, 68
Kokoda Campaign
  battle at Isurava, 251, 408
  cost of victory, 254
  counterattack, 252–255
  regaining Kokoda, 252
  retreating over the Kokoda Trail, 250–251
  significance, 254, 408–409, 418
  stalemate at Buna, Gona and Sanananda, 253–254
  trapping the Japanese at Oivi–Gorari, 253
*Kokoda* (film), 418
*Königsberg* (German cruiser), 150
Korean War
  27th Commonwealth Brigade, 311
  advancing to Yalu River, 312
  air war, 311
  Australia's commitment, 310
  battle of Kapyong, 313–314, 410
  brainwashing prisoners, 316
  capture of Maryan San, 315
  casualties, 318
  contribution of 3 RAR, 309–318
  as the 'forgotten war', 318
  holding on at the Hook, 317–318
  involvement of Australian Navy, 308, 317
  involvement of Chinese Air Force, 311
  involvement of Chinese Army, 312–318
  the Jamestown Line, 315–316
  Korea 1950–53, **309**
  outbreak, 308
  retreating to Seoul, 312–313
  role of UN, 308
*Kormoran* (German merchant raider), 188, 417
Kressenstein, Colonel Freiherr Kress von, 125
Krueger, General Walter, 255, 270
Kruger, Paul (President, Transvaal), 56, 67
Kurdish people, 372
Kurdistan, humanitarian relief, 382–383
Kuwait
  1991 Gulf War, 381
  Australian headquarters for ADF units in region, 386
  invasion by Iraq, 378–379

## • L •

Laden, Osama bin, 385
Lalor, Peter, 43
Lamb, Lieutenant Colonel Jimmy, 177
Lancaster bombers, 27, 208
Lancaster House Agreement, 365

Land Army, 297
landmine clearing, 371
Lang, Jack, 287
Lark Force, 230
Lavarack, Lieutenant General Sir John, 139, 164, 182–184, 192, 193, 234, 237
Lawrence, T E ('Lawrence of Arabia'), 132
Lea, General Sir George, 331
League of Nations, 152, 158
Leane, Brigadier General Ray, 139
Leary, Vice-Admiral Herbert, 236
Leggatt, Lieutenant Colonel William, 233
Legge, Major General James, 76, 83, 101, 107, 111, 113
Lerew, Wing Commander John, 230
Lewis, Major General Duncan, 388
Lewis, Essington, 293
Liberal Party, 289
Light Horse tradition, 122–124
  charge at Beersheba, 129–130, 406
Lincoln bombers, 325, 328
Little, Captain Robert, 149
Littler, Corporal Bryan, 333
Lloyd, John, 252
Lone Pine, 98–99
Long, Gavin, 274
Long Tan Day, 345
Lord Haw Haw, 194
Ludendorf, Field Marshal Erich, 137, 138, 146
Lustreforce, 174, 178
Lyon, Lieutenant Colonel Ivan, 279

## • M •

McAliney, Lance Corporal Shannon, 372
MacArthur, General Douglas
  arrival in Australia, 236
  battles in New Guinea, 246, 248, 251, 252, 253, 254–255, 257, 258, 262, 264, 266–267, 267, 274
  commander of UN force in Korea, 308, 310–313
  as Commander-in-Chief of South West Pacific Area, 290–291
  and conscription, 289
  forces under his command, 236–237
  and occupation of Japan, 308
  operations in Borneo, 277–278, 280
  operations in the Philippines, 270–273
  reputation, 238, 287
  return of Australian troops from Middle East, 202
  sidelining of Australian forces, 269, 271
  surrender of Japan, 283
Macarthur, John, 41
McBride, Phillip, 310
McCarthy, Captain Peter, 364
McCay, Major General Sir James Whiteside, 59, 84, 92, 95, 107, 113, 405
McDaniel, Lieutenant Colonel Dan, 386
McDevitt, Ben, 376
MacDonald, General Sir Arthur, 29
McDonald, Major General Bruce, 331
McEwen, John, 288
Mackay, Lieutenant General Sir Iven, 98, 169, 170, 174, 175, 176, 237, 259, 262
MacLaurin, Colonel Henry, 84, 94
McMahon, William, 420
McNamara, Air Commodore Frank, 132
McNarn, Major General Maurie, 388
Macquarie, Lachlan (Governor), 41
Madden, Private 'Slim', 316
Magic intercepts, 241
Makin, Norman, 288
Malaya
  1941–42, **224**
  independence from Britain, 329
  reinforcing, 186, 187, 222–223
Malayan Communist Party (MCP), 324–325
Malayan Emergency
  bombing the jungle, 325
  Briggs Plan, 324–325
  casualties, 328
  countering the 'CTs', 324–325
  deployment of Australian troops, 326–327
  Federal Priority Operations, 326
  Framework operations, 326
  Malayan states, 1950, **327**
  RAAF involvement, 325
  tracking and ambushing in the jungle, 328
Malaysia, proposal for Federation, 329
Malaysian conflict with Indonesia
  Australian commitment to assist with defence, 330
  Australian patrolling of borders of Borneo, 331–332
  defence support from Britain, 329
  patrol of Borneo's borders by Australian troops, 331–332
  proposal for Federation of Malaysia, 329
  RAN involvement, 333–334
  Sarawak, Sabah, Brunei and Kalimantan, **330**
  securing the peace, 334
  Special Air Service's secret missions, 332–333
Malta, 322–323
Man with the donkey, 97
Manchurian campaign, 282
Mannix, Daniel, 113

Manpower Directorate, 294, 297
Maori Wars, 43, 50
maps
   Afghanistan — areas of operations involving Australians, **387**
   Allied dispositions 19 May 1941, **179**
   Allied invasion of Syria, 1941, **183**
   Allied withdrawal from Greece, **175**
   Australian Corps offensive, Northern France, August–October 1918, **145**
   Borneo and the Philippines, **270**
   Cyrenaica and northern Egypt, **191**
   Eastern New Guinea, **247**
   Eastern New Guinea and the Solomon Islands, **240**
   El Alamein area, **197**
   envelopment of Huon Peninsula, **259**
   German offensive, northern France, March–April 1918, **138**
   Iraq — areas of operations involving Australians, **383**
   Korea 1950–53, **309**
   Malaya and Singapore 1941–42, **224**
   Malayan states, 1950, **327**
   Middle East theatre 1940–41, **168**
   northern approaches to Australia, **229**
   Northern Palestine and southern Syria, 1917–18, **132**
   peacekeeping missions 1947–2007, 362
   Persian Gulf and Gulf of Oman, **380**
   Phuoc Tuy Province, Bien Hoa and Long Khanh provinces, 341–343, **342**
   Sarawak, Sabah, Brunei and Kalimantan, **330**
   Sinai Desert and southern Palestine, 1917–18, **125**
   South Vietnam showing ARVN corps zones, **338**
   Southern Africa 1895–1902, **57**
   territories of Papua and New Guinea including Bougainville, **274**
   Western Front 1916–17, **109**
maritime patrol aircraft, 27
Martin, Pilot Officer Colonel K E, 217
Maygar, Lieutenant Colonel Leslie, 69
Medal for Gallantry (MG), 35, 374
medals
   for bravery, 35
   campaign or service medals, 34
   categories, 34
   for good work, 35
   issued under Australia system, 34
   issued under Imperial system, 34
   rosettes and bars, 35

Mediterranean Expeditionary Force, 90
Member of the Order of Australia (AM), 35
Member of the Order of the British Empire (MBE), 35
Menzies Government (Liberal–Country Party Coalition)
   decision to send troops to Vietnam, 339–340
   national service scheme for CMF, 322–323
   and occupation force in Japan, 305
   re-election, 355
Menzies Government (UAP)
   Advisory War Council, 287
   and the Brisbane Line, 289, 419
   building wartime industries, 293
   rationing, 294
   response to outbreak of Second World War, 161–163
   War Cabinet, 286
Menzies, Robert, 161
   and British War Cabinet, 290
   policy making, 288
   reluctance to send troops to Greece, 174
   reputation, 162
   resignation as prime minister, 187
merchant navy, during Second World War, 296–297
Mesopotamia, 148
Messines, 115, 120
Meteor 8 jet fighters, 311
Methuen, Lieutenant General Lord, 57, 60
Metson, Corporal John, 251
Middle East, commitment to support British in early 1950s, 322–323
Middle East theatre — Second World War. *See also* North Africa Campaign
   1940–41, **168**
   capture of Bardia, 168–170
   capture of Giarabub, 171
   capture of Tobruk, 170
   Cyrenaica campaign, 171
   scaling down of Australian forces, 196
Middleton, Pilot Officer Rawdon, 215
MiG-15 jet fighters, 311
Mikawa Gunichi, 249
Mike Force battalions, 339
Milford, Major General Edward, 258, 281
military acronyms and abbreviations, 23
Military Cross (MC), 35
military history, forms of, 17–18
military leaders
   role, 395
   top ten Australians, 396–404
military ranks, 33–34
military service, nature of, 30

military speak, 23
military training
　prior to First World War, 77
　universal training, 76
militia, during Second World War, 163, 246, 289
Milne Force, 248
Minister for Defence, role, 24
Mirage fighters, 334
Mitsuo, Rear Admiral Fuchida, 232
Monash, General Sir John
　reputation as a military leader, 204, 400, 415–416
　service in First World War, 59, 87, 97, 100, 106, 115, 139, 140, 142, 144, 145, 146, 151, 407, 415–416
Mont St Quentin, 146, 407
Montagnard battalions, 337, 339
*Montevideo Maru*, 231
Montgomery, Michael, 417
Montgomery, Field Marshal Sir Bernard, 189, 199–202, 409
Moor, Major Hatherly, 62
Morant, Lieutenant Harry 'Breaker', 18, 69–70, 414
moratorium marches, 356
Morris, Major General Basil, 237, 248
Morshead, Lieutenant General Sir Leslie
　reputation as a military leader, 401
　service in Second World War, 191–193, 196–197, 201–202, 409
Moten, Brigadier Murray, 255–256, 257
Mountbatten, Admiral of the Fleet Lord, 290
Mucke, Lieutenant Helmuth von, 86
Mugabe, Robert, 365
Muller, Captain Karl von, 86
Multinational Force and Observers (MFO), 364, 375
munitions manufacturing, 161, 293
Munitions Supply Board, 293
Munro, General Sir Charles, 102
Murdoch, Keith, 101
Murray, Lieutenant Colonel Henry ('Mad Harry'), 143
Murray, Major General John, 191
Murray, General Sir Archibald, 124, 125, 126, 127, 128, 129
Mussolini, Benito, 168
Mustang fighters, 311
mustard gas, 119
Myall Creek massacre, 47, 48

● *N* ●

Namibia, 369–370
Nashos. *See* National Servicemen
national development, following Second World War, 300
National Liberation Front, 344
National Service Scheme
　to bolster CMF, 322–323
　introduction in 1964, 339–340, 355
National Servicemen, 31, 343, 347
Native Police, 46–48
Nauru, Australian occupation, 82
naval defence
　after Federation, 77–78
　at Federation, 74, 77
　limiting of following end of First World War, 158
　under Singapore Strategy, 159
naval training, 78
Navy Reservists, 31
New Britain, 82
New Britain Force, 255
New Caledonia, coup, 167–168
New Guinea
　Australian control after First World War, 152
　Australian occupation, 82
　seizing of German colonies, 80–82
New Guinea Battles (1942–44)
　air attacks on Wewak, 260
　battle at Wau, 255–256
　battle of Guadalcanal, 249
　battle of Savo Island, 249
　capture of Kaiapit, 265
　capture of Salamaua, 257–258
　capture of Sattelberg, 263
　Death Valley, 265
　destroying Japanese shipping in the Bismarck Sea, 256–257
　Eastern New Guinea, **247**
　envelopment of Huon Peninsula, **259**
　figuring out jungle warfare, 254–258
　Finisterre Range offensive, 264–267
　Finschhafen campaign, 262–264
　forcing the Japanese from the Huon Peninsula, 262–264
　halting Japan's south Pacific offensive, 246–251
　Japanese capture of Kokoda, 248
　Japanese landing at Buna, 248
　Mandang, 266–267
　Milne Bay victory, 249–250
　overview, 245
　paratroops secure Nadzab, 261
　retreating over Kokoda trail, 250–251
　seizing of Japanese base at Lae, 258–261
　Shaggy Ridge, 265–266
　training and preparation for Lae campaign, 259–260

# Index

New Guinea Force, 248, 254, 259, 260
New Ireland, Australian occupation, 82
New Zealand, casualties in First World War, 103, 151
New Zealand Infantry Brigade, 88
New Zealand Mounted Rifles Brigade, 88, 107, 124, 128, 129
Nimitz, Field Admiral Chester, 243
Nimmo, Lieutenant General Robert, 363
no-man's land, 117
non-combat military service overseas, 16–17
non-commissioned officers (NCOs), 33
Normandy landing, 216–217
North Africa Campaign
 Cyrenaica and northern Egypt, **191**
 El Alamein, 196–202, **197**
 overview, 189–190
 preventing the Germans from reaching the Nile, 196–199
 RAAF contribution, 198–199
 Rats of Tobruk, 194
 retreat from Benghazi, 190–192
 Ruin Ridge, 198
 siege of Tobruk, 192–195
 Tel el Eisa, 197–198
North Atlantic Treaty Organization (NATO), 386
North Vietnamese Army (NVA), 339, 344, 351, 352, 353
Northcott, Lieutenant General Sir John, 304, 305
NSW Colonial Forces, 74
NSW Corps (Rum Corps), 40, 41
NSW Lancers, 58–59, 60, 61, 63
NSW Marine Light Infantry, 53
NSW Medical Corp, 59, 61, 63
NSW Mounted Police, 47
NSW Mounted Rifles, 61, 63, 64, 68

Ochiltree, Lieutenant Colonel James, 326
O'Connor, Lieutenant General Sir Richard, 168, 170, 171
O'Donnell, Colonel Jake, 348
O'Dowd, Major Bernard, 314
Okinawa, 282
Old Guard (NSW), 231
Onslow, Brigadier General George Macarthur, 133, 135
Operation Bel Isi, 369
Operation Jaywick, 279
Operation Rimu, 279

Orme, Major General Craig, 367
Osborn, Brigadier Bruce, 369
Osmena, Sergio, 271
Owen, Evelyn, 293
Owen submachine guns, 293
Oxenbould, Chris, 380
Ozawa, Vice-Admiral Jizaburo, 272

P3-C Orion maritime patrol aircraft, 334
Pacific War (1941–45). *See also* New Guinea Battles (1942–44)
 1944 campaigns that crushed Japan, 281–282
 Aitape offensive, 277
 arrival of US servicemen in Australia, 235–239
 attack on Darwin, 232
 Battle of the Coral Sea, 242
 Battle of Leyte Gulf, 271–272
 Battle of Midway, 243–244
 battles in Borneo, 277–281
 beginning, 222–223
 Borneo and the Philippines, **270**
 Bougainville offensives, 275–276
 Eastern New Guinea and the Solomon Islands, **240**
 fall of Singapore, 226–228
 garrisoning the islands to the North, 228–235
 guerilla war in Timor, 233
 invasion of Java, 234
 invasion of Malaya, 223–226
 Japanese surrender, 283
 Japan's intentions, 239–242
 joining the British Pacific Fleet in Japanese waters, 282–283
 Kota Bharu, 222
 liberation of Philippines, 270–273, 281
 Lingayen Gulf, 272
 loss of Ambon, 231–232
 loss of Rabaul, 230–231
 massacre at Parit Sulong, 226–227
 mopping up operations in New Guinea and the islands, 273–277
 northern approaches to Australia, **229**
 overview, 220, 221–222
 overview of final year, 269–270
 Pearl Harbor, 222
 punishing war criminals, 283–284
 submarine attack in Sydney Harbour, 243
 territories of Papua and New Guinea including Bougainville, **274**
 treatment of prisoners of war by Japanese, 228

Pacific War *(continued)*
  watching over Rabaul, 276
  Wewak offensive, 277
Pacific War Councils, 290
Page, Earle, 288, 290
Palestine Campaign
  Anzac Mounted Division, 124–125, 125, 126, 128, 129, 130, 131, 135
  attacks on Amman, 132–133
  Australian Mounted Division, 129, 130, 133, 134
  capture of Beersheba, 129–130
  capture of Damascus, 134–136
  capture of Jerusalem and Jericho, 130–131
  capture of Magdhaba and Rafah, 126
  casualties, 126, 128, 129
  defence of Egypt, 124–127
  Desert Column, 126, 129
  Desert Mounted Corps, 129, 133, 134
  first battle at Gaza, 128
  Imperial Camel Corps Brigade, 126, 127, 129, 133
  Imperial Mounted Division, 127–128, 129
  Northern Palestine and southern Syria, 1917-18, **132**
  overview, 121–122
  role of aircraft, 131–132
  Romani battle, 125–126
  second battle at Gaza, 128–129
  Sinai Desert and southern Palestine, 1917–18, **125**
  Surafend, 136
Panzer Army Africa, 196
Papua New Guinea, conflict with Bougainville, 368
Parbury, Lieutenant Colonel Philip, 184
Patey, Rear Admiral Sir George, 78, 80, 81, 82
patrol boats, 25
Payne, Warrant Officer Keith, 337
Peace Monitoring Group (Bougainville), 368–369, 375
peacekeeping commitments
  Australia as an 'international good citizen', 377
  Australia's contribution to peacekeeping missions 1947–2007, 362
  overview, 360, 361
peacekeeping missions
  Afghanistan, 371
  Bougainville, 368–369
  Cambodia, 370–371
  Cyprus, 364–365
  East Timor, 374–376
  end of Iran-Iraq war, 366–367
  enforcing peace, 371–376
  Indonesia, 362–363
  Kashmir, 363
  keeping Arabs and Israelis apart, 363–364
  Namibia, 369–370
  rebuilding shattered nations, 369–371
  Rwanda, 373–374
  Sinai Desert, 364, 377
  Solomon Islands, 376
  Somalia, 372–373
  UN berets and helmets, 375
  Western Sahara, 367–368
  Zimbabwe, 365
Pearl Harbor, 221, 222
Percival, Lieutenant General Arthur, 222, 223, 227
Persian Gulf, 185
Persian Gulf, and Gulf of Oman, **380**
Philippines, 270–273, 281
Phillip, Captain Arthur (Governor), 41, 44–45
Phillips, Major General Peter, 352
phosgene gas, 119, 120
Pilcher, Lieutenant Colonel Thomas, 60
pilots, aces, 148, 199, 212
Pinjarra massacre, 47
Plumer, General Sir Herbert, 68, 115, 116
Pockley, Captain Brian, 82
police. *See* Australian police
Porter, Major General Selwyn, 280
Potts, Brigadier Arnold, 250
Pozières, 110, 111, 120
pre-emptive strikes, 22
Price, Colonel Tom, 52, 61
prisoners of war
  in Korean War, 316
  treatment by Japanese, 228
propaganda campaigns, 194

Queensland Mounted Infantry, 61, 63, 66, 68, 125
Queensland Permanent Military Forces, 125

Rabaul, 230–231
Radford, Admiral Arthur, 319
Radford–Collins agreement, 31
Ramsay, Major General Alan, 264, 273, 276
Ramsey, Brigadier Wayne, 373
RAN College (Geelong), 78
rationing and restrictions, 294–295
Rats of Tobruk Association, 194
Rawlinson, General Sir Henry, 109, 110, 145, 146
Raws, Lieutenant Alexander, 111
RE8 reconnaissance aircraft, 131, 148

# Index

Red Cross, Voluntary Aid Detachments, 298
refugees, following Second World War, 300
Regional Assistance Mission to Solomon Islands (RAMSI), 376
Regular Army. *See also* Royal Australian Regiment, 31, 306, 307
Regular Navy personnel, overseas service, 31
*Remo* (Italian ship), 165
reparations, First World War, 152
Retired List, 363
Returned Servicemen's League, 296
Rey, General Koos de la, 66
Reynolds, Henry, 414
Ricardo, Lieutenant Colonel Percy, 60
Richardson, Major General John, 51
*Richelieu* (French battleship), 167
Ridgeway, General Matthew, 312–313
Roberts, Field Marshal Lord, 58, 61, 62, 63, 64, 67
Robertson, Lieutenant General Sir Horace ('Red Robbie'), 169, 170, 305, 309
Rommel, Erwin, 171, 189, 190, 191, 192–193, 196, 409
*Romolo* (Italian ship), 165
Roosevelt, Franklin, and return of Australian troops from Middle East, 202, 235
Rosenthal, Major General Sir Charles, 59, 140, 143
Ross, Lieutenant Colonel David, 382
Ross, Major Robert, 40
Rowell, Lieutenant General Sir Sydney, 178, 248, 251
Royal Air Force (RAF), 149, 204
Royal Air Force Palestine Brigade, 131
Royal Australian Air Force (RAAF)
  aircraft and personnel prior to Second World War, 161, 206
  Article XV squadrons, 209–210
  bombing operations, 213–218
  categories of aircraft, 27
  contribution to Second World War, 203
  deployment to Malta, 323
  early struggle for survival, 205–206
  fighter squadrons, 211–212
  flying boat squadrons, 212–213
  formation, 147–148, 205
  front-line personnel, 32
  involvement in enforcing sanctions in Iraq, 385
  involvement in Korean War, 308, 311
  involvement in US-led invasion of Iraq, 388–389
  involvement in war against terrorism, 386
  in New Guinea campaigns, 271
  Non-Article XV squadrons, 209–210
  and occupation of Japan, 305, 308
  operation prior to 1976, 28
  ranks, 33–34
  squadrons in Europe and Middle East in Second World War, 209–210
  squadrons, wings and groups, 28
  structure and permanent strength following Second World War, 306
Royal Australian Air Force Nursing Service (RAAFNS), 298
Royal Australian Artillery, formation, 52
Royal Australian Navy (RAN)
  battle of Leyte, 272
  enforcement of sanctions against Iraq, 380, 384
  first victory, 86
  formation, 73, 78
  front-line personnel, 32
  involvement in 1991 Gulf War, 381
  involvement in Korean War, 308, 317
  involvement in Malaysian defence, 333–334
  involvement in US-led invasion of Iraq, 388–389
  in the Mediterranean, 166
  modernisation prior to Second World War, 160–161
  operation prior to 1976, 28
  protection of coastal trade, 165–166
  ranks, 33–34
  role, 24
  service in First World War, 149–150
  ships, 24–25
  and Singapore Strategy, 159, 160
  sinking Italian ships, 166
  structure and permanent strength following Second World War, 306
  support for war against terrorism, 386
Royal Australian Regiment
  1st Battalion (1 RAR), 315–317, 327, 328, 340, 341, 352, 372
  2nd Battalion (2 RAR), 317–318, 326–327, 328
  3rd Battalion (3 RAR), 309–318, 327, 328, 330–331, 351–352
  4th Battalion (4 RAR), 331, 348, 357
  5th Battalion (5 RAR), 341, 353
  6th Battalion (6 RAR), 341, 349
  8th Battalion (8 RAR), 356
  service in Vietnam, 346
Royal Flying Corps, 149, 204
Royal Military College (Duntroon), 76, 85
Royal Naval Air Service, 149, 204, 205
Royal Navy, 77, 149–150
Royal Navy Auxiliary Squadron, 77
Royston, Brigadier General 'Galloping Jack', 126
Rudd Government, defence policy, 390
Rudd Labor Government, defence policy, 15
Rum Corps, 40, 41

Rum Rebellion, 41
Rush, Trooper Harold, 99
Russell, Sergeant Andrew, 387
Russian Revolution, 137
Russo-Japanese war, 76, 78, 79
Rwanda genocide, 373–374
Rwanda Patriotic Army (RPA), 37
Ryrie, Major General Sir Granville, 87, 97, 123, 124, 126, 127

• S •

Sabah, **330**
Sabi (explosives detection dog), 391
Sabre fighters, 311, 328, 334
Saddam Hussein, 366, 378, 382, 387
salients, 110, 115
saluting, 33
Sanders, General Otto Liman von, 91, 100, 133, 134, 135
Sanderson, Lieutenant General John, 370–371
Sandford, Lieutenant Colonel Augustus, 81
Sandover, Brigadier Ray, 181
Sarawak, **330**
Saunders, Captain Reg, 314
Sautot, Henri, 168
Savage, Sister Nell, 297
Save Our Sons, 356
Savige, Lieutenant General Sir Stanley, 169, 174, 257, 258, 273, 275–276
Scherger, Air Chief Marshal Sir Frederick, 267, 340, 401–402
Scott, Lieutenant Colonel Jack, 231
Scullin Government, 160, 287
Scullin, James, 288
SEATO (South East Asia Treaty Organization), 323
Second Australian Imperial Force. *See* Australian Imperial Force (Second AIF)
Second Indochina War. *See* Vietnam War
Second World War. *See also* names of specific campaigns, theatres or battles; Pacific War (1941–45)
   Australian contribution, 156, 157
   Australia's entry into war, 161–162
   balancing the war effort, 291–292
   building wartime industries, 293
   casualties, 299–300
   civilian involvement in Australia, 285–286
   cooperation with allies, 290–292
   cost, 299–300
   domestic politics, 289–290
   early signs of approaching war, 160
   first battles involving Australians (1940–41), 165–171
   impact on shaping the nation, 15, 299–300
   marshalling of nation's resources, 292–295
   outbreak and spread of war, 157
   the phoney war, 162
   treaty with Japan, 318
   volunteer work in support of war effort, 299
   women in the armed services, 298
   women in the workforce, 297
seige of Tobruk, 32
Serong, Brigadier Francis (Ted), 336–337
service medals, 34
servicepeople
   amateurs, regulars and nashos, 30–31
   the 'diggers', 30
   on the front-line, 31–32
   and nature of military service, 30
   role of women, 30
*Shake Hands with the Devil* (memoir), 373
Shalders, Vice Admiral Russell, 380
Shedden, Sir Frederick, 280, 291
Sheean, Ordinary Seaman Teddy, 233
Sherrin, Sergeant Chad, 347–348
ship-building, 293
ships. *See* names of specific ships, e.g. HMAS *Sydney*
*Shoho* (Japanese aircraft carrier), 242
*Shokaku* (Japanese aircraft carrier), 242, 243
Short Sunderland flying boats, 208
Sidi Barrani, 168
signals intelligence, 241
Simpson, Warrant Officer Ray, 337
Sinai Desert
   1917–18, **125**
   peacekeeping mission, 364, 377
Sinclair-MacLagan, Major General Ewen, 84, 91, 92, 116, 139, 140, 144, 405
Singapore
   1941–42, **224**
   fall to Japanese, 226–228
Singapore Strategy, 159, 160, 186, 222
Six Days War, 364
Skinner, Lieutenant Colonel Roy, 364
slang, originating from First World War, 148
Slater, Major General Mick, 376
Smith, Brigadier General Clement, 127, 129
Smith, Lieutenant Colonel Harry, 344
Smith, Captain Keith, 132
Smith, Captain Ross, 131–132
Smuts, Field Marshal Jan, 204

Smyth, Major General Sir Neville, 113
Snowy Mountains Hydro Electricity Scheme, 300
Solomon Islands, 376
Somalia, guarding aid workers, 372–373
Sopwith Camels, 148
South Pacific Peacekeeping Force, 368
South West Africa People's Organisation (SWAPO), 369–370
South-East Asia, Australia's involvement in regional conflicts, 321–322
Southern Africa 1895–1902, **57**
Special Air Service (SAS)
  in Afghanistan, 386
  enforcement of weapons inspections in Iraq, 385
  invasion of Iraq, 389
  operations in Vietnam War, 349
  secret missions in Borneo, 332–333
  in Somalia, 373
Special Forces Task Groups
  in Afghanistan since September 2005, 390–392
  Australian Reconstruction Task Force in Afghanistan, 391
  initial operations in Afghanistan (Operation Slipper), 386–387
  Mentoring and Reconstruction Task Force in Afghanistan, 391
  for US-led invasion of Iraq, 388–389
Special Reconnaissance Department, 270
Spee, Admiral Maximillian Graf von, 80
Spence, Major Alexander, 233
Spence, Wing Commander Lou, 311
Spender, Percy, 310, 318
Spitfires, 27
Spruance, Vice-Admiral Raymond, 243
SS *Chicago*, 243
SS *Enterprise*, 243
SS *Hornet*, 243
SS *Houston*, 234
SS *Lexington*, 242
SS *Midway*, 381
SS *Missouri*, 283
SS *Pfalz*, 81
SS *Ranger*, 381
SS *Yorktown*, 242, 243
Stanner, W E H, 49
Stevens, Major General Sir Jack, 273, 277
Steyn, Martinus (President, Orange Free State), 56, 68
Stirling bombers, 208
Stoker, Lieutenant Commander Henry, 93–94
Stopford, Lieutenant General Frederick, 98, 101
strategic bombing, 204, 217–218, 282

strike-breaking
  by militia, 52, 75
  by Regular Army, 307
Sturdee, Lieutenant General Sir Vernon, 235, 273
submarines, 25, 166, 243
Sudan, 51
Suez Crisis, 363
Sukarno, President, 329
Sunderland flying boats, 27, 208, 212–213
supply ships, 25
Sydney Harbour, colonial defences, 41–42
Synnot, Admiral Sir Anthony, 29
Syrian Campaign
  Allied invasion, 183–184, **183**
  capture of Damascus, 184–185
  capture of Damour, 185
  French counterattack at Merjayoun, 184
  purpose, 182

Taliban
  Australian involvement in operations in Afghanisan, 386–387, 390–392
  support for Al Qaeda, 385
  US-led attacks against, 385
tank warfare, at Hamel, 144
tanks, described, 26
Tarakan, 278–279
Taylor, Brigadier Harold, 227
tear gas, 120
technological advances, impact on First World War, 117
terrorism, September 11 attacks, 385
Teshima, General Futsataro, 283
Theodore, Edward, 296
Third Ypres, 115–117, 120
Thomson, Brigadier David, 331
Thurgar, Major Jack, 365
Thursby, Admiral Cecil, 93
Timor, guerilla war with Japanese, 233
Timor-Leste, 375, 376
Tobruk
  capture of, 170
  siege of, 192–195
Tol massacre, 230
Tomahawk fighters, 199
Tovell, Brigadier Ray, 191
transport aircraft, 27
trench warfare
  conditions during Gallipoli Campaign, 93, 96, 98, 99

trench warfare *(continued)*
  in Korean War, 315
  no man's land, 117
  on Western Front, 110–111, 115, 118
Truman, Harry, 310, 313
Truscott, Squadron Leader Keith, 212
Tunbridge, Colonel Walter, 66

### • U •

*Uebi Scebeli* (Italian submarine), 166
United Australian Party (UAP), 289
United National Military Observer Group in India and Pakistan (UNMOGIP), 363
United Nations
  coalition force to drive Iraq out of Kuwait, 381
  dealing with threats to international peace, 378
  enforcing peace, 371–376
  formation and role, 303, 306
  peacekeeping role, 361–362
  sanctions against Iraq, 379
United Nations Advance Mission in Cambodia, 370
United Nations Force in Cyprus (UNFICYP), 364
United Nations Iran–Iraq Military Observer Group (UNIIMOG), 366–367
United Nations Mine Clearance Training Team (UNMCTT), 371, 375
United Nations Special Commission on Iraq (UNSCOM), 383–385, 389
United Nations Transitional Administration (East Timor), 375
United Nations Transitional Authority in Cambodia (UNTAC), 370
United Nations Truce Supervision Organisation (UNTSO), 363–364
United States
  attack on terrorist targets in Afghanistan, 385
  September 11 terrorist attacks, 385
  War on Terrorism, 385
universal training, 76
US Presidential Citation, 314, 345

### • V •

Vasey, Major General George, reputation as a military leader, 174, 175, 176, 177, 179, 252, 253, 259, 261, 265–266, 402–403
Vaughan-Evans, Major Carol, 373–374
Veale, Brigadier William, 233
Verdun, 108, 109
Versailles Treaty, 153
Vials, Major Harry, 66

Vichy Government, 167, 168, 182
Vickers Wellington bombers, 208
Victoria Cross for Australia, 35
Victoria Cross (VC)
  first awarded to an Australian, 64
  purpose of award, 35
Victorian Bushmen, 68
Victorian Mounted Rifles, 61, 62, 69
Victory Suit, 295
Viet Cong, 335, 336, 343, 344, 348, 349, 351, 352, 353
Vietnam, division into north and south sections, 323
Vietnam Veterans' Remembrance Day, 345
Vietnam War
  1st Australian Task Force (1 ATF), 342–347, 349–354
  advising and training the South Vietnamese Army, 336–339
  arrival of first battalion, 341
  artillery, 349–350
  Australian tactics, 341
  barrier minefield (Graham's Folly), 345–346
  base at Nui Dat, 343
  battle at FSPB Balmoral, 352
  battle at FSPB Coral, 352
  Battle of Long Tan, 344–345, 349, 411
  casualties, 338, 339, 341, 345, 348, 351, 352, 357
  cavalry squadron, 347
  decision to send troops, 339–340
  dominating Phuoc Tuy Province, 341–343, **342**
  fighting at Binh Ba, 353–354
  Fire Support Patrol Bases (FSPB), 350, 352
  grunts, 346–347
  helicopter support, 350
  increase in forces, 341
  infantry activities, 346–350
  Mike Force battalions, 339
  Montagnard battalions, 337, 339
  moratorium marches, 356
  national service scheme, 339–340
  operations of the different Australian services, 28
  overview, 335–336
  patrolling and ambushing, 347–348
  protest and dissent, 355–357
  RAAF involvement, 354
  RAN involvement, 354–355
  SAS operations, 349
  search and destroy operations, 348–349
  South Vietnam showing ARVN corps zones, **338**
  street fighting in Baria and Long Dien, 351–352
  Tet Offensives, 351–354
  withdrawal of Australian troops, 419–420
  withdrawal of troops, 356–357

Villers-Bretonneux, 120, 140–142
voluntary service, 30–31
Volunteer Defence Corps, 296

# • W •

Walker, Major General Harold ('Hooky'), 96, 98, 107, 111
Walker, Lieutenant Colonel Theo, 181
Walker, General Sir Walter, 329
Walker, General Walton, 312
Waller, Captain Hector, 166
War Cabinets. *See* Australian War Cabinet; British War Cabinet
war criminals, 283–284
war graves
  in France, 153
  at Gallipoli, 153
war memorials
  to First World War, 153
  in overseas locations, 19
War on Terrorism, 385
Ward, Eddie, 289, 419
Warfe, Colonel Peter, 373
Warner, Nick, 376
warrant officers, 33
wars, where Australians have fought, 12
wartime industries, 293, 294
Waterloo Creek massacre, 47
Watson, William, 64
Wavell, Field Marshal Sir Archibald, 23, 164, 168–169, 173–174, 176, 182, 190, 224, 234, 290
weapons of mass destruction (WMD), 382, 387, 388, 389
Webb, Sir William, 283
Weir, Sergeant Roy, 333
Western Alliance
  Australia's control over its own troops, 22–23
  Australia's cooperation with allies in Second World War, 290–292
  Australia's involvement in wars to support allies, 16
  reasons for supporting, 14
Western Australian Mounted Infantry, 62, 63, 68
Western Desert Force, 168, 171
Western Front
  1916–17, **109**
  Amiens, 145–146
  artillery techniques, 118–119
  Australian Corps offensive, August–October 1918, **145**
Broodseinde attack, 116
Bullecourt, 114
coining of term, 106
counteroffensive that won the war, 142–147
Dernancourt, 139–140
dominance of artillery, 118–119
Flanders, 114–117
Fromelles, 110–111
gas attacks, 119–120
German offensive of March–April 1918 (Michael Offensive), 137–142, **138**
Hamel, 144
Hazebrouck, 140
Hindenburg Line, 113–114, 138, 146–147
Menin Road attack, 116
Messines, 115, 120
Mont St Quentin, 146, 407
Peaceful Penetration, 142
Polygon Wood attack, 116
Pozières, 110, 111, 120
a single Australian force, 117
the Somme, 109–110
Third Ypres, 115–117, 120
trench warfare, 110–111, 115, 118
use of new technology, 117
Villers-Bretonneux, 120, 140–142, 406, 406–407
Western Sahara, 367–368
Wet, General Christian de, 68
Wheatley, Warrant Officer Kevin, 337
White, Lieutenant Colonel Alexander, 99, 113
White Australia Policy, 76, 153, 158
White, Lieutenant Colonel John, 327
White, Osmar, 251
White, General Sir Cyril Brudenell, 77, 83, 102, 204
Whitehead, Brigadier David, 201, 278
Whitlam Government, and withdrawal of troops from Vietnam, 419–420
Wilcox, Craig, 414
Williams, Able Seaman Bill, 82
Williams, Captain Moreton, 81
Williams, Air Marshal Sir Richard, 131, 205
Wilmot, Chester, 194
Wilson, Brigadier General Lachlan, 133, 135
Wilson, Field Marshal Sir Henry Maitland ('Jumbo'), 174, 184
Wilson, Woodrow, 152
Wilton, General Sir John, 341, 403–404
Windeyer, Major General Sir Victor, 200, 260, 262, 280
Windschuttle, Keith, 414
women in the armed forces
  roles, 30
  in the Second World War, 298

Women's Australian Auxiliary Air Force (WAAAF), 298
Women's Royal Australian Naval Service (WRANS), 298
Wooten, George, 171, 192, 259, 260, 263, 280
World War I. *See* First World War
World War II. *See* Second World War

*Yamashiro* (Japanese battleship), 272
Yamashita, General Tomoyuki, 223, 227

'Yellow Peril', 158
Yeomanry Brigades, 128
Yeomanry Mounted Division, 129
Yugoslavia, 174, 372

Z Special Force, 279
Zeppelins, 204
Zimbabwe, Commonwealth Monitoring Force, 365
*Zuikaku* (Japanese aircraft carrier), 242, 243

# Notes

# FOR DUMMIES

## Health, Fitness & Pregnancy

0-7314-0596-X
$34.95

1-74031-094-2
$39.95

0-7314-0760-1
$34.95

1-74216-984-8
$39.95

1-74031-011-X
$39.95

1-74031-173-6
$39.95

0-7314-0595-1
$34.95

0-7314-0644-3
$39.95

1-74031-042-X
$39.95

1-74031-103-5
$39.95

1-74216-946-5
$39.95

1-74216-972-4
$39.95

For Dummies, the Dummies Man logo, Making Everything Easier! and related trade dress are trademarks or registered trademarks of Wiley. All prices are GST-inclusive and subject to change without notice.

## Business & Investment

0-7314-0991-4
$39.95

1-74216-852-3
$39.95

1-74216-971-6
$39.95

1-74216-939-2
$34.95

1-74216-943-0
$39.95

0-7314-0724-5
$39.95

1-74216-853-1
$39.95

0-7314-0715-6
$39.95

1-74216-859-0
$32.95

0-7314-0746-6
$29.95

0-7314-0940-X
$39.95

1-74216-941-4
$36.95

For Dummies, the Dummies Man logo, Making Everything Easier! and related trade dress are trademarks or registered trademarks of Wiley. All prices are GST-inclusive and subject to change without notice.

# FOR DUMMIES

## Reference

1-74216-982-1      0-7314-0723-7      1-74216-945-7      0-7314-0909-4
$39.95             $34.95             $39.95             $39.95

1-74216-925-2      0-7314-0722-9      0-7314-0784-9      0-7314-0752-0
$29.95             $29.95             $34.95             $34.95

## Technology

0-470-49743-2      0-7314-0761-X      0-7314-0941-8      1-74031-159-0
$34.95             $39.95             $39.95             $39.95

For Dummies, the Dummies Man logo, Making Everything Easier! and related trade dress are trademarks or registered trademarks of Wiley. All prices are GST-inclusive and subject to change without notice.

Godfrey Charles Mundy
*Mounted Police and Blacks* 1852
Lithograph on paper, 10.9 × 18.2 cm (image), 30 × 43.8 cm (sheet)
© Australian War Memorial ART50023
This image depicts the killing of Aborigines by British troops at Slaughterhouse Creek, in north central New South Wales, in 1838. Between 60 and 300 Aborigines were killed. The European casualty was a corporal, speared in the leg. The incident is an example of the frontier wars described in Chapter 3.

The New South Wales contingent, bound for Sudan, departing from Circular Quay, Sydney, in March 1885. As described in Chapter 3, it was the first time a formed Australian military unit had departed for service overseas. It would not be the last. (AWM A05215)

Mounted troops from the Victorian Imperial Bushmen crossing a watercourse during the Boer War. The unit served in South Africa between May 1900 and June 1901 (see Chapter 4). (AWM P00268.004)

Stores, limbers and soldiers on Anzac Beach at Anzac Cove, Gallipoli. Note the small size of the cove and the hills up which the troops advanced during the first day of the landing on 25 April 1915 (see Chapter 6). (AWM A03050)

In the trenches at Lone Pine, Gallipoli, after the attack between 6 and 9 August 1915 (see Chapter 6). Australian and Turkish dead are on the parapet. On the right is Captain Leslie Morshead, later to become Lieutenant General Sir Leslie Morshead, commander of the 9th Division at Tobruk and El Alamein (see Chapter 12). (AWM02025)

Machine gunners, probably from the 46th Battalion, in action at Pozières in 1916. Three Australian divisions fought near Pozières during the Somme offensive in July–August 1916 (see Chapter 7). (AWM P07670.003)

George Lambert
*Battle of Romani, 4 August 1916* 1925–27
Oil on canvas, 121.5 × 244.5 cm
© Australian War Memorial ART09556

For a night and a morning the light horsemen fought a gradual withdrawal during the battle of Romani. When the Australians and New Zealanders counterattacked the following morning the Turks turned and fled (see Chapter 8).

An unidentified Australian soldier rescuing a fallen comrade lying on muddy ground beside the duckboards at Chateau Wood in the Menin Road area. The Australians took part in the grinding offensive along the Menin Road towards Passchendaele, Flanders, in September–October 1917 (see Chapter 7). (AWM E04599)

Gassed Australians awaiting medical attention at a dressing station at White Chateau, near Villers-Bretonneux on 27 May 1918. A month earlier the Australians had recaptured Villers-Bretonneux in one of the outstanding military attacks of the war (see Chapter 9). (AWM E04852)

The Australian Light Horse raising dust near Megiddo during the advance to Damascus in September 1918. The Australians took part in one of the great cavalry sweeps in history (see Chapter 8). (AWM B00256)

German prisoners resting with a wounded comrade, along with members of the Australian 60th Battalion, at one of the access entrances to the Mont St Quentin Canal Tunnel, 1 October 1918. A few days earlier Australian and American troops had broken through the Hindenburg Line and captured the entrance to the tunnel (see Chapter 9). (AWM E03476)

Charles Bean, working on files in his Victoria Barracks office, Melbourne, while writing his monumental *Official History of Australia in the War of 1914–18*. His work set the standard for military history in Australia (see Chapter 1). (AWM 105389)

Frank Norton
HMAS Sydney *in action with Italian cruiser* 1942
Medium oil on composite board, 55.4 × 70.8 cm
© Australian War Memorial ART23692
The Australian cruiser HMAS *Sydney* in action near Cape Spada, Mediterranean Sea, 19 July 1940. The Italian cruiser *Bartolomeo Colleoni* is on fire. The British destroyer *Hyperion* closes in on the stricken ship, while *Sydney* is in pursuit of another Italian cruiser (see Chapter 10).

An Australian artillery battery shelling a Vichy French position during the attack on Damour, Lebanon, in July 1941 during the Syrian campaign (see Chapter 11). (AWM 008624)

An infantry section from the 9th Australian Division occupying a front-line position during the siege of Tobruk, August 1941 (see Chapter 12). (AWM 041790)

Australian infantry breaking through barbed wire entanglements in the Western Desert. The Australians fought in several major campaigns in North Africa between January 1941 and November 1942 (see chapters 10 and 12). (AWM 010580)

William Dargie
*Attack by 2/24th Battalion, El Alamein at night, 25–26 October 1942* 1973
Oil on canvas, 152 × 274.6 cm
© Australian War Memorial ART27821
In the battle the 9th Division drew onto itself the might of the German panzers, enabling the British tanks to break through the enemy line elsewhere (see Chapter 12).

General Douglas MacArthur, Commander-in-Chief of the South West Pacific Area, with General Sir Thomas Blamey and the Australian Prime Minister, John Curtin, in March 1942. MacArthur commanded all American and Australian forces in the Australian area and became Curtin's principal military adviser (see Chapter 17). (AWM 042766)

The Australian cruiser HMAS *Australia* under air attack during the Battle of the Coral Sea, 7 May 1942. The battle prevented the Japanese invasion force from reaching Port Moresby (see Chapter 14). (AWM 044238)

Members of the 39th Battalion on parade at Menari in the Owen Stanley Range, Papua, 22 September 1942. The bedraggled but proud militiamen of the battalion had been in action against the advancing Japanese for almost a month (see Chapter 15). (AWM 013289)

Australian troops on patrol at Milne Bay, New Guinea, in October 1942, soon after they had stopped the Japanese attempt to seize the airfields and had forced the Japanese to withdraw (see Chapter 15). (AWM 013339)

A landing ship tank (LST) pushes ashore on the New Guinea coast to deliver troops and equipment during the Aitape–Wewak campaign in 1945 (see Chapter 16). (AWM OG0971)

A Second World War poster depicting six women representing the WRAN, AWAS, WAAAF, AWLA, AAMWS and a munitions worker. For the first time Australian women served in the armed forces in roles other than as nurses (see Chapter 17). (AWM ARTV00332)

A Lancaster bomber of No 463 Squadron RAAF of Bomber Command being loaded with 1000-pound bombs before a raid over enemy territory. In the Second World War it was more dangerous to serve in Bomber Command than in the infantry (see Chapter 13). (AWM UK1217)

Lieutenant Colonel Charles Green, Commanding Officer of the 3rd Battalion, the Royal Australian Regiment (left), with Brigadier Basil Coad, commander of the 27th Commonwealth Brigade, near Chongju, North Korea, on 29 October 1950. Green was killed the following evening (see Chapter 18). (AWM HOBJ1648)

Infantrymen of D Company, 2nd Battalion, the Royal Australian Regiment, heading into the jungle for an eight-day patrol during Operation Shark North, Malaya, May 1956. The battalion served in Malaya for two years (see Chapter 19). (AWM HOB/56/0480/MC)

A Royal Air Force Westland Whirlwind helicopter inserts Australian soldiers from 2 Squadron, Special Air Service (SAS) Regiment to begin a patrol in Sarawak, Borneo, in 1966. During the response to Indonesia's 'Confrontation' Commonwealth troops crossed into Indonesia in secret Claret operations (see Chapter 19). (AWM P05221.001)

Soldiers from C Company 5th Battalion, the Royal Australian Regiment, assist a comrade who has been wounded by a booby trap grenade, during operations in Phuoc Tuy Province, South Vietnam, October 1966. By that time two Australian battalions were serving in Vietnam (see Chapter 20). (AWM COA/66/0877/VN)

Australian Centurion tanks and armoured personnel carriers moving along a road towards the village of Binh Ba, South Vietnam, June 1969. Tanks and infantry dislodged a strong North Vietnamese Army group which had entered the village (see Chapter 20). (AWM BEL/69/0389/VN)

Soldiers from the 4th Field Regiment, part of the International Force East Timor (INTERFET), on patrol near the town of Suai, East Timor, 16 November 1999. The INTERFET deployment was the largest single Australian military undertaking since the Second World War (see Chapter 21). (AWM P03184.263)

An Australian Light Armoured Vehicle (ASLAV) of the 2nd Cavalry Regiment on patrol in Baghdad near the sculpture *The swords of Qadisiyyah*, also called *The hands of victory*, in May 2003. The troops were part of the security detachment responsible for protecting Australian diplomats in Iraq (see Chapter 22). (AWM P04101.800)

Soldiers from the Operational Mentor and Liaison Team on patrol with the Afghan National Army in the Baluchi Valley, Afghanistan, in January 2010. Australian troops have served continually in Afghanistan since 2005 (see Chapter 22). (© Commonwealth of Australia, reproduced with permission.)

www.ingramcontent.com/pod-product-compliance
Lightning Source LLC
LaVergne TN
LVHW080309260326
834688LV00038B/1028